INTRODUCTION TO COMPU[illegible] GENERAL EQUILIBRIUM MODELS

Computable general equilibrium (CGE) models are widely used by governmental organizations and academic institutions to analyze the economywide effects of events such as climate change, tax policies, and immigration. This book is a practical, how-to guide to CGE models that is suitable for use at the undergraduate college level. Its introductory level distinguishes it from other available books and articles on CGE models. The book provides intuitive and graphical explanations of the economic theory that underlies a CGE model and includes many examples and hands-on model exercises. It may be used in courses on economic principles, microeconomics, macroeconomics, public finance, environmental economics, and international trade and finance, because it shows students the role of theory in a realistic model of an economy. The book is also suitable for courses on general equilibrium models and research methods, and for professionals interested in learning how to use CGE models.

Mary E. Burfisher is a Distinguished Visiting Professor at the United States Naval Academy, Annapolis, Maryland. She has also served as a senior economist for the Economic Research Service of the U.S. Department of Agriculture in Washington, D.C. Dr. Burfisher is a consultant on computable general equilibrium models and agricultural policy for U.S. governmental agencies and international organizations. She is the author or editor of numerous monographs, books, and articles on international agricultural and trade policies. Dr. Burfisher was a Fellow of the Global Trade Analysis Project (GTAP) at Purdue University from 2003 to 2010 and received the Quality of Communication Award from the American Agricultural Economics Association. She earned her Ph.D. in economics from the University of Maryland.

INTRODUCTION TO COMPUTABLE GENERAL EQUILIBRIUM MODELS

MARY E. BURFISHER
United States Naval Academy, Annapolis, Maryland

CAMBRIDGE UNIVERSITY PRESS
Cambridge, New York, Melbourne, Madrid, Cape Town,
Singapore, São Paulo, Delhi, Mexico City

Cambridge University Press
32 Avenue of the Americas, New York, NY 10013-2473, USA

www.cambridge.org
Information on this title: www.cambridge.org/9780521139779

First published 2011
Reprinted 2012

A catalog record for this publication is available from the British Library.

Library of Congress Cataloging in Publication Data

Burfisher, Mary E., 1955–
Introduction to Computable General Equilibrium Models / Mary E. Burfisher.
p. cm.
Includes bibliographical references and index.
ISBN 978-0-521-76696-8 (hardback) – ISBN 978-0-521-13977-9 (paperback)
1. Equilibrium (Economics) – Econometric models. I. Title.
HB145.B86 2011
339.501´5195–dc22 2010050361

ISBN 978-0-521-76696-8 Hardback
ISBN 978-0-521-13977-9 Paperback

For my family

Contents

Text Boxes

About This Book

Objectives

This book will introduce you to computable general equilibrium (CGE) models. A CGE model is a powerful analytical tool that can help you to gain a better understanding of real-world economic issues. CGE models are a class of economic model that over the past twenty-five years has gained widespread use in the economics profession, particularly in government. Economists today are using these models to systematically analyze some of the most important policy challenges and economic "shocks" of the twenty-first century, including global climate change, the spread of human diseases, and international labor migration.

Since the early 1990s, prominent CGE models have been built and maintained at the U.S. International Trade Commission, the Economic Research Service of the U.S. Department of Agriculture, the World Bank, and other national agencies and international organizations to provide ongoing economic analytical capability. These models have come to play an important part worldwide in government policy decisions. For example, the models' predictions about prices, wages, and incomes factored heavily in the debate about the terms of the North American Free Trade Agreement, the Kyoto Protocol, and China's entrance into the World Trade Organization. CGE-based analyses have also helped the United States and other governments anticipate and design responses to substantial changes in the availability of key resources, ranging from petroleum to people.

CGE models are comprehensive because – whether they are detailed or very simplified – they describe all parts of an economy simultaneously and how these parts interact with each other. The models describe the efficiency-maximizing behavior of firms and the utility-maximizing behavior of consumers. Their decisions add up to the macroeconomic behavior of an economy, such as changes in gross domestic product (GDP), government tax revenue and spending, aggregate savings and investment, and the balance of

Prologue Table 1. *Modeling and Data Resources Used in This Book*

Resource	Source
RunGTAP CGE model	Download from GTAP.org
GTAPAgg7-global database aggregation utility	Download from GTAP.org
U.S. 3x3 database	Create using GTAPAgg7

trade. As might be expected, such models can require large databases and they contain sophisticated model code. Yet despite their complexity, continuing advances in modeling software and database development are making CGE models increasingly accessible and intuitive. Minimizing the technical entry barriers to CGE modeling has freed economists to focus on the models' economic behavior and the economic insights that can be derived from their results. These innovations have also made CGE models an ideal laboratory in which economics students can learn to manipulate, observe, and deepen their knowledge of economic behavior.

This book is designed to provide a hands-on introduction to CGE models. You will draw on theory from microeconomics, macroeconomics, international trade and finance, public finance, and other areas of economics, as you observe how producers and consumers in the CGE model respond to various changes in market conditions that we refer to as "model experiments." The guided model exercises will show you how to build and use a demonstration CGE model to assess the economywide effects of such economic shocks as the elimination of agricultural subsidies, global elimination of trade barriers, labor immigration, and changes in a tax system. By the end of the book, you will have begun to develop your skills as both a producer and a consumer of professional CGE-based economic analysis.

The book introduces the CGE models and databases that are used by professional economists. We will study the key features of "standard" CGE models, which are static (single period), single- and multicountry models, with fixed national endowments of factors of production. Most textbook examples and model exercises use RunGTAP, a user-friendly, menu-driven interface (Horridge, 2001) of the GTAP (Global Trade Analysis Project) CGE model. RunGTAP may be downloaded at no charge from the GTAP Web site (Prologue Table 1). The GTAP CGE model is an open model developed by Hertel and Tsigas (1997) and is written in the GEMPACK software.

The GTAP project also maintains a global database that CGE modelers rely on as a data source for many types of CGE models. The database is built on data contributions from CGE modelers around the world, which GTAP then organizes and balances into a consistent, global database. The 7.0

version of the database, used in this book, describes 113 countries or regions and 57 industries in 2004. Modelers may use GTAPAgg, a freeware program developed by Horridge (2008b) and available from the GTAP project, to aggregate the global database into smaller sets of regions and industries that are relevant for their research. In this book and in the model exercises, most examples use a small-dimension, two-region aggregation of the database that describes the United States and an aggregate rest-of-world region.

Organization

This book covers eight topics beginning with an introduction to CGE models (Chapter 1), their elements and structure (Chapter 2), and the data that underlie them (Chapter 3). Chapters 4–6 focus on the microeconomic underpinnings of CGE models. Chapter 4 describes final demand by households, government, and investors and the demand for imports and exports. Chapter 5 describes supply, focusing on the technology tree and the producer's cost-minimizing demand for intermediate and factor inputs. Chapter 6 covers additional aspects of factor markets, including factor mobility, factor endowment and productivity growth, factor substitutability, and factor employment assumptions. Trade topics, including theorems on the effects of endowment changes and world prices, are covered in Chapter 7. Chapter 8 explores public finance topics related to trade and domestic taxes.

Chapters 1–8 adhere to a common template, consisting of:

- Chapter text (e.g., "Introduction to Computable General Equilibrium Models")
- Text boxes
- Chapter summary
- Key terms (e.g., "stock" and "flow")
- Practice and review exercises
- Model exercise

Text boxes introduce examples of classic, innovative, and influential CGE-based economic analyses that relate to chapter topics. These summarized articles offer practical examples of how the concepts that you are learning about in the chapter are operationalized in CGE models. Practice and review exercises review and reinforce the central themes of the chapter.

Model exercises linked to each chapter provide step-by-step direction and guidance to help you to develop your modeling skills (Prologue Table 2). The modeling problems are general enough to be suitable for use with almost any standard CGE model, but their detailed instructions are compatible with RunGTAP. The first three model exercises guide you in creating a database, setting up your CGE model, and learning core modeling skills. You may use the demonstration model developed in the first model exercise

Prologue Table 2. *Chapters and Related Model Exercises*

Chapter	Model Exercise
1. Introduction to CGE Models	Set up the GTAP Model and Database
2. Elements of a CGE Model	Explore the GTAP Model and Database
3. The CGE Model Database: A Social Accounting Matrix	Run the GTAP Model
4. Final Demand in a CGE Model	Soaring Food Prices and the U.S. Economy
5. Supply in a CGE Model	Food Fight – Agricultural Production Subsidies
6. Factors of Production in a CGE Model	How Immigration Can Raise Wages
7. Trade in a CGE Model	The Doha Development Agenda
8. Taxes in a CGE Model	The Marginal Welfare Burden of the U.S. Tax System
	Challenge: Successful Quitters: The Economic Effects of Growing Antismoking Attitudes

to replicate almost all results reported in the tables in Chapters 1–8 of the book. Exercises 4–8 are case studies that begin with a discussion of a timely topic or influential CGE analysis such as labor immigration and U.S. tax policies. They demonstrate how to design model experiments and how to use economic theory to select and interpret model results. A ninth "challenge exercise" introduces advanced students to macroprojections and uncertainty about economic shocks.

Resources for New CGE Modelers

We recommend that beginning modelers start by reading articles and monographs, both current and classic, that provide general introductions to, or critiques of, CGE models. Particularly recommended as introductory treatments are Piermartini and Teh (2005), McDaniel et al. (2008), Shoven and Whalley (1984), Bandara (1991), Francois and Reinert (1997), Robinson et al. (1999), Devarajan et al. (1990, 1997), and Borges (1986). Breisinger, Thomas, and Thurlow (2009); Reinert and Roland-Holst (1992); and King (1985) provide introductions to social accounting matrices, which are the databases that underlie CGE models.

As your skills progress, we recommend that you read the intermediate-level treatments in Kehoe and Kehoe's (1994) primer on CGE models and Dervis, de Melo, and Robinson's (1982) introduction to open economy CGE models. Hosoe, Gasawa, and Hashimoto (2010) introduce students at an intermediate level to CGE models, focusing on models coded in General Algebraic Modeling Software (GAMS). Some books and articles that describe specific CGE models are also useful for new modelers, who will recognize many of the same features in those models as in the standard CGE model that we study in this book. Hertel and Tsigas (1997) provide an overview of the GTAP model. Lofgren, Harris, and Robinson (2002) describe the International Food Policy Research Institute's (IFPRI) standard single-country CGE model and database. De Melo and Tarr (1992) describe the structure and behavior of their CGE model of the United States. For more advanced students, Shoven and Whalley (1992) provide a practical introduction to CGE models, and Scarf and Shoven (2008) present a collected volume of case studies that describe different aspects of CGE models.

Because CGE modeling is a dynamic field of research, the best way to keep abreast of developments in CGE modeling and in the applications of CGE models is to review working papers and conference papers, in addition to economic journals. The GTAP Web site, at www.gtap.org is a useful source for up-to-date information on CGE-based research papers, CGE model databases, and research tools and utilities related to the GTAP model and data. All papers presented at annual GTAP conferences are posted online, providing students with access to unpublished papers and work in progress by many leading CGE modelers, using many types of CGE models. Perusing recent conference papers can give you ideas for timely research topics and experiment designs for your own research projects.

The International Food Policy Research Institute (IFPRI), which developed the "IFPRI standard" CGE model, has published many studies based on variations of that model as well as papers about model databases and database construction. These publications are available from the IFPRI Web site at www.ifpri.org.

Many international organizations, such as the World Bank, and national government agencies, such as the U.S. Department of Agriculture, also produce and post CGE-based working papers and research products. In addition, the GAMS Web site, at www.gams.org maintains a library of simple CGE models that can be downloaded and run using the free demonstration versions of GAMS. Also, the United States Naval Academy hosts the Tools for Undergraduates "TUG-CGE" model (Thierfelder, 2009), a GAMS-based CGE model designed for undergraduate use.

For the Instructor

The book is designed for use in a one-semester class that is spent primarily doing hands-on model exercises and independent research, with the book used as background reading. The exercises are all fully portable. They are

Prologue Table 3. *Recommended Sequences for Courses of Different Lengths*

Chapter	One Semester Course	6-Week Course	1-Week Course
1. Introduction to CGE Models	0.5 weeks	0.5 weeks	Omit
2. Elements of a CGE Model	1 week	0.5 weeks	0.25 day
3. CGE Model Data: Social Accounting Matrix	1 week	1 week	0.5 day
4. Demand in a CGE Model	1.5 weeks	0.5 weeks	0.5 day
5. Supply in a CGE Model	1.5 weeks	0.5 weeks	0.5 day
6. Factors of Production in a CGE Model	1 week	Optional	Omit
7. Trade in a CGE Model	1.0 weeks	0.5 weeks	0.5 day
8. Taxes in a CGE Model	1.5 weeks	0.5 weeks	0.75 day
Independent Research	6 weeks	2 weeks	2 days

designed to use free materials downloaded from the Internet so they are suitable for students to carry out in computer labs or on their personal computers. The ideal classroom setting is one that promotes student teamwork and ongoing discussion among students and teachers while students carry out model exercises.

The book can also be used in condensed courses, with our recommendations for selecting and paring materials described in Prologue Table 3. For courses of all lengths, we recommend a generous allotment of time for model exercises and independent research because students will then learn by doing. If the book is used as a supplementary hands-on resource for economic theory courses, such as macroeconomics or international trade, we suggest that the teacher cover Chapters 1–3 and their related model exercises and then assign only the chapter and exercise that is relevant to the course. Most teachers are likely to find that some or all of Chapter 8 on taxes is relevant because taxes are a policy lever that governments use to address many economic problems.

Acknowledgments

This book was made possible by the support of three institutions. I am most grateful to the National Science Foundation and especially to Dr. Myles G. Boylan, Program Director in the Course, Curriculum and Laboratory Improvement Program of the Division of Undergraduate Education, who encouraged this project from its inception. I deeply appreciate the support provided to me by the United States Naval Academy, where I was privileged to be a Distinguished Visiting Professor while writing this book. The Global Trade Analysis Project (GTAP), particularly Thomas Hertel and Terrie Walmsley, have been tremendously generous in their encouragement and support of this project. I am also deeply grateful to Karen Thierfelder, a longtime friend and colleague, and to Sherman Robinson, who has been a generous teacher and friend. I have learned much about models and policy analysis from our long and rewarding collaboration. Victoria Greenfield, Kurtis Swope, and Katherine Smith – my colleagues at the Academy – acted as beta testers and reviewers and provided insightful critiques and many helpful suggestions and edits on earlier drafts of the book. I owe a special thanks to my students at the Naval Academy, who over the course of four years uncovered many errors and oversights, and who often provided fresh takes on CGE models and economic theory. My editor, Scott Parris, and Adam Levine and Tilak Raj at Cambridge University Press facilitated this project in every way possible while guiding it through to publication. I also thank Roger Betancourt, Cheryl Christensen, Neil Conklin, Praveen Dixit, Aziz Elbehri, Cheryl Flax-Davidson, Rae Jean Goodman, Kenneth Hanson, Barry Krissoff, Gene Mathia, Sara Pastor, Alan Pocinki, Ken Reinert, David Skully, Agapi Somwaru, and Deborah Tanno, each of whom, in different ways, helped to bring this project to fruition. Channing Arndt, Rob McDougall, Jeffrey Round, Marcelle Thomas, Marinos Tsigas, Dominique van der Mensbruggh, Frank van Tongeren, and three anonymous reviewers provided many helpful ideas, corrections, and suggestions.

All remaining errors are my own responsibility, and I encourage readers to contact me about them or to offer their comments or suggestions on the book.

This material is based upon activities supported by the National Science Foundation under Agreement No. DUE-0632836. Any opinions, findings, and conclusions or recommendations expressed are those of the author(s) and do not necessarily reflect the views of the National Science Foundation.

1

Introduction to Computable General Equilibrium Models

This chapter introduces students to computable general equilibrium (CGE) models, a class of economic model that describes an economy as a whole and the interactions among its parts. The basic structure of a CGE model and its database are described. We introduce a "standard" CGE model and provide a survey of CGE model applications.

Economic Models, Economists' Toys

When an economist wants to study the economic behavior observed in the complex world around us, the first step is often to build an economic model. A model can focus an analysis by stripping down and simplifying real world events into a representation of the motivations of the key players in any economic story. Some amount of context and interesting detail must be left out as the economist distills a model rich enough to explain events credibly and realistically, but simple enough to put the spotlight on the essential actions in the story. When an economist succeeds in building a model, he or she now has a tool that can be manipulated. By playing with this "toy" representation of economic activity, the economist can learn more about the fundamentals behind an event and can study likely outcomes or possible solutions.

There are many kinds of economic models. The type of model that we will be studying is a ***Computable General Equilibrium (CGE)*** model. It is an "economywide" model because it describes the motivations and behavior of all producers and consumers in an economy and the linkages among them. It depicts firms that respond to demand by purchasing inputs and hiring workers and capital equipment. The income generated from sales of firms' output ultimately accrues to households, who spend it on goods and services, taxes and saving. Tax revenue and savings lead to government and investor spending. The combined demand by private households, government, and investors is met by firms who, to complete the ***circular flow of income and***

Table 1.1. *Bicycle Industry Model*

Model Equations Type	General Notation	Numerical Function
Supply equation:	$Q_s = G(P_i, P)$	$Q_s = -4P_i + 2P$
Demand equation:	$Q_d = F(P, Y)$	$Q_d = 2Y - 2P$
Market clearing constraint:	$Q_s = Q_d = Q$	
Endogenous Variables		
Q = Quantity of bikes		
P = Price of bikes		
Exogenous Variables		
P_i = Prices of inputs (e.g., tires, steel)		
Y = Income		

spending, buy inputs and hire workers and capital used in their production processes. Such a comprehensive model may seem to be very complex but we hope that its deconstruction in the following chapters will reveal it to be a relatively simple, "toy" representation of our complex world.

As a point of departure for our study, we begin by examining a toy partial equilibrium model. Suppose we are asked to build an economic model to analyze the supply and demand for bicycles. We can draw on our microeconomic theory to introduce a supply equation to describe bicycle production. First, we use general functional notation to express that the quantity of bicycles that producers supply, Q_s, is related to the prices of bicycle inputs, P_i, such as rubber tires, and the market price of bicycles, P. With this general functional notation, we know only that there is a causal relationship among the variables, but not its size or whether it is positive or negative. We can also draw on microeconomic theory to introduce a demand equation. Again using general notation, we express that the quantity of bicycles that consumers demand, Q_d, is a function of their income, Y, and the price of bicycles. Finally, we know from economic theory that a market economy will tend toward market-clearing; that is, the price of bicycles will adjust until the quantity that producers supply equals the quantity that consumers demand. To describe this equilibrium in the model, we introduce the market-clearing constraint, $Q = Q_s = Q_d$; the equilibrium quantity of bicycles supplied and demanded must be equal.

The three equations describing the bicycle industry model, expressed in general functional notation, are listed in Table 1.1. The model has two ***exogenous*** variables: input prices, P_i, and consumer income, Y. Their values are determined by forces outside the model, and we take them as given. The model has two ***endogenous*** variables: the equilibrium quantity, Q, and the price, P, of bicycles. Their values will be determined as solutions to our model's equations.

Using our bicycle industry model with general functional notation, we can draw these qualitative conclusions about the effects of changes in our exogenous variables on the endogenous variables: A change in income, Y, will affect the quantity of bicycles that consumers demand, while a change in input prices, P_i, will affect the quantity of bicycles that producers supply. Given our market clearing constraint, a change in either exogenous variable will lead to a change in the price of bikes until the quantities of bikes that are supplied and demanded are again in equilibrium.

Our model becomes more useful if we have sufficient data on the supply and demand for bicycles to estimate the sign and size of the relationships among the variables. We can then express our model equations in specific and numerical functional form, such as: $Q_d = 2Y - 2P$, which is a linear demand function. With this information, we can now say that the quantity of bicycles demanded can be calculated as two times income minus two times the price of bicycles. Perhaps we also estimate this linear supply function for bicycle supply: $Q_s = -4P_i + 2P$. We now have a quantitative model that describes both supply and demand and is capable of yielding numerical solutions.

If we are now given values for our exogenous variables, Y and P_i, we can solve our model to find the initial, market-clearing values for the two endogenous values, P and Q. If, for example, we know that the value of Y is ten and P_i is four, then we can substitute these values into our equations and solve for the market clearing quantity of two bicycles at a price of $9 each.

We can learn a great deal about the bicycle industry by using the model to conduct a model experiment. We carry out an experiment by changing an exogenous variable in the model, Y or P_i. When we change one exogenous variable at a time, we are using our model of the bicycle industry to conduct a controlled experiment. This "what-if" scenario helps us to isolate and understand the role of a single factor, such as income, in explaining the changes in the bicycle quantities and prices that we observe in our model. We can also now offer quantitative conclusions such as "if we double income, bicycle production will increase to twelve and the price of bicycles will rise to $4."

What Is a Computable General Equilibrium Model?

A CGE model is a system of equations that describe an economy as a whole and the interactions among its parts. Despite its comprehensiveness, it is much like the bicycle model. It is based on equations derived directly from economic theory, which will look familiar to students from their courses in microeconomics and macroeconomics. The equations may describe producers' supply or consumer demand, or be familiar macroeconomic identities such as "GNP = C + I + G + E − M." Like the bicycle model, a CGE model includes exogenous and endogenous variables and market clearing constraints. All of the equations in the model are solved simultaneously to find an economywide equilibrium in which, at some set of prices, the quantities of supply and demand are equal in every market.

To conduct experiments with a CGE model, the economist changes one or more exogenous variables and re-solves the CGE model to find new values for the endogenous variables. The economist observes how the exogenous change, or "economic shock," affects the market equilibrium and draws conclusions about the economic concern under study – be it a rise in the price of bicycle tires, or fuel, or labor immigration.

A CGE model differs from our model of the bicycle industry since it represents the whole economy, even if at times in a very stylized and simplified way. A CGE model describes production decisions in two or more industries – not just one, as in the bicycle model. A CGE model also includes demand for all goods and services in the economy, not just for bicycles. While the ***partial equilibrium*** model assumes income and prices in the rest of the economy are fixed, a CGE model describes how changes in the demand and supply for a good such as bicycles can lead to changes in employment and wages, and therefore in households' income. It also describes changes in prices for other goods and services in the economy, such as bicycle inputs and the products that compete with bicycles in consumer demand. A CGE model also includes all sources of demand, not only from producers and private households but also from other economic agents – the government, investors, and foreign markets. Because a CGE model depicts all of the microeconomic activity in an economy, the summation of these activities describes the macroeconomic behavior of an economy, including its gross domestic product (GDP), aggregate savings and investment, the balance of trade, and, in some CGE models, the government fiscal deficit or surplus.

We can learn more about the basic features of a CGE model by considering the meaning of each component of its name: "computable," "general," and "equilibrium."

Computable

The term *computable* in CGE models describes the capability of this type of model to quantify the effects of a shock on an economy. As an economist, you can generally rely on economic theory to help you anticipate a directional change. For example, if you are asked to describe the expected effect of a reduction in a U.S. tariff, you are likely to argue that it will lower the price of the import, leading to an increase in the quantity demanded of imports and a decrease in the quantity demanded for the domestic, import-competing variety. However, policy makers or industry advocates may want to know if this effect will be large or small.

The equations of a CGE model utilize data for an actual economy in some base year, such as the U. S. economy in 2004. In this case, the utility functions incorporate data on U.S. consumer preferences in 2004. The production function for each industry is based on U.S. firms' technology – inputs and production levels – in 2004. Because the equations in a CGE model incorporate real data about an actual economy, the model's new equilibrium values following an experiment enable you to quantify in a realistic way the anticipated value of the impact on the economy, such as a $25 million or $2.5 billion change in an industry's output.

The ability to quantify the values associated with the outcomes of various "what if" scenarios allow the economist to make a powerful contribution to debates about economic policy. CGE modelers have provided influential analyses of the costs and benefits of government policies, such as trade agreements like NAFTA, emissions control programs, and the agreement to allow China's WTO membership. CGE models have also been used to quantify the effects of market shocks including oil price hikes and labor migration.

General

In a CGE model, the term *general* means that the model encompasses *all* economic activity in an economy simultaneously – including production, consumption, employment, taxes and savings, and trade – and the linkages among them. For example, if higher fuel prices change the cost of producing manufactured goods such as bicycles, books, cars, and TVs, then the prices of these goods will rise. The demand response of consumers will lead to changes throughout the economy. For example, consumers may buy fewer bicycles, cars, and TVs, but buy more Kindles and e-books. The changes in consumer demand and industry output will then affect employment, incomes, taxes, and savings. In an open economy, the fuel price hike also may lead to changes in trade flows and in the exchange rate; the latter is a macroeconomic shock that will in turn affect the whole economy.

One way to depict the interrelationships in a CGE model is to describe them as a circular flow of income and spending in a national economy, as shown in Figure 1.1. You may recall this circular flow diagram from your macroeconomics class. To meet demand for their products, producers purchase inputs such as rubber tires and bicycle seats. They also hire factors of production (labor and capital) and pay them wages and rents. The factor payments ultimately accrue to private households as wage and capital rental income. Households spend their income on goods and services, pay taxes to the government, and put aside savings. The government uses its tax revenue to buy goods and services, and investors use savings to buy capital investment goods for use in future production activities. The combined demand

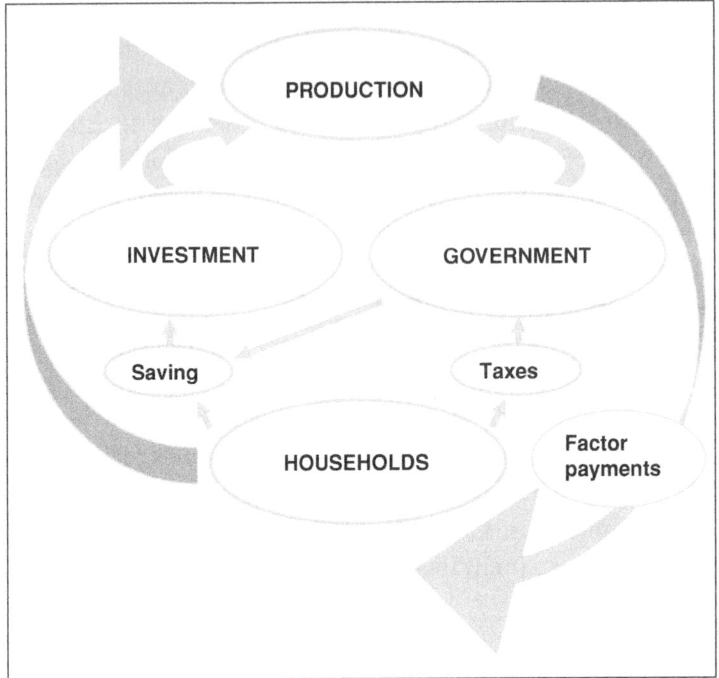

Figure 1.1. The circular flow of income and spending in a national economy

for goods and services from households, government, and investment constitutes final demand in the economy. Firms produce goods and services in response to this demand, which in turn determines input demand, factor employment levels, households' wage and rental income, and so forth, in a circular flow. If we introduce trade in this circular flow, we would account for the role of imports in meeting some of the domestic demand, and we would add export demand as an additional source of demand for domestic goods. Finally, we can think of policies such as taxes and subsidies as "price wedges" that increase or lower the prices of goods between buyers and sellers, or as transfers that directly affect households' level of income and therefore their levels of consumption, savings, and taxes.

A general equilibrium model describes all of these interrelationships in an economy at once: "Everything depends on everything else." An important caveat to "everything" is that CGE models are "real" models. A real model does not include money, describe financial markets or changes in overall price levels (like inflation or deflation), or reflect the effects of monetary policy such as an increase in the money supply. Instead, a real model measures all variables in terms of physical quantities and the relative prices at which goods are exchanged for each other, such as three books per DVD.

It is likely that most of your economics coursework so far has presented partial equilibrium models. A partial equilibrium model describes economic motives and behavior in one industry, like the bicycle industry, or of one type of economic agent, such as consumers, and holds prices and quantities in the rest of the economy constant. A partial equilibrium analysis is similar to placing a magnifying glass over one part of the economy and assuming that the action in the rest of the economy is either not important or not changing at the moment. This focus on a specific part of the economy allows economists to develop richly detailed analyses of a particular industry or economic activity, but the trade-off is that important, interdependent links with the rest of the economy are not taken into account. These linkages are particularly important if the industry or other aspect of economic activity under study is large relative to the rest of the economy.

Equilibrium

An economy is in ***equilibrium*** when supply and demand are in balance at some set of prices, and there are no pressures for the values of these variables to change further. In a CGE model, equilibrium occurs at that set of prices at which all producers, consumers, workers, and investors are satisfied with the quantities of goods they produce and consume, the number of hours they work, the amount of capital they save and invest, and so forth. Producers have chosen input and output levels that have *maximized their efficiency* given the costs of inputs such as fuel and equipment, their sales prices, and the technological constraints of their production processes. Consumers have *maximized their utility*, or satisfaction, by purchasing the most satisfying bundle of products – such as books, bicycles, cars, and TVs – given their budgets and the prices of consumer goods. The CGE model's equilibrium must also satisfy some important macroeconomic, market-clearing constraints; generally these require that aggregate supply of goods and services equals aggregate demand, all workers and the capital stock are employed, and national or global savings equals investment.

The CGE modeler conducts an experiment by creating "disequilibrium" – that is, by changing an exogenous variable in the model. For example, the modeler may specify an increase in an import tariff. This shock will change the economy – consumers are likely to buy fewer imports and more of the domestic product, and domestic firms are likely to expand their production to meet growth in demand. When running a model experiment, the CGE modeler is like a billiard player who hits one ball, causing reactions and interactions among all of the balls on the table, and who must wait to see where all the balls come to rest. All of the CGE model equations must be re-solved to find new solution values for all of the endogenous variables in the model. The new values represent a new equilibrium in which the supply is again equal to demand at some set of prices. The CGE model that we will study does not show the adjustment process; we do not watch as the billiard balls traverse the table. This is an important point to keep in mind as you use a CGE model to conduct policy analysis.

A Standard CGE Model

CGE models come in all shapes and sizes. Despite this diversity, most models share the same core approaches to depicting supply and demand, factor markets, savings and investment, trade, and taxation. In this book, we concentrate on these shared, core elements as we introduce you to a "standard" CGE model, which is a static (single-period), single or multicountry CGE model with a fixed endowment of factors of production, such as labor and capital.

A ***static*** CGE model provides a before- and after-comparison of an economy when a shock, such as a tax, causes it to reallocate its productive resources in more or less efficient ways. Static models can tell a powerful story about the ultimate winners and losers from economic shocks. However, a noteworthy drawback is that they do not describe the adjustment path. The adjustment process may include periods of unemployment and dislocation that could exact a high societal price, regardless of the size of expected benefits in the new equilibrium

A standard CGE model assumes that an economy's factors of production are in fixed supply, unless they are changed as a model experiment. For example, the size of the labor force is assumed to be fixed, and the available quantity of capital equipment does not change. Often, models depict a medium-run adjustment period following a model shock. This period is long enough to allow the fixed supplies of factors to change the industries in which they are employed in response to changes in wages and capital rents, but too short for long-run changes in factor productivity or capital stock accumulation to take place.

We consider both single and multicountry CGE models in the following chapters. ***Single-country*** models describe one country in detail, with a simple treatment of its export and import markets. ***Multicountry*** CGE models contain two or more countries (or regions) and describe their economies in full, including each country's production, consumption, trade, taxes, tariffs, and so on. The economies in multicountry models are linked to each other through trade and sometimes through capital flows.

No one CGE model can have all of the features that we describe in the following chapters. Rather, our intent is to provide you with a solid foundation in CGE modeling basics that will equip you to understand or to work with almost any standard CGE model. Later, you can build on this foundation to learn about and appreciate the ramifications of differences in among CGE models and the capabilities of more sophisticated or special-purpose models. We describe some of these more sophisticated models and the frontiers of CGE modeling in text boxes throughout the book, and in our concluding chapter.

CGE Model Structure

A CGE model consists, essentially, of a set of commands. Some of the commands simply provide the model preliminaries. They define sets, parameters, and exogenous and endogenous variables. We discuss these elements of a CGE model in detail in Chapter Two. Other commands present the economic equations of the model. These are typically organized into blocks related to:

- consumption
- production
- factor markets (e.g., capital and labor)
- international trade
- taxation

We explore each of these economic components of a CGE model separately and in depth in Chapters 4 through 8.

CGE Model Database

A CGE model's database describes the circular flow of income and spending in a national economy during a specific time period, usually a year, such as 2004. The database reports the values of all goods and services that are produced and the income generated from their sale. It describes households' income and their spending, government tax revenue and outlays, savings and investment spending, and international trade. CGE model databases typically use data from official national accounts.

Of course, the database does not report every individual transaction that takes place in an economy during a year, such as your purchase of shoes last month. CGE model databases must aggregate or sum up economic activity into a tractable number of transactions. Industries are therefore aggregated into representative groups of industries, such as agriculture, manufacturing, and services. Households' transactions are often summed into those of a single, representative household, or into a small number of household types, perhaps categorized by income class, geographical location, or demographic characteristics. The goods and services consumed in the economy are also aggregated into broad categories of commodities, such as food, manufactures, and services.

Every researcher must decide how to aggregate economic activity in his or her database, balancing the need for detail, for example on specific industries

Text Box 1.1. The GTAP Global Database
"Chapter 1: Introduction." (Hertel and Walmsley, 2008)

The Global Trade Analysis Project (GTAP) database, developed and maintained by researchers at Purdue University, is a publicly available resource (www.gtap.org) that provides the core data sets required by CGE models. These data include input-output tables, bilateral trade flows, transport costs, tax and tariff information, and all other data that comprise the Social Accounting Matrices (SAMs) used in CGE models. Version 7.0 of the GTAP database, released in 2008, describes 113 countries or regions and fifty seven commodities in a 2004 base year. The GTAP global database is regularly updated every three to four years and is reliant on broad participation by a network of database users who donate data.

that are relevant to the research question, with the benefits that a small, highly aggregated database offers in terms of experimenting with the model, and understanding and communicating model results. Many CGE modelers use the global CGE model database developed by Global Trade Analysis Project (GTAP) (see Text Box 1.1). Modelers typically aggregate this database in ways that are relevant to their research question. For example, we use the GTAP database to develop a small, three-sector, three-factor database for 2004 for the United States and an aggregated rest-of-world region, to use for demonstration throughout this book. The three sectors are agriculture, manufacturing, and services; and the three factors of production are land, labor, and capital.

The model database provides the values of all exogenous variables and parameters, and the initial equilibrium values of all endogenous variables. The database is typically maintained in a computer file separate from the CGE model, which is written in general functional notation. This approach makes it easier for the researcher to use the same general CGE model, but swap databases when the country, sectors, or factors under study change.

CGE Model Applications

CGE models have been applied to the study of a wide and growing range of economic problems. A comprehensive guide to their applications is well beyond the scope of this book, or indeed, of any one survey article. Nevertheless, there are several noteworthy books, articles and surveys that can provide you with a solid introduction to this growing body of literature. The early CGE model applications were mainly to tax policies in developed countries and to development policy in developing countries. Recommended surveys of this early literature are Shoven and Whalley (1984) and Pereira and Shoven (1988), who survey CGE-based analyses of taxation in developed countries. deMelo (1988) and Bandara (1991) review CGE analyses of trade and development policy in developing countries and Decaluwe and Martens (1988) provide a survey of CGE-based country studies. These classic surveys remain of interest for new modelers because they served as introductions of CGE models to the economics profession and thus include overviews of the core structure and behavior of CGE models.

By the early 1990s, many CGE modelers began to focus on trade liberalization within regional free trade areas and at the global level. Informative surveys of this literature include Robinson and Thierfelder (2002) and Bouet (2008). CGE models were also applied to the study of regions and states. Partridge and Rickman (1998) survey approaches to developing regional CGE models that describe economic activity at sub-national levels. More recent examples of regionalized CGE models are the USAGE-ITC model of the United States, developed by Dixon, Rimmer and Tsigas (2007) and studies of Morocco (Diao et al., 2008) and of Ethiopia (Block et al., 2006). Also, see Taylor et al. (1999) who developed an interesting CGE model of a village in Mexico.

More recently, CGE models have begun to make important contributions to the analysis of climate change and the evaluation of mitigating policies and adaptive behaviors. Bergman (1988 and 2005) and Bhattacharyya (1996) survey the CGE-based climate change literature and Burniaux and Truong (2002) detail the modeling approaches to climate change in several prominent CGE models. More recent contributions to climate analysis are the major CGE-based research programs based on the EPPA Model developed at the Massachusetts Institute of Technology (Paltsev, et al. 2005), and CIM-EARTH, an open CGE model developed at the University of Chicago and Argonne National Laboratory (Elliott, et al., 20101a).

The growing diversity of CGE model applications means that many innovative studies are not readily categorized into the broad areas described in surveys. Some examples that may help you to appreciate the breadth of recent CGE model applications include analyses of the economic effects of AIDS/HIV (Arndt, 2002), tourism and climate change (Berrittella et al., 2004), growing antibiotic resistance (Keogh et al., 2009), consumer aversion to genetically modified foods (Nielson, Thierfelder, and Robinson, 2001), and the modernization of retail food shopping in India (Landes and Burfisher, 2009). As you undertake a literature review for your own research project, you will discover many innovative and creative ways that CGE models are being applied today.

Summary

A CGE model is a system of equations that describes an economy as a whole and the interactions among its parts. Its equations describe producer and and consumer behavior and impose market clearing constraints, and they are solved for the set of prices at which the quantities of supply and demand are in equilibrium. A model experiment perturbs this equilibrium, and the model is re-solved for new market-clearing prices and quantities. In this book, we study a "standard" CGE model, which is static (single-period), single- or multicountry model with fixed national supplies of the factors of production (e.g., labor and capital). CGE models have been applied to the study of a wide and growing range of economic problems, including taxation, economic development, trade policy, climate change, tourism, and disease.

Key Terms

Computable general equilibrium model
Circular flow of income and spending
Equilibrium
Multicountry model
Partial equilibrium model
Single-country model
Static model

PRACTICE AND REVIEW

1. Solve the bicycle model.

   A CGE model is solved to find the set of prices at which quantities supplied are equal to the quantities demanded. In this exercise, you are asked to solve a partial equilibrium model of the bicycle industry for the market-clearing price and quantities.

   Model equations:

$$Q_d = 2Y - 2P$$
$$Q_s = -4P_i + 2P$$
$$Q_s = Q_d$$

   Exogenous parameters:

$$Y = 6$$
$$P_i = 1$$

   Solve for the base values of the two endogenous variables:

   P____________________

   $Q_s = Q_d$ _______________

2. Carry out a model experiment.

   Model experiments change the value of an exogenous variable(s) or parameter(s), and the model solve for new values for the model's endogenous variables. Assume that the exogenous variable in the bicycle model, income, Y, has increased from six to eight. Solve for the new equilibrium values of the endogenous variables:

P ________________

$Q_s = Q_d$ ____________

3. Partial vs. General Equilibrium Analysis of the Bicycle Industry

How important is a general equilibrium perspective in economic analysis? Is it possible that conclusions based on a partial equilibrium analysis could be wrong in either magnitude or the direction of change? In this exercise, you are asked to use your economic theory to make predictions about changes in the output price and output level of the bicycle industry following a price shock to one of its inputs – rubber tires. First, you will consider only the effects on supply and demand for bicycles – this is a partial equilibrium analysis that could be drawn from the simple bicycle model we developed in this chapter. Then you will be asked to consider some general equilibrium dimensions of the problem, and to compare these results with the partial equilibrium analysis. You are simply asked to reach *qualitative* conclusions about the general equilibrium impacts of an increase in the price of rubber tires.

Assume that the market is perfectly competitive, so that bicycle producers are price-takers in both input and product markets. This is shown in Figure 1.2, where D^1 is the demand for bicycles and S^1 is the initial supply of bicycles. In the initial equilibrium, at point A, 20 bicycles are supplied and demanded at a price of $1.00 per bike.

Consider the effects of the increase in price of rubber tires on bicycle production and sales price. An increase in input costs shifts the supply upward to S^2, because producers must now charge a higher price for any given quantity of bicycles. (We could also say that the supply curve shifts left, because a smaller quantity can be

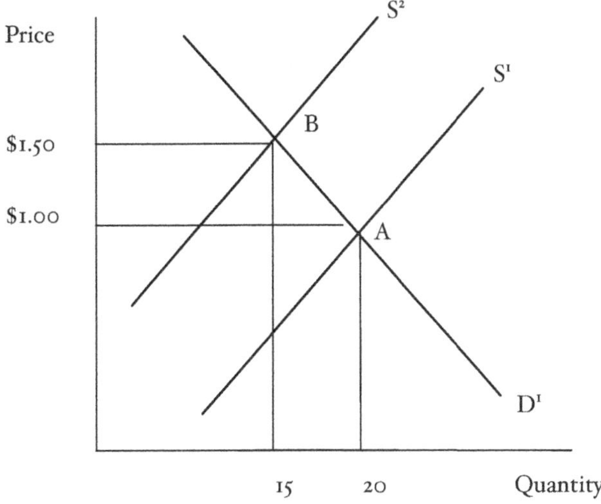

Figure 1.2. Effects of higher rubber tire prices on the domestic bicycle industry

Table 1.2. *Partial versus General Equilibrium Analysis*

	Bicycle Equilibrium Price is Higher/lower than $1.50	Bicycle Supply/demand Equilibrium is Greater/less than 15	Which Curve Shifts and in which Direction?
Increase in price of rubber tires	**$1.50**	**15**	**Supply – upward/left**
Bicycle workers accept lower wages	higher/lower	greater/less than	
Consumer demand shifts to imported bicycles	higher/lower	greater/less than	
Decline in exports causes depreciation and higher imported input costs	higher/lower	greater/less than	
Bicycle seat price falls due to fall in demand from bicycle producers	higher/lower	greater/less than	

produced for any given price.) The increase in price causes the quantity demanded to fall, shown as a movement along the demand curve, D^1. At the new equilibrium, at point B, the bicycle price has increased by 50 percent, to $1.50, and the quantity demanded has fallen by 25 percent, to 15.

This is a partial equilibrium analysis of the bicycle industry. The results are reported in the first row of Table 1.2. You will use these base results for comparison with your general equilibrium results.

Next, consider the interactions between the bicycle industry and the rest of the economy – a general equilibrium analysis. Analyze each of the following circumstances, *each independent of the rest.* Show how each of these factors individually can lead to an outcome that modifies the result of your partial equilibrium analysis.

Start by describing how each of the factors below causes a shift in either the supply curve, S^2, or the demand curve, D^1 and results in a new equilibrium price and quantity of bicycles. In Table 1.2, compare the new equilibrium with the results reported in the first row of the table, which describe point B. When you are done, look at the entries in the table and consider how your general equilibrium analysis compares with the partial equilibrium results.

In this thought exercise, you consider each of the factors individually. In a CGE model, all of these forces influence model results simultaneously. As you progress through this book and learn how to interpret your CGE model results, you may want to return to this exercise to remind yourself of some of the most important factors that may explain your new equilibrium.

1. Bicycle workers are highly specialized and unable to find work easily in other industries. Due to their limited job mobility, they choose to accept a drastic reduction in their wage to retain their jobs. The wage cut lowers the cost of bicycle production.

2. Imported bicycles are now cheaper than those made in the domestic industry. Because customers find imported bicycles to be almost indistinguishable from domestic ones, the domestic price increase causes the market share of imports to increase relative to domestically produced bicycles. Assume that the demand curve reports only demand for domestically produced bikes.
3. Assume that the higher price of rubber has increased the cost of production of autos, Tupperware, and many other products, causing exports of these goods to fall and the domestic currency to depreciate. Most of the steel used to produce bicycles is imported. How will depreciation influence your input costs and the supply curve for bicycles?
4. Any decline in your bicycle production reduces your demand for all of your inputs. Because you are the only industry that uses bicycle seats, your reduced production causes their price to drop. How will the falling price of your input from this "upstream" industry affect your supply curve, sales price and output level?

2

Elements of a Computable General Equilibrium Model

In this chapter, we deconstruct the computable general equilibrium model and describe its core elements. These include sets, endogenous and exogenous variables, exogenous parameters, behavioral and identity equations, and model closure. We describe prices, price normalization and the numeraire. We explain how the CGE model runs, including the processes of calibrating and solving the model, and carrying out an experiment.

A computable general equilibrium (CGE) model is a system of mathematical equations that describes an economy as a whole, and the interactions among its parts. A model this comprehensive is more complex than the bicycle industry model that we built in Chapter 1, but it need not be a "black box." In this chapter, we deconstruct the CGE model and describe its core elements. We show that a CGE model and the simple bicycle model share many features, such as exogenous and endogenous variables, market-clearing constraints, and identity and behavioral equations. We describe how the price of a single commodity changes as the product moves along the supply chain from producers to consumers. We explain the practice of normalizing prices and the role of the price numeraire. We introduce model closure, which is the decision about which variables are exogenous and which are endogenous. We also describe how the CGE model runs by explaining the sequence of model calibration, model solution, and model experiment.

In this chapter, our objective is to introduce, at a general level, the model's elements and mechanics. Even so, for many students, it may suffice to skim this chapter and return to it as needed as your modeling skills progress. For now, we also set aside any consideration of the economic theory that governs behavior in the model. Here, we do not consider how the model describes the motivations behind producers' decisions about how much to produce or consumers' decisions about how much to buy, or a nation's choice between consumption of its domestic production and imported goods. Of course, the economic properties of a CGE model are its real heart and soul but they also present a much broader area of study; most of the other chapters in this book address this study.

Sets

A CGE model starts by introducing sets. ***Sets*** are the domain over which parameters, variables, and equations are subsequently defined. For example, we can define set *i* as industries, which in the 3x3 U.S. database consists of agriculture, manufacturing, and services. If "QO" is output, then we can define a variable QO_i, which is the output quantity defined over the set *i*. That is, QO_i is a vector with three elements. It includes the output of agriculture, output of manufacturing, and output of services. To refer to only one element in set *i*, for example, the quantity of agricultural output, we express the variable as $QO_{\text{"agriculture"}}$, where one element of set *i*, in this case agriculture, is identified in quotes.

Similarly, we might define a different variable, PS, over the same set *i*, where PS is the producer price. If our equation refers to PS_i, then we are referring to the producer prices of agriculture, manufacturing, and services. To refer to the price of services alone, we would identify the set element in quotes, as $PS_{\text{"services"}}$.

Different variables in the CGE model can have different set domains. For example, our model might also include a set *f* that contains two factors of production – labor and capital. In that case, we could define variable PF_f as the price of factor *f*. The variable is a vector with two elements – labor wage and capital rent. Variables may also have more than one domain. For example, variable $QF_{f,i}$ is the quantity of factor *f* employed in the production of good *i*. The variable is a matrix, with *f* rows and *i* columns.

In multi-country CGE models, set notation related to bilateral trade usually follows the convention that the first country name is the source country and the second country name is the destination country, i.e., variable $QM_{i,r,s}$, describes QM quantity of commodity *i* imported from country *r* by country *s*. For example, $QM_{\text{"agriculture","USA","ROW"}}$ refers to imports of agriculture from the United States by the rest-of-world region. It is equal to $QE_{\text{"agriculture","USA","ROW"}}$, which is the quantity of agricultural goods exported from the United States to the rest-of-world region.

Endogenous Variables

Endogenous variables have values that are determined as solutions to the equations in the model, similar to the equilibrium price and quantity of bicycles in our simple partial equilibrium model of Chapter 1. Examples of endogenous variables in CGE models are prices and quantities of goods that

Text Box 2.1. Math Refresher – Working with Percent Changes

CGE model results are usually reported as the percent change from initial, or base, values. The following are three useful mathematical formulae for working with percent change data:

1. ***Percent change in a variable*** is the new value minus the base value, divided by the base value, multiplied by 100.

   Example: If the labor supply, L, increases from a base value of 4 million to 6 million, then:

   $$\text{Percent increase in L} = (6 - 4)/4 = 0.5 * 100 = 50$$

2. ***Percent change in the product of two variables*** is the sum of their percent changes.

   Example: GDP = P * Q, where P is the price and Q is the quantity of all goods in the economy. If P increases 4 percent but Q decreases 2 percent, then:

   $$\text{Percent change in GDP} = 4 + (-2) = 2$$

3. ***Percent change in the quotient of two variables*** is the dividend (numerator) minus the divisor (denominator).

   Example: Per capita GDP is GDP/N, where N is population. If GDP grows 1 percent and N grows 2 percent, then:

   $$\text{Percent change in GDP/N} = 1 - 2 = -1$$

are produced and consumed, prices and quantities of imports and exports, tax revenue, and aggregate savings.

When describing CGE model results, our notational convention in this book is to describe the level of a variable (e.g., the quantity of a good produced or its price) in upper or lower case letters and to denote the percent change in a variable in lower case italics. For example:

Variable $QO_{\text{“mfg”}}$ = quantity of manufacturing output

Variable $qo_{\text{“mfg”}}$ = percent change in quantity of manufacturing output

A CGE model usually has the same number of endogenous variables as independent equations. This is a necessary (although not a sufficient) condition to ensure that the model has a unique equilibrium solution.

Exogenous Variables

Exogenous variables have fixed values that do not change when the model is solved. For example, if the labor supply is assumed to be an exogenous variable, then the labor supply will remain at its base quantity, both before and after a model experiment.

Model Closure

Modelers decide which variables are exogenous and which are endogenous. These decisions are called ***model closure***. An example of a closure decision is the modeler's choice between (1) assuming that the economy's labor supply is exogenous, and an endogenous wage adjusts until national labor supply and demand are equal, or (2) assuming that the economywide wage is exogenous, and an endogenous labor supply adjusts until national labor supply and demand are equal.

To illustrate the important concept of model closure, assume that we are studying the effects of a decline in the demand for computers, which causes the computer industry's demand for workers to fall. If we assume the nation's total labor supply is exogenous (i.e., fixed at its initial level), then economy-wide wages will fall until all laid-off computer workers are reemployed in other industries. However, if the closure instead defines the economywide wage as exogenous (and fixed at its initial level), then the loss of jobs in the computer industry may cause national unemployment. Because a change in the size of a country's labor force changes the productive capacity of its economy, its gross domestic product (GDP) will decline more in a CGE model that allows unemployment than in a model whose closure fixes the national labor supply.

Because the choice of closure can affect model results in significant ways, modelers try to choose closures that best describe the economy they are studying. CGE models usually have a section of model code that lists model closure decisions. In the Global Trade Analysis Project (GTAP) model, for example, one of the tabbed windows on the model's front page is titled "Closure." The closure page lists all of the exogenous variables, and the remainder is endogenous.

Exogenous Parameters

CGE models include ***exogenous parameters*** that, like exogenous variables, have constant values. CGE models contain three types of exogenous parameters: tax and tariff rates, elasticities of supply and demand, and the shift and share coefficients used in supply and demand equations.

Tax and Tariff Rates

Tax and tariff rates are typically calculated by the CGE model from the model's base data. For example, a CGE model database reports the value of imports in world prices and the amount of tariff revenue that is paid to the government. The model calculates the exogenous parameter – the import tariff rate – as:

Value of tariff revenue/Value of imports in world prices * 100
= Import tariff rate.

If the tariff revenue is $10, and the world price of the import (including freight and other trade costs) is $100, then consumers pay $110 and the model calculates a tariff rate of 10 percent.

Modelers can change tax and tariff rates as a model experiment to analyze "what if" scenarios. For instance, the modeler may want to know what would happen in the economy if the government reduces the import tariff rate. As an experiment, the modeler lowers the tariff and re-solves the CGE model to find the resulting prices and the new quantities that are demanded and supplied.

Elasticity Parameters

Elasticities are exogenous parameters in a CGE model that describe the responsiveness of supply and demand to changes in relative prices and income. The magnitudes of model results stem directly from the size of the elasticities assumed in the model. For example, suppose that the National Chefs' Association has asked you to study the possible effects of economic growth on the demand for restaurant meals. If consumer demand for restaurant meals is assumed to be very responsive to income changes (so the income elasticity of demand parameter is high), then even a small increase in income will lead to a relatively large increase in the demand for restaurant services. However, if the income elasticity is assumed to be low, then even large economic growth will have only a small effect on the quantity of demand for restaurant services.

Because of the importance of elasticities to model results, modelers try to choose parameters based on a careful review of relevant econometric studies that estimate supply and demand elasticities. Often, however, the links between a CGE model's parameter requirements and the elasticities available in the literature are weak. Econometric studies may include different categories of commodities from those in the CGE model; they may be estimated using different functional forms; and the estimates themselves may be statistically weak. For these reasons, many CGE modelers also carry out "sensitivity analysis" of their model results to alternative sizes of elasticities. First, they run their model experiment with their assumed elasticity parameter. Next, they repeatedly change the values of one or more elasticities and rerun both the model and the experiment. They then compare the new experiment results with the results of the first experiment to determine whether their findings hold true across a reasonable range of elasticity values.[1]

The types of elasticities used in CGE models vary because they depend on the types of production and utility functions assumed in the model. Some elasticities may not be the types that you are familiar with from your microeconomics studies. In the following two sections, we describe the supply and demand elasticity parameters used in many CGE models and show how each influences the slope or shift in supply or demand curves. A CGE model generally utilizes some, but not all, of these parameters.

Supply Elasticity Parameters

Factor Substitution Elasticity. This parameter, σ_{VA}, relates to demand for factors of production, e.g., labor, L, and capital, K. It describes the flexibility of a production technology to allow changes in the quantity ratios of factors used in the production of a given level of output as relative factor prices change. For example, the parameter describes the ease with which producers in an industry can hire more labor and use less capital when the wage falls relative to the price of machinery and equipment.

The elasticity – one for each industry *i* in the model – describes the percent change in the quantity ratio of factor inputs given a percent change in their inverse price ratio:

$$\frac{\%\ \text{change}\ \dfrac{L_i}{K_i}}{\%\ \text{change}\ \dfrac{r}{w}}$$

where L_i and K_i are labor and capital employed in industry i, and r and w are the economy-wide capital rent and wage. The parameter's value ranges from zero to infinity. For example, an 0.5 percent factor substitution elasticity means that a 2 percent increase in capital rents relative to wages will lead to a 1 percent increase in the ratio of labor to capital quantities in the production process. As the parameter value approaches infinity, labor and capital become perfect substitutes. One worker can always be substituted for the same amount of capital with no reduction in the level of output. When the parameter is zero, the factors are complements, and producers must use a fixed ratio of capital and labor, regardless of changes in wages compared to rents.

[1] In Model Exercise 8, you will use an automated utility developed for the GTAP model by Arndt and Pearson (1998) to systematically analyze the sensitivity of model results to alternative values of elasticity parameters. This utility considerably simplifies this reiterative process of sensitivity analysis.

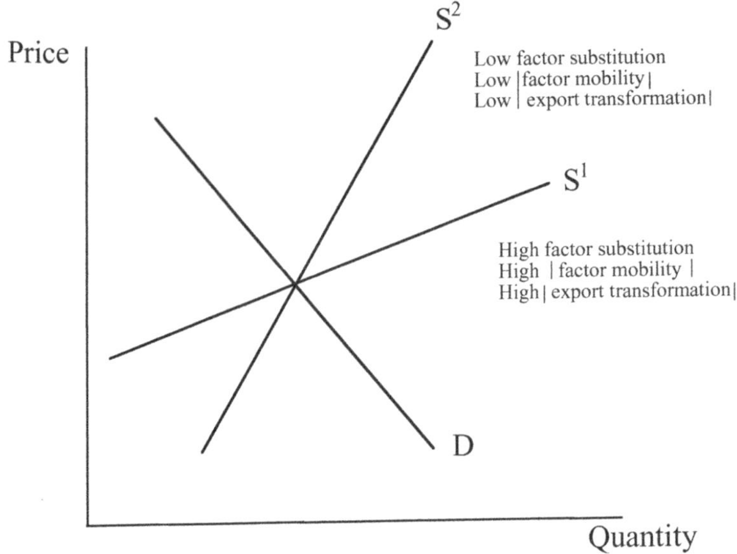

Figure 2.1. Effects of supply elasticity parameters on the slope of the supply curve

Producers who can more readily substitute among factors have a more elastic industry supply curve, such as curve S^1 in Figure 2.1, where the axes represent output quantity and output price. When this industry increases its output, producers can keep the costs of production low by switching to lower cost factor inputs. For example, an industry with a flexible technology (a high factor substitution elasticity) can become more mechanized if its expansion causes wages to increase by more than capital rents. An industry with a more rigid technology, and a low factor substitution elasticity, is described in Figure 2.1 by the less elastic, and steeper, supply curve, S^2.

Factor Mobility Elasticity. This elasticity parameter, σ_F, relates to factor supply. It describes the ease with which a factor moves across industries in response to changing industry wages or rents. For example, it describes the willingness of a worker to move to another industry if it offers higher wages than his current job.

One elasticity is defined for each factor in the CGE model. It governs the percent change in the share of the national factor supply employed in industry *i* given a percent change in the economy-wide average factor price relative to the industry wage, w_i, or rent, r_i. For example, the labor mobility elasticity describes the share of the labor force employed in industry *i* as a function of its wage relative to the economy-wide wage:

$$\frac{\%\ \text{change}\ \dfrac{L_i}{L}}{\%\ \text{change}\ \dfrac{W}{W_i}}$$

The parameter value can range between zero (factors cannot move between sectors) and negative one (factors move proportionately to a change in relative factor prices). The lower range restriction of negative one reflects that the factor supply function, in those CGE models that explicitly include one, is used to describe relatively inflexible factor movements. As an example, an elasticity of minus 0.5 percent means that a 2 percent increase in the wage in the computer industry relative to the average wage, results in a 1 percent increase in the share of the labor force employed in computers.

When an industry employs factors that move sluggishly (with low absolute values of the mobility elasticity), its supply curve becomes relatively steep, like S^2 in Figure 2.1, where the axes represent output quantity and output price. This is because its wage and rental costs must rise sharply to attract the additional factors needed to increase production. The more mobile factors are and the larger the parameter's absolute value, the more elastic is the industry's supply curve, such as S^1 in Figure 2.1.

Export Transformation Elasticity. This parameter, σ_E, relates to an industry's export supply. It describes the technological ability of an industry to transform its product between the varieties sold in the domestic and export markets. For example, it describes how easily automakers could shift production between models for the home market and models that are more popular in foreign markets.

For each industry *i,* the elasticity measures the percent change in the ratio of the export quantity, QE, to the quantity sold domestically, QD, given a percent change in the ratio of the domestic price, PD to the free on board (*fob*) export price, PE:

$$\frac{\%\text{ change }\dfrac{QE_i}{QD_i}}{\%\text{ change }\dfrac{PD_i}{PE_i}}$$

One export transformation elasticity is defined for each industry, with a value that ranges from zero to negative infinity. For example, a minus 0.8 percent parameter value means that a 2 percent increase in the domestic price relative to the export price will lead to a 1.6 percent decline in the quantity ratio of exports to domestic sales in producers' total output.

If the parameter has a low absolute value, then the resources used in the production of one variety are relatively difficult to transform into the production of the other variety. For example, to increase their production of exports, producers must shift toward greater use of relatively unsuitable inputs from the production of the domestic variety. This raises the cost of expanding export sales and therefore limits the export supply response. In

Figure 2.1, assuming that the axes represent export quantity and export price, the lower the absolute value of the export transformation elasticity, the less elastic (and steeper) is the industry's export supply curve such as S^2 in Figure 2.1. When the export transformation parameter is high in absolute value, then producers can readily expand their export output with less upward push on their costs of production. Their export supply curve is therefore more elastic, such as S^1.

Demand Elasticity Parameters

Income Elasticity of Demand. This elasticity parameter describes the effect of a change in income upon demand for a commodity. One parameter is defined for each consumption good *i* in the model. It measures the percent change in the quantity demanded, Q, given a percent change in income, Y:

$$\frac{\%\text{ change } Q_i}{\%\text{ change } Y}$$

Income elasticity parameter values between zero and one indicate necessity goods, such as food, for which demand grows by proportionately less than growth in income. Parameter values greater than one describe luxury goods, for which demand grows by proportionately more than growth in income. A unitary income elasticity assumes that consumer demand changes by the same proportion as a change in income.

In CGE models, goods are usually "***normal***"; that is, income elasticities are positive so that an increase in income leads to an increase in demand for a good. Not all CGE models allow the modeler to specify an income elasticity of demand. Often, the models assume utility functions in which the income elasticity of demand is "hardwired" to have a value of one. See Chapter 4 for a more complete discussion of this point. In Figure 2.2, a change in income could be shown as a shift in the demand curve, where the axes represent the quantity of the consumption good and its consumer price. The higher the income elasticity, the larger is the rightward (leftward) shift in the demand curve for any given increase (decrease) in income.

Own- and Cross-Price Substitution Elasticities. These parameters measure the responsiveness of consumer demand to changes in the price of commodities. The own-price elasticity measures the percent change in quantity demanded for good *i* given a percent change in its consumer price, P:

$$\frac{\%\text{ change } Q_i}{\%\text{ change } P_i}$$

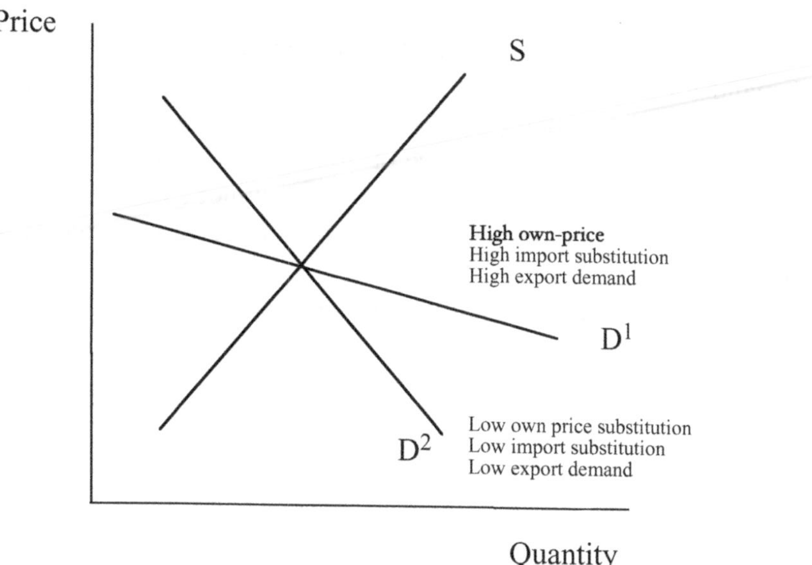

Figure 2.2. Effects of demand elasticity parameters on the slope of the demand curve

CGE models generally assume that the ***Law of Demand*** holds; that is, an increase in the price of a good causes the quantity demanded to fall, so the own-price elasticity of demand is negative. When consumer demand is price sensitive, the own-price parameter is large in absolute terms. The demand curve for good is relatively elastic, such as curve D^1 in Figure 2.2, where the axes describe the quantity demanded of good *i* and its consumer price. When the own-price elasticity parameter is low, then the demand curve becomes less elastic, such as D^2.

A cross-price elasticity of demand measures the percent change in demand for a good *i* given a percent change in the consumer price of another good, *j*:

$$\frac{\%\text{ change } Q_i}{\%\text{ change } P_j}$$

The cross-price elasticity is positive when the two goods are easily substituted (like brown sugar and dark brown sugar), negative when the goods are ***complements*** (like left shoes and right shoes), and zero when demand for one good is ***independent*** of the price of the other good. In Figure 2.2, a change in the price of a ***substitute*** good can be shown as a shift in the demand curve for consumption of good *i*. The larger the positive cross-price substitution elasticity parameter, the larger the rightward (leftward) shift in the demand curve as the price of the substitute good falls (rises).

Import Substitution. This elasticity parameter, σ_M, relates to consumer demand for imports. It describes consumers' willingness to shift between imported (QM) and domestically produced varieties in their consumption of commodity *i* as the relative price of domestic (PD) to imported (PM) varieties changes. For example, it describes a consumer's willingness to shift from an imported car to a domestic model when the relative price of the import rises.

The parameter is calculated as the percent change in the quantity ratio given a percent change in their inverse price ratio:

$$\frac{\%\ \text{change}\ \dfrac{QM_i}{QD_i}}{\%\ \text{change}\ \dfrac{PD_i}{PM_i}}$$

Its value may range between zero and infinity. For example, if the substitution elasticity is two, then a 1 percent increase in the price of the domestic relative to the imported variety will lead to a 2 percent increase in the ratio of the import relative to the domestic quantity for a given consumption level. Assume that the axes in Figure 2.2 describe quantities of imports and the import price. When the import substitution parameter has a low value, import demand is inelastic, shown as D^2 in Figure 2.2. As the parameter value increases, the import demand curve becomes more elastic, such as D^1.

Export Demand Elasticity. Single-country CGE models describe the rest of the world's demand for a country's exports as a function of its export price. Usually, when its export price rises relative to the world price, θ, the country's foreign sales will fall. An export demand elasticity parameter is defined for each exported commodity *i* in the CGE model. It describes the percent change in the share of country's exports, QE, in world trade, QW, given a percent change in the ratio between the average world price, PXW, and the exporter's price:

$$\frac{\%\ \text{change}\ \dfrac{QE_i}{QW_i}}{\%\ \text{change}\ \dfrac{PXW_i}{PE_i}}$$

An increase in the exporter's price relative to the world price causes its export quantity and world market share to decline. The larger the elasticity parameter value, the larger the decline in its exports as the country's relative export price increases. The export demand elasticity ranges from zero to infinity. A parameter value that approaches infinity describes a small country, and a parameter value near zero describes a very large country in world markets. In Figure 2.2, if we assume that the axes represent the quantity of a country's export good and its export price, then a high value of the export demand elasticity parameter is shown as the very elastic demand curve, D^1, for a small country's exports. A low parameter value is described by the relatively inelastic export demand curve of a large country, D^2.

Shift and Share Parameters

Shift parameters and ***share parameters*** are exogenous values used in the supply and demand functions in a CGE model. As an example, consider the shift and share parameters in a Cobb-Douglas production function. This function is used in many CGE models to describe the production technology of an industry:

$$QO = A(K^{\alpha}L^{1-\alpha})$$

where QO is the output quantity. Parameter A is a shift parameter whose value is greater than zero and that describes the productivity of capital, K, and labor, L, in the production process. Parameter α is a share parameter, ranging between zero and one. It measures the share of K in the total income received by labor and capital from their employment in the industry. Labor's income share parameter is $1 - \alpha$.

Parameter A is called a shift parameter because a change in its value causes the industry supply curve to shift to the right or the left. For example, if the shift parameter increases in value, perhaps from $A = 5$ to $A = 10$, then factors are more productive, and the same quantity of K and L can produce a larger quantity of output. This change in the shift parameter is described by the rightward shift in the supply curve from S^1 to S^2 in Figure 2.3. CGE modelers can change the value of the shift parameter in the production function as a model experiment to describe changes in the productivity of one or more inputs.

Other share parameters in the production and consumption functions in a CGE model include the shares of commodities in consumers' total consumption; shares of imported and domestic varieties in the demand for commodities; and the shares of domestic and export sales in total industry output.

Model Calibration

The *model* ***calibration*** procedure calculates the shift and share parameters used in the production and utility functions in the CGE model so that the

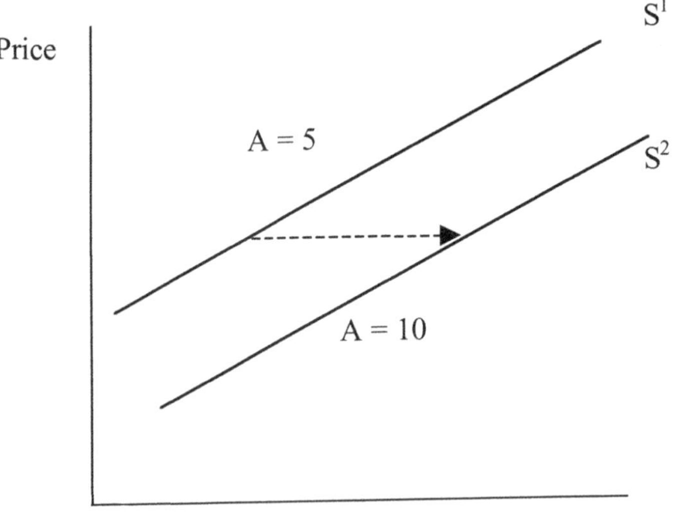

Figure 2.3. Effect of an increase in the shift parameter value on the supply curve

solutions to the equation replicate the initial equilibrium as reported in the base data. The calibrated model solution is then used as the benchmark equilibrium, against which the results of model experiments are compared. The inputs to the calibration process are the CGE model database, which describes an economy in an initial equilibrium; the model's production or utility functions (such as a Cobb-Douglas production function), and the elasticity parameters assumed by the modeler.

As an example of the calibration procedure, let's again consider a CGE model that assumes this Cobb-Douglas production function:[2]

$$QO = A\,(K^{\alpha}L^{1-\alpha})$$

Suppose the model database reports that the industry employs thirty units of capital, K, and seventy units of labor, L, with per unit wages and rents of one dollar each, at a total factor cost of \$100. The base-year output quantity, QO, is 109 units. The model calibration process first calculates the share parameters α and $1-\alpha$. The share of capital, α, in total factor payments of \$100 is 0.3, and the income share of labor, $1-\alpha$, is 0.7. With these share parameters, and the given values of QO, K, and L from the model database, the calibration process then solves for A:

$$109 = A\,(30^{.3}70^{.7})$$

[2] Note that the modeler does not need to specify any elasticities in the case of a Cobb-Douglas production function because these are implied by the properties of the function: the own-price elasticity of demand for each factor is negative one, and the cross-price elasticities of demand for capital and labor are zero.

whose value is two. You can also verify for yourself that the production function, with these calibrated shift and share parameters, reproduces the base year output of 109.

The calibrated shift and share parameters used in the model's production and utility functions always remain at their initial values, even though actual shares may later change as the result of model experiments. Modelers sometimes change the shift parameters used in production functions to analyze the effects of productivity shocks. Sometimes, too, modelers change calibrated share parameters as an experiment. Two interesting examples of this approach are Kuiper and van Tongeren (2006), summarized in Text Box 2.2, who change the import share parameters; and Nielson, Thierfelder, and Robinson (2001), summarized in Text Box 4.1, who change consumer budget share parameters.

Equations

CGE models have behavioral and identity equations. ***Behavioral equations*** describe the economic behavior of producers, consumers, and other agents in the model based on microeconomic theory. You may recognize some of the behavioral supply and demand equations in the model from your economics coursework. For example, CGE models include a behavioral equation that describes how firms minimize the costs of inputs to produce a specific level of output, given input and output prices and subject to the technological constraints of their production process.

CGE models also include a utility function that describes the combinations of goods that consumers prefer. The choice of utility function, for example, Cobb-Douglas or Stone-Geary, depends on which best describes consumer preferences in the country under study. Given consumers' preferences, a behavioral equation describes how they choose quantities of goods that maximize their utility subject to the prices of goods and their budget. Additional behavioral equations in the CGE model explain the demand for imports and the supply of exports.

Identity equations define a variable as a mathematical function (sum, product, etc.) of other variables. Identity equations therefore hold true by definition. If the value of any one of the variables in the identity equation changes, then one or more of the other variables must also change in order to maintain the equivalence. For some equations, model closure is the choice made by the modeler as to which variable adjusts to maintain the identity.

Identity equations act as constraints in a CGE model to ensure that the model solves for a market-clearing set of prices at which quantities supplied and demanded are equal. The equations are similar to the market-clearing constraint in our bicycle model of Chapter 1, that $Q_d = Q_s$.

Text Box 2.2. The Small Share Problem and the Armington Import Aggregation Function

"An Empirical Approach to the Small Initial Trade Share Problem in General Equilibrium Models." Kuiper and van Tongeren (2006).

What is the research question? CGE-based analyses of trade liberalization describe the effects of eliminating trade barriers on import quantities. The majority of these analyses assume an Armington import aggregation function. The "small share problem" is due to the scaling effect of the share parameter α in the Armington import demand equation:

$$\frac{M}{Q} = \alpha \frac{P_M}{P_Q}^{-\rho}$$

where M is the import, Q is the composite commodity (the sum of imported and domestically produced varieties), P_M and P_Q are the prices of the import and the composite commodity, respectively, and parameter ρ is related to the import substitution elasticity parameter. Parameter α is the initial quantity share of imports in the consumption of commodity Q. Its value is calculated during model calibration and does not change following a model experiment. Notice that if the initial import share is small, then even a large change in the relative price of the import, or a large increase in the size of the import substitution parameter, can result only in small changes in the import share of consumption. This scaling effect may lead to unrealistically small import quantity results in trade liberalization simulations that cause the import price to fall. Could a gravity model provide an empirical basis for changing the share parameters as part of trade liberalization experiment?

What is the model innovation? The researchers develop a gravity model to identify the role of trade barriers in bilateral trade flows. They use the gravity model to simulate trade liberalization and estimate changes in bilateral trade shares. Then, they modify their GTAP model to adjust the calibrated trade shares to those of the gravity model results as part of a trade liberalization experiment.

What is the model experiment? The authors eliminate global import tariffs and export subsidies (1) with and (2) without changes in import share parameters.

What are the key findings? The adjustments shift bilateral trade flows, causing some regions to gain larger shares of the world market following trade reform and other regions to lose market share, compared to a standard CGE model analysis. Adjusting the import share parameters does not change the size of global welfare effects by very much.

An example of a market-clearing identity equation from the GTAP model is this expression:

$$qo_f = \sum_j SHR_{f,j}\, qfe_{f,j}$$

The equation states that the percent change in the national supply, *qo*, of the mobile factor, *f*, must equal the weighted sum of percent changes in demand, *qfe*, for factor *f* by industry *j*, where $SHR_{f,j}$ is each industry's share in national employment of factor *f*. That is, it imposes the constraint that aggregate supply must equal aggregate demand for each factor *f*.

Macroclosure

CGE models include an identity equation that imposes the constraint that total savings is equal to total investment. Some multicountry models impose this constraint at the global level. Other single and multicountry models impose it at the national level. ***Macroclosure*** describes the modeler's decision about which of the two macroeconomic variables – savings or investment – will adjust to maintain the identity that savings equals investment.

Standard, static CGE model rely on an identity equation to model savings and investment because these behaviors are determined largely by macroeconomic forces, such as monetary policy and expectations about future economic conditions, that are outside the scope of a real CGE model.[3] Nevertheless, the models must account for them in some way because savings and investment are part of the circular flow of income and spending, with effects on the real economy. Investment affects the production side of the economy because investors buy capital equipment that is produced by industries. Savings affects the demand side of the economy because households and the government allocate some share of their disposable income to savings, which affects their demand for goods and services.

CGE models may differ in whether savings or investment is assumed to adjust to maintain the savings-investment identity. In some models, such as the default closure in the GTAP model, the savings rate (the percentage of income that is saved) is assumed to be exogenous and constant, so the quantity of savings changes whenever income changes. Investment spending then changes to accommodate the change in supply of savings. A model with this closure is called savings-driven, because changes in savings drive changes in investment. An advantage of this closure is that a nation's savings rate remains the same as the rate observed in the base year. This is appealing if we think that base year savings rates reveal the subjective preferences of a country's households and government.

In other CGE models, the aggregate value of investment is fixed at its initial level, and savings rates are assumed to adjust until savings are equal to

[3] For a more detailed discussion of macroclosure and savings and investment, see Lofgren, et al. (2002), Hertel and Tsigas (1997), Robinson (1991), and Dewatripont and Michel (1987). Shoven and Whalley (1984) discuss the effect of closure in predetermining model results.

investment spending. A model with this closure is called investment-driven. This closure is well suited for the study of countries in which governments use policies that influence savings rates to achieve targeted investment levels.

To demonstrate how this macroclosure decision can matter, assume that a country's income increases. In a savings-driven model, households save a fixed share of their income, so income growth will cause savings to increase and therefore investment spending to rise. In an investment-driven model, investment is fixed, so the supply of savings is also fixed. In this case, consumers will spend, rather than save their additional income. Because households and investors are likely to prefer different types of goods, the two alternative closures will lead to a different commodity composition of demand. The savings-driven model is likely to result in an increase in production of machinery and equipment, which is what investors prefer to buy. An investment-driven model is likely to result in an increased demand for consumer goods, like groceries, apparel, and consumer electronics.

Some CGE models, such as those in the Dervis, de Melo, and Robinson (1982) tradition, specify additional macroclosure rules to describe the current account balance and the government fiscal balance. These macroclosure decisions address components of national savings. The current account closure describes whether foreign savings inflows (the current account) are exogenous and the exchange rate is endogenous, or vice versa. An exogenous current account closure fixes the supply of foreign savings (the current account deficit or surplus) at its initial level and the exchange rate adjusts to maintain it, whereas a fixed exchange rate makes foreign savings endogenous. The government budget closure describes whether government savings (the federal deficit) is endogenous and government spending is fixed, or vice versa.

Modelers choose macroclosure rules that best describe the economy under study. The rules also offer researchers the flexibility to explore macroeconomic policy shocks in a CGE model, such as currency devaluation or pay-go federal budget rules. See, for example, Cattaneo, Hinojosa-Ojeda, and Robinson's (1999) methodical study of the effects of alternative macroeconomic policies in Costa Rica, which are simulated by running the same policy shock with different macroeconomic closures (Text Box 2.3).

Normalizing Prices

The value of output of good X is the product of its prices times its quantity. For example, the value of production of apples is the product of their price (say, $1.50 each) and the quantity of apples (ten), which is $15. The database of a CGE model comprises only value flows. It reports the value of output of each good in the model, but not their quantities or prices. It reports the

Text Box 2.3. Macro Closure and Structural Adjustment in Costa Rica
"Costa Rica Trade Liberalization, Fiscal Imbalances, and Macroeconomic Policy: A Computable General Equilibrium Model." (Cattaneo, Hinojosa-Ojeda, and Robinson, 1999).

What is the research question? In the 1980s, Costa Rica signed structural adjustment agreements with the World Bank that included trade liberalization, elimination of producer and consumer subsidies, and other policy reforms. How might the broader reform program that Costa Rica must carry out temper the gains from the trade liberalization component?

What is the CGE model innovation? The authors develop a multihousehold SAM for Costa Rica for 1991. Using the IFPRI standard CGE model, they vary macroclosure rules to describe alternative ways to implement structural adjustment commitments.

What is the experiment? A single trade liberalization experiment, that removes all import tariffs and export taxes, is carried out under two alternative foreign savings closures: fixed foreign savings and an endogenous exchange rate versus a fixed exchange rate and endogenous foreign savings. Both scenarios are also conducted with three alternative closures for government savings: loss of trade tax revenue causes the government to run a deficit; and the government budget balance is fixed with trade tax revenue replaced by a corporate income tax or by a retail sales tax.

What are the key findings? Trade liberalization generates efficiency gains for the economy as a whole, and changes in the distribution of income across households are small. However, there are trade-offs that the government must face to maximize these potential gains. The scenarios offer a blueprint for government policy, recommending reduced government expenditures and higher retail sales taxes to offset the significant loss of trade tax revenues.

value of factor inputs, such as labor, but not the number of workers who are employed or their wage rates. However, you will see that a CGE model reports the results of model experiments for both quantities and prices. For example, a new production subsidy may increase the quantity of X that is produced by 5 percent but cause its price to fall by 2 percent. How does a CGE model develop price and quantity data if its database contains only value data?

CGE models translate value data into price and quantity data by ***normalizing*** prices. This procedure converts most of the initial, or base, prices in the model into $1 or one unit of the currency used in the model.[4]

[4] This practice is attributed to Arnold Harberger (1964), who normalized the prices and quantities of factors in a general equilibrium analysis of the U.S. income tax.

Table 2.1. *Normalizing the Price and Quantity of Apples in a CGE Model*

	Base Values for Apples			50% Increase in Apple Quantity		
	Price	Quantity	Value	Price	Quantity	Value
Actual market data	.5	6	3	.5	9	4.5
Normalized data	1	3	3	1	4.5	4.5

Quantities of goods and of factors of production (e.g., labor and capital) are then interpreted as the quantity per $1 or unit of currency.

Let's use a simple example of apples to show how prices are normalized. According to the actual market data reported in Table 2.1, apples cost fifty cents each and the initial quantity demanded is six, so the value of apples sold in the market is $3. In a CGE model database, we know only the value of apples sales, which is $3. By normalizing prices, we describe the apple price as $1 and the quantity as the unit quantity per dollar, which is three. That is, each quantity unit of apples in the model is two actual apples.

Normalizing prices does not affect our results. To illustrate this point, consider what happens if the sales quantity of apples increases by 50 percent. If we use actual market data, then the value of sales increases to $4.50 (nine apples times fifty cents). When we use the normalized data, we get the same answer. The apple quantity rises 50 percent, from three to 4.5 units of apples, and 4.5 apples times $1 equals $4.50.

The practice of normalizing data considerably reduces the information needed to build a CGE model database without losing the capability of the CGE model to generate results for prices, quantities, and values. This approach also means that most, but not all, prices in a CGE model have an initial value of one. Some prices in the CGE model are adjusted to include taxes or subsidies and these initial prices do not equal one. An example is the domestic consumer price of imports. If the normalized world import price is $1 and the import tariff is 10 percent, then the initial domestic consumer price of imports in the CGE model is $1.10.

Price Linkages

If you purchase a shirt in China for $14 that is imported from Brazil, you probably realize that the Brazilian company that manufactured the shirt does not receive $14 for it. The difference between the price that you pay in China and that received by the producer includes any export taxes that the Brazilian firm paid to its government, the costs of transporting the shirt between Brazil and China, and any import tariffs and sales taxes that you

Table 2.2. *Prices in a Multicountry CGE Model*

Type of Price	Defined Over Sets	Definition
Producer price (*ps*)	i,r	Cost of production, includes production tax or subsidy
Consumer price (*pp*)	i,r	Producer price plus sales tax (domestic variety) and bilateral *cif* import price plus import tariff and sales tax (import variety)
Bilateral import price (*pcif*)	i,r,s	Exporter's bilateral export price plus *cif* trade margins, excluding tariff.
Bilateral export price (*pfob*)	i,r,s	Exporter's domestic producer price plus export tax
World import price (*pim*)	i,r	Trade-weighted sum of bilateral *cif* import prices in country *r*
World export price (*piw*)	i,r	Trade-weighted sum of bilateral *fob* export prices in country *r*
Global price (*pxw*)	i	Trade-weighted sum of all countries' bilateral export prices

Notes: *i* is the set of commodities, *r* is the exporting country and *s* is the importing country. The corresponding variable names used in the GTAP model (in percent change terms) are listed in the first column, in parentheses.

paid to your own (Chinese) government. We omit discussion of the costs of wholesale and retail services incurred in bringing the shirt from the port to your department store.

A CGE model reports several prices for a single commodity, such as a shirt, because it tracks goods and prices all along the supply chain between producers and consumers (Table 2.2). The ***producer price*** is the sales price received by the producer. In a competitive market, it is equal to the cost of production, inclusive of any taxes or subsidies entailed in the production process. The Brazilian shirt, for example, may cost $8 to manufacture, so the Brazilian producer price is $8. Some Brazilian shirts are sold in the domestic market. In this case, Brazilian consumers pay $8 plus any sales tax that the Brazilian government imposes. If we assume that the sales tax is $2 per shirt, then the ***consumer price*** for a Brazilian-made shirt in Brazil is $10.

Figure 2.4 describes prices for goods that are traded internationally. In this example, Brazil's ***bilateral fob export price*** to China is a "free on board" value. An ***fob*** value is the value of the export good when placed on board the ship at the Brazilian port of departure. It is the producer price plus any export taxes or subsidies on its sales to China. In Figure 2.4, the Brazilian

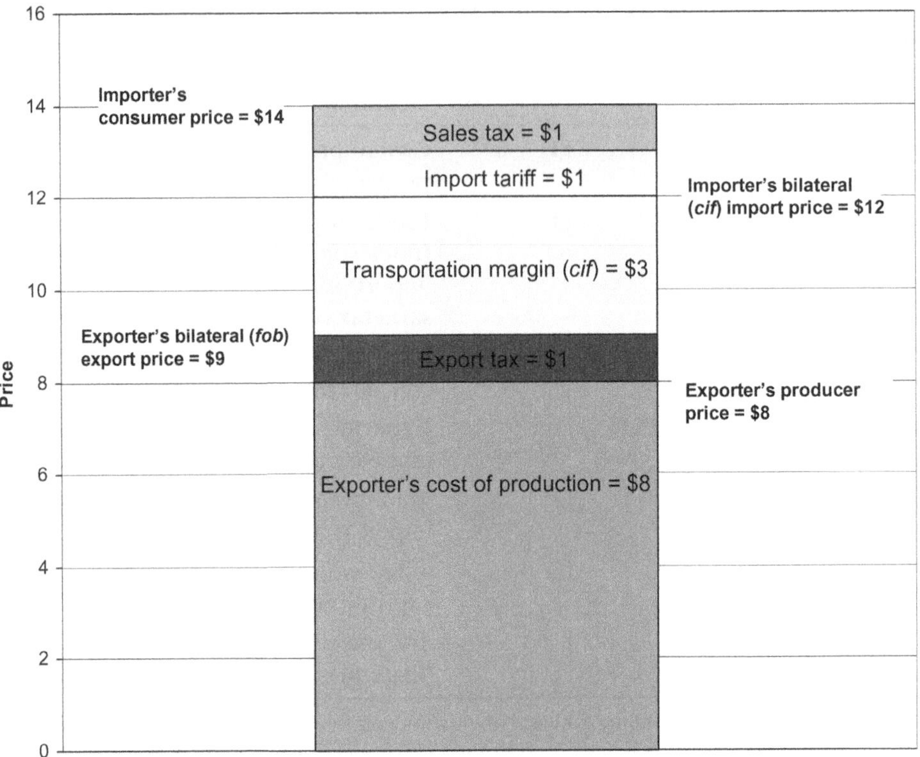

Figure 2.4. Price linkages in international trade

producer pays $1 per shirt in export taxes on sales to China, so its bilateral *fob* export price is $9 per shirt.

Imports incur insurance and freight charges, also called trade margin costs, to move goods from the exporter's port to that of the importer. Suppose that the trade margin cost for shipping the shirt to China totals $3. China's ***bilateral cif import price*** (i.e., cost plus insurance and freight) for a shirt from Brazil, is therefore $12. The *consumer price* of the Brazilian shirt in China is its bilateral *cif* import price plus any import tariffs and sales taxes imposed by the Chinese government. Assuming that China has a tariff of $1 on the Brazilian shirt and imposes a $1 sales tax on its consumers, then the consumer price of the Brazilian shirt in China totals $14. Notice that the consumer price of the Brazilian shirt is higher in China ($14) than in Brazil ($10); the difference is because of trade margin costs, import tariffs, and the difference in sales taxes in the two countries.

Multi-country CGE models with bilateral trade flows report bilateral *fob* export and *cif* import prices for every commodity traded between every pair of trading partners in the world. Tracking bilateral export and import prices allows the modeler to take into account that taxes, tariffs, and trade margin costs may diverge among trade partners. It also allows the modeler to take into account that many products are differentiated by country of origin. For example, French consumers may think that oranges from Spain are different than oranges from Israel. As a result, France may import oranges from both Israel and Spain. There also can also be two-way trade in the same product. For example, Spain may export oranges to Israel and Israel may export oranges to Spain.

A country's ***world export price*** and ***world import price*** are the trade-weighted sum of its bilateral *fob* export and bilateral *cif* import prices for each good. Brazil's world export price of shirts, for example, is the trade-weighted sum of its bilateral *fob* export prices of shirts sold to China, the United States, and all other countries to which it exports. A **trade weight** is the share of a destination country in an exporter's total export quantity, or the share of a source country in an importer's total import quantity.

As an example, let's calculate the world export price of Brazil's shirts. Suppose China accounts for 75 percent of Brazil's total quantity of shirt exports, at a Brazilian bilateral export price of $10 per shirt (this includes Brazil's export tax). Suppose the United States accounts for the remaining 25 percent of shirt exports, but there is no Brazilian export tax on its sales to the United States. Brazil's bilateral export price to the United States is therefore only $8 per shirt. Brazil's world export price for shirts is calculated as:

China	.75 * $10 = $7.50
United States	.25 * $8 = $2.00
World price	$7.50 + $2.00 = $9.50

Brazil's world import price for each good would be calculated in a similar fashion; this time the trade weights would be the quantity shares of each source country in Brazil's total imports of a commodity.

Finally, the ***global price*** of a good, such as shirts, is the trade-weighted sum of all of the bilateral, *fob* export prices of all countries in the world. The weights are the shares of each bilateral trade flow in the total quantity of global trade in that good.

Numeraire

A CGE model describes only relative prices. To express all prices in relative terms, the modeler chooses one price variable in the CGE model to remain fixed at its initial level. This price serves as the model's ***numeraire***, a benchmark of value against which the changes in all other prices can be measured (see Text Box 2.4).

As an example, consider a model with three goods: agriculture, services, and manufacturing. The producer prices of manufactured goods and services could be measured in terms of – or relative to – the price of the agricultural good, which we have selected to be the numeraire. Initially, the producer

Text Box 2.4. The Numeraire and Walras' Law

CGE modelers can be more confident that their model has a feasible and unique solution if it is "square;" that is, if the number of variables and equations in the model are equal. When we fix one price to serve as the numeraire, we are dropping one variable from our model. Are we therefore causing the number of variables to be one fewer than the number of equations? The answer is no, and it rests on Walras' Law.

Leon Walras was a 19th century economist who studied the interconnectedness among all markets in an economy. He focused in particular on the problem of whether a set of prices exists at which the quantity supplied is equal to the quantity demanded in every market simultaneously. His theoretical, general equilibrium model was much like the standard, "Walrasian" CGE model that we are studying. They share the features that: (1) producers are profit-maximizers who sell their goods in perfectly competitive markets at zero economic profit; (2) consumers are utility-maximizers who spend all of the income they receive from their production and sale of goods; and (3) prices adjust until demand for each commodity is equal to its supply. Based on these assumptions and market-clearing constraints, Walras' Law states that, for the economy as a whole, the aggregate value of excess supply in the economy must be matched by the aggregate value of excess demand. This is essentially because producers plan to sell that value of goods that will enable them to afford their desired purchases. A shortfall in their actual sales (excess supply) therefore results in an equal shortfall between their actual and desired consumption (excess demand).

An implication of Walras' Law is that equilibrium in the last market follows from the supply-demand balance in all other markets. As a result, the equations in his model were not all independent. One equation was redundant and had to be dropped – but this meant his model had one more variable than the number of equations. Walras' solution was to fix one price in the model to serve as numeraire, making his model "square" once again. He could now solve for the market-clearing set of relative prices.

To make their models square, CGE modelers, too, usually drop one equation and fix one price variable to serve as numeraire. Any equation can be dropped without influencing results if the model is homogenous of degree zero in prices (as they usually are). In practice, modelers usually omit the macroeconomic market-clearing equation that defines aggregate savings (S) to be equal to aggregate investment (I). As an alternative, some modelers fix a numeraire but keep the redundant equation and add an additional variable called "Walras," i.e., S = I + Walras. If all markets in the CGE model are in equilibrium, then the Walras variable's value will equal zero. Such a variable can be useful to the modeler as a way to check that all markets are in equilibrium in the base data and model solutions.

prices of all three goods are \$1, because they have been normalized. Let's assume that after a model shock, the producer price of the numeraire (agriculture) remains at \$1 (it must, because it is the numeraire) but the producer price of the manufactured good has doubled; the relative producer price of manufactures is now $2/1 = 2$.

Because the exchange ratios of all goods are specified relative to the numeraire, you can also compare the prices of non-numeraire goods – in this case, the price of manufactured goods relative to services. Assume that the price of services increased only 20 percent, then its relative price in terms of agriculture is $1.20/1 = 1.20$. The price of services (1.20) has fallen relative to manufacturing (2).

You can choose any price in the CGE model to be the numeraire. Your choice of numeraire has no impact on real, or quantity, variables that result from an experiment. Some modelers define the numeraire to be the consumer price index (CPI), which is calculated as the weighted sum of initial consumer prices, where the weights are each good's base budget share in the consumption basket. Other modelers select a producer price index or an index of the prices of domestically produced, nontraded goods. In the GTAP model, the default numeraire is an index of global wages and rents for labor, capital, and other factors.

Structure of a CGE Model

The programming code of a CGE model can be lengthy, so it is a common practice to organize it into a small number of blocks that accomplish different tasks.[5] Although this organization can vary among models, the structure of most CGE models and the steps required to run the model and an experiment are similar to those described in Figure 2.5.

A CGE model often opens with one or more blocks of code whose task is to introduce and define each of the sets, exogenous and endogenous variables, and exogenous parameters used in the model. The modeler must define each of these elements in the model code before the model can recognize and use them.

For example, model code may define an endogenous variable, the quantity of imports of commodity *i*, as:

$$QM_i = \text{imports of commodity i}$$

[5] Models tend to get more complex as their analytical capabilities are enhanced. Two examples of relatively simple CGE models are the Cameroon model, developed by Condon, et al. (1987), and the ERS/USDA model developed by Robinson, et al. (1990). Both can be downloaded from the GAMS model library at www.gams.com. Students can run the models by downloading a demonstration version of GAMS software.

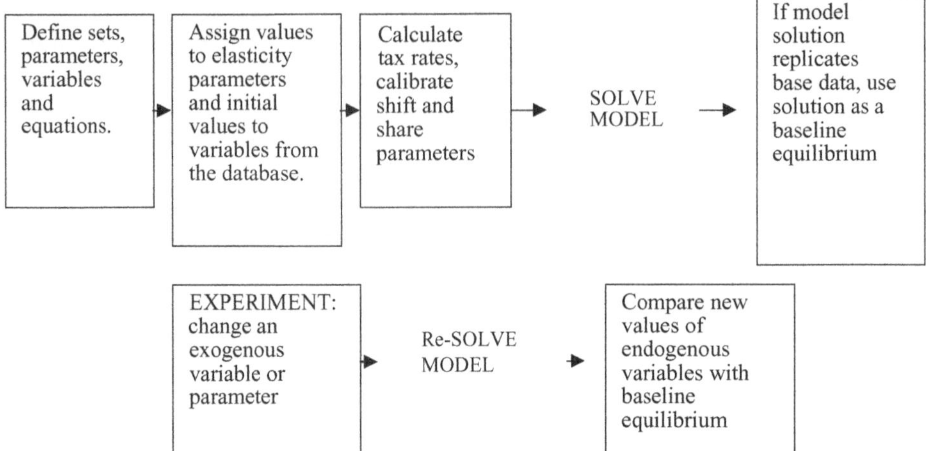

Figure 2.5. Structure of a CGE model and experiment

Once the model code defines the variable QM_i, all subsequent model code, such as equations, can recognize it. If an equation or other types of model commands refer to a set, parameter, or variable that has not yet been defined, the model will fail to solve.

Next, a CGE model has programming code whose task is to assign initial values to variables from the model database and to define elasticity parameter values. For instance, now that QM_c has been defined, it can be assigned its value from the database, such as:

$$QM_i = 552$$

Once sets, parameters, and variables have been defined and values have been assigned, the model can calculate tax rates and calibrate the shift and share parameters. CGE model equations are now numerical equations, similar to our bicycle model, which can be solved to find the equilibrium values of prices and quantities. This calibrated model solution should exactly replicate the original database. For example, we expect the model's solution value for the import quantity of good *i*, QM_i, to be 552, which was its initial value in the database. If the CGE model can reproduce the initial data, then the economist can be confident that the model is capable of explaining the prices and quantities observed in the initial equilibrium. The calibrated model solution then becomes the baseline against which experiment results are compared.

Now the modeler is ready to carry out an experiment. An experiment involves changing the value of at least one of the exogenous parameters or variables, such as the import tariff on agricultural imports. This change in the economy – a "shock" – is a controlled experiment in which the only change in the economy is the value of the exogenous parameter or variable, as specified in the experiment. The modeler re-solves the model, which recalculates new equilibrium values for all endogenous variables. The new solution values for the endogenous variables are compared with the baseline solution values from the calibrated model. The resulting changes in variables' values, such as a 5 percent decline in the quantity of imports compared to the base value, describe the effects of the economic shock on the economy.

Summary

In this chapter, we described the elements of standard CGE models, focusing only on their mechanics and leaving the study of their economic behavior for Chapters 4–8. For many students, this chapter can serve as a practical reference guide that you can return to as your modeling skills progress and questions arise.

CGE models of all types share many common features. They include behavioral equations that describe the behavior of producers and consumers, identity equations that impose market-clearing constraints, and macroclosure rules that govern the savings and investment balance. CGE models follow the convention of normalizing prices so that the value data in the model database can be used to describe both prices and quantities. CGE models report several prices for a single commodity because the models track prices at all points in the supply chain that links producers and consumers. All prices in the model are relative and expressed in terms of the numeraire. In most CGE models, the program code first defines the names of the sets, endogenous and exogenous variables, and exogenous parameters used in its equations. Next, the model assigns numerical values from the database to all variables and defines elasticity parameter values. Blocks of equations then describe the model's economic behavior. The calibration procedure utilizes model equations, the initial database, and elasticities to solve for shift and share parameter values that yield a model solution that replicates the initial base data. This calibrated model solution becomes the baseline equilibrium against which the results of experiments are compared.

Key Terms

Behavioral equation
Bilateral *fob* export price
Bilateral *cif* import price
Calibration
Complement
Consumer price
Cost, insurance, freight (*cif*)
Cross-price elasticity of demand
Elasticity
Endogenous variables
Exogenous parameters

Exogenous variables
Export demand elasticity
Export transformation elasticity
Factor mobility elasticity
Factor substitution elasticity
Free on board (*fob*)
Global price
Identity equation
Import substitution elasticity
Income elasticity of demand
Independent good
Law of Demand
Macroclosure
Model closure
Normal good
Normalized price
Numeraire
Own-price elasticity
Producer price
Set
Substitute
Trade weight
World export price
World import price

PRACTICE AND REVIEW

1. Assume a set of consumer goods *i* with three elements: agriculture, manufacturing, and services. If P is the consumer price, use set notation to express these variables:

   Consumer price for set *i* ______________________________
   Consumer price of manufactures ________________________

2. If QM is import quantity, define QM ("AGR", "USA", "Brazil"):
   ____

3. Review the role of supply elasticities in a demand shock.
   a. Draw a graph of the supply and demand for one good. Label the supply curve S^1 and the demand curve D^1. Label the axes and the initial equilibrium.
   b. Draw a second supply curve that shows the industry with a more elastic supply, that has the same equilibrium as S^1 and D^1. Label the second supply curve S^2.
   c. Assume that an income tax cut increases disposable income and consumer demand. Draw a new demand curve, labeled D^2, and label the two new equilibria along S^1 and S^2.
   d. In a paragraph, (1) explain the difference between the two market equilibria and (2) identify the elasticity parameters in a CGE model that can cause S^2 to be more elastic than S^1.

Table 2.3. *Normalized Prices and Quantities of Apples*

	Base Values			50% Change in Quantity			
							% Change
	Price	Quantity	Value	Price	Quantity	Value	in Value
Actual	4	6		4	9		
Normalized	1			1			

4. Review the role of demand elasticities in a supply shock.
   a. Draw a graph of the supply and demand for one good. Label the supply curve S^1 and the demand curve D^1. Label the axes and the initial equilibrium.
   b. Draw a second demand curve that shows the consumer with a less elastic demand curve, that has the same equilibrium as S^1 and D^1. Label it D^2.
   c. Assume a supply shock, such as favorable weather, that increases the supply of a good. Draw the new supply curve, labeled S^2, and label the two new equilibria along D^1 and D^2.
   d. In a paragraph, (1) explain the difference between the two market equilibria and (2) identify the elasticity parameters in a CGE model that can cause D^2 to be more elastic than D^1.
5. Normalize prices.
   Assume that the apple sales quantity has increased by 50 percent. Calculate the percent change in the value of apple sales in the first row of Table 2.3. Next, normalize apple prices and quantities and calculate the percent change in value of sales. Demonstrate that this result is the same for both actual and normalized data.
6. Calculate a trade-weighted world import price.
   Use the data in Table 2.4 to calculate the U.S. world import price for corn:
   a. Calculate the bilateral U.S. *cif*, import price for its corn imports from each trade partner.
   b. Calculate the trade-weighted, bilateral *cif* import price U.S. imports from each trade partner.
   c. Calculate the U.S. world import price as the sum of the trade-weighted bilateral *cif* import prices.

Table 2.4. *Calculating the U.S. World Import Price of Corn*

	France	Germany	South Africa
Exporter's market share of U.S. corn imports	50	25	25
Exporter bilateral (fob) export price	$1.25	$0.85	$1.90
Trade margin	$0.25	$0.15	$0.10
U.S. bilateral import price			
Trade-weighted bilateral import price			

3

The CGE Model Database: A Social Accounting Matrix

In this chapter, we describe the computable general equilibrium (CGE) model database. The database reports the value of all transactions in an economy during a period of time. The database can be organized and displayed as a Social Accounting Matrix (SAM), a logical framework that provides a visual display of the transactions as a circular flow of national income and spending. The SAM's microeconomic data describe transactions made by each agent in the economy. When aggregated, the SAM's microdata describe the economy's macroeconomic behavior. The SAM's microdata can also be used to calculate descriptive statistics on an economy's structure and tax rates.

Introduction to the Social Accounting Matrix

The database of a CGE model reports the value of all transactions in the circular flow of national income and spending in an economy over a specified period of time, usually a year. The model database that we use throughout this book, for demonstration, describes economic activity in the United States and the rest-of-world economies during 2004.

A CGE model's database can be organized into a table called a ***Social Accounting Matrix*** (SAM) (see Text Box 3.1). The SAM table is a logical arrangement of the model's database to provide an easy-to-read, visual display of the linkages among ***agents*** in the economy. Agents typically include industries, factors of production (e.g., labor and capital), household consumers, the government, and the rest-of-world region, which supplies imports and demands exports.

A SAM is a square matrix of data. It is square because every economic agent in the economy has both a column account and a row account. The SAM's column accounts record each agent's spending. Row accounts record each agent's sources of income. Therefore, every cell in the SAM matrix describes a single transaction as being simultaneously an expenditure by an agent's column account and the receipt of income by an agent's row account.

Text Box 3.1. Key Features of a SAM

- A SAM is a square matrix because each agent has both a column and a row account.
- Column accounts record spending.
- Row accounts record income.
- Each cell in the SAM is simultaneously an expenditure by an agent and a source of income to an agent.
- For each agent, total expenditure (column account total) must equal total income (row account total).

This procedure for recording transactions visually records how any single transaction links agents in the economy.

Table 3.1 shows a simple example of the SAM accounting framework. There are two agents: a farmer and a baker. Each agent has both a row account and a column account. The farmer's expenditure of $1 on bread is reported in his column (expenditure) account, "Farmer spending," and his income of $1 from the sale of wheat to the baker is reported in his row (income) account, "Farmer income." The baker's expenditure of $1 on wheat is reported in the column account "Baker spending;" and her income of $1 from the sale of bread to the farmer is reported in the row account, "Baker income." Note that the $1 that the farmer spends on bread is simultaneously the $1 earned by the baker on the sale of bread. This single cell therefore reports both sides of the same transaction. Finally, the incomes of the farmer and the baker of $1 are equal to their expenditures of $1.

The SAM format enables the modeler to verify visually that the initial database is balanced. A SAM is balanced when every agent meets this constraint: Total spending (its column sum) equals total income (its row sum). For example, by comparing the baker's column sum with her row sum you may easily verify that her income of $1 is equal to her expenditure of $1. When income is equal to spending in every account, then the economy's aggregate spending is equal to its aggregate income, and the database describes an economy in an initial equilibrium. A CGE model requires a balanced database

Table 3.1. *A Two-agent SAM*

	Farmer Spending	Baker Spending	Total Income
Farmer income		Baker buys $1 wheat from farmer	Farmer income = $1
Baker income	Farmer buys $1 bread from baker		Baker income = $1
Total spending	Farmer spending = $1	Baker spending = $1	

as an initial starting point. As we will see in later chapters, model shocks will disturb this equilibrium. Price, supply and demand will then readjust until the economy is in a new equilibrium in which income again is equal to expenditure for all agents in the economy.

Accounts in a SAM

The SAMs used in CGE models usually contain more accounts than in our simple example of the transactions between the farmer and the baker. SAMs contain accounts that describe the incomes and spending of all agents in the model. Additional accounts describe income transfers among agents such as tax payments by labor to the government. SAMs also include a financial account to describe the sources of national savings and investment spending.

Throughout this book, we will study a SAM for the United States in 2004 (Appendix Table). In this SAM, the circular flow begins with a description of the production process. (It does not matter in which order accounts are presented in a SAM, although it is the convention that the ordering of row accounts is the same as that of columns.) The SAM reports each industry's purchases of intermediate inputs and payments to the labor and capital that it employs. In turn, wage and capital rental payments provide income to households. The SAM reports all tax revenue paid to the government and the value of household plus government savings (or dissaving), which funds investment spending. Together, households, government, and investors purchase goods and services, which leads back to demand for industries' output and their spending on inputs and factors. The SAM also reports trade and foreign savings inflows or outflows.

The accounts included in SAMs often differ across CGE models. They may differ in dimensions; that is, in their number of industries, factors of production, or household types. For example, some SAMs may have accounts that divide an economy into two industries, such as mining and nonmining industries, while other SAMs may have accounts for 400 or more industries. The U.S. SAM that we study in this book has three industries – agriculture, manufacturing, and services; three factors – land, labor and capital; and one household type. That is why we call it the U.S. 3x3 SAM.

SAMs' accounts can differ, too, because the structure and theory of the CGE models in which they are used differ. A SAM and its CGE model must be consistent with each other. For example, one CGE model may include a regional household while another model does not. Their SAMs will differ in that case – one will include row and column accounts for a regional household while the other will not. Note, too, that even when the accounts of two SAMs are identical, the location of data in their cells can differ. This point is particularly important for tax data. Taxes' cell locations describe the transactions in the CGE model on which each tax is assumed to be levied. For example, a retail sales tax should appear as a cost in the household consumer's spending column.

Studying the accounts and the cell locations of data in your SAM model is a good first step in learning about your CGE model. This study can help you to identify both visually and intuitively the industries and agents in your model, their economic interrelationships, and the activities on which taxes are levied.

Table 3.2 presents a summary of the accounts typically found in SAMs. This summary, and the U.S. SAM that we will study, are compatible with the Global Trade Analysis Project (GTAP) CGE model, which we use for demonstration throughout this book. You can use the U.S. 3x3 SAM to follow along as we discuss each of the accounts in a SAM in detail.

Production Activities

A production **activity** is a domestic industry engaged in the production of a good or service. An activity's column account describes all of its expenditures on the inputs used in its production process. For example, the column account for the U.S. agricultural activity records its purchases of imported and domestically produced intermediate inputs. These include agricultural inputs such as seeds, manufactured inputs such as fertilizer, and services such as bookkeeping. The remaining inputs – the sum of wages, rents, and tax expenditures – is called an industry's ***value-added***. The column sum for an activity is the value of its ***gross output***. Gross output is value-added plus the costs of all intermediate inputs. In the U.S. 3x3 SAM for 2004 (see Appendix Table), for example, the value of gross output by the agriculture production activity is $434 billion.

An activity's row account records where the industry sells its output. Production activities are usually assumed to sell their entire output to a commodity account. This transaction is explained more fully in the description of commodity accounts.

Sometimes, the same good is produced in more than one way. Agricultural production in Arizona, for example, may require types of irrigation equipment not needed by farmers in California. A modeler interested in studying the two types of agricultural industries can expand the SAM by dividing the agricultural production activity into two separate activity accounts, each with its own row and column. In our example, separate Arizona and California agriculture column accounts would report purchases of very different types of inputs, even though the two activities produce the same type of output. Their row accounts would report their sales of an identical product to the same commodity account – "agriculture."

Table 3.2. *Accounts in a Social Accounting Matrix with a Regional Household*

		Commodities				Final Demand						
	Production Activities	Import Variety	Domestic Variety	Factors	Taxes	Regional Household	Private Households	Government	Savings–Investment	Trade Margins	Rest-of-World	Total
Production activities			Domestic production									Domestic sales
Commodities Imports	Demand for imported intermediates						Demand for imports	Demand for imports	Demand for imports			Aggregate demand
Domestic	Demand for domestic intermediates						Demand for domestic	Demand for domestic	Demand for domestic	Export of trade margins	Exports	
Factors of production	Factor payments											Factor income
Taxes	Taxes on productionoutput, factor use, inputs	Import tariff	Export tax	Income tax			Sales tax	Sales tax	Sales tax			Tax revenue
Regional household				Net factor income	Tax revenues							Aggregate income
Private household						Household income						Private household income
Government						Government income						Government income
Savings–investment				Depreciation		Domestic savings				Foreign savings	Foreign savings	Savings
Trade margins		Trade margins on imports										Foreign exchange outflow
Rest-of-world		Imports										
Total	Gross value of production	Aggregate supply		Factor expenditure	Tax expenditure	Aggregate expenditure	Private consumption expenditure	Government consumption expenditure	Investment expenditure	Foreign exchange inflow		

Text Box 3.2. Disaggregated Production Regions and Households in a SAM for Morocco

"Policy Options and Their Potential Effects on Moroccan Small Farmers and the Poor Facing Increased World Food Prices: A General Equilibrium Model Analysis." (Diao, Doukkali, and Yu, 2008).

What is the research question? World food prices have increased sharply over recent years and do not appear likely to return to 2000–03 levels. How will higher food prices affect different production regions and household types in Morocco, which is dependent on food imports for a large share of its domestic consumption?

What is the CGE model innovation? The authors modify the IFPRI standard CGE model to account for disaggregated production regions and households in the SAM. They construct a SAM for Morocco that divides each agricultural production activity account into six agroecological regions, each with a different production technology. The household accounts in the SAM are disaggregated into ten representative groups consistent with the income deciles of rural and urban households.

What is the model experiment? World import and export prices of food are increased, based on price projections from the U.S. Department of Agriculture. Three mitigating policy options are modeled: (1) import tariff reforms, (2) import subsidies to the poor, and (3) compensatory direct transfer payments (negative income taxes) to poor households.

What are the key findings? Direct transfers to poor consumers combined with increased public investment in agriculture to improve productivity, is a win-win strategy for Morocco's agricultural producers and consumers.

Modelers sometimes use this technique of subdividing activity accounts in order to create CGE models that subdivide a national economy into regions. Text Box 3.2 describes a research project in which the CGE modelers subdivided the activity accounts of a SAM for Morocco to describe the production of the same agricultural good in different regions and using different production technologies.

Commodities

A **commodity** is an economy's total supply of a good or service from domestic production and imports, combined. For example, the U.S. supply of the commodity "automobiles" is the sum of domestically produced varieties, such as Ford Tauruses, plus imported varieties, like Japanese Toyotas.

In the SAM, commodity column accounts might be thought of as wholesale packagers who purchase goods and services from domestic producers and combine them with imported varieties to create the "bundle," or composite commodity, that consumers purchase. In the U.S. 3x3 SAM, for example, the agricultural commodity account describes the sourcing of agricultural goods from imports and domestic production. The agricultural commodity is composed of $434 billion worth of domestically produced agricultural products and $177 billion worth of agricultural imports (shown as the column totals of the imports and domestic commodity columns). The total supply of the agricultural commodity is $611 billion.

The commodity row accounts show where goods are sold. Thus, while the activity accounts in the SAM describe the supply side of the model, the commodity row accounts describe the demand side of the model. Production activities, households, government, and investors all demand commodities, and some share of domestic production is used to satisfy export demand. In the U.S. SAM, for example, the domestic variety of the agricultural commodity is sold to production activities as an intermediate input ($24 + $229 + $70 = $323), to private households ($60 billion), to the government ($1 billion), and as exports ($50 billion).

Each of the domestic customers may demand different proportions of the imported and domestic varieties in their commodity bundle. In the U.S. SAM, for example, $2 billion of the imported variety and $24 billion of the domestically produced variety of the agricultural commodity are purchased by the agricultural production activity. The import share in its use of agricultural inputs is 2/26 *100 = 8 percent. Private households purchase $9 billion of the imported variety of agriculture and $60 billion of the domestically produced variety. In this case, households import 13 percent of their total agricultural consumption.

In most CGE models, each good or service has both an activity account and a matching commodity account. That is, if there is an electricity production activity account, there is also an electricity commodity account to which it is sold. However, this one-to-one correspondence is not necessary. Some production activities can have multiple products, such as a livestock operation that produces beef and cowhides. In this case, the livestock activity account could sell its output to separate beef and leather commodity accounts. Or, if we disaggregated manufacturing production activities by all fifty U.S. states, a single commodity account called "manufacturing" could purchase the same output, "manufacturing," from fifty different manufacturing production activities.

Factors of Production

Factors of production are the resource endowments of land, labor, and capital that are combined with intermediate inputs such as steel, rubber gaskets and electronic components, to produce goods and services. The factors in the U.S. 3x3 SAM are labor, capital, and land. Some modelers further subdivide these factor types. For example, labor may be divided into skilled and unskilled workers, or land divided into cropland and forest, or irrigated and nonirrigated. You can visualize the disaggregation of factors in a SAM by imagining that there is a new factor column and a matching row account for each additional factor in the model.

The row account for each factor reports the income it receives from the production activities in which it is employed. Production activities pay wages to labor and rents to capital and land. In the U.S. 3x3 SAM, for example, the manufacturing production activity pays $1,109 billion in wages to its labor force and $467 billion in rents to capital equipment.

The factor column accounts report factor expenditure. In the U.S. 3x3 SAM, for example, the land column account reports that $31 billion in land factor income flows to the regional household, and $3 billion is spent on income taxes. The capital income account in addition records capital depreciation as an expenditure in the savings-investment row account.

Taxes

The tax row accounts in a SAM describe the economic activities on which taxes are levied and the amount of tax revenue that is generated. For example, in the U.S. 3x3 SAM, production activities pay production taxes (from their column accounts) to the production tax row account. The agricultural production activity spends $4 billion on this tax. Tax column and row sums report the value of total revenue from each tax, which is paid by the column account for each tax to the regional household account. In the U.S. SAM, for example, production taxes generate a total of $469 billion in revenue and income taxes generate $1,693 billion in revenue.

Regional Household

A regional household is a macroeconomic account found in some SAMs and CGE models. It is similar to the concept of GDP from the income side and from the expenditure side. It is row describes the sources of aggregate national income from factor incomes and taxes, and its column describes allocation to aggregate domestic spending by private households and government, and to national savings.[1] In the U.S. 3x3 SAM, for example, the regional household accrues factor incomes (net of income tax) along its row account: $31 + $5,397 + $1,632 = $7,060 billion. It also earns tax income from trade taxes, sales taxes, factor use, production, and income taxes, for a total regional income of $10,628 billion. The regional household column account shows how national income is allocated to spending by private households

[1] The regional household account differs from GDP because it excludes depreciation. For example, in the U.S. 3x3 SAM, regional household income is $10,627.9 billion, GDP is $11,673.4 billion, and depreciation is $1045.5 billion.

($8,233 billion) and government ($1,810 billion) and to domestic savings ($585 billion, combining private and public savings).[2]

Private Households

The **private household** row and column accounts describe the income and spending of all of the individuals in an economy, aggregated into a single, representative "household." The private household row account receives after-income-tax income from the regional household's column account. Households spend this income in its entirety on goods and services and related sales taxes, as described in the household's column account. Private household consumption is usually a large component of an economy's final demand for goods and services. In the U.S. 3x3 SAM, for example, households spend $8,233 billion, which dwarfs spending by government and investors.

Sometimes, SAMs (and their related CGE models) disaggregate the single household into several representative household types. They may be disaggregated according to criteria such as sources of income (perhaps one type earns low-skilled wages, and the other type earns high-skilled wages), or location (e.g., rural or urban), or expenditure patterns (e.g., high or low share of spending on food). Disaggregating households allows the modeler to analyze the distributional effects of an economic shock across different household types. For example, a new tax may benefit rural households but impose a burden on urban households.

You can visualize a SAM with many households by imagining that the single private household row and column accounts in the U.S. 3x3 SAM are disaggregated into *n* household row accounts and *n* household column accounts, each describing the different income sources and expenditure patterns of *n* household types.

Government

The **government** row and column accounts report government income and its expenditure on goods and services. In the U.S. 3x3 SAM, the government account receives $1,810 billion from the regional household, and spends it almost exclusively on services.

Savings-investment

This row account reports the sources of a nation's savings. In the U.S. 3x3 SAM, the savings row account shows the accumulation of saving from

[2] Breisinger, Thomas, and Thurlow (2009), Reinert and Roland-Holst (1997) and Pyatt and Round (1985) offer nontechnical introductions to SAMs without a regional household account.

domestic sources ($585 billion). Foreign savings ($536 + $32 = $568 billion) equals the trade balance in goods and services and in trade margin services. Depreciation of the existing capital stock, which totals $1,046 billion, is also recorded. The investment column account records investors' purchases of the goods and services that will be used in future production activities, and related sales taxes. In the U.S. 3x3 SAM, investment spending totals $2,198 billion. The SAM does not indicate in which industries the investment goods are installed.

Trade Margins

These accounts describe the insurance, and freight charges which are incurred when goods are shipped by air, sea, or overland from an exporting country to the importing country. These costs raise the price of imports relative to the price received by the exporters. The exporter's margin exclusive-price is called the free on board, or *fob* price. The importer's margin-inclusive price is called the *cif* price. The difference between the *cif* and *fob* values of imports is the trade margin.

In the SAM, there are trade margin accounts for both imports and exports. For imports, the trade margin row account records the freight and insurance costs incurred for each imported good. For example, the United States spends $9 billion on margin services to import $167 billion worth of agricultural products. It spends a total of $56 billion on trade margin charges on its total imports. The exports trade margin column account reports the value of trade margin services produced by the United States and exported for use in global trade.[3] The United States exports $24 billion in margin services. Because trade margins are essentially the export and import of a type of service, a country has a balance of trade in trade margin services. It is the value of trade margin exports minus trade margin imports and reported as a foreign capital inflow or outflow in the savings-investment row. The United States has a trade deficit in margin services, resulting in a foreign savings inflow of $32 billion.

Rest-of-World

This account describes trade and investment flows between a country and the rest of the world (ROW). The row account in the SAM shows the home country's foreign exchange outflow, which is its spending on each import valued in ROW's *fob* world export prices. The ROW column account reports the home country's foreign exchange inflow, or export sales of each commodity, valued in the home country's *fob* world export prices. The column

[3] Export margin data are not tracked bilaterally in the GTAP database from which our SAM is derived.

account also records the balance of trade as a payment by, or inflow from, the rest-of-world to the savings-investment account. The balance of trade is the difference between the *fob* values of the home country's total exports and total imports. When the country runs a trade deficit (its imports exceed its exports), its foreign savings inflow is positive. In this case, the country is borrowing from abroad and the foreign savings inflow increases its supply of savings. When a country runs a trade surplus (the value of its exports exceed the value of its imports), its foreign savings inflow is negative. In effect, it is lending its capital to foreigners. In the U.S. 3x3 SAM, imports of goods and services worth $1,601 billion and exports of $1,056 trillion result in a foreign savings inflow to the United States (a trade deficit) of $536 billion.

Microeconomic Data in a SAM

A SAM database presents microeconomic data. Microeconomic data describe a nation's economic activity in detail. For example, the SAM's microeconomic data on production describe the amount spent by each industry on each type of intermediate and factor input, and each type of tax. Its data on domestic demand describe expenditure on each type of commodity by each agent in the economy. Microeconomic data on trade describe the commodity composition of imports and exports. Even when the modeler chooses to summarize an economy into a relatively small number of industries or factors, we still consider the SAM to be a presentation of microeconomic data.

Macroeconomic Data in a SAM

Macroeconomic data provide a summary description of a nation's economic activity. Some of the row sums and column sums of the SAM are macroeconomic indicators. For example, the column sum of the private household account reports an economy's total private consumption expenditure, and the row sum of the ROW account reports total imports of goods and services. We can also aggregate other microeconomic data in the SAM to calculate descriptive macroeconomic statistics, such as the gross domestic product (GDP). Developing macroeconomic indicators from the data in a SAM is a useful exercise because it illustrates how the macroeconomic behavior of an economy rests on the microeconomic behavior of firms and households. (Text Box 3.3 provides an interesting example of a group of modelers who work in the opposite direction. In their research, they impose long-run growth projections for macroeconomic variables, such as the labor force, as an experiment, and then solve for the resulting microeconomic structure of the economy.)

Text Box 3.3. Macroeconomic Projections in a CGE Model of China
"China in 2005: Implications for the Rest of the World." (Arndt, et al. 1997).

What is the research question? In 1992, the Chinese economy was projected to triple in size over the next thirteen years. How will China's rapid growth affect its competing exporters in world trade and its import suppliers?

What is the CGE model innovation? The authors simulate the projected growth rates in macroeconomic variables (population, capital stock, and productivity) and analyze the resulting effects on the microeconomic composition of industry supply, demand, and trade in fifteen regions, including China, in the GTAP CGE model. The authors also carry out a systematic analysis of the sensitivity of their results to alternative values of import substitution elasticities, and they decompose welfare effects using the GTAP welfare decomposition utility.

What is the experiment? The experiment imposes cumulative projected growth rates of macroeconomic variables. The results describe the level and microeconomic structure of the fifteen economies in 2005. An alternative experiment assumes a lower growth rate of Chinese factor endowments that eliminates growth in its per capita GDP. The results of this alternative scenario for 2005 are deducted from those of the first scenario to identify the effects of China's rapid economic growth.

What are the key findings? Based on net-trade positions and likely changes in world prices, China's growth has an adverse impact on other developing countries. However, from a broader perspective that considers terms-of-trade benefits, efficiency gains, and factor endowment effects, China's growth benefits twelve of the other fourteen regions in the model, a result that is robust to a wide distribution of assumed trade elasticity values.

In the following examples, we use microeconomic data from the U.S. 3x3 SAM to calculate three important macroeconomic indicators: GDP from the income and expenditure sides, and the savings-investment balance.

GDP from the Income Side

GDP from the income side reports the sources of total national income from (1) the wages and rents that production activities pay to the factors (e.g., labor and capital) that they employ (reported on a net, or after-income tax, basis), and (2) total tax revenues in the economy:

$$\text{GDP} = \text{Factor income} + \text{tax revenue}$$

We calculate this macroeconomic indicator using data from the U.S. SAM's row accounts, which report income flows:

Factor payments = 8,106 =

Land factor payments: 34

Labor factor payments: 68 + 1,109 + 5,667 = 6,844

Capital factor payments: 122 + 467 + 2,332 = 2,921

Minus income taxes: 3 + 1,446 + 244 = 1,693

Plus taxes = 3,570 =

Import tariffs: 1 + 24 = 25

Export taxes: 2

Sales taxes on imported variety: 1 + 47 + 0 = 48 (from sales tax row totals)

Sales taxes on domestic variety: 2 + 178 + 45 = 225 (from sales tax row totals)

Factor use taxes: − 3 + 1, 021 + 90 = 1, 108 (from factor use tax row totals)

Production taxes: 4 + 42 + 43 = 469

Income taxes: 3 + 1,446 + 244 = 1,693

Thus, U.S. GDP from the income side is:

GDP = 8,106 + 3,570 = 11,673 billion (adjusted for rounding)

GDP from the Expenditure Side

GDP from the expenditure side is a macroeconomic indicator that reports the allocation of national income across four aggregate categories of final demand: private household consumption expenditure, C, investment expenditure, I, government consumption expenditure, G, and net exports, E–M. You may recall this important equation, called the national income identity equation, from your macroeconomics studies:

GDP = C + I + G + (E-M)

We calculate GDP from the expenditure side using data from the U.S. SAM's column accounts, which report expenditure flows:

C = demand for commodities + sales taxes
= total private consumptionexpenditure

C = (9 + 415 + 60 + 60 + 1, 104 + 6,392) + (1 + 35 + 0 + 2 + 115 + 41)
= 8,233

Text Box 3.4. Distributing National Effects to the State-Level in a CGE Model of the United States
"Disaggregation of Results from a Detailed General Equilibrium Model of the U.S. to the State Level." (Dixon, Rimmer and Tsigas, 2007)

What is the research question? The USAGE-ITC, developed at the U.S. International Trade Commission, is a recursive dynamic CGE model descended from the Monash and ORANI models of Australia. It has more than 500 U.S. industries and multiple U.S. trade partners. However, U.S. policymakers are often concerned with the impacts of national policies at the state level. Can an already large, national-level model be solved to also yield results for state-level variables?

What is the CGE model innovation? The authors develop a "top-down" approach to disaggregating national results to the state level. First, a static version of the CGE model is used to solve for variables at the national level, including employment, private and government consumption, trade, real GDP, and industry output and employment. Then, state-level results are computed using an "add-in" program. The program describes the impacts for each state as the change in the national-level variable plus a state-specific deviation term. This approach ensures that state-level impacts sum to the national level, however results at the state-level do not feed back to affect national-level variables.

What is the model experiment? The authors test their approach using an illustrative experiment in which the United States removes all import tariffs and quotas.

What are the key findings? The authors focus on employment effects, concluding that differential employment impacts across states reflect not only the shares of industries in employment in each state, but also states' proximities to ports and to other high- or low-growth states.

$$I = \text{demand for commodities} + \text{sales taxes} = \text{total investment expenditure}$$

$$I = (0 + 237 + 3 + 0 + 628 + 1{,}315) + (0 + 5 + 0 + 0 + 10 + 1) = 2{,}198$$

$$G = \text{demand for commodities} = \text{total government consumption expenditure (governments usually don't pay tax)}$$

$$G = (0 + 1 + 1 + 1 + 2 + 1{,}805) = 1{,}810$$

The trade margin costs incurred in shipping goods to an importing country raises the costs of its imports. These margins are therefore included when calculating expenditures on imports. On the export side, a country's sale of the trade margin services used in global shipping is an export of a type of service so, just like the export of any product, these sales are included in the value of its total exports. The GDP calculation excludes import tariffs and export taxes, however, because these are already embedded in the values of exports and imports reported in the final demand columns of the SAM.

$$E = \text{exports} + \text{exports of trade margins}$$
$$E = (50 + 756 + 259) + 24 = 1{,}089$$
$$M = \text{imports} + \text{trade margins on imports}$$
$$M = (167 + 1{,}203 + 230) + (9 + 47 + 0) = 1{,}657$$

Thus, U.S. GDP from the expenditure side is:

$$GDP = 8{,}233 + 2{,}198 + 1{,}810 + (1{,}089 - 1{,}657) = \$11{,}673 \text{ billion.}$$

Savings-Investment and the Balance of Trade

Recall from your macroeconomic coursework that by rearranging the expression for GDP from the expenditure side, we can derive this macroeconomic identity equation to describe the relationship between a nation's *domestic* savings, S_D, its investment spending net of depreciation, I_N, and its trade balance, $E - M$:

$$S_D - I_N = E - M$$

We can use data from the SAM to calculate the balance of trade and the savings-investment balance, and check that this relationship holds true in the U.S. 3x3 SAM, where:

S_D = domestic savings = 585, and

I_N = Investment spending minus depreciation = 2,198 − 1,046 = −$1,152

and E and M are already known from our calculation of GDP from the expenditure side. Thus, we can verify that in our database, the gap between domestic savings and net investment equals the trade deficit:

585 − 1,152 (adjusted for rounding) = 1,089 − 1,657 = −$568 billion

Structure Table

As a SAM's dimensions become larger, with an increased number of industries, factors, household types, or taxes, it becomes more challenging to fully understand or describe the complex economy that it depicts. (See Text box 3.4.) One way to develop an overview of an economy without losing the detailed information available in the SAM is to construct a ***structure table***. The table uses the microeconomic data in the SAM to describe the economy in terms of shares. For example, it reports the shares of each commodity in households' total consumption and the shares of each commodity in a country's total exports. Share data will enable you to make quick comparisons and to identify the most important features of the economy that you are studying.

You are likely to find yourself often referring to your structure table as you define experiments and interpret your model results.

Table 3.3 presents an illustrative structure table constructed from the data in the U.S. 3x3 SAM. We can use the structure table to make observations like these about the U.S. economy:

- The United States now has a service economy. Services account for 81 percent of GDP, 83 percent of labor employment and 79 percent of household spending.
- U.S. agriculture is a "capital-intensive" industry; capital accounts for a larger share (54 percent) of its factor costs than labor or land, and the capital share in factor costs is higher in agriculture than in other industries.
- U.S. manufacturing and services production are relatively "labor-intensive." The industries spend far more on labor (73 percent) than on capital inputs, and labor's share in their factor costs is higher than in agriculture.
- The United States imports more than 30 percent of its food supply but households spend only 1 percent of their budget on food.
- Trade is very important to U.S. manufacturing – imports account for 22 percent of U.S. consumption of manufactured goods, and exports for 14 percent of manufacturing output

You can follow the steps described below to construct a structure table for the country that you are studying. We demonstrate how each type of indicator is constructed, using data from the U.S. 3x3 SAM as an example, and we explain how each indicator can be useful as you begin to run model experiments and interpret your results.

Industry GDP

The GDP for industry *a* is calculated from the SAM's activity and tax column accounts as:

Factor payments by a + taxes on factor use, output, sales, and trade of a

Using agriculture as an example, we can calculate the GDP for U.S. agriculture from data in the U.S. 3x3 SAM as:

Agricultural factor payments = 34 + 68 + 122 = 224
Agricultural taxes = 3
Factor use taxes in agriculture = −3 + 5 −1 = 1
Sales taxes paid by agricultural activity on imported inputs = 0
Sales taxes paid by agricultural activity on domestic inputs = −1 −1 −4 = −6
Production tax on agricultural activity = 4
Import tariffs on agriculture = 1
Export taxes on agriculture = 0
Sales tax on final demand for imported and domestic agriculture = 1 + 2 = 3
Agricultural GDP = 224 + 3 = 226 (adjusted for rounding)

Table 3.3. *Structure Table for the United States in 2004*

	Industry GDP	Industry Shares	Factor Shares in Industry Factor Costs			Industry Shares in Factor Employment		
	$US billion	in GDP	Land	Labor	Capital	Land	Labor	Capital
Agriculture	226	2	14	32	54	100	1	4
Manufacturing	2,007	17	0	73	27	0	16	16
Services	9,441	81	0	73	27	0	83	80
Total	11,673	100	na	na	na	100	100	100

	Commodity shares in:							
	Domestic Demand				Trade			
	Intermediate Demand	Private Household Consumption	Government Consumption	Investment Demand	Exports	Imports	Import Share of Domestic Consumption	Export Share of Domestic Production
Agriculture	5	1	0	0	5	11	32	12
Manufacturing	37	20	0	40	69	75	22	14
Services	58	79	100	60	26	14	2	2
Total	100	100	100	100	100	100	8	5

Source: GTAP v.7.0 U.S. 3x3 database.

Industry Share in GDP

The share of industry *a* in total GDP is calculated as:

Industry *a's* GDP/ GDP * 100

The share of U.S. agriculture in GDP is therefore:

226/11,673 * 100 = 2

The relative size of an industry in total GDP is among its most important economic characteristics. The larger its size relative to other industries, the greater is the impact of a shock in that industry on the rest of the economy. Given the small size of agriculture in the U.S. economy, do you think that a policy shock, such as the removal of agricultural production subsidies, would have significant effects on the U.S. economy as a whole? Probably not, although it may be a difficult shock to absorb for those engaged in agriculture.

Factor Shares in Industry Factor Cost

Factor cost shares describe which factors are most important in an industry's total factor costs. For example, capital equipment such as drills and pumps typically account for a far larger share of the factor costs of the petroleum extraction industry than labor. Factor cost shares are calculated for each factor *f* for each industry *a* from data in the production activity column accounts. An industry's factor costs include the wages and rents that it pays directly to each factor plus factor use taxes such as Social Security:

(factor payment plus factor use tax for factor *f* in industry *a*)/total factor cost in industry *a* * 100

As an example, we calculate the factor cost share for labor employed in the U.S. manufacturing industry as:

Labor cost share in mfg. = labor payment plus labor use tax in mfg./ total factor cost in mfg. * 100

$$(1{,}109 + 166)/(1{,}109 + 467 + 166 + 15) * 100 = 73$$

Thus, labor accounts for 73 percent of factor costs in U.S. manufacturing.

Factor cost shares in an industry matter when there are shocks that change the relative price or the productivity of a factor. For example, consider an industry such as wearing apparel, which spends far more on wages than it does on capital equipment. If there is an increase in the labor supply that causes wages to fall, then the apparel industry's factor costs will fall by proportionately more than in the petroleum extraction industry, from our previous example. The apparel industry's proportionately larger factor cost savings are likely to lead to an increase in its output and in its size relative to the petroleum industry, depending on consumer demand.

Industry Shares in Factor Employment

Industry shares in factor employment describe where an economy's land, labor, and capital endowments are employed. The shares are calculated for factor f and industry a from the income data in the factor rows of the SAM:[4]

Factor payment to factor f in industry a/sum of factor payments to f by all industries * 100

Using data from the U.S. 3x3 SAM, we calculate industry employment shares for labor as:

Labor payment in agriculture/sum of activity payments to labor 68/(68 + 1,109 + 5,667) * 100 = 1
Labor payment in manufacturing/sum of activity payments to labor 1,109/(68 + 1,109 + 5,667) * 100 = 16
Labor payment in services/sum of activity payments to labor 5,667/(68 + 1,109 + 5,667) * 100 = 83

Most U.S. labor is employed in services (83 percent) and just 1 percent is employed in agriculture.

Industry shares in factor employment are useful to know because the larger an industry's employment share, the larger is the impact on the economywide wage and rent when there is a change in its production and factor demand. For example, with 83 percent of U.S. labor employed in the service sector, a decline in the production of services would likely have a larger effect on national employment and wages than would a decline of similar proportion in agricultural output. Less employment in services could cause the average U.S. wage to fall because the loss of even a small proportion of service jobs means that a relatively large share of the U.S. work force must look for new employment.

[4] Most CGE models include data on the value of factor payments or earnings, but not factor quantities, such as number of workers or acres of land. We can only infer industry shares in employment from income data if we assume that all workers and all capital equipment receive the same wages and rents across all industries. In this case, each dollar that any production activity pays to a factor buys the same factor quantity. This is the simplifying assumption made in many CGE models. However, wages and rents are often observed to differ across industries. Many doctors, for instance, earn more per hour than programmers. In this case, two production activities may pay the same amount of wages and rents, but employ different quantities of workers and equipment. Some CGE models account for wage or rent differentials across industries, but their databases must also include factor quantity data.

Commodity Shares in Domestic Demand

Firms, private households, government, and investors usually demand different types of goods and services. For instance, all households purchase food while investors rarely buy food and instead purchase mostly heavy machinery and equipment for use in factories and other businesses. The shares of each commodity *i* (which includes domestic and imported varieties) in total spending by each agent *d* describe an economy's consumption patterns. Because sales taxes are part of the purchase price, the calculation of commodity shares also includes that tax.

Commodity shares for each agent and commodity are calculated from the spending data reported in the agents' columns in the SAM:

Expenditure by agent *d* on commodity *i* plus sales taxes/total consumption expenditure by agent *d* * 100

Using private household spending on the manufactured commodity as an example, the share of the manufactured commodity in total private household spending is calculated as:

$$(415 + 1{,}104 + 35 + 115)/8{,}233 * 100 = 20$$

When consumption patterns differ among agents, the same shock can affect each of them in different ways. For example, if the same sales tax is levied on all private sector purchases of services, the impact on households will be proportionately greater than on investors, because households consume more services than investors, as a share of their spending. Alternatively, taxes may be levied in a targeted way based on consumption shares. For example, a tax code may be designed to impose higher sales taxes on the types of goods that are purchased mainly by businesses, or by high-income households.

Commodity Shares in Exports and Imports

Commodity shares in the value of total exports and total imports describe the commodity composition of trade. The shares of each commodity *i* in total exports are calculated from data in the SAM's column accounts for export margins and the rest-of-world. The export margins are included because margins are a type of service export. Export taxes are excluded because they are already embedded in the export value reported in the commodity row of the SAM:

export of *c*/total commodity exports plus total margin exports * 100

Using manufacturing as an example, and data from the U.S. 3x3 SAM, the share of manufacturing in total exports is:

$$756/(24 + 50 + 756 + 259) * 100 = 69$$

Thus, manufactured products account for most of U.S. exports of goods and services.

The share of each commodity *i* in the value of total imports is calculated using data from the column accounts of the imported variety of each commodity. The value of imports is inclusive of trade margins, but excludes import tariffs:

Import plus trade margin on import of commodity *i* /
total commodity imports plus total trade margins on imports * 100

Using agriculture in the United States as an example, its share in total U.S. imports is:

$$(9 + 167)/(9 + 167 + 47 + 1{,}203 + 230) * 100 = 11$$

Import Share of Domestic Consumption

The share of imports in the total value of total consumption of commodity *i* by firms, private households, government, and investors combined, determines the strength of the linkage between events in world markets and domestic consumers. Consider the effect of an increase in world oil prices. Countries that depend on imports for a large share of their domestic petroleum consumption will experience a greater shock to their economy than would countries that import very little oil. Calculating import shares of consumption must take into account the sales taxes paid on both varieties of commodity c.

The import share of consumption of commodity *i* is calculated as:

Total domestic demand plus sales tax for the imported variety of *c*/total domestic demand plus sales taxes for imported plus domestic varieties of commodity *c* * 100.

Using U.S. manufacturing from the U.S. 3x3 SAM as an example, the import share in domestic consumption of the manufactured commodity is calculated from data in the commodity rows and sales tax rows:

Total domestic demand for imports of mfgs. = 629 + 450 + 1 + 242 = 1,322

where:

Intermediate demand for mfg. import = (12 + 393 + 216) + (0 + 3 + 5) = 629
Private household demand for mfg. import = 415 + 35 = 450
Government demand for mfg. import = 1
Investment demand for mfg. import = 237 + 5 = 242.

We leave it as an exercise for you to verify that the value of total domestic consumption of the manufactured commodity (imported plus domestic varieties) = 5,972. The import share of domestic consumption of manufactured goods is therefore:

$$1{,}322/5{,}972 * 100 = 22$$

Given a 22 percent share of imports in U.S. consumption of manufacturing, what do you think would happen if a foreign export tax causes the price of manufactured imports by the United States to rise sharply? The effect will probably be significant (and negative) because imports constitute a large part of aggregate U.S. demand for manufactures.

Export Share of Production

Similar to the case of imports, the share of exports in the total value of production of good *i* determines the strength of the linkage between world markets and domestic producers. Because the revenue that producers get from export sales includes export taxes (or subsidies), the calculation of the export share of production also includes that payment. Export margins are not included as a cost to exporters, since these freight and insurance charges are assumed to be paid by importers. The export share of production of each good or service is calculated from data in the domestic commodity row, and the rest-of-world column in the SAM:

(Exports of good *i*)/Domestic sales of *i* * 100.

Using U.S. agriculture as an example, we calculate the export share of production as:

$$(50)/434 * 100 = 12$$

Because U.S. farmers export 12 percent of their output, how do you think they are likely to be affected by a foreign import subsidy and a resulting increase in foreign demand? Because exports do not represent a very large share of U.S. production, the impact is likely to be positive but rather small.

Tax Data in a SAM

Import tariffs and taxes on exports, sales, production, and factor use, all drive a wedge between the prices received by sellers and the prices paid by buyers. Income taxes effectively reduce the wage and rents earned by labor, capital, and other factors of production. The tax data in the SAM report the value of taxes paid by each agent and the total amount of tax revenue generated by each tax in the model. The location of tax data in the cells of the SAM reveal the economic activity on which each tax is levied.

Developing a ***tax structure table*** using the tax data in the SAM will enable you to gain an overall perspective on the importance of these policies in the economy that you are studying. A tax structure table expresses the tax flow data in terms of tax rates. For example, if the SAM reports that consumers pay ten cents in import tariffs on the import of $1 of textiles, then the tax structure table will report a 10 percent import tariff rate on textiles (since 10 cents/$1 * 100 = 10 percent).

Many of your experiments will entail changes in tax and tariff rates. The tax structure table provides a foundation for your analysis that helps you to define your experiments and interpret your model results. For example, if all else is equal, the removal of a tax with a high initial rate is likely to have a larger effect on quantities in the model than removal of a tax with a low rate. A tax structure table also facilitates a comparison of your model and results with those of other researchers.

We describe in Chapter 8 how to calculate each type of tax and subsidy rate using data in the SAM. For now, we simply present a tax structure table based on data from the U.S. 3x3 SAM, as an example (Table 3.4).

The SAM and Economic Models

The SAM framework was developed to support economic models of national income and spending. The models were not initially CGE models, but **multiplier models**, used for economywide economic planning and the analysis of linkages between an economy's industry structure and the distribution of income across different types of households.[5] The modelers developed the SAM framework as a way to organize and display national accounts data in a format that depicts the circular flow of income and spending that interconnects all parts of an economy.

A key contribution made by multiplier models is their ability to calculate the direct and indirect effects of an economic shock on the quantities of supply and demand in an economy. The direct effect is the change in the economic activity that is shocked. For example, the direct effect of a tax on auto production may be to reduce auto output by ten cars. The indirect effects are the changes in related activities that occur because industries rely on other industries to supply their inputs or buy their outputs, and because a change in output of any industry leads to changes in employment, incomes

[5] See Pyatt and Round (1985) for a discussion of the development of SAMs in the Cambridge Growth Project and their use in multiplier models. Breisinger, Thomas, and Thurlow (2009) provide excellent and intuitive instructions for developing a multiplier model using a SAM.

Table 3.4. *Tax Structure Table for the United States, 2004*

Type of Tax	Tax Rate and Agent that Pays the Tax							
	Agriculture	Manufacturing	Services	Private Households	Investment	Land	Labor	Capital
	Commodity accounts							
Import tariff								
Agriculture	0.48	0.48	0.48					
Manufacturing	1.91	1.91	1.91					
Services	0.00	0.00	0.00					
Export tax	0.01	0.29	0.00					
	Production activities							
Sales tax – imports								
Agriculture	−4.10	0.01	0.02	6.38	0.00			
Manufacturing	−2.01	0.67	2.25	8.49	1.91			
Services	−2.82	0.00	0.00	0.02	0.00			
Sales tax – domestic								
Agriculture	−4.02	0.00	0.05	4.07	0.00			
Manufacturing	−0.99	0.73	3.69	10.40	1.61			
Services	−3.73	0.27	0.12	0.44	0.05			
Factor use tax								
Land	−9.48	0.00	0.00					
Labor	7.19	15.00	15.00					
Capital	−1.05	3.253	3.25					
Production tax	1.00	0.80	2.83					
Income tax						8.35	21.13	8.35

Notes: Positive rate denotes a tax; a negative rate denotes a subsidy.
Source: GTAP v.7.0 U.S. 3x3 database.

and taxes, and final demand. For example, if, according to the SAM, each car requires four tires, then automakers will reduce their demand for tires by forty. An indirect effect is the reduction in tire output and the employment of tire workers, based on the number of workers required per tire as described in the SAM. In addition, the loss of employment for auto and tire workers will reduce household incomes and demand for items such as clothing and restaurant meals, thereby leading to indirect effects on the apparel and food service industries, too.

Multiplier models essentially trace the effects of an exogenous shock in one or more parts of the SAM throughout the rest of the SAM as an accounting procedure. Producers adjust the quantity of their output to meet any changes in demand and consumers adjust their demand in response to any change in income. Prices are fixed and there are no limits on the supply of labor, capital or other productive resources.

The multiplier, similar to the fiscal multiplier you may have studied in macroeconomics, calculates the sum of successively smaller rounds of adjustment to a shock until the economy is again in equilibrium. In our example, the decline in income to workers in the auto and tire industries will reduce their demand for all types of goods, including autos, leading back to a further decline in auto production, perhaps by two autos. This reduces automakers' demand for tires by eight, causing incomes and demand to fall again, and so on, until the size of successive adjustments fall to zero.

CGE models represent the next generation of economywide models because they describe changes throughout the SAM as the result of producers maximizing their efficiency and consumers maximizing their utility. Productive resources are in limited supply and firms' competition for them will affect their prices. Instead of a multiplier process, the CGE model solves for a new set of prices at which supply and demand are again in equilibrium, based on the optimizing behavior of producers and consumers. Each cell in the SAM matrix therefore corresponds to an economic equation in the CGE model. In the chapters that follow, we reinforce this connection between the SAM database and optimizing behavior in the CGE model by prefacing our study of the economic behavior in each part of the CGE model with a description of the corresponding data in the SAM.

Summary

In this chapter, we described the SAM, a logical format used to organize and display CGE models' databases as a circular flow of income and spending in an economy. The SAM is a square matrix because each of its accounts is described by both a row, which records income, and a column, which describes spending. Each cell of the SAM describes a transaction simultaneously as an expenditure by a column account and as an income source to a row account. A SAM is balanced when the total income for each account (its row total) is equal to its total spending (its column total). A balanced SAM describes an economy in equilibrium. The accounts and the location of data in the cells of the matrix vary among SAMs because a SAM corresponds to the structure and theory of the CGE model in which it is used. Using a three-industry, three-factor SAM for the United States in 2004 as an example, we calculated macroeconomic indicators and developed a structure table and tax table. These tables are a useful way to summarize the microeconomic data in the SAM and they inform experiment design and the analysis of model results.

Key Terms

Activity
Agent
Commodity
Factor of production
GDP from the income side
GDP from the expenditure side
Gross value of output
Intermediate input
Regional household
Trade margin
Social Accounting Matrix
Structure table
Tax structure table
Value added

PRACTICE AND REVIEW

1. Based on data in the manufacturing activity column in the U.S. 3x3 SAM:
   a. What is the gross output of the manufacturing activity?
   b. What is the total value of the intermediate inputs used in the production of manufacturing, including sales taxes? Which intermediate input accounts for the largest share of input costs, including sales taxes? Calculate its cost share.
   c. What is the total value of taxes paid by the manufacturing production activity? On which input is the tax payment largest?
   d. Based on Table 3.4, on which factor input in manufacturing is the tax rate highest?
2. Based on data in the manufacturing commodity column in the U.S. 3x3 SAM:
   a. What is the value of the imported supply of the manufactured commodity (including import tariff and import margin)?
   b. What is the value of the supply from the domestic variety (including export taxes)?

   c. What is the total, or aggregate, supply of the manufactured commodity in the United States?
3. Based on data in the manufacturing commodity rows in the U.S. 3x3 SAM:
   a. Where is the imported variety of the manufactured commodity sold? List each sale and calculate the value of total sales.
   b. Where is the domestic variety of the manufactured commodity sold? List each sale and calculate the value of total sales.
   c. Accounts in a SAM are balanced when supply or income (the row total) is equal to demand or spending (the column total). Are the supplies of the imported and the domestic manufactured commodities equal to the value of their sales? Check the rest of the accounts in the SAM. Are all of the accounts in the SAM balanced?
4. Based on data for the services production activity in the U.S. 3x3 SAM:
   a. Which factor has the largest cost share in the production of services? Show your calculations.
   b. What is the amount of services' production tax? Is output taxed or subsidized?

4
Final Demand in a CGE Model

In this chapter, we describe final demand by domestic agents – private households, government, investors – and by the export market. Data in the Social Accounting Matrix (SAM) describe agents' incomes and the commodity composition of their spending. The computable general equilibrium (CGE) model depicts demand by domestic agents as a two-stage decision. First, consumers decide on the quantities of each commodity in their consumption basket. Second, an "Armington" import aggregation function describes their choice between domestic and imported varieties of each commodity. We survey functional forms commonly used in CGE models to describe private household preferences. We also introduce the concept of "national welfare," which is the monetary value of changes in a nation's well-being following an economic shock.

The U.S. economic stimulus package, implemented in the 2009 recession, was designed to increase government spending in order to compensate for sharp declines in spending by private households and investors, and in export sales. These four categories of demand – private households, investment, government, and exports – constitute the demand side of an economy. They are called components of ***final demand*** since the goods and services that are consumed are in their end-use; they are not further combined or processed into other goods and services. An economy's structure can change when the categories of aggregate final demand change in relative size because each type of final demand usually purchases different goods and services. For example, households purchase items like groceries and entertainment, whereas investors purchase mainly machinery and equipment, and governments mostly purchase services. The increased share of the government in U.S. final demand as a result of the stimulus program is thus likely to change the types of goods demanded in the U.S. economy, at least in the short term.

In this chapter, we learn how the SAM's data describe each component of final demand. We then study how each final demand agent is assumed to behave in the CGE model. Our discussion in this chapter mostly focuses

Table 4.1. *Final Demand Data in The U.S. 3x3 SAM ($U.S. Billions)*

	Private Household	Government	Savings-Investment	Trade Margin Export	Rest-of-World
Imports					
Agriculture	9	0	0	0	0
Manufacturing	415	1	237	0	0
Services	60	1	3	0	0
Domestic					
Agriculture	60	1	0	0	50
Manufacturing	1,104	2	628	0	756
Services	6,392	1,805	1,315	24	259
Sales taxes–imports					
Agriculture	1	0	0	0	0
Manufacturing	35	0	5	0	0
Services	0	0	0	0	0
Sales tax–domestic					
Agriculture	2	0	0	0	0
Manufacturing	115	0	10	0	0
Services	41	0	1	0	0
Savings–Investment	0	0	0	32	536
Total	8,233	1,810	2,198	56	1,601

Source: GTAP v.7.0 U.S. 3x3 database.

on commonalities among CGE models, including the concept of "commodities," the two- (or three-) stage budgeting decision and the measurement of national welfare. CGE models differ widely in their descriptions of private households' consumption behavior, making it difficult to characterize a "standard" CGE model in this respect. Thus, we survey four functional forms commonly used in CGE models to describe private households' preferences, and we explain the differences among these functions that are of practical importance for the modeler.

Final Demand Data in a SAM

Table 4.1 presents data on final demand from the U.S. 3x3 SAM. The table reproduces the column accounts (omitting the rows with zeros) that record expenditures by domestic consumers – which include private households, government, and investors – and by the rest of world.

Consumers demand commodities, such as "agriculture," which are composed of the domestic and imported varieties of a good. In the U.S. 3x3 SAM, consumers' column accounts separately record their spending on the imported and domestic variety of each of the three commodities (agriculture, manufacturing, and services). For example, U.S. private households spend a total of $69 billion on the agricultural commodity, composed of $9 billion worth of imported agricultural goods and $60 billion of the domestic variety. Private households also spend $1 billion on retail sales taxes on the imported variety and $2 billion on retail sales taxes on the domestic variety. The total value of private household expenditure on all commodities, including sales taxes, is $8,233 billion. The column accounts for the U.S. government and investors similarly report their total spending on commodities plus sales taxes.

The export trade margin's column account reports U.S. exports of insurance and freight (*cif*) services used in global trade. Expenditures reported in the rest-of-world's column account report foreign purchases of U.S. goods, which are valued in U.S. *fob* export prices (i.e., excluding trade margin charges). Both of these column accounts include, in addition, payments to the savings-investment row account. The payments report the balance of trade in margin services and in other goods and services. A positive value indicates a foreign exchange inflow (a balance of trade deficit), and a negative value indicates a foreign exchange outflow (a balance of trade surplus). In the U.S. SAM, the positive numbers signal that the United States has trade deficits in both trade margin services, and in goods and services, which sum to $568 billion.

We can use the final demand data in the SAM to calculate ***budget shares***. A budget share is the share of a commodity in the consumer's total spending. For example, private households' spending on imported manufactured goods (including the sales tax) accounts for 5.5 percent of their total spending.

Income Data in a SAM

CGE models impose the constraint that spending on goods and services, taxes and savings must equal income. You may recognize this model constraint from your microeconomic theory, in which spending is subject to a budget constraint. Indeed, you may recognize this constraint from managing your own finances, as you decide how to allocate your after-tax income to purchases and to savings. Because final demand is constrained by income in the CGE model, it is worthwhile also to examine the income data in a SAM.

Data in Table 4.2 report the row accounts from the U.S. 3x3 SAM that describe income flows. Income originates from the employment of factors by production activities. The land factor, for example, earns a total of $34 billion, paid from the activity columns to the land factor row. Of this amount, the land column account reports that $3 billion is spent on land-based income taxes and the remaining, after-tax income of $31 billion is paid to the regional

Table 4.2. *Income Flows in The U.S. 3x3 SAM ($U.S. Billions)*

	Total Production Activities	Land	Labor	Capital	Income Tax	All Other Taxes	Regional Household
Land	34						
Labor	6,844						
Capital	2,921						
Income tax		3	1,446	244			
All other taxes	1,639						
Regional household		31	5,397	1,632	1,693	1,875	
Private household							8,233
Government							1,810
Savings–investment				1,046			585
Total	11,438	34	6,844	2,921	1,693	1,875	10,628

Note: The production activities' column sums the agriculture, manufacturing, and services activities columns of the U.S. 3x3 SAM.
Source: GTAP v.7.0 U.S. 3x3 database.

household's row account. Labor earnings of $6,844 billion are also divided between income taxes and payments to the regional household. Capital earnings of $2,921 billion are paid to income taxes and the regional household and, in addition, are expended on savings (this payment measures the depreciation of capital equipment and machinery).

The regional household's row account shows its accumulation of $7,060 billion in after-tax factor income ($31 plus $5,397 plus $1,632 billion), income taxes ($1,693 billion), and all other taxes combined ($1,895 billion). National income, excluding depreciation, therefore totals $10,628 billion. National income is then allocated by the regional household's column account to the three categories of domestic spending: Private households receive (and spend) $8,233 billion, the government receives (and spends) $1,810 billion, and $585 billion is saved (this includes combined household savings and government savings).[1]

Two-Stage Domestic Final Demand

In most CGE models, domestic consumers make their consumption decision in two stages, depicted in Figure 4.1. In the first stage, shown at the top level in the figure, they decide on the quantity of each commodity in their

[1] In the GTAP model that corresponds to this SAM, the allocation of regional household income is determined by a demand system that allows the shares of private households, government, and savings in national income to change. In most CGE models without a regional household account, private household income is equal to factor income, government income is equal to tax revenues, and investment spending is equal to savings.

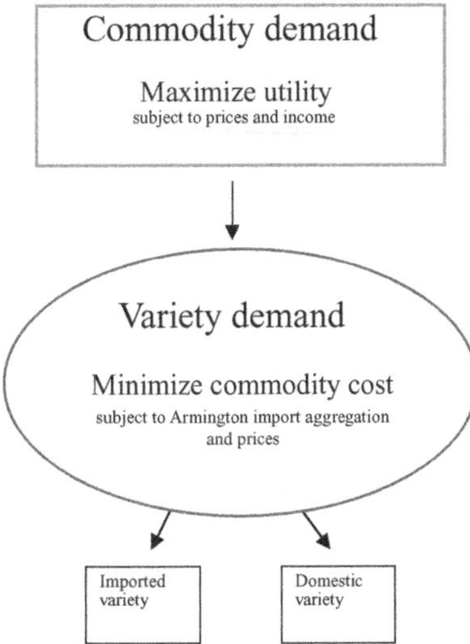

Figure 4.1. Two-stage domestic final demand

consumption basket, such as the amount of food and the number of books. Their choice depends upon their subjective preferences. For example, consumers may prefer a large quantity of food relative to books. These preferences are described by a ***utility function,*** an equation that quantifies how much utility, or satisfaction, consumers derive from any given combination of consumption goods. Given their utility function, consumers select the basket of goods that generates the maximum achievable satisfaction given the prices of the goods and their budgets.

In the next stage, consumers minimize the cost of their commodity bundle by deciding on the shares of domestic and imported varieties that comprise each commodity. For example, once a consumer has decided on the quantity of food in her basket, she next decides on the amounts of domestically produced or imported food that she prefers, given their relative prices. This decision is governed by an ***Armington import aggregation function,*** named after the economist Paul Armington (1969), who developed this type of sourcing decision in an applied economic model.

Some CGE models have an additional stage that describes the lowest-cost sourcing of imports from alternative suppliers for a given quantity of a commodity import. For example, once the consumer decides on the quantity of imported shoes that he prefers, he then chooses the least-cost bundle of imported shoes from competing suppliers, such as Italy or Japan. Since this additional stage in consumer decision making is identical to that between the aggregate import and the domestic variety, for brevity, we omit further discussion of it. (See Text Box 4.1 for another example of an additional stage

Text Box 4.1. Consumer Aversion to GM Foods
"Genetically Modified Foods, Trade and Developing Countries."
(Nielson, Thierfelder, and Robinson, 2001).

What is the research question? Genetically modified (GM) seeds used in agricultural production have raised yields and increased pest resistance. Their use lowers production expenses by reducing the need for costly chemical and fertilizer inputs. However, some consumers, especially in developed countries, are concerned about the possible, unknown health effects of GM foods and prefer not to purchase them. How might consumer aversion to GM foods affect developing countries that produce and export these crops?

What is the CGE model innovation? The authors develop a database on trade and production of GM crops that they use to disaggregate the rows and columns of the SAMs' activity and commodity accounts for grains and oilseeds into GM and non-GM varieties. They also introduce an additional stage of the consumer budget allocation decision into an eight-region, global version of the International Food Policy Research Institute (IFPRI) standard CGE model. At the top level, a Cobb-Douglas utility function describes consumers as spending a fixed share of their budgets on grain and oilseed commodities. At the second level, a CES utility function describes consumers' choice between the GM and non-GM varieties of each commodity.

What is the model experiment? GM adoption is described as a 10 percent increase in total factor productivity and a 30 percent reduction in the use of chemical intermediate inputs in the GM grains and oilseed sectors. The authors present two alternative approaches to describe the aversion to GM foods by consumers in developed countries. First, they assume that consumers become less sensitive to prices, which is modeled as a reduction in the substitution elasticity between GM and non-GM varieties. Second, they assume a structural shift in demand by imposing a very low, fixed 2 percent budget share parameter for the GM variety. They reduce the share parameter by changing the base data in the SAMs and recalibrating the model.

What are the key findings? Adoption of GM crops provides farmers in developing countries with productivity benefits that lead to large welfare gains. Consumer preferences in developed countries do not diminish these gains since bilateral trade patterns adjust, and GM and non-GM products are redirected according to preferences in the different markets.

in consumer decision making; in this case related to the genetic attributes of food products.)

Most of our discussion in this chapter describes the utility-maximizing behavior of private households at the first stage of their consumption decision. We treat this stage of government and investment demand for commodities very briefly since many CGE models describe their preferences in a

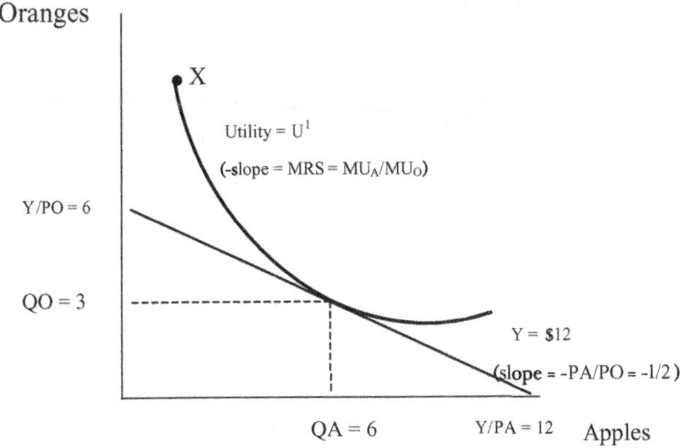

Figure 4.2. Consumer utility function with a budget constraint

simple fashion, by assuming that the initial budget shares in their consumption baskets remain fixed.[2] For example, if the government spends 10 percent of its budget on agricultural commodities, it will continue to spend 10 percent of any sized budget on agricultural commodities. Or, if agricultural prices rise by 10 percent, the government will reduce the quantity of agricultural goods that it purchases by 10 percent so that the agricultural budget share remains constant. This simple specification of government spending reflects the view that economic theory does not fully explain government outlays. In the case of investment, the standard, one-period CGE model that we are studying does not account for intertemporal calculations or expectations about the future that influence today's investment decisions. Consequently, this fixed-share allocation rule for investment demand is a transparent approach that simply replicates the demand for capital goods observed in the model's base year and reported in the SAM.

Utility-Maximizing Private Households

Private households in CGE models are assumed to be utility maximizers who allocate their income across commodities based on their preferences and subject to their budget and commodity prices. To illustrate their behavior, suppose that a household consumer has a total income of $12 (and does not save or pay taxes) that it allocates to purchasing two commodities: apples, QA, with a price, PA, of $1, and oranges, QO, with a price, PO, of $2. Figure 4.2 describes the consumer's decision on how much to buy of each good. The downward-sloping, straight line, Y, in the figure is the household's

[2] This is a Cobb-Douglas utility function. See Lofgren, et al. (2002) for a discussion of alternative treatments of government and investment demand.

budget constraint. It shows all combinations of the two commodities that he can purchase for \$12. For example, points on this line include such combinations as two apples (\$2) plus five oranges (\$10) for a total of \$12; or ten apples (\$10) plus one orange (\$2) for a total of \$12.

A budget constraint drawn to the right of Y represents expenditures greater than \$12; a budget constraint drawn to its left represents expenditures of less than \$12. A utility-maximizing household that earns \$12 will always choose a basket of goods along its \$12 budget constraint. More is always better, but the household cannot afford to reach higher budget lines, and at lower budget lines, it foregoes some achievable consumption. We observe this behavioral assumption of the CGE model in the model's SAM database where, in the initial equilibrium, the income (the row total) for the household account is equal to its expenditure (the column total). This equivalence also will hold true in any post-shock model equilibrium.

If all income is spent on oranges, where Y meets the vertical axis, then quantity Y/PO, or $12/2 = 6$, oranges can be purchased. If all income is spent on apples, where Y meets the horizontal axis, then quantity Y/PA, or $12/1 = 12$, apples can be purchased. The slope of the budget constraint is calculated from the ratio of these two quantities (i.e., the rise over the run of the budget line) as $-6/12 = -1/2$. The sign is negative because the budget constraint is downward sloping; an increase in apples expenditure leads to a decrease in orange expenditure. Its slope can also be expressed as the price ratio of apples (the good on the horizontal axis) to oranges (the good on the vertical axis), since $-(Y/PO)/(Y/PA) = -PA/PO = -1/2$.

With so many feasible combinations that cost \$12, the household's choice of apple and orange quantities depends on how it ranks its preferences for goods and services – that is, its utility function. We can plot this function on a graph as an ***indifference curve***, such as U^1 in Figure 4.2. The indifference curve shows all possible combinations of apples and oranges that yield the same level of utility. Indifference curves drawn to the right of U^1 represent higher levels of utility while those drawn to its left represent lower levels of utility.

The slope of the indifference curve describes the consumer's willingness to substitute apples with oranges, or the ***marginal rate of substitution*** (MRS). Imagine, for example, that the consumer has ten oranges and only two apples at point X on the indifference curve. Based on his preferences, the consumer would be willing to forego two oranges as he moves down his indifference curve and consumes one more apple, so the MRS of oranges for one additional apple is two. As the consumer moves further down his indifference curve, and quantity of apples consumed increases, he becomes more "apple satiated." His willingness to give up oranges in exchange for an additional apple diminishes and the MRS falls. We can also express the MRS as the ratio of the ***marginal utility*** of apples (i.e., the utility derived from consuming

Text Box 4.2. A Macro-Micro CGE Model of Indonesia
"Representative Versus Real Households in the Macroeconomic Modeling of Inequality." (Bourguignon, Robilliard, and Robinson, 2003).

What is the research question? CGE models with disaggregated households contain two or more "representative" household types. These models can describe differences in the income effects of economic shocks across types of households but imply that households within each type are all affected in the same way. However, household survey data show that changes in income inequality within each household type are at least as important as cross-type changes. Could a macro-micro analysis more realistically describe the effects of shocks on the distribution of income in a country?

What is the CGE model innovation? The authors combine the IFPRI standard CGE model with a micro-simulation model based on a survey sample of 9,800 households in Indonesia. They estimate reduced-form equations that explain households' work and occupational choices as a function of exogenous parameters such as wage, age, and education. The CGE model is solved for the effects of an economic shock on endogenous variables such as wages. These CGE model results are then used as the exogenous parameters in the equations of the micro-model to analyze impacts at the household level.

What is the model experiment? The authors explore two alternative macroeconomic shocks: a 50 percent decline in the world price of Indonesia's main commodity exports and a 30 percent decline in foreign savings inflows, similar to the effect of the 1998 financial crisis. Each CGE model scenario is run under three alternative government closures: the shares of government, investment, and private consumption in aggregate spending remain the same (suggesting a successful structural adjustment program); government spending adjusts to maintain the base government budget balance; and value-added taxes adjust to maintain the base government budget balance.

What are the key findings? The macro-micro model leads to distributional effects that are different in size, and sometimes even in sign, than a CGE model with representative households. The differences reflect that the macro-micro model accounts for phenomena that are known to be important in explaining household adjustments and resulting distributional changes, including changes in types of occupation, combinations of income sources, and differences in consumption behavior within household types.

one more apple) to the marginal utility of oranges: MU_A/MU_O.[3] As more apples and fewer oranges are consumed, the marginal utility derived from

[3] The MRS is equivalent to the ratio of marginal utilities (MU_A/MU_O) because, if d refers to a marginal change, then the slope at any point on the indifference curve is $-dQO/dQA$, which is the rise over the run. The marginal utility of A is dU/dQA and of O is dU/dQO, so the ratio $MU_A/MU_O = (dU/dQA)/(dU/dQO) = dQO/dQA$, which is the negative of the slope of the indifference curve, or the MRS.

eating yet one more apple falls, and the marginal utility derived from an additional orange increases as fewer oranges are consumed. The ratio MU_A/MU_O therefore falls as the consumer moves down his indifference curve.

Consumers maximize their utility by choosing the combination of apples and oranges that provides the highest attainable utility curve given their budget constraint. In Figure 4.2, this is shown as the tangency between the budget constraint Y and indifference curve U^1, where the consumer chooses three oranges ($6) and six apples ($6) at a total cost of $12. At this tangency, the slope of the budget constraint (the ratio of prices) and the slope of the indifference curve (the ratio of marginal utilities) are equal: $MU_A/MU_O = PA/PO$. Rearranging, $MU_A/PA = MU_O/PO$. This means that the consumer maximizes utility when the marginal utility per additional dollar spent on each good is equal. If not, the consumer will spend more on the good that yields a higher marginal utility and less on the other good until their marginal utilities are equalized.

In some CGE models, household consumers are assumed to be cost minimizers instead of utility maximizers. They allocate their purchases to achieve a given level of utility with the minimum possible expenditure at given prices. Imagine that, in Figure 4.2, the consumer seeks the lowest attainable budget line with the slope $-PA/PO = -1/2$, while constrained to remain on the U^1 indifference curve. It should be evident that utility maximization and cost minimization are equivalent ways to describe consumer choice, and will yield the same ratios of demand quantities for a given level of utility.

Demand Response to Income Changes

Economic shocks in static CGE models usually lead to changes in income and in relative prices. Consumers respond by changing the quantities of goods and services that they purchase. We first consider the effect of income changes on quantities demanded. The indifference curve U^1 in Figure 4.3a describes the household's preferences for combinations of apples and oranges. The initial equilibrium is at the tangency of the budget constraint and the U^1 indifference curve, at quantities QO^1 and QA^1. An increase in income, holding relative prices fixed, shifts the budget constraint outward. It shifts outward in a parallel fashion since the price ratio of oranges and apples has not changed. An increase in income allows the consumer to increase his purchases of both goods to quantities QO^2 and QA^2, and therefore to achieve a higher level of utility, U^2. An additional increase in income shifts the budget constraint out further, enabling the consumer to increase the quantities purchased and to achieve utility of U^3. Notice that Figure 4.3a describes a utility function in which income growth causes the quantity demanded of both goods to increase by the same proportion. For example, a 10 percent increase in income,

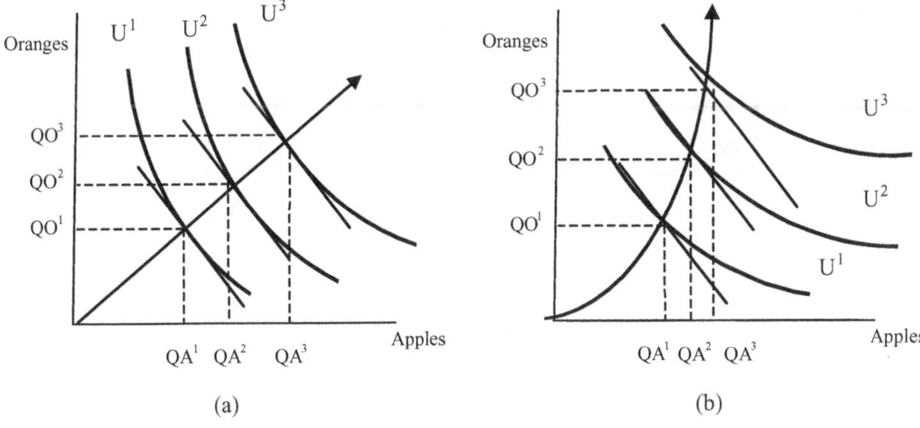

Figure 4.3. (a) Effects of income growth on consumer demand – homothetic utility function. (b) Effects of income growth on consumer demand – nonhomothetic utility function.

holding prices constant, would result in a 10 percent increase in demand for both oranges and apples. This is a ***homothetic*** utility function with income elasticities of demand of goods equal to one. As income grows, with prices constant, an expansion path plots the locus of tangencies between the budget constraint and a mapping of successively higher indifference along a straight line emanating from the origin. Many CGE models assume homothetic utility functions.

Some CGE models assume ***nonhomothetic*** utility functions, such as that drawn in Figure 4.3b. Nonhomothetic functions allow income elasticities of demand to differ from one. Some goods may be ***luxuries***, with income elasticities greater than one; others may be ***necessities*** with income elasticities of less than one. If oranges are a luxury and apples are a necessity, then income growth, with constant prices, will lead to an increase in the ratio of oranges to apples in the consumption basket. In this case, the expansion path veers toward oranges as income grows.

Demand Response to Relative Price Changes

Economic shocks in standard CGE models usually lead to larger changes in relative prices than in income, so it is worthwhile to examine carefully how demand quantities are assumed to respond to price shocks in these models. A key determinant is the ***elasticity of substitution in consumption***, denoted by parameter σ_C. The elasticity expresses the percentage change in the quantity ratio of good Y to good X given a percentage change in the price ratio of good X to good Y. Returning to our example of apples and oranges, the larger is the elasticity of substitution, the more willing is the consumer to shift to apples from oranges as the relative price of apples falls.

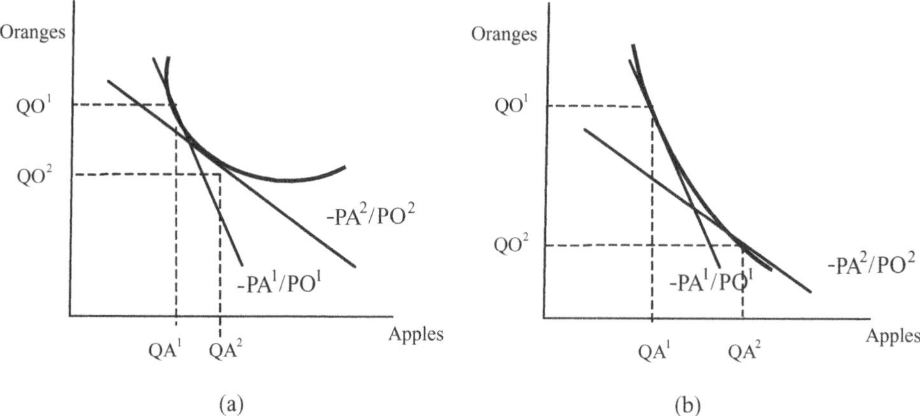

Figure 4.4. (a) Effects of price change on consumer demand, low substitution elasticity. (b) Effects of price change on consumer demand, high substitution elasticity.

Parameter σ_C describes the curvature of the indifference curve. When the parameter value is small, then the indifference curve is sharply convex, as in Figure 4.4a. In this case, an outward rotation of the budget constraint, as the price of apples falls relative to oranges, causes a relatively small change in the consumption basket, from QO^1 and QA^1 to QO^2 and QA^2. Intuitively, the more curved is the indifference curve, the faster the ratio of the marginal utility from an additional apple relative to that of an additional (MRS) falls as the ratio of apple to orange consumption rises. Therefore, the consumer is not very willing to give up oranges for an additional apple when the relative price of apples falls. When parameter σ_C is large, then the indifference curve is flatter, as in Figure 4.4b. The consumer will readily trade off oranges for an additional apple, with small effects on the fruits' relative marginal utilities. Therefore, the same decline in the relative price of apples will lead to a larger increase in the ratio of apples to oranges in the consumer's basket.

Sometimes, consumer preferences are quite rigid – for example, consumers usually buy right and left gloves in pairs. A fall in the price of right-hand gloves will not change the ratio in which gloves are purchased since most consumers require right- and left-handed gloves in a fixed proportion. Such preferences are described by a Leontief utility function, whose elasticity of substitution is zero and whose indifference curve has an L-shape. Other consumers may be completely flexible in their preferences; for example, any brand of bottled water is equally satisfactory. If a consumer is always willing to trade off the same quantity of one good for the other, then the MRS between the products is constant. Since the goods are perfect substitutes, the elasticity of substitution approaches infinity and the indifference curve is drawn as a straight line.

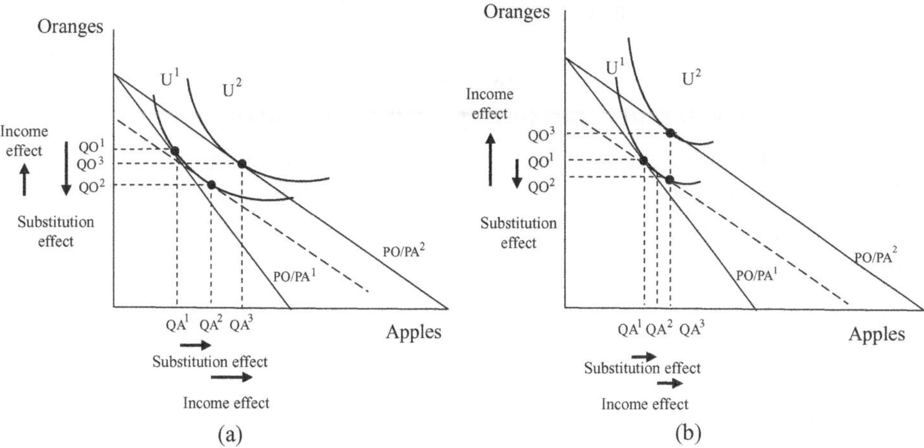

Figure 4.5. (a) Effects of price change on consumer demand – net and gross substitutes. (b) Effects of price change on consumer demand – net substitutes and gross complements.

We can decompose the effect of a price change on demand quantities into two components. First, if we assume that the own-price elasticity is negative (which is the case in standard CGE models), then the price change will cause consumers to shift the composition of their basket toward the cheaper good at any given level of utility. This is the substitution effect of a price change. It describes the movement of a consumer along the initial indifference curve as relative prices change, holding utility constant. Figure 4.5a illustrates the substitution effect of a price shock. In this example, the consumer initially purchases an orange quantity of QO^1 and an apple quantity of QA^1, at the U^1 level of utility. Suppose the price of apples falls to PO/PA^2, but the consumer is constrained to remain at the same level of utility. The dotted line, drawn parallel to the new price line, is the new price ratio. The substitution effect is the movement of the consumer along the initial indifference curve to the new basket of QO^2 and QA^2.

The second component is the effect of a price change on the consumer's purchasing power. If the price of apples falls, consumers now have money left over from purchasing their original basket. They can allocate this additional purchasing power toward buying more apples, more oranges, or more of both. The income effect of a price change measures the effect of the change in purchasing power on the consumption basket, holding relative prices constant. In Figure 4.5a, the income effect is the change from QO^2 and QA^2 to QO^3 and QA^3, at the new price ratio PO/PA^2.

By decomposing the income and substitution effects of a price change, we can describe apples and oranges as ***net substitutes*** (measuring only the substitution effect) and ***gross substitutes*** or ***gross complements*** (measuring the combined substitution and income effects). Two goods are net substitutes when a fall in the price ratio of good X to good Y cause an increase in the quantity ratio of good X to good Y, holding utility constant (i.e., remaining on the initial indifference curve). In our example in Figure 4.5a, apples and oranges are net substitutes because the fall in the relative price of apples causes the ratio of apples to oranges to increase, holding utility constant. CGE models typically assume that goods are net substitutes in consumption.

Two goods are gross substitutes if a decline in the price of one good causes demand for the second good to fall, and gross complements if demand for the second good rises. In Figure 4.5a, apples and oranges are gross substitutes. Although the income effect leads to increased demand for both fruits, the substitution effect dominates the income effect and causes the quantity of oranges demanded to fall when the price of apples declines. Figure 4.5b describes the case of gross complements. Oranges and apples are still net substitutes but now the income effect dominates the substitution effect on oranges, so the quantity of oranges demanded increases when the price of apples falls. Gross complementarity is more likely to occur when the price change affects a good that is important in the consumer's total expenditure, so that purchasing power changes substantially; when income elasticities are large, or when the substitution effect is small because the indifference curve is very convex.

Comparing Utility Functions Used in CGE Models

Our discussion of income and prices effects has emphasized how assumptions about consumer preferences, as described by utility functions and depicted in the curvature of indifference curves, determine how consumer demand responds to changes in income or in prices. CGE modelers therefore try to choose utility functions and elasticity parameter values that best describe consumer preferences in the economy that they are studying. Sometimes a modeler may need to trade off some degree of realism for feasibility when describing consumer demand. This is particularly true of modelers who want to use a standard CGE model and the utility function or demand system that it assumes, without extending the model's theory or programming. Flexibility to specify demand elasticity parameter values varies, too, since in some utility functions, these values are a "hard wired" part of the functional form or constrained in the CGE model. For these reasons, it is useful for modelers to study the functional forms commonly used to describe consumer preferences in CGE models and to understand the practical implications for their model results.

We compare four functions that are widely used in standard CGE models: the Cobb-Douglas, Stone-Geary/Linear Expenditure System (LES), Constant Elasticity of Substitution (CES) utility functions, and the Constant Difference of Elasticities (CDE) demand system (Table 4.3).

Table 4.3. *A Comparison of Functional Forms that Describe Consumer Preferences in CGE Models*

Utility Function	Elasticity			Budget Shares	
	Income	Own-price	Substitution	Price Change	Income Change
Cobb-Douglas	Homothetic	Negative own-price	Net and gross substitutes	Fixed	Fixed
Stone-Geary/Linear Expenditure System (LES)	Quasi-homothetic	Negative own-price	Net substitutes, gross complements	Flexible	Flexible
Constant Elasticity of Substitution (CES)	Homothetic	Negative own-price	Net and gross substitutes	Flexible	Fixed
Constant Difference of Elasticities (CDE)	Non-homothetic	Negative own-price	Net substitutes, gross substitutes or complements	Flexible	Flexible

Notes: We assume that the Frisch parameter in the Stone-Geary utility function is greater than negative one, and the elasticity of substitution parameter in the CES utility function is greater than zero. See Technical Appendix 4.1 on parameter value restrictions.

The simplest (but most restrictive) is the Cobb-Douglas utility function. The function itself implies values for elasticity parameters that the modeler cannot change. For all goods, the Cobb-Douglas own-price elasticity is minus 1, and the elasticities of substitution and income are one. A unitary, negative own-price elasticity means that a change in price leads to an opposite change in quantity of an equal proportion. For example, a 10 percent increase in the apple price leads to a 10 percent reduction in apple quantity demanded. Since the quantity change in apples exactly offsets the price change, the apple budget share does not change. And, since there is no change in spending on apples, the quantities of oranges and any other goods do not change either when the apple price falls. The function therefore implies that budget shares for all goods remain fixed as relative prices change. The homothetic Cobb-Douglas utility function also implies that, if income increases 10 percent, the quantities demanded of every good also increase by 10 percent. Therefore, the budget shares of each commodity in the consumer basket remain constant when incomes alone change. Since consumers make the same substitutions in response to relative price changes at any income level, all goods are also gross substitutes.

The other three functional forms allow the CGE modeler to define one or more elasticity parameters whose values lie within specified ranges (see the Technical Appendix to this chapter). The Stone-Geary utility function differs from the Cobb-Douglas function in that it accounts for a minimum subsistence level of consumption, but above that level, preferences are described by a Cobb-Douglas utility function. For this reason, all goods are gross complements because an increase in the price of a good that meets minimum subsistence requirements means that the quantities of all discretionary goods must fall. Therefore, budget shares may vary. The Stone-Geary function is ***quasi-homothetic*** because only the demand quantities for goods that exceed subsistence levels change by the same proportion as income. Thus, budget shares of subsistence goods increase when incomes fall, and decrease when incomes rise. The smaller the share of subsistence goods in the consumption bundle, the larger is the share of the bundle that is described by a Cobb-Douglas utility function, and the more homothetic the function becomes.

The Constant Elasticity of Substitution is a homothetic utility function that allows the modeler to specify explicitly the elasticity of substitution parameter that defines the shape of the indifference curve. The name of the function, constant elasticity of substitution, derives from the fact that the substitution elasticity parameter has the same value at all points along its indifference curves and at all income levels. CGE models usually allow the modeler to define only one substitution elasticity parameter that describes identical pairwise substitutability among all goods in the consumption basket. Therefore, all goods are net substitutes (unless parameter σ_C is defined to be zero),

Text Box 4.3. Consumer Fear and Avian Flu in Ghana
"Economywide Impact of Avian Flu in Ghana: A Dynamic CGE Model Analysis." (Diao, 2009).

What is the research question? HPAI H5N1 (also known as avian flu) has attracted considerable public attention because the virus is capable of producing fatal disease in humans. Control measures have focused on its prevention and eradication in poultry populations by culling flocks, but this has not prevented a sharp fall in poultry demand by fearful consumers. Are there cost-effective and evidence-based measures that both reduce disease risk and protect the livelihoods of the small-holder farmers who account for most poultry production in Ghana?

What is the model innovation? The author develops a SAM for Ghana for 2005 that divides national production into four agro-ecological zones and ninety representative households classed by income and rural or urban location. The model is a recursive dynamic version of the IFPRI standard CGE model, which assumes the quasi-homothetic Stone-Geary utility function. Consumer aversion to chicken is simulated by reducing poultry meat's marginal budget share, a calibrated parameter in the utility function. This results in a smaller increase in poultry meat demand for any given increase in income.

What is the experiment? The production effect of avian flu is modeled as a decline in the poultry sector's capital stock (which represents the culling of chickens) that reduces production by 10 percent for periods of one to three years, an outcome that is consistent with studies of this industry. Little is known of the virus' potential effects on consumer attitudes so the demand shock is described as a change in the marginal budget share parameter that reduces poultry demand by 40 percent from the baseline time path, for periods of one to three years.

What are the results? A decline in poultry production causes a shortage in poultry supply and tends to push producer prices upward. But the decline in consumer demand tends to cause producer prices to fall. Thus, model results show little change in poultry prices due to avian flu but much lower levels of both supply and demand.

and their budget shares may change when relative prices change. Because the utility function is homothetic, consumers make the same substitutions in response to relative price changes at any income level, so all goods are also gross substitutes.

An important and useful characteristic of the Constant Difference of Elasticities demand system is that it is nonhomothetic. As incomes change, consumers can purchase proportionately more luxury goods and spend a smaller share of their budget on necessities, depending on the income elasticity of demand specified for each good. Its nonhomotheticity makes the CDE demand system especially well suited to analyze experiments in which there are large income effects. Commodities are net substitutes but the presence

Table 4.4. *U.S. Private Household Default Demand Parameters in U.S. 3x3 Database*

	Income Parameter (IINCPAR)	Substitution Parameter (SUBPAR)
Agriculture	0.25	0.74
Manufactures	0.88	0.24
Services	1.04	0.22

Source: GTAP v.7.0 U.S. 3x3 database.

of income effects means that goods can be either gross substitutes or gross complements. For example, a fall in the relative price of a necessity good with a large budget share is likely to shift consumption toward the necessity good, but the price savings will also provide a significant boost to a household's purchasing power. This income effect will cause the quantity demanded of luxury goods to increase and that of the necessity good to fall. If this income effect is large enough, the necessity and luxury goods can be gross complements. The CDE demand system also has the flexibility to specify different pair-wise substitution possibilities in models that include more than two commodities.

We illustrate the practical significance of the choice of utility function and parameter values by comparing the model results of the same experiment when making three different assumptions about consumer preferences. Our experiment is a 10 percent increase in the productivity of factors used in the production of services. This simulates an income increase in the U.S. economy and causes the price of services to fall relative to other goods. We use the GTAP model, which has a CDE demand system because we can choose CDE parameter values that will transform the CDE function into CES and Cobb-Douglas utility functions. However, we cannot replicate the Stone-Geary utility function because it includes parameters for subsistence spending that are not accounted for in the CDE demand system.

The CDE system allows the modeler to define income and substitution parameter values. These parameters are not exactly the same as income and compensated own-price elasticities of demand, but are closely related to them.[4,5] The CDE parameter values for the United States in our 3x3 database are reported in Table 4.4. The INCPAR parameter values for the United States indicate that private household demand for services is relatively sensitive to income changes, but demand for agriculture (which is

[4] A compensated own-price elasticity describes the consumer's demand response to a price change net of the income effect; it is the movement along an indifference curve.

[5] Formulae that describe the relationship between these parameters and income, own-price and cross-price elasticities are derived by Hanoch (1975). For a detailed discussion of the CDE demand system, see McDougall (2003), Surry (1993) and Hertel, et al. (1991).

Table 4.5. *Effects of a 10 Percent Increase in Total Factor Productivity in the Services Sector on Private Household Demand Assuming Different Consumer Preferences (% Change From Base)*

	Consumer Price (*pp*)	Consumer Demand Quantity (*qp*)	Expenditure on Commodity	Budget Share
Constant Difference of Elasticities (CDE)				
Agriculture	−0.57	1.82	0.25	0.89
Manufacturing	−3.65	4.82	1.17	0.81
Services	−9.45	9.59	0.14	−0.22
Constant Elasticity of Substitution (CES)				
Agriculture	0.44	4.61	4.17	3.92
Manufacturing	−3.70	6.24	2.54	2.44
Services	−9.57	9.18	−0.39	−0.50
Cobb-Douglas				
Agriculture	−0.62	1.03	0.41	0.0
Manufacturing	−3.62	4.03	0.41	0.0
Services	−9.39	9.80	0.41	0.0

Notes: We use the Johansen solution method.
Source: GTAP v.7.0 U.S. 3x3 database.

mainly foodstuffs) is not very sensitive to income changes. As the substitution parameter value becomes larger, the negative own-price and positive cross-price compensated elasticities become larger. Based on the SUBPAR parameter values, U.S. private households are relatively price sensitive with respect to their food purchases, but less so with respect to purchases of services and manufactures.

We first carry out the model experiment using the CDE demand system. Then, we redefine income parameters and substitution parameters to correspond with a CES utility function (with a low, 0.5 elasticity of substitution) and re-run the model experiment.[6] We repeat these steps for the Cobb-Douglas utility function.

In all three model experiments, national income increases by a small amount, about 0.5 percent, which suggests that income effects on demand will be small. Other model results are reported in Table 4.5. In all three cases, the consumer price of services falls substantially relative to the prices of agricultural and manufactured goods. However, consumer responses differ in the three cases, reflecting different assumptions about consumer preferences.

[6] To describe a CES function, we define CDE utility function income parameters for all commodities and regions to be one and define all substitution parameters to be 0.5, which describes a relatively low elasticity of substitution and a highly convex indifference curve. To describe a Cobb-Douglas utility function, we define all income parameters as one, and all substitution parameters as zero. See Hertel, et al. (1991).

With the CDE function, income growth favors a disproportionate increase in quantity demanded for services, a luxury good, which reinforces the substitution toward services as their relative price falls. Nevertheless, the budget share of services falls because more services can be purchased at a lower total cost, and the budget shares of agriculture and manufactured goods increase. With the homothetic CES function, the income effect leads to a small, proportionate increase in the quantity demanded for all three commodities, which contributes to a more evenly balanced growth within the basket, compared to the CDE case. Still, as in the CDE case, the price effect causes consumers to substitute toward the consumption of services. The net effect is an increase in budget shares for agriculture and manufactured goods while the budget share of services declines. In the case of the Cobb-Douglas function, budget shares are fixed by assumption and quantities demanded for each good change by the same proportion as income. As a result, the quantities of services that consumers demand increase substantially relative to agriculture and manufacturing.

The differences in results from this simple modeling demonstration are potentially important. For example, if you were an agricultural producer, how would you assess the potential benefits to farmers of productivity gains in the U.S. services industry? Your conclusion will differ depending on the functional form and the elasticity parameter values that are assumed in the CGE analysis that you consult. Based on the CDE demand system, you may conclude that demand quantities for agricultural products will grow, but by substantially less than for other products. Based on the CES function, you may expect to participate more fully in the demand stimulus created by the service sector's productivity gains. However, based on Cobb-Douglas preferences, you may expect growth in demand for your agricultural product to be rather modest.

The right utility function for any specific analysis will depend on the research question and the flexibility offered by the CGE model to specify the utility function and the elasticity parameter values that best describe the economy under study. In general, homothetic functions are appropriate when income changes are small, as in our example, but nonhomothetic functions are better suited for shocks in which income changes are relatively large. The choice of elasticity parameter values that describe substitutability and income effects should be made with care and ideally be grounded in the empirical literature.

Import Demand

The second stage of the consumer's decision making determines the sourcing of each commodity. How much of the demand will be met by the domestically produced variety and how much will be imported? In most CGE models,

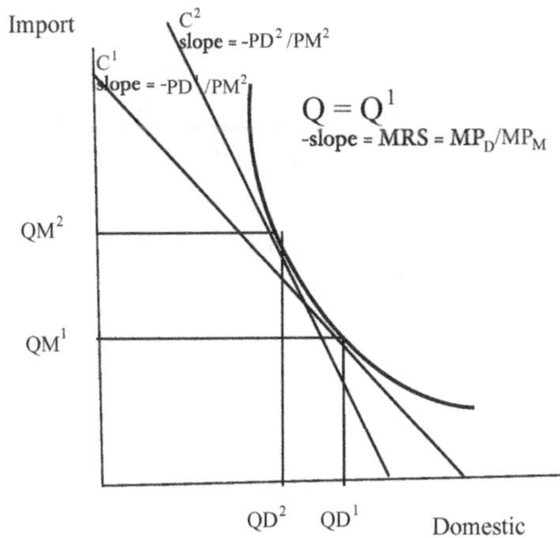

Figure 4.6. Armington aggregation function

the allocation between domestic products and imported goods reflects the assumption that the two varieties are imperfect substitutes. For example, Chilean consumers may feel that imported Chinese apples differ in flavor and texture from local apples. Chinese apples may be more suitable for baking in pies, while the Chilean variety is best eaten raw. These preferences would explain why there is two-way trade in apples between Chile and China and why the prices of the two types of apples may differ. Many CGE models describe these preferences using an ***Armington import aggregation function***. The function describes how imported and domestic apple varieties are combined to produce the composite commodity, "apples," that is demanded by Chilean consumers.

The aggregation function can be drawn as an ***isoquant***, shown as curve Q in Figure 4.6. The isoquant is similar to an indifference curve in many respects. It describes all possible quantity combinations of the imported and the domestic varieties that produce the same level of output of Q, the composite commodity. The further the isoquant lies from the origin, the larger is the quantity of Q that it represents. The negative of its slope at any point describes the MRS, which measures the quantity of imports, QM, that can be exchanged for a one-unit increase in the quantity of the domestic good, QD, holding Q constant. We can also express the MRS as the ratio of the ***marginal product*** of each variety in the production of Q, MP_D/MP_M.[7] The marginal product is the contribution to output of an additional unit of either input, holding the other input quantity constant. As the consumer moves down the isoquant, and production of Q becomes more intensive in the use of QD,

[7] The MRS is equivalent to the ratio of marginal products (MP_D/MP_M) because the slope at any point on the isoquant is $-dQM/dQD$, and since the marginal product of QD is dQ/dQD and of QM is dQ/dQM, the ratio $MP_D/MP_M = (dQ/dQD)/(dQ/dQM) = dQM/dQD$, which is the negative of the slope of the isoquant, or the MRS.

the marginal product of QD falls relative to the marginal product of QM. For example, when the consumption basket is composed mostly of Chilean apples, the addition of yet one more eating apple is not as useful to the consumer as the addition of a Chinese baking apple.

The ***Armington import substitution elasticity***, σ_M, describes the curvature of the isoquant. The smaller is σ_M, the less substitutable are QM and QD in the production of Q and the more curved is the isoquant. Each additional unit of QD relative to QM causes a relatively large decline in the ratio MP_D/MP_M. Price changes must therefore be quite large to motivate consumers to give up imports for an additional unit of the domestic variety. In the limit, when the import substitution elasticity has a value of zero, the isoquant has the L-shape of a "Leontief" function and QM will not be substituted for an additional unit of QD, regardless of any change in their relative prices. When the varieties are good substitutes, and σ_M is large, then the isoquant is relatively flat, showing that imports are easily substituted for the domestic variety, with little effect on the ratios of their marginal products in the production of Q. As the parameter value approaches infinity, the isoquant becomes linear and the two varieties become perfect substitutes.

C^1 is an ***isocost*** line with a slope of $-PD^1/PM^1$, where PD is the price of the domestic good and PM is the domestic *cif* consumer price of the imported good. The isocost line shows all combinations of the two goods that cost the same amount. Isocost lines that lie further from the origin represent higher costs. C^2 is a second isocost line, depicting price ratio PD^2/PM^2 .

The consumer minimizes the cost of producing Q by choosing the quantities of imports and domestic goods described by the tangency between the isoquant and the lowest achievable isocost line. In the initial equilibrium shown in Figure 4.6, the consumer chooses quantities QM^1 and QD^1 at a cost of C^1. At the tangency, the ratios $MP_D/MP_M = PD^1/PM^1$. Rearranging (by multiplying both sides by MP_M/PD^1), $MP_D/PD^1 = MPM/PM^1$. This means that costs are minimized when an additional dollar spent on the domestic or imported variety yields the same additional quantity of the composite good, Q. Suppose that the price of imports declines relative to the price of the domestic variety, as shown by the isocost line C^2. The least-cost ratio of input quantities shifts to QM^2/QD^2. The magnitude of the change in the quantity ratio, QM/QD, relative to the change in the price ratio, PD/PM, is determined by isoquant's curvature and the value of the import substitution elasticity parameter.

We explore the behavior of the Armington aggregation function in a CGE model by running an experiment that increases the price of imports relative to domestic goods while assuming different import substitution parameter values. We use the GTAP model and the U.S. 3x3 database to examine the effects of a five percent increase in the world import price of U.S. manufactured imports. The results, reported in Table 4.6, show that when

Table 4.6. *Effects of a 5 Percent Increase in the World Import Price of U.S. Manufactures on the Import/Domestic Quantity Ratio in Consumption (% Change From Base)*

	Armington Import Substitution Elasticity for Manufacturing		
U.S. Manufacturing	0.8	1.2	4
Import quantity (*qiw*)	−0.7	−2.6	−2.9
Domestic quantity (*qds*)	0.7	1.3	1.4
Import/domestic quantity ratio	−1.4	−3.9	−4.3

Source: GTAP model, GTAP v.7.0 U.S. 3x3 database.

the goods are relatively poor substitutes, with an import substitution elasticity of 0.8, the ratio of imports to domestic goods in the consumption of manufactures falls only 1.4 percent. When goods are assumed to be readily substitutable, with a parameter value of four, the quantity response is much larger – the ratio of imports to domestic goods declines by 4.3 percent.

As you might imagine, the sizes of import substitution elasticities are an important consideration for CGE modelers who study the effects of price changes, such as tariff reforms, on production and trade. Indeed, these elasticities have received much attention in the CGE-based literature on trade policy because of the potential sensitivity of model results to the assumed parameter values. Modelers try to address these concerns by grounding their selection of parameters values in the econometric literature, and in some studies, by estimating their own elasticity parameters.[8] Modelers may also test and report the sensitivity of their results to alternative values of the parameter, as we do in this experiment.

Export Demand

Export demand is the demand by foreign consumers for the home county's exports. The treatment of foreign demand in a CGE model depends on whether the model is a multicountry model or a single-country model.

The multicountry case is straightforward: The demand for exports from country X by country Y is simply the demand for imports by country Y from country X. This is the case even when the global economy is aggregated into two regions, for example, the United States and rest-of-world, as in the model we use for demonstration. The slope of the foreign demand curve for

[8] Estimation and critiques of Armington import substitution elasticities include McDaniel and Balistreri (2003); Erkel-Rousse and Mirza (2002); Gallaway, McDaniel, and Rivera (2000); Hummels (1999); Brown (1987); and Shiells, Stern, and Deardorff (1986). See Reinert and Roland-Holst (1992); Shiells and Reinert (1993), and Hertel, et al. (2004a) for examples of studies in which CGE modelers estimated the Armington import demand elasticities used in their models.

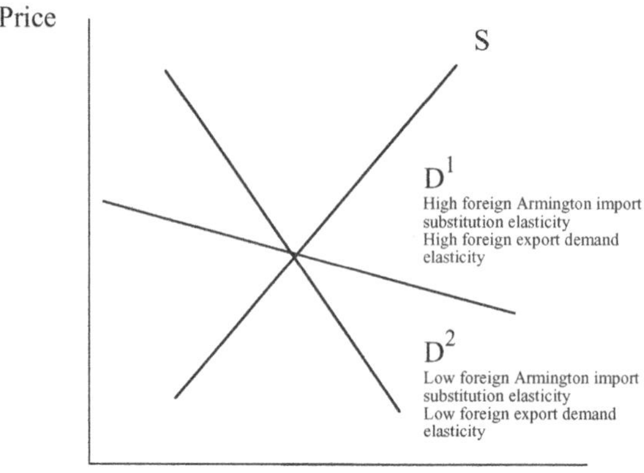

Figure 4.7. Elasticity parameters and the export demand curve

a country's export good therefore depends in part on the foreign country's Armington import substitution elasticity. The larger its value, the more elastic is its import demand and therefore the more elastic is the exporter's export demand curve.

Figure 4.7 illustrates the effect of foreign Armington elasticity parameters on a country's export demand. In the figure, S is the home country's supply of exports, D^1 describes a relatively elastic export demand curve (high foreign import substitution parameter) and D^2 describes a relatively inelastic export demand curve (low foreign import substitution parameter). For example, foreign countries' import substitution elasticities for dry milk powder are likely to be very high, because all varieties are nearly identical. The U.S.'s export demand curve for dry milk powder is therefore probably similar to demand curve D^1. In this case, even a small increase in the relative world export price of the U.S. variety can lead foreigners to make a large substitution toward their own domestic product. Conversely, a low foreign import substitution elasticity implies an inelastic export demand curve for U.S. dry milk powder.

Single-country CGE models do not describe the foreign economy or foreign import substitution preferences. Instead, the home country's export demand for each good is usually described using a simple expression:

$$QE/QW = (PXW/PE)^{\theta}$$

where QE is the country's export quantity and QW is global trade in that good, so QE/QW is the country's market share in world trade. PXW is the average global price, which is the trade-weighted sum of bilateral *fob* export prices of the good from all suppliers and PE is the *fob* world export price of the exporter's variety. Given the assumption that goods are differentiated by country of origin, a country's world export price can differ from the prices of its competitors. For example, the U.S. world export price for its corn, a yellow type used mainly for animal feed, can differ from the world export price of Mexico's corn, a white variety used mainly for food.

In the single-country model, a country can be assumed to be either ***small*** or ***large*** in its world export market by selecting the appropriate ***export demand elasticity***, denoted by θ. This parameter measures the percent change in a country's market share given a percent change in the ratio of the global price to its world export price. When a country is small, it is reasonable to assume that any change in its export quantity is too small to affect the global price level. PXW remains fixed and the export demand elasticity approaches infinity. Any change in the country's world export price relative to the global price therefore results in large changes in export quantity and market share, so its foreign demand curve is relatively flat. For example, if Uganda raises the price of its textile exports, it will not affect the world price level, but it is likely to cost Uganda a large portion of its market share in the world textile trade. Its output quantity will decline and, moving down its supply curve, its marginal costs will fall until Uganda's world export price is again equal to the prevailing global price.

When the single country is assumed to be large in world markets, then its world export price can affect the global price level and its foreign demand elasticity is assumed to be low. In this case, a change in the exporter's world price relative to the average global price causes only a small change in its market share. For example, suppose that a drought reduces Mexico's export supply of white corn and leads to an increase in its world export price. The lower the foreign demand elasticity, the less willing are foreigners to change their quantity of corn imports from Mexico as its price rises, and the steeper is Mexico's downward sloping foreign demand curve.

Consumer Welfare

"Are you better off today than you were four years ago?" This was the defining question of the 1980 presidential campaign in the United States. How you can tell that you are better off? Economists answer this question by quantifying a "money metric" measure of the change in a nation's well-being, or welfare, following an economic shock. Such a measure has a cash value, such as $14 billion, that describes the welfare change in terms of an income equivalent. In this example, we could say that a nation's consumers are now just as well off as if they had been given an additional $14 billion to spend before an economic shock. Such a measure is useful because it allows us to make unambiguous comparisons of alternative polices or other shocks. For example, we can conclude that a policy that increases national welfare by $14 billion leaves it better off than one that increases its welfare by $5 billion. CGE models are particularly well-suited to quantifying welfare effects because they describe the effects of a shock on all prices and quantities in an economy. In fact, the measurement of welfare effects is one of the most important contributions that CGE models have made in empirical economic analysis.

In this section, we describe two approaches that are commonly used to measure welfare effects in standard CGE models that have a single, representative household. We start with the most intuitive, which is the money metric equivalent of changes in "real," or the quantity of, consumption of goods and services. A quantity-based measure has intuitive appeal because it is based on the idea that larger quantities of consumption make people better off. This welfare measure includes only changes in quantities, and not the value of consumption, because value changes might be due only to price changes. For example, if I buy one candy bar both before and after a new policy changes its price from $1 to $2, the value of my consumption has doubled but my real consumption has remained the same – one candy bar.

We calculate the ***real consumption***, RC, welfare measure as the difference between the cost of the new basket, Q^2, and the cost of the initial basket, Q^1, valuing both baskets at the same, preshock consumer prices, P^1 for each good *i*:

$$\text{RC welfare} = \sum_i P_i^1 Q_i^2 - P_i^1 Q_i^1$$

Because the RC measure holds prices constant at their initial levels, a change in its value reflects only changes in quantities consumed. When the result is positive, real consumption has increased between periods one and two, and when the result is negative, real consumption has declined.

We can infer that an increase in real consumption is a welfare gain by drawing on the theory of revealed preference. At P^1 prices, the cost of Q^2 exceeded that of Q^1. Basket Q^2 was unaffordable and Q^1 was chosen. Following the shock, both Q^1 and Q^2 are affordable but Q^2 must be preferred because it is chosen. The cost difference between the baskets is equivalent to the additional income that the consumer would have needed to be able to afford the preferred basket, Q^2, at preshock prices.

All goods in the consumer basket are included in the welfare measure because a shock in one industry can affect prices and quantities throughout an economy. As an example, an import tariff reform may lower the consumer price of imported t-shirts. When the t-shirt price falls, you can either buy a larger quantity of t-shirts or, if you prefer, you can spend the money that you have saved on t-shirts to buy more of other types of goods, such as books and DVDs. Therefore, the welfare measure must account for t-shirts, books, DVDs and any other goods in your basket, even though the import tariff policy affects only t-shirts.

Table 4.7. *Calculating the Real Consumption Measure of Welfare*

	Initial Price	Initial Quantity	New Quantity	Cost of Initial Quantity at Initial Prices	Cost of New Quantity at Initial Prices
T-shirts	$1.00	10	12	$10.00	$12.00
Books	$1.00	12	16	$12.00	$16.00
DVDs	$1.00	3	8	$3.00	$8.00
Total	–	–	–	$25.00	$34.00

Table 4.7 illustrates how to calculate the real consumption welfare measure. Let's assume that we have used a three-good CGE model to analyze the effects of removing the import tariff on imported t-shirts. The original consumption basket is composed of ten t-shirts, twelve books and three DVDs. It costs a total of $25. The tariff removal causes all three consumer prices to change (these prices need not be reported). In this case, the removal of the t-shirt tariff enables the consumer to buy more of all three goods. At the original prices, the new consumption basket would have cost $34.00, or $9.00 more than the initial basket. There is a welfare gain of $9.00, which is equivalent to the additional income the consumer would have needed to purchase the new basket at the preshock prices.

Some CGE modelers take a different approach, and instead develop an ***equivalent variation***, EV, welfare measure. It, too, is a money metric measure but instead of comparing the cost of pre- and post-shock consumption quantities, it compares the cost of pre- and post-shock levels of consumer utility, both valued at base year prices. Because a CGE model contains a utility function, it is straightforward to calculate and compare the utility derived from different baskets of goods. For example, suppose the removal of the t-shirt tariff causes price changes that enable consumers to afford a new basket of goods that increases their utility from U^1 to U^2. The EV welfare effect measures the change in income that consumers would have needed to afford the new level of utility at preshock prices.[9] A positive EV welfare result indicates a welfare gain, and a negative result is a welfare loss.

To demonstrate step-by-step how to calculate an EV measure of welfare, we use a two-good example of apples, QA, and oranges, QO. Let's assume that consumer preferences in our CGE model are described by a Cobb-Douglas utility function:

$$U = QA^{\alpha}QO^{1-\alpha}$$

[9] Compensating variation is an alternative utility-based measure of welfare that compares the cost of the new versus the old utility when both are valued in post-shock prices. Similarly, the real consumption measure of welfare can be calculated by comparing the costs of two baskets when both are valued in post-shock prices.

where parameter α is the budget share for apples and, $1 - \alpha$, is the budget share for oranges. Our model will then specify the utility-maximizing demand functions for each commodity, which are derived from the utility function. In our example, the demand functions for any expenditure level, Y, and for any prices of apples, PA, and oranges, PO, are:

$$QA = \alpha(Y/PA)$$
$$QO = (1 - \alpha)(Y/PO)$$

If we assume that apples and oranges each account for a 50 percent budget share, expenditure in the base period is 100, and the initial price of apples is four and of oranges is two, then the utility function is:

$$U = QA^{.5}QO^{.5}$$

and the utility maximizing quantities of apples and oranges are:

$$QA = .5(100/4) = 12.5$$
$$QO = .5(100/2) = 25.0$$

Now we are ready to run a model experiment. Let's assume that the economic shock has caused the apple price to fall to two but that the orange price and total expenditure remain unchanged. Based on our model's demand functions, we solve for the new, utility-maximizing quantities. Using these demand functions, verify that the quantity of apples demanded increases to twenty-five whereas the quantity of oranges demanded is still twenty-five.

To calculate the equivalent variation welfare effect, our first step is to calculate the base level of utility, U^1, by substituting the base quantities for apples and oranges into the utility function:

$$U^1 = 12.5^{.5} * 25^{.5} = 17.7$$

Next, we calculate the new utility level, U^2, by substituting the new quantities into the utility function:

$$U^2 = 25^{.5} * 25^{.5} = 25.0$$

Then, we solve for the expenditure level required to achieve the new utility level at base prices by substituting the expressions for apple and orange quantities into the utility function, and solving for the total expenditure, Y. Notice that our equation incorporates the new utility level (twenty-five) and the base year prices:

$$U^2 = 25.0 = [.5 * (Y/4)]^{.5} * [.5 * (Y/2)]^{.5}$$
$$Y = \$141.6$$

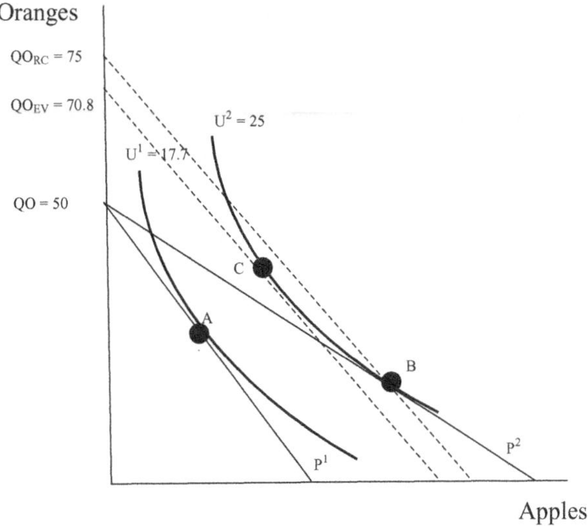

Figure 4.8. Alternative measures of consumer welfare

Last, we calculate the EV welfare measure, which is the change in expenditure that would have been required for consumers to afford the U^2 level of utility at preshock prices:

$$\$141.4 - \$100 = \$41.6.$$

For comparison, verify that the real consumption measure of welfare in this example is \$50.

The RC and the EV welfare measures are closely related. We illustrate this point in Figure 4.8, which describes and compares the results from our two-good example of apples and oranges. In the figure, the initial equilibrium is at point A on the U^1 indifference curve, given the initial price ratio between apples and oranges of P^1. The decline in the apple price is shown by the rotation of the price line to P^2. This causes the utility maximizing consumer to choose the consumption basket at point B, which provides a higher level of utility on the U^2 indifference curve. Using the real consumption measure, we can ask: "How much additional income would have been required to purchase the new basket, B, at the original prices?" The answer is shown as the vertical distance between the original budget line, and a budget line that is parallel to P^1 and goes through point B. Its intercept on the vertical axis at point QO_{RC} measures the total level of expenditure on basket B in terms of oranges, which is \$2 * 75 oranges = \$150.

Now suppose that, instead, we allowed the consumer to choose the least-cost basket of apples and oranges that generated the same U^2 level of utility as basket B, again at original prices. Given the consumer's preferences (shown by the curvature of the isoquant), that least cost bundle is at point C. Using the equivalent variation welfare measure, we can ask, "How much additional income would have been required to purchase a basket that yields the new utility level, U^2, at the original prices?" The answer is shown as the vertical distance between the original budget line, and a budget line that is parallel to P^1 and goes through point C. Its vertical intercept at point QO_{EV} describes total expenditure on basket C in terms of oranges, which is $2 * 70.8 oranges = $141.60. In this case, if original prices had actually prevailed in period two, the consumer would have substituted between apples and oranges, spending less money on a basket, C, that was as satisfying as basket B.

The welfare measure that values the change in real consumption is the distance QO-QO_{RC}. It is 25 oranges, valued at $50. It exceeds the welfare measure that values the change in utility, shown by the distance QO-QO_{EV}, which is 20.8 oranges, or $41.60.

You may verify for yourself that as the elasticity of substitution becomes smaller, and indifference curve is more sharply curved, the distance between the EV and RC intercept becomes smaller. In fact, the two approaches yield identical results when the elasticity of substitution is zero, as in a Leontief fixed-proportion utility function, with L-shaped indifference curves.

CGE models can differ in their approaches to welfare measurement in other ways, too. For example, the GTAP model measures equivalent variation welfare effects on behalf of the regional household. It therefore includes the combined changes in the utility of household consumers and government from their purchase of goods and services, and in addition includes domestic savings. Savings is included because it represents future consumption possibilities. In other CGE models, without a regional household, the welfare measure often describes only changes in quantities or utility from current consumption by private household consumers and may or may not also include investment spending. The modeler must then assume compatible macroclosure rules that fix the quantities purchased by government and perhaps of investors at their base levels.[1] It is well worth your time to study and understand the welfare measure used in your model, particularly so because this important summary measure is often presented as the "bottom line" of CGE-based analyses.

Summary

Final demand is the demand for goods and services for end use by private households, government, investors and foreign markets. Data in the row

[1] See Lofgren et al. (2002) for a discussion of the links between welfare measures and model closure.

accounts of the SAM describe the sources of income for each domestic agent and investment in the CGE model. Data in the column accounts of the SAM describe how their income is spent on commodities, and report export sales to the foreign market.

CGE models describe consumer demand as a two-stage decision. In the first stage, consumers allocate their income across commodities to maximize their utility, or satisfaction, given their preferences, budgets and prices. When income or prices change, consumers readjust their basket of commodities to again maximize their utility. We describe and compare four functional forms commonly used in CGE models to describe private households' preferences: Cobb-Douglas, Stone-Geary/LES, and CES utility functions, and the CDE demand system. Most CGE models describe the first stage of government and investment demand very simply by assuming that they spend a fixed share of their budgets on each commodity (i.e., a Cobb-Douglas utility function). In the second stage of the consumption decision, consumers minimize the cost of their consumption basket by choosing between imported and domestic products. This allocation is described by an Armington import aggregation function. In this chapter, we also describe and compare export demand in multicountry and single country models and introduce the concept of national welfare, demonstrating how to calculate real quantity and equivalent variation welfare measures.

Key Terms

Budget constraint
Budget share
Elasticity, (Armington) import substitution (σ_M)
Elasticity export demand (θ)
Elasticity, substitution in consumption (σ_C)
Equivalent variation
Final demand
Gross complements
Gross substitutes
Homothetic utility function
Import (Armington) aggregation function
Indifference curve
Isocost
Isoquant
Large country
Luxury good
Marginal product
Marginal rate of substitution

Necessity good
Net substitutes
Nonhomothetic utility function
Small country
Utility function
Welfare

PRACTICE AND REVIEW

1. Using data from the U.S. 3x3 SAM,
   a. Trace the sales of U.S.-produced agricultural goods in final demand:
      C__________ I__________ G__________ E__________
   b. Trace the sales of U.S. service-produced commodities:
      C__________ I__________ G__________ E__________
   c. In a few sentences, describe the differences in final demand for agriculture and services.
2. Using data from the U.S. 3x3 SAM,
   a. Calculate the budget shares of U.S.-produced goods in households' private consumption expenditure (including sales taxes):
      Agric: __________ Mfg: __________ Serv: __________
3. Explain the difference between a homothetic and a nonhomothetic utility function. If you are conducting a study of foreign aid inflows and economic growth in a developing country, explain some of the differences in model results that you might expect to see when using the two utility functions.
4. Using a graph of the Armington aggregation function, explain the role of the Armington import substitution elasticity in determining the quantities demanded for imports and exports if the removal of a tariff causes the relative price of the import to fall. Compare the outcome in a case with a high substitution parameter value and a low parameter value.
5. Calculate the real consumption welfare effect using the data in Table 4.8. Has welfare improved or declined as a result of the price changes?

Table 4.8. *Practice and Review Calculation of the Real Consumption Welfare Measure*

	Initial Price	Initial Quantity	New Quantity	Cost of Initial Quantity at Initial Prices	Cost of New Quantity at Initial Prices
Agriculture	$1.00	5	6		
Manufacturing	$1.00	5	4		
Services	$1.00	2	8		
Total	–	–	–		

Technical Appendix 4.1: Elasticity Parameters in Utility Functions

Table 4.9 describes the elasticity parameters that are required for four functional forms commonly used in CGE models to describe private households' preferences. The table describes the restrictions usually placed on the elasticity parameter values to ensure that the CGE model can be solved for a unique solution. The table also includes a brief explanation of different parameter values.

Table 4.9. *Elasticity Parameter Values in Utility Functions Commonly Used in CGE Models*

	Modeler Input	Parameter Restrictions	Parameter Values
Cobb-Douglas	None	None	Unitary (negative) own-price; zero cross-price, and unitary substitution and income elasticities are implied by the utility function.
Stone-Geary/Linear Expenditure System (LES)	Frisch parameter (ratio of total expenditure to discretionary expenditure)	$-1 \leq$ Frisch $\leq \infty$	All expenditure is discretionary: Frisch $= -1$ All expenditure is on subsistence requirements: Frisch $= \infty$
	Expenditure elasticity by commodity (E_i).	$0 \leq E_i \leq \infty$	Luxury goods: $E_i > 1$ Necessity goods: $0 \leq E_i < 1$
	Stone-Geary/LES collapses to a Cobb-Douglas utility function when Frisch $= -1$ and all $E_i = 1$.		
Constant Elasticity of Substitution (CES)	Elasticity of substitution by commodity (σ_i)	$0 \leq \sigma_i \leq \infty$	Leontief complements: $\sigma_i = 0$ Perfect substitutes: $\sigma_i = \infty$
	CES collapses to a Cobb-Douglas utility function when all $\sigma_i = 1$; and to a Leontief utility function when all $\sigma_i = 0$.		
Constant Difference of Elasticities (CDE)	$INCPAR_i$ – a parameter related to the income elasticity of demand for good i.	$0 < INCPAR_i$	Larger $INCPAR_i$ parameter value implies larger income elasticity of demand. Income insensitive (necessity) goods: $0 < INCPAR_i < 1$ Income sensitive (luxury) goods: $1 < INCPAR_i$ Homothetic demand: $INCPAR_i = 0$ for all *i*
	$SUBPAR_i$ – a parameter related to the compensated own and cross-price elasticities of substitution, defined for good i.	Either $SUBPAR_i < 0$ or $0 < SUBPAR_i < 1$ for all *i*	Larger $SUBPAR_i$ parameter value implies larger (absolute value) of compensated own-price elasticity. Leontief complements: SUBPAR $= 1$ for all i. Goods become substitutes as $SUBPAR_i$ and $SUBPAR_j$ become smaller. Independent goods: SUBPAR $= 0$ for all i.
	CDE collapses to a Cobb-Douglas utility function when all $INCPAR_i = 1$ and $SUBPAR_i = 0$; to a Leontief utility function when $INCPAR_i = 1$ and $SUBPAR_i, = 1$; and to a CES utility function when all $INCPAR_i = 1$ and SUBPAR are identical for all i.		

5

Supply in a CGE Model

In this chapter, we examine the supply side of an economy as represented in computable general equilibrium (CGE) models. The production data in the Social Accounting Matrix (SAM) depict the production process, in which firms combine intermediate inputs with factors of production to produce goods and services. We use these data to calculate input-output coefficients, and forward and backward linkages. CGE models break down the production technology into parts, depicting how subprocesses are nested within the overall production process. Within each nest, behavioral equations describe producers' efficiency-maximizing input demands and output levels, subject to their production technology. Export transformation functions, used in some CGE models, describe the allocation of production between domestic and export markets.

In 2009, the United States government offered financial assistance to its auto manufacturers to help them survive a deep recession and a freefall in consumer demand for cars. The bailout was controversial in part because the government seemed to be choosing to support a particular manufacturing industry. The government response was that the aid package not only helped save the jobs of autoworkers but also preserved jobs in the many industries that supply parts to the automakers and that sell and service autos. This part of the U.S. economic stimulus program built on the idea that an injection of support into one part of the economy would move in a circular flow to the rest of the economy, starting with the strong interindustry linkages between automakers and other manufacturing and service sectors.

In this chapter and the next, we explore the supply side of the economy as represented in a CGE model, emphasizing the linkages among industries through their demands for intermediate inputs and their competition for the factors of production. We start with an examination of the production data in the SAM. The activity column accounts of the SAM describe the inputs used in industries' production processes and the activity row accounts describe the use of industries' outputs as inputs for other industries. In the CGE model, producers are assumed to maximize their efficiency, subject to the flexibility

Table 5.1. *Production Inputs in the U.S. 3x3 Micro SAM ($U.S. Billions)*

	Activities			
SAM entry	Agric.	Mfg.	Services	Definition
Commodities – total	212	3,411	5,574	Intermediate inputs
Agric. imports	2	160	6	
Mfg. imports	12	393	216	
Services–imports	1	16	149	
Agric.–domestic	24	229	70	
Mfg.–domestic	66	1,533	1,141	
Services–domestic	109	1,079	3,991	
Factors–total	223	1,576	7,999	Factor payments (Value-added)
Land	34	0	0	
Labor	68	1,109	5,667	
Capital	122	467	2,332	
Factor use taxes–total	1	182	926	Factor use taxes (Value-added)
Land	−3	0	0	
Labor	5	166	850	
Capital	−1	15	76	
Sales tax	−6	17	52	Sales taxes (Value-added)
Production tax	4	42	423	Production tax (Value-added)
Total	434	5,227	14,974	Gross value of output

Note: Sales taxes rows in the SAM are aggregated into a single sales tax row.
Source: GTAP v.7.0 U.S. 3x3 database.

afforded by their technological production process, as they choose inputs and their levels of output. We describe technologies and producer behavior in detail in this chapter and conclude by describing how producers are assumed, in some CGE models, to allocate their output between domestic and export sales.

Production Data in a SAM

Production activities use inputs to produce goods and services. Inputs are of two types: ***intermediate inputs*** (such as electronic components for a television or computer) and the ***primary factor inputs*** (land, labor, and capital) that are necessary to turn these intermediate inputs into final products. The activity columns in a SAM report the value of all intermediate and factor inputs and any taxes paid (or subsidies received) in the production of industry output.

To illustrate, Table 5.1 presents the three production activity columns from the U.S. 3x3 SAM (omitting the rows with zeros). Each column of the table shows the expenditure by that industry on all of its intermediate and factor inputs and on taxes. According to Table 5.1, U.S. agricultural producers spend $212 billion (with rounding) on intermediate inputs. These are composed of $26 billion of agricultural commodities ($2 billion are imported and $24 billion are produced domestically), $78 billion of imported and domestic manufactured inputs, and $110 billion of imported and domestic services. Notice that the table also shows how each type of good is used as an input into the other industries. The production of manufacturing, for example, requires substantial amounts of agricultural inputs.

In addition to intermediate inputs, U.S. agricultural production requires $223 billion of factor inputs, which include $34 billion for land, $68 billion for labor, and $122 billion for capital services. On net, U.S. agricultural producers pay $1 billion in taxes on their use of factors, which includes $3 billion in subsidies on land and capital use (which have negative factor use taxes). Agricultural producers received an additional $6 billion in subsidies to purchase intermediate inputs (a negative sales tax). Finally, because production taxes change producers' costs, the activity column also reports the production taxes paid (or subsidies received) by an industry. In agriculture, producers pay $4 billion in production taxes.

The contributions of factors (and including all tax and subsidies) to increasing the value of the industry's finished goods is called the industry's "value-added." For example, farm labor adds value to the agricultural and other intermediate inputs that are used to produce farm products. In U.S. agriculture, value-added totals $222 billion (i.e., $223 + $1 − $6 + $4 = $222 billion) Value-added plus the $212 billion value of intermediate inputs equals the gross value of output of U.S. agriculture of $434 billion.

Input-Output Coefficients

The data reported in the activity columns of the SAM can be used to calculate a useful descriptive statistic called an ***input-output coefficient***. These coefficients describe the ratio of the quantities of intermediate and factor inputs per unit of output. They are calculated by dividing every cell of Table 5.1 by its column total – the gross value of output.[1]

In Table 5.2, we display the input-output coefficients based on the U.S. 3x3 SAM (omitting the tax rows of the SAM). For example, the input-output coefficients for the agriculture activity indicate that .03 units of imported manufactured inputs are required per unit of output, and .05 units of domestically produced agricultural inputs are required, and so on.

[1] The SAM reports value data so the input-output coefficients are value shares. But recall from Chapter 2 that if we normalize the data by assuming that it reports quantities per dollar, then we can interpret our input-output coefficients as ratios of input and output quantities.

Table 5.2. *U.S. Input-Output Coefficients*

	Production Activities		
	Agric.	Mfg.	Services
Intermediate inputs			
Agric.–imports	0.00	0.03	0.00
Mfg.–imports	0.03	0.08	0.01
Services–imports	0.00	0.00	0.01
Agric.–domestic	0.05	0.04	0.00
Mfg.–domestic	0.15	0.29	0.08
Services–domestic	0.25	0.21	0.27
Factor Inputs			
Land	0.08	0.00	0.00
Labor	0.16	0.21	0.38
Capital	0.28	0.09	0.16

Source: GTAP v.7.0 U.S. 3x3 database.

Input-output coefficients allow us to describe the ***intermediate input intensity*** or ***factor intensity*** of a production activity. A sector is "intensive" in the intermediate and factor inputs whose input-output coefficients are highest. For example, U.S. agriculture is capital-intensive because it uses more units of capital per unit of output than of land or labor. This knowledge can be useful if we want to design experiments or predict and interpret model results. For example, what if the U.S. government asks us to identify and study input subsidies that would most benefit farmers? Based on our input-output table, we could choose to focus our study on subsidies to services or capital inputs, because these are the inputs in which agricultural production is most intensive.

We can also use input-output coefficients to make scale-neutral comparisons of input intensities across industries and countries. For example, we could compare the capital input-output ratio between U.S. agriculture, .28, and U.S. services, .16. We can conclude that U.S. agriculture is more capital intensive than services because it has a higher capital-output ratio. The comparison is scale neutral because we can make this observation without confusing it with the observation that services, the largest sector in the U.S. economy, accounts for vastly more capital usage than agriculture.

Input-output coefficients in addition describe linkages among industries through their demands for intermediate inputs. ***Upstream*** industries are the activities that produce goods that are used as inputs into other ***downstream*** industries – as if products flowed downstream on a river from a producer toward the industries that use them as inputs. Auto parts suppliers, for example, are an upstream industry that produces parts used downstream by auto assembly industries. Based on the U.S. 3x3 SAM, services is the major upstream industry providing intermediate inputs into agriculture and manufacturing.

In a CGE model, intermediate input linkages are a potentially important channel through which a shock in one industry can affect the rest of the economy. For example, consider a shock that lowers the price of services. Given the input-output coefficients reported in Table 5.2, we can see that this shock will lower the input costs of all sectors in the U.S. economy, but particularly of services and agriculture, which use services inputs most intensively.

Input-output coefficients sometimes are used to identify the sectors that are most intensive in their total requirements for intermediate inputs. This information may be useful for policymakers who want to know which industry exerts the strongest "pull" on the rest of the economy through its demand for intermediate goods. A stimulus program or development plan that targets growth in that industry could be particularly effective in spurring economywide growth because its expansion will increase demand for products produced upstream. We can compare the intensities of sectors' demands for intermediate inputs by calculating a ***backward linkage index*** for each industry. The index is the sum of the input-output coefficients for all intermediate goods used in an industry. It is called a "backward" index because we are looking backward at where the inputs for this industry came from. For agriculture, we use the input-output coefficients in Table 5.2 to calculate the index as:

$$\text{Backward linkage index for agriculture} = .03 + .05 + .15 + .25 = 0.48.$$

This shows that agricultural output requires .48 units of intermediates per unit of final product. Verify that the backward index for services is .37. A comparison of the two index values indicates that, relative to its size, increased agricultural output exerts a greater pull on the economy as a whole than increased production of services.

A similar concept is the ***forward linkage index***. The index describes the role of industries in providing inputs into downstream industries. Lowering the cost of inputs exerts a "push" on other sectors of the economy by lowering their costs of production. The index is the share of an industry's output that is used as intermediate inputs by other industries. It is called a "forward" index because we are looking forward to where the inputs from this industry are used. The index is calculated using data from the SAM on demand for domestically produced intermediates and industry output. For example, the forward linkage index for agriculture, calculated from the values in domestic agriculture's row account in Table 5.1, is:

$$\text{Forward index for agriculture} = \$24 + \$229 + \$70/\$434 = 0.74.$$

Verify that the forward index for manufacturing is .52. A comparison of the two index values indicates that, relative to their size, increased agricultural output exerts a greater push force on the U.S. economy than an increase in manufacturing output.

These interindustry linkages often play an important role in explaining the results of economic shocks in a CGE model. However, as we will demonstrate in this chapter, a CGE model accounts for additional aspects of intermediate demand that are also important to consider. These include the relative size of each sector in the economy, the potential for imports to supplant domestic products in meeting demand for intermediates, and the ability of producers to substitute toward cheaper intermediate inputs in their production process.

Producer Behavior in a CGE Model

Behavioral equations in a CGE model govern producers' decisions about their input quantities and levels of output. In some models, producers are assumed to be cost-minimizers who choose the least-cost level of inputs for a given level of output, given input and product prices and technological feasibility. Other CGE models describe producers as profit maximizers who choose quantities of both inputs and output, given input and product prices and subject to technological feasibility. The two approaches are just two sides of the same coin; both describe producers as maximizing their efficiency. Our discussion in the following sections mostly describes a cost-minimizing producer.

In addition to maximizing their efficiency, other important assumptions about producers that are commonly made in standard CGE models are that markets are perfectly competitive. Individual producers cannot influence the market prices of outputs or inputs, and they sell their output at their cost of production, making zero profits (in the economic sense). In many standard CGE models, production is also assumed to exhibit constant returns to scale. Thus, an increase of the same proportions in all inputs leads to an increase in output of the same proportion.

Technology Tree and Nested Production Functions

Because a producer's economic decisions on input and output levels are constrained by the firm's physical production technology, let's first explore in some detail how technological processes are described in a standard CGE model, before we consider economic choices any further. Technology defines the physical production process by which intermediate inputs, such as rubber tires and engines, are transformed by machinery and workers into a final product, such as an auto. This physical relationship is depicted by a ***production function***. CGE models typically separate the production function into parts. In a diagram, it looks a lot like an upside down tree. The trunk of the ***technology tree*** describes the final assembly of a good or service.

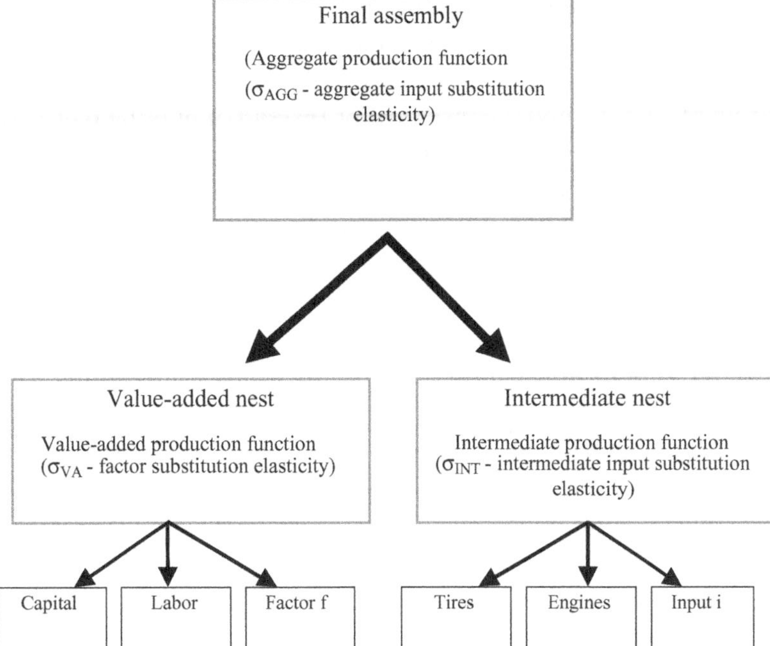

Figure 5.1. Technology tree for a nested production functions

Each tree branch is a subprocess with its own production function, or technology. The branches are called ***nested production functions*** because these smaller production processes are "nested" within the larger process of producing the final product. The twigs describe every input into the production process; each sprouts from the subprocess in which it is nested.

Figure 5.1 shows a technology tree that is typical of those assumed in standard CGE models. Notice how the figure shows two levels of the production process. At the bottom level are two nested production functions. The separate nests describe how the producer can combine labor and capital (and any other factors) into a value-added bundle that contains factor inputs, and how intermediate inputs, such as tires and engines, are combined to form an intermediate bundle. Moving above, an aggregate production function describes how the producer combines the value-added bundle with the intermediate bundle to make the final product, such as an auto.

A nested production function is a useful approach when the technologies of the component processes are substantially different. For example, an automaker may find that it is easy to substitute between workers and mechanized assembly equipment within the value-added bundle but that it is difficult to substitute more tires for one less steering wheel within the intermediate bundle. Nested production functions allow the modeler to describe realistically the different ways that subsets of inputs are combined with each other during the production process.

An additional advantage of nesting is that the selection of input combinations within each nested process is independent of the contents of other nests. This assumption about their separability simplifies the database and the solution of a CGE model considerably. Instead of making pair wise decisions among all inputs, the producer is instead assumed to make one decision about the contents of the intermediate bundle, a separate decision about the contents of the value-added bundle, and another decision about the ratio of the intermediate and value-added bundles in the final product. Changing the ratios of inputs within the intermediate bundle will not influence the ratios of inputs within the value-added bundle.

The specific type of production function, such as a Cobb-Douglas or Constant Elasticity of Substitution, that is assumed in each nest and for the final assembly, is determined by the modeler. A standard approach in CGE models is to assume functions that allow some substitution among factors of production in the value-added nest, but fixed input-output ratios in the intermediate nest and between the valued added and intermediate bundles. Later in this chapter, we describe in more detail the different types of production functions and their assumptions about input substitutability.

Sometimes, modelers choose to add additional nests to the production technology. CGE-based analyses of energy use and climate change, for example, usually add one or more levels of nesting to the value-added nest. Although the specific nesting structure varies across models, in general, climate models include nests that describe the substitution possibilities between labor, capital, and a bundle of energy inputs. Additional nests then describe substitution possibilities among different types of energy within an energy bundle, such as coal, oil, or gas. An advantage of adding nests is that it allows the modeler to describe subsets of inputs as complements, instead of substitutes, within the production process. Technical Appendix 5.1 provides a more detailed discussion of nesting in CGE models of climate change.

Intermediate Input Demand

Now we are ready to study the producer's economic decisions, focusing on one nest at a time. We start with the demand for intermediates, which has the simplest technology. This is because CGE modelers typically assume that intermediate inputs are used in fixed proportions to produce the bundle of intermediate goods. This means that, for any given input bundle, the producer has no ability to substitute more of one intermediate input for another.[2]

[2] This treatment is widely used in CGE models. However, some models provide the modeler with the flexibility to define a nonzero elasticity of substitution between intermediate inputs. In this case, the

Text Box 5.1. Climate Change, Emissions Taxes, and Trade in the CIM-EARTH Model
"Trade and Carbon Taxes" (Elliott, et al. 2010b).

What is the research question? Climate change is a function of global CO_2 emissions and the most efficient strategy to control them is to impose a uniform carbon tax wherever emissions occur. However, this approach presents a free-riding problem because nations have an incentive to not comply while gaining the benefits of reduced emissions elsewhere. How will carbon tax policies perform, given international trade, if countries adopt different carbon emissions tax rates?

What is the CGE model innovation? The researchers use CIM-EARTH, an open-source, recursive-dynamic, global CGE model with the GTAP v.7.0 database. The model places energy in the value-added nest, and extends that nest to describe substitution possibilities among energy sources in the production of goods and services.

What is the model experiment? The authors define four scenarios: (i) the baseline time path is business as usual, with no carbon tax; (ii) a carbon tax is applied uniformly across the globe; (iii) a carbon tax is applied to emissions only in Kyoto Protocol Annex B countries (who have pledged to cut emissions); and (iv) a carbon tax is applied to Annex B countries in combination with complete border tax adjustments that rebate their emissions taxes on exported goods and impose tariffs on emissions embodied in their imported goods. Carbon taxes in the last three scenarios range from $4 to $48 per ton of CO_2.

What are the key findings? A carbon tax applied worldwide at a uniform rate of $48 per ton of CO_2 reduces emissions by 40 percent from 2020 levels. Increasing tax rates yield ever smaller reductions in emissions because the least-costly carbon-reducing steps are taken first. A carbon tax imposed only in Annex B countries generates little more than one-third of the emission reduction achieved with a uniform, global tax, due in part to substantial "carbon leakage" as production shifts to nontaxing countries. With full import and export border tax adjustments, carbon leakage is halted.

For example, the production of an auto requires a bundle of intermediate inputs like rubber tires, engines, and mirrors. Furthermore, these inputs are ordinarily used in a fixed ratio. For each auto, the intermediate bundle must include four tires, one engine, and three mirrors. If the producer wishes to make another auto, he needs another bundle of auto parts – adding another wheel without an additional engine and so on, would not increase the number of intermediate bundles. This technology is often called a ***Leontief fixed proportions production function***. It is named after Wassily Leontief, an economist well known for his work on interindustry linkages in an economy.

technology in the intermediates nest is similar to that in the value-added nest, described in the next section.

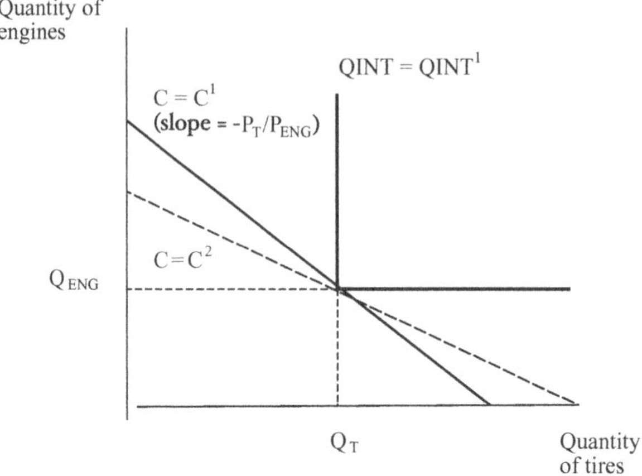

Figure 5.2. Nested production function – intermediate input demand

This type of intermediate production function offers a reasonable description of many intermediate production activities.

A Leontief production function is depicted graphically as an L-shaped curve, QINT, in Figure 5.2. The curve is an ***isoquant*** that shows all combinations of two inputs – in this case, tires and engines – that can be used to produce bundles of intermediate car parts of quantity $QINT^1$. The further an isoquant lies from the origin, the higher is the number of intermediate bundles that it represents. You can see from the isoquant's L-shape that increasing the amount of either tires or engines without increasing the quantity of the other input will not change the quantity of intermediate input bundles from level $QINT^1$.

The straight line in Figure 5.2, C, is an ***isocost*** line. It shows all combinations of engines and tires that cost the same total amount. The closer an isocost line lies to the origin, the lower is the total cost or outlay on tires and engines. The slope of an isocost line describes the ratio of input prices – in this case, the ratio of the tire price to the engine price, $-P_T/P_{ENG}$. The producer minimizes the cost of producing the input bundle $QINT^1$ when he operates at a point of tangency between the $QINT^1$ isoquant and the lowest attainable isocost line, which is C^1 in Figure 5.2, using the input bundle Q_{ENG} and Q_T.

The important property of a Leontief production function for CGE modelers to remember is that when relative input prices change, there is no change in the lowest-cost ratio of inputs for any level of QINT. Adding more of just one of the inputs would increase costs without increasing the number of intermediate bundles produced because the inputs must be used in fixed proportions. For example, assume that the price of tires falls relative to the price of engines, shown by the isocost curve, C^2. The lowest cost bundle of

Table 5.3. *Changes in Intermediate Input Demand When Relative Input Prices Change, with a Fixed Quantity of Intermediate Input Bundles (% Change From Base)*

	Production Activity		
Intermediate Input	Agriculture	Manufacturing	Services
Agriculture	0.00	0.00	0.00
Manufacturing	0.00	0.00	0.00
Services	0.00	0.00	0.00

Note: Because we assume that σ_{AGG} is zero, the change in demand for input i by activity j, remaining on the original isoquant, is approximately $qf_i - qo_j$.
Source: GTAP model, GTAP v.7.0 U.S. 3x3 database.

tires and engines remains unchanged. Because the ratio of input quantities does not change when input price ratios change, we say that the ***elasticity of intermediate input substitution elasticity*** σ_{INT}, of a Leontief production function is zero.

We demonstrate how a Leontief intermediate production function determines input demands in a CGE model by carrying out an experiment that changes relative intermediate input prices. We use the Global Trade Analysis Project (GTAP) model and the U.S. 3x3 database to run an experiment that imposes differing domestic sales tax rates of 5 percent on agriculture, 10 percent on manufactures, and 2 percent on services. Results, reported in Table 5.3, demonstrate that when holding output constant (i.e., we remain on isoquant $QINT^1$), there is no change in the quantities or ratios of intermediate inputs as their relative prices change. Thus, given a Leontief technology, the original proportions remain the least-cost mix of intermediate inputs for a given level of intermediate input bundles. However, if the output quantity changes, say by 5 percent, then demand for each intermediate input will also change by the same proportion, 5 percent, leaving the intermediate input ratios unchanged.

Factor (Value-Added) Demand

CGE models specify a ***valued-added production function*** to describe the technology in the nest in which producers assemble their bundle of factors (i.e., the combination of labor, capital, and other factors used in the final assembly stage). Most CGE modelers assume that producers have some flexibility with regard to the composition of the value-added bundle. For example, although the assembly of an auto requires fixed proportions of four tires and one engine, the mix of capital and labor used to assemble the parts into an auto is somewhat variable. The assembly process can use a lot of

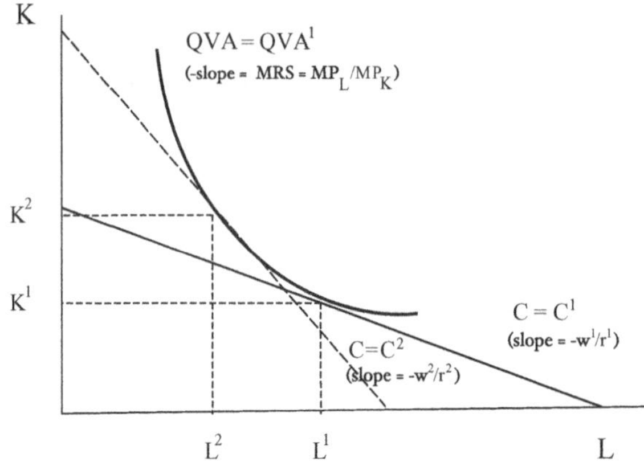

Figure 5.3. Nested production function – factor demand

manual labor and little machinery, or the process can be highly mechanized, depending on the relative cost of workers and equipment.

Figure 5.3 illustrates how producers choose the cost-minimizing factor ratio for a given quantity of value-added bundles. In the figure, an isoquant, QVA, describes the value-added production function. It depicts all technologically feasible combinations of two factors, capital, K, and labor, L, that can be used to produce the same value-added bundle, such as QVA^1. The negative of the slope at any point along the isoquant describes the marginal rate of substitution (MRS) between the two inputs. The MRS measures the amount by which capital could be reduced if the quantity of labor is increased by one unit, while keeping output constant. We can also express the MRS as the ratio of the marginal product of labor to the marginal product of capital, or MP_L/MP_K in the production of QVA.[3]

To visualize these concepts, assume that the producer described in Figure 5.3 moves downward along the isoquant, using less capital and more labor in the production of the value-added bundle. Notice that as the ratio of capital to workers declines, a smaller quantity of capital can be substituted for each additional worker to produce the same QVA. As an example, assume that the automaker moves downward on its isoquant, employing more labor and using less assembly equipment. As an increasing number of workers shares fewer assembly tools, each additional worker becomes a less productive input to the value added requirements of an auto, relative to an additional unit of equipment and tools. That is, as the K/L ratio falls, so does the inverse ratio of their marginal products, MP_L/MP_K.

[3] This is because, if d refers to a marginal change in quantity, then the slope at any point on the isoquant is $-dK/dL$, which is the rise over the run. Because the marginal product of L is dQVA/dL and of K is dQVA/dK, then the ratio $MP_L/MP_K = (dQVA/dL)/(dQVA/dK) = dK/dL$, which equals the MRS.

The isocost line, such as C^1 in Figure 5.3, describes all combinations of labor and capital that can be purchased for the same total cost. Its slope depicts the relative wage and capital rent at initial factor prices, w^1/r^1. The producer minimizes the cost of producing QVA^1 at the tangency between the isoquant and the lowest achievable isocost line, C^1, using input ratio L^1/K^1. At their tangency, the ratio of marginal products is equal to the price ratio: $MP_L/MP_K = w^1/r^1$. Rearranging (by multiplying both sides by MP_K/w^1), then $MP_L/w^1 = MP_K/r^1$. Input costs are minimized for a given QVA when the marginal product from an additional dollar spent on labor is equal to the marginal product from an additional dollar spent on capital inputs. If not, producers will spend more on the more productive factor input and less on the other input, until their marginal products per dollar spent are equalized.

Now consider how the cost-minimizing factor input ratio changes if there is an increase in wages relative to capital rents. The rise in the wage-rental price ratio is shown in Figure 5.3 by the dotted isocost line, C^2, with slope $-w^2/r^2$. As workers become relatively expensive, the producer can reduce costs by substituting them with machinery. In Figure 5.3, inputs L^2 and K^2 become the cost-minimizing ratio of capital to labor in the production of QVA^1.

The ***elasticity of factor substitution***, σ_{VA}, describes the relationship between changes in the capital-labor input ratio and the inverse ratio of their marginal products – that is, the curvature of the isoquant. When σ_{VA} is very large, the technology is flexible, and the isoquant becomes flatter. In this case, even large changes in factor intensities have little effect on factors' marginal products. Producers can therefore make large shifts in their capital-labor ratios to take advantage of changing relative factor prices without experiencing a sizeable change in either input's marginal product. For example, if wages fall relative to rents, an automaker could hire more labor and use far fewer tools, without causing labor productivity to decline relative to that of assembly equipment.

CGE modelers usually express σ_{VA} in terms of factors' prices instead of their marginal products but the two concepts are equivalent. Parameter σ_{VA} is the percentage change in the quantity ratio of capital to labor given a percentage change in the wage relative to capital rents. In the limit, when σ_{VA} approaches infinity, factors are perfect substitutes in the production process, and the isoquant is a straight line. In this case, a decrease in one input can always be offset by a proportional increase in another input without affecting either input's marginal product. A change in relative factor prices will therefore lead to large changes in factor proportions. At the other extreme, a parameter value of zero describes a value-added isoquant with an L-shape. With this technology, capital and labor are Leontief complements that must be used in fixed proportions. A change in relative factor prices does not result in a change in the factor ratio. For most industries, substitutability is

Table 5.4. *Factor Substitution Effects of a 5 Percent Increase in the Labor Tax in Manufacturing, with Different Factor Substitution Elasticities, Holding Output Constant (% Change from Base)*

	Manufacturing Activity	
	Capital-labor Ratio ($qf_K - qf_L$)	Wage/rental Ratio ($pfe_L - pfe_K$)
Elasticity = 1.2	0.68	.55
Elasticity = 8.0	2.42	.30

Source: GTAP model, GTAP v.7.0 U.S. 3x3 database.

likely to fall between these two extremes. Balistreri, McDaniel, and Wong's (2003) review of the econometric literature on this parameter found a range of estimated values clustered around a value of one.

Many CGE models use a constant elasticity of substitution (CES) valued-added production function to describe the value-added production technology, similar to the CES utility function studied in Chapter 4. It derives its name from the fact that the factor substitution elasticity remains constant throughout an isoquant (i.e., at any given factor input ratio). CGE modelers are usually restricted to specifying one elasticity parameter for each industry that governs all pairwise substitutions among the factors of production in the model.

The most important thing to remember about a value-added production function is that the ratio of factor input quantities can change when the relative prices of inputs change. Note, too, that if we allow substitution of one primary factor for another in the production process, the input-output coefficients for the factors, shown in Table 5.2, also change. This is not the case for the input-output coefficients for intermediate inputs when their ratios are assumed to be fixed (the "Leontief fixed proportions").

To illustrate these value added concepts, we use the GTAP model and the U.S. 3x3 database to explore the effects on factor input ratios when the cost of labor increases relative to the cost of capital. Our experiment is a 5 percent increase in the tax on labor employed in the manufacturing activity. We compare the effects of the tax when we assume a low factor substitution elasticity in manufacturing of 1.2 versus a large value 8, holding the quantity of value added bundles constant (i.e., remaining on the same isoquant). You can visualize this experiment in Figure 5.3 by imagining that we are observing the producer substituting between the two inputs along (a) a highly curved isoquant in the case of the low substitution elasticity value, and (b) a flatter isoquant in the case of a high elasticity value.

Our model results illustrate that the larger the elasticity parameter value, the larger is the producers' shift toward capital as labor costs rise (Table 5.4). Notice, too, that wages do not rise as much relative to rents when the

Text Box 5.2. Climate Variability and Productivity in Ethiopia
"Impacts of Considering Climate Variability on Investment Decisions in Ethiopia." (Block, Strzepek, Rosegrant, and Diao, 2006).

What is the research question? Extreme interannual rainfall variability that causes droughts and floods is common in Ethiopia. A model that describes climate using mean climate conditions (a deterministic model) does not capture the effects of year-to-year changes and extreme weather events. Would a stochastic model that incorporates both annual variability and the probabilities of extreme weather events result in different and more realistic estimates of production and climate effects on an economy?

What is the CGE model innovation? The authors develop annual climate-yield factors (CYF) by crop and agricultural zone within Ethiopia. The calculation of CYF's uses data on crop sensitivity to water shortages and 100-years of monthly rainfall data by zone. It also includes a flood factor, which decreases the CYF if the year is significantly wet or if the probability of flooding is high. CYF factors are used as multipliers of the technological productivity parameter in the production functions in the CGE model, which is an extension of the IFPRI standard CGE model.

What is the experiment? The 100 years of CYF data are divided into nine 12-year time periods from 1900 to 2000. The authors explore four time path scenarios for the 2003–15 period: (i) a base scenario assumes historic, exogenous growth in endowments and productivity with no new policy initiatives, (ii) an irrigation scenario adds to the base case the government's plans for expanded irrigation acreage, (iii) an investment scenario adds to the base case a planned increase in government spending on infrastructure, and (iv) a combined scenario assumes both irrigation and investment plans are realized. Model results are stochastic in the sense that all four scenarios are run assuming nine alternative weather patterns, producing an ensemble of outcomes.

What are the key findings? In the deterministic model, use of mean climate conditions is adequate when modeling drought, but this approach significantly overestimates the country's welfare when there are floods, which not only reduce agricultural yields but also lead to longer-term damage to roads and infrastructure and sustained losses in output.

production technology is more flexible. This is because even a large increase in the capital-labor ratio causes only a small change in the productivity (and price) of each input.

Combining Intermediate Inputs and Factors

At the top level of the assembly process, the producer combines the bundle of intermediate inputs with the bundle of factors to produce the final output. This aggregate technology is described by a production function in which the two bundles can be substituted according to an ***aggregate input elasticity of substitution***, σ_{AGG}, similar to the value-added production function. In practice, this final stage of production is usually depicted as a Leontief fixed proportions technology, with σ_{AGG} assumed to equal zero. For any level of output, Q, a fixed ratio of intermediate bundles and factor bundle is required. The addition of another bundle of intermediates without also adding a bundle of factors (or vice versa), will not increase output.

Input Prices and Level of Output

Until now, we have explained how the cost-minimizing producer can (or cannot) substitute among inputs as their relative prices change, to produce a given level of output, and we have remained on the same isoquant. However, in our general equilibrium framework, a change in input prices will usually lead to a change in output prices and in consumer demand. As a result, the level of output can change, too, whenever input prices change. The producer may shift to a higher output level, on an outer isoquant, or reduce his output, on an inner isoquant. These output changes will also affect the quantities of inputs required, although not their ratios.

First, let's consider in more detail how a change in the price of an input works through consumer demand in the CGE model to affect the level of output. Labor union concessions, for example, might lower wage costs for automakers. If their technology allows it, automakers will substitute more labor for less equipment in their production process at any given production level. The more that producers can substitute toward labor (i.e., the larger is the elasticity of factor substitution), the lower their production costs will become. As production costs fall, then in perfectly competitive markets, so will auto prices. This point is illustrated in Figure 5.4 as the downward shift in the supply curve from S^1 to S^2. The movement from equilibrium Point A to Point B shows that the same quantity of output is now produced at a lower cost. Depending on consumer preferences, lower auto prices will stimulate consumer demand, so auto production and auto prices will increase, as shown by the movement from Point B to Point C. Increased output, in turn, leads to an increase in demand by the same proportion for all inputs. That is, a 10 percent increase in auto output will lead to a 10 percent increase in demand for both autoworkers and assembly equipment, as well as all intermediate inputs.

In Figure 5.5, we show more generally how the effects of a change in one input price – in this case, a fall in capital rent – on demand for both factor inputs can be decomposed into ***substitution effects*** and ***output effects***. (The alert student will find similarities between this exposition and our discussion of income and substitution effects on consumer demand in Chapter 4.) In the

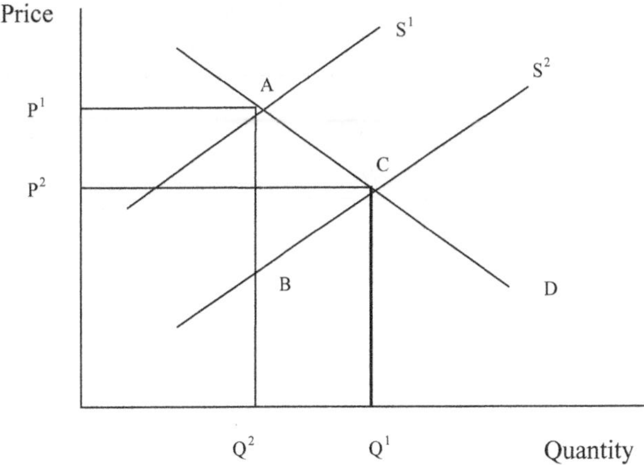

Figure 5.4. Input prices and level of output

figure, QO^1 is the initial level of output of QO, which is produced using the factor input ratio K^1/L^1. (You may notice that we have drawn the figure to show K and L as inputs into QO, instead of QVA, the value-added bundle. This is possible because we assume that the top of the nest requires a fixed proportion of value-added bundles in the production of QO.)

The slope of the isocost curve, C^1, describes the initial ratio of wages to rents, w/r^1. A fall in the price of capital is shown as isocost curve C^2, with slope $-w/r^2$. A decline in the cost of capital lowers the cost of production and leads to higher demand for the final product. Output increases to QO^2, using factor inputs quantities of K^3 and L^3.

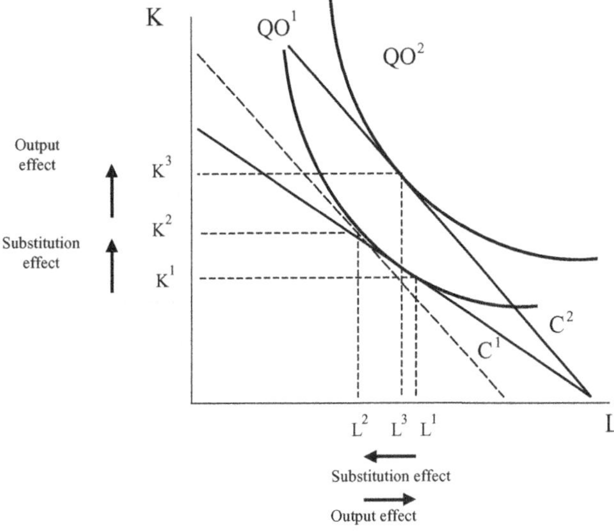

Figure 5.5. Input demand and output levels

Table 5.5. *Effects of a Fall in the Price of Capital Relative to Labor on Input Demand in U.S. Services Industry*

Input	Substitution Effect ($qf - qo$) or ($qfe - qo$)	Output Effect (qo)	% Change Input Demand (qf or qfe)
Intermediate inputs			
Agriculture	0.0	2.1	2.1
Manufacturing	0.0	2.1	2.1
Services	0.0	2.1	2.1
Factor inputs			
Capital	7.6	2.1	9.7
Labor	−2.7	2.1	−0.6

Note: The substitution effect is approximately $qfe - qo$.
Source: GTAP model, GTAP v.7.0 U.S. 3x3 database.

To measure the substitution effect, imagine that producers continue to produce QO^1 but purchase inputs at the new price ratio, shown as the dotted line drawn parallel to isocost curve C^2. The substitution effect measures the movement along the QO^1 isoquant to the tangency between the isoquant and the new isocost curve. As the relative price of capital falls, more capital and less labor are used in the production of QO^1. This change in the factor ratio, from L^1 and K^1 to L^2 and K^2, is the substitution effect. The movement from L^2 and K^2 to L^3 and K^3 is the output effect. It measures the change in factor demand due to the change in production quantity from QO^1 to QO^2, holding the factor prices constant at the new price ratio. The expansion of output leads to a proportionate increase in demand for both inputs.

To explore these concepts in a CGE model, we use the GTAP model with the U.S. 3x3 SAM to run an experiment in which capital rents fall relative to wages. The experiment assumes a 10 percent increase in the U.S. capital stock, which reduces economywide capital rents by 6.8 percent and increases U.S. wages by 0.2 percent. The percentage rise in the wage/rental ratio is therefore $0.2 - (-6.8) = 7.0$.

For brevity, we describe the results only for the U.S. services industry. The lower price of capital reduces the cost of the value-added bundle used in the production of services. In the new equilibrium, the consumer price of services declines by 1.6 percent, demand for domestically produced services increases 1.9 percent, and production of services rises 2.1 percent.

The effects on service's intermediate and factor input are reported in Table 5.5. The output effect increases demand for all intermediate and factor inputs by the same proportion as the change in services output, 2.1 percent. In the intermediate bundle, the substitution effects are zero because we assume a Leontief intermediate production technology with fixed input-output ratios.

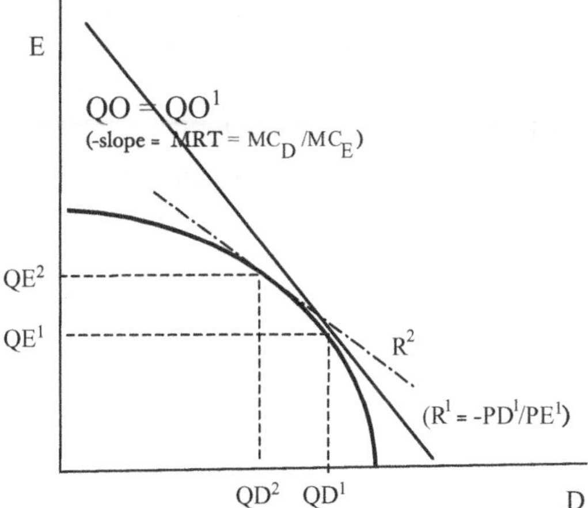

Figure 5.6. Export transformation function and a change in relative prices

In the value-added bundle, the substitution effect results from an increase in the wage-rental ratio, which causes the production of services to become more capital intensive. In total, the combined substitution and output effects stimulate service's demand for capital. In the case of labor, the negative substitution effect on labor demand outweighs the positive output effect and results in a decline in services' demand for labor.

Export Supply

In CGE models, an increase in price in the export market relative to that in the domestic market usually leads a producer to shift sales of his product toward exports, and vice versa. However, in some CGE models, the variety that is exported and the variety that is sold domestically are assumed to be two different goods, and the producer may not be able to readily transform his product line between them. Perhaps electric clocks require different electrical plugs when used in different countries, or a food item like beef may need to meet different consumer safety standards in each market. CGE models in which goods are differentiated by destination markets include an ***export transformation function*** to describe the technological flexibility of producers to transform their product between export and domestic sales.[4]

We depict the function as a ***product transformation curve***, shown in Figure 5.6. It shows all technologically possible combinations of the export, QE, and domestic, QD, varieties that can be produced from a given level of resources

[4] Mainly GAMS-based CGE models include export transformation functions. An early example is the single-country Cameroon model developed by Condon, et al. (1987). Others with this export treatment include the ERS-USDA CGE model (Robinson, et al. 1990), the IFPRI standard model (Lofgren, et al. 2002), the GLOBE model (McDonald, et al. 2007) and the TUG-CGE model (Thierfelder, 2009).

and that comprise the composite output quantity, QO. Perhaps QE and QD are European and American styles of the electric clocks, and QO is the total supply of electric clocks. The farther the transformation curve, QO, lies from the origin, the larger is the quantity of production of QO.

The most obvious difference between this function and the value-added production function that we have already studied is that the export transformation curve is drawn concave to the origin, while isoquants are convex. As we will show, its concave shape means that an increase in the price of QD or QE *increases* its use in the production of QO, whereas with the convex isoquant, an increase in an input price *decreases* its use.

The export transformation curve is otherwise similar in many respects to the value-added isoquant. The negative of its slope at any point describes the ***marginal rate of transformation*** (MRT), which measures the producer's ability to substitute QE for QD in the production of a given level of QO. We can also express the MRT as the ratio of the marginal costs of QD and QE in the production of QO, or MC_D/MC_E.

You can visualize why the two expressions for the curve's slope are equivalent by imagining a point on the curve in Figure 5.5 at which production is almost entirely specialized in exports. As the producer shifts toward domestic sales, the value of MRT becomes larger, because more units of QE must be given up for each additional unit of QD that is produced. This is because the inputs that are most productive when used in QD, and the least productive when used in QE, are the first to be shifted as QD output increases. As output of QD expands further, it draws in less and less productive inputs and QE retains only its most productive inputs. Therefore, the marginal cost of producing QD rises and the marginal cost of producing QE falls as production shifts toward QD.

The line in the figure, R^1, with slope $-PD^1/PE^1$, is an ***isorevenue*** line, where PD is the sales price of the good in the domestic market and PE is the *fob* export sales price. The isorevenue line shows all combinations of QE and QD that generate the same amount of producer revenue from the sale of QO. The further this line from the origin, the higher is producer revenue.

The producer's problem is to choose the ratio of export and domestic varieties for a given QO that maximizes his revenue – shown by the achievement of the highest attainable isorevenue line on any given product transformation curve. In Figure 5.6, revenue from output QO^1 is maximized at output ratio QE^1/QD^1. At this point, the transformation curve and the isorevenue line are tangent and $MC_D/MC_E = PD^1/PE^1$. Rearranging (by multiplying both sides by MC_E/PD^1) revenue is maximized where $MC_D/PD^1 = MC_E/PE^1$. That is, each additional dollar of revenue from QE and QD incurs the same marginal cost. If not, producers will produce more of the variety whose marginal cost is lower, and less of the variety whose marginal cost is higher, relative to its price.

Assume that the relative price of exports increases, as shown by the dotted line R^2 in Figure 5.6. The revenue-maximizing producer will increase the ratio of exports to domestic sales in output QO^1, to ratio QE^2/QD^2. The size of this quantity response depends on the curvature of the transformation curve, which is defined by the ***export transformation elasticity***, σ_E. The parameter defines the percentage change in the ratio of exports to domestic goods given a percentage change in the ratio of the domestic to the export sales price. It has the varieties are perfect substitutes in the composition of Q, then the transformation parameter has a negative value that approaches minus infinity and transformation curve becomes linear. In this case, a small change in the price ratio will result in a large change in the product mix.

CGE models that describe export transformation generally assume a constant elasticity of transformation (CET) function to describe the producer's decision-making.[5] The CET function derives its name from the fact that the export transformation elasticity is constant throughout the product transformation curve, and at any level of QO.

We illustrate the properties of an export transformation function in a CGE model by running an experiment that increases the world export price of U.S. manufactured goods by 5 percent. We use the U.S. 3x3 database in the TUG-CGE model, a single country model developed by Thierfelder (2009) that contains a CET export transformation function.[6] We compare the effects of the price shock on the quantity ratio of exports to domestic goods, using two different values of the export transformation elasticity parameter. As the parameter becomes larger and the transformation technology is more flexible, a 5 percent increase in the world export price elicits a larger export supply response from U.S. manufacturers (Table 5.6). Notice, too, that total output increases more when producers are relatively flexible in shifting toward export opportunities. Because the inputs are relatively suitable for use in the production of either variety, the marginal cost of producing additional exports does not rise as fast as in the low-elasticity case.

Summary

In this chapter, we examine production data in the SAM and producer behavior in the CGE model. Data in the SAM describe each industry's production

[5] See Powell and Gruen (1968) for a detailed presentation on the CET function.

[6] World export and import prices are assumed to be exogenous variables in this single-country CGE model.

Table 5.6. *Effects of a 5 Percent Increase in the World Export Price of U.S. Manufactured Exports on the Production of Exported and Domestic Varieties (% Change from Base)*

	Export Transformation Elasticity	
U.S. Manufacturing	0.8	4.0
Export/domestic price ratio	6.0	5.5
Export/domestic production ratio	4.9	24.5
Total manufacturing output	2.7	6.2

Source: TUG-CGE, GTAP v.7.0 U.S. 3x3 database.

technology, reporting its use of intermediate and factor inputs and any taxes paid or subsidies received. We use the SAM's production data to calculate input-output coefficients that describe the units of intermediate and factor inputs required per unit of output. Input-output coefficients are useful for characterizing production activities' intermediate factor-intensities, comparing input intensities across industries, and describing inter-industry linkages from upstream to downstream industries. We also use data in the SAM to calculate indices of forward and backward linkages among industries, another measure of industry interdependence.

CGE models break down the production technology into subprocesses that, when diagrammed, look like an upside-down tree. The trunk is the assembly of the final good; its branches are the subprocesses that are nested within the overall production process; and its twigs are the inputs used in each subprocess. Each subprocess and final assembly has its own production technology, cost-minimization equation, and input substitution elasticity parameter. In the intermediates' nest, producers decide on the cost-minimizing levels of intermediate inputs, and in the value-added nest, producers choose the cost-minimizing levels of factor inputs. Some CGE models include export transformation functions, which describe how producers allocate their output between exports and sales in the domestic market.

Key Terms

Backward linkage index
Downstream industries
Elasticity of export transformation
Elasticity of factor substitution
Elasticity of intermediate input substitition
Export transformation function

Factor intensity
Forward linkage index
Input-output coefficient
Isocost
Isoquant
Isorevenue
Leontief fixed-proportion production function
Nested production function
Output effect
Product transformation curve
Substitution effect
Technology tree
Upstream industries
Value-added production function

PRACTICE AND REVIEW

1. Use the U.S. SAM (in the Appendix), to describe the production technology of the U.S. services sector:

   Total intermediate inputs ______________________
   Total factor payments ______________________
   Total tax (and subsidy) ______________________
   Value-added ______________________
   Gross value of output ______________________

2. Data in exercise Table 5.7 describe the inputs purchased by manufacturing and services for their production process. Calculate the input-output coefficients for the two industries and report them in the table. Answer the following questions:
   a. In which factor is the production of manufacturing most intensive?
   b. In which factor is the production of services most intensive?
   c. Which industry is more labor intensive?
   d. Describe the upstream and downstream role of manufacturing.
3. Assume that you are CEO of a small firm. The introduction of a universal health insurance program has eliminated your health premium payments and lowered your cost per worker. Use a graph that describes your cost-minimizing choice of capital and labor shares in the value- added bundle, explain how the new program will change the labor-capital ratio in your production process, for a fixed level of value-added.
4. Consider the following results reported in Table 5.8, from a model with a nested production function. Can you infer from the results the percentage change in the industry's production, the possible types of production functions used in the each nest, and the likely change in relative factor prices that accounts for these results?

Table 5.7. *Input-Output Coefficients Exercise*

	Inputs Into Production		Input-Output Coefficients	
	Manufacturing	Services	Mfg.	Services
Labor	12	12		
Capital	8	18		
Manufacturing	10	50		
Services	20	20		
Gross value of output	50	100		

Technical Appendix 5.1: Inputs as Substitutes or Complements – Energy Nesting in Climate Models

The production functions used in CGE models describe inputs as substitutes or Leontief complements in the production process. However, in some cases, it may be more realistic to describe some inputs as true complements in the sense that an increase in one input price causes demand for the other input to fall. The presence of complementary inputs is especially important in the analysis of climate change. Climate change modelers often want to represent some degree of substitutability between capital and energy, yet characterize them as overall complements, at least in the short run. Capital-energy substitution assumptions are important because the estimated costs of reducing carbon emissions are lower the more flexible are production technologies.

CGE models used for climate change analysis typically move energy from the intermediate bundle into the value-added (VA) nest. Some models, including the example we study in this appendix, combine capital and energy into a composite bundle, KE, that is combined with labor in the VA nest, as illustrated in Figure 5.7. The modeler then adds a nest to describe how capital and energy are combined to produce the KE bundle. Other models combine capital and labor into a bundle, KL, that is combined with E. Both model

Table 5.8. *Effects of a Change in Factor Price on An Industry's Input Demand*

Input	Substitution Effect	Output Effect	% Change in Input Demand
Agriculture	0	3.5	3.5
Manufacturing	0	3.5	3.5
Services	0	3.5	3.5
Capital	−4	3.5	−0.5
Labor	6	3.5	9.5

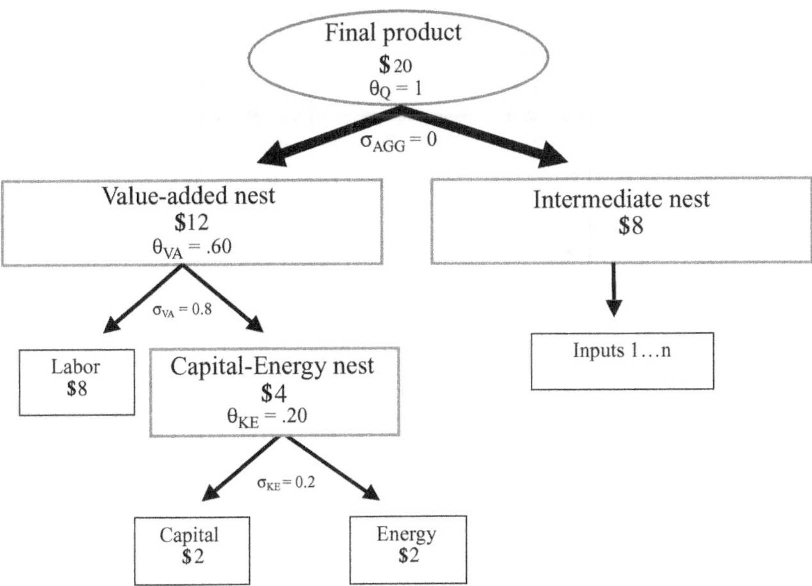

Figure 5.7. Technology tree with a KE-L nest

types usually add additional nests to describe substitution among energy types which, for brevity, we do not discuss.

Adding a KE nest to the value-added production function is a technique that allows modelers to describe K and E as overall complements while still allowing for a realistic amount of KE substitution. Suppose the price of energy rises. Within the KE nest, the quantity of energy demanded will fall and demand for capital will rise, to the extent that capital can be substituted for energy. Substitutability within the KE nest is likely to be quite low. For example, most machinery needs a certain amount of electricity to run properly. If the unit cost of the KE bundle still rises, then the producer will shift toward labor and away from the KE bundle in the higher level, VA nest. As demand for the KE bundle falls, demand for both capital and energy will fall by the same proportion. If the within-KE substitution effect dominates, then an increase in the energy price will cause demand for capital to rise – K and E are overall substitutes. If the VA substitution effect dominates, and the rise in the energy price causes demand for capital to fall – then K and E are overall complements.

Keller (1980) developed a formula to calculate the overall substitution parameter for nested inputs like capital and energy, σ^*_{KE}. His formula defines the parameter as a function of all three substitution effects – within KE, σ_{KE}; within VA, σ_{VA}; and at the top level of aggregation, σ_{AGG} – and of each nest's share in the total cost of the final product. Table 5.9 demonstrates how the overall substitution parameter is calculated, using the data shown in

Table 5.9. *Within-Nest and Overall Capital-Energy Substitution Parameters*

	Substitution Parameter			Share in Total Cost of Production			Overall K-E Substitution
	KE nest (σ_{KE})	VA nest (σ_{VA})	VA-Intermediate (top) nest (σ_{AGG})	KE (θ_{KE})	VA (θ_{VA})	Q (θ_Q)	σ^*_{KE}
Formula: $\sigma_{KE}(\theta_{KE}^{-1}) - \sigma_{VA}(\theta_{KE}^{-1} - \theta_{VA}^{-1}) - \sigma_{AGG}(\theta_{VA}^{-1} - \theta_Q^{-1}) = \sigma^*_{KE}$							
Base case	0.2	0.8	0	0.2	0.6	1	−1.66
High KE cost share	0.2	0.8	0	0.5	0.6	1	0.13
High KE substitution	0.9	0.8	0	0.2	0.6	1	1.83

Figure 5.7.[7] In this example, the cost share of the KE bundle, $\theta_{KE,}$ is \$4/\$20 = 0.20, and the KE substitution parameter is 0.2. The cost share of the VA bundle, θ_{VA}, is \$12/\$20 = 0.6 and the L-KE substitution parameter is 0.8. The elasticity parameter, σ_{AGG}, between VA and intermediate inputs, is zero. The cost share of the final product itself, θ_Q, is one.

Using Keller's formula, capital and energy inputs are overall complements, with an overall substitution elasticity parameter of minus 1.66. As illustrations, a change in the cost shares that gives more weight to the within-KE process causes its substitution effect to dominate, so capital and energy become overall substitutes, with a parameter value of .13. A change in relative elasticities, making capital and energy more substitutable in the KE nest, also causes the two inputs to become overall substitutes, with a parameter value of 1.83.

7 For a more general statement of this formula for any number of nesting levels, see Keller (1980) and McDougall (2009).

6

Factors of Production in a CGE Model

In this chapter, we explore factor markets in a computable general equilibrium (CGE) model. Data in the Social Accounting Matrix (SAM) on factors of production describe factors' sources of employment and income. Important factor market concepts in the CGE model are factor mobility assumptions, the effects of factor endowment and productivity growth, complementary and substitute factors, full-employment versus unemployment model closures, and the links between factor supply and industry structure and between industry structure and factor prices.

Factors of production are the labor, capital, land, and other primary resources that producers combine with intermediate inputs to make goods and services. A nation's ***factor endowment*** is its fundamental stock of wealth because factors represent its supply of productive resources. In Chapter 5, we considered production activities' demand for factors and how these adjust with changes in relative factor prices or output levels. Many other dimensions of factor markets in a CGE model also deserve study.

In the next sections, we describe factor markets in CGE models in detail, focusing on those aspects that are of greatest practical importance for CGE modelers. We begin by studying the factor market data in the SAM. Then we consider the behavior of factor markets in the CGE model. We explain factor mobility assumptions, which govern the readiness of factors to change their employment in response to changing wages and rents across industries. We explore the effects of changes in the supply, or endowment, of factors, and contrast it with changes in the "effective" endowment when factor productivity changes. We study the implications of assuming production functions, or industry technologies, that treat factors as complements (low factor substitutability) versus substitutes (high factor substitutability). We describe the CGE model's closures rules that specify full employment versus factor unemployment and demonstrate the importance of this assumption for model results. Finally, we examine the links between factor markets and the industry structure of an economy. We study how a change in factor

Table 6.1. *Factors of Production Data in the SAM ($U.S. billions)*

	Production Activities			Factors		
	Agriculture	Manufacturing	Services	Land	Labor	Capital
Land	34	0	0			
Labor	68	1,109	5,667			
Capital	122	467	2,332			
Income tax	0	0		3	1,446	244
Regional household	0	0		31	5,397	1,632
Savings–investment	0	0	0	0	0	1,046
Total	na	na	na	34	6,844	2,921

Source: GTAP v.7.0 U.S. 3x3 database.

endowments leads to changes in the industry structure, and we examine how changes in industry structure leads to changes in factor prices and factor input ratios across industries.

Factors of Production Data in a SAM

Each factor of production has its own row and column account in a SAM. For example, in the U.S. 3x3 SAM, there are three factors of production: land, labor, and capital (Table 6.1). The factor row accounts describe the receipt of income earned from employment in agriculture, manufacturing, and services activities. For example, land receives $34 billion from employment in agricultural production. Labor receives income from all three production activities: $68 billion from employment in agriculture, $1,109 billion from employment in manufacturing, and $5,667 billion from employment in services. Capital also receives income from all three production activities.

The SAM's factor column accounts report the disposition of factor income. First, there are income taxes based on factor earnings. Land rental income incurs $3 billion in taxes. In this database, the $1,446 billion in labor income tax includes payroll taxes such as Social Security. The SAM, and the CGE model that we use for most of our examples in this book, assume that their after-tax factor earnings are paid to a regional household, a macroeconomic account. Capital pays $244 billion in income taxes. In addition, the capital account column reports depreciation as a cost that is allocated to the investment-savings account. Capital's remaining income is paid to the regional household account.

CGE models generally have at least two factors of production. Often, researchers disaggregate factors into many more types. For example, they may disaggregate labor into skilled and unskilled workers or urban and rural workers. Modelers also may disaggregate the capital account to separate capital equipment and structures from natural capital resources such as coal and oil. Sometimes, CGE modelers disaggregate land into types, such as cropland versus grazing land, or irrigated and nonirrigated land. You can visualize factor market disaggregation in a SAM by imagining that instead of a single labor row and labor column account, there are, for example, two labor rows and two labor columns – one each for skilled and unskilled labor. By disaggregating factors, the researcher who is interested in factor markets can pursue a richer analysis of some types of economic shocks. For example, a labor economist may be interested in differentiating the effects of immigration on skilled versus unskilled wages.

Factor Mobility

Factor mobility describes the ease with which labor, capital, and other factors can move to employment in different production activities *within a country* as wages and rents change across industries. Some multicountry CGE models also allow factor mobility *across* countries, which changes nations' factor supplies. A CGE model of this type supported a recent World Bank analysis of global labor immigration, summarized in Text Box 6.1. In this chapter, we assume a nation's factors are in fixed supply, except when we explicitly consider, as in the next section, the ramifications of a change in factor endowments.

In a CGE model, factors are called ***fully mobile*** if they are assumed to move among jobs until wage and rent differentials disappear. For example, if workers perceive that one industry offers a higher wage than another, some number of them will exit the low-wage industry, causing its wage to rise, and enter the high-wage industry, causing its wage to fall. Their movement will continue until wages in the two industries are equal. Full factor mobility is probably a realistic view of labor and capital markets in the medium run or long run because transition costs, such as retraining and job search costs, become less important when they are amortized over a longer time horizon. Younger workers, for example, may decide it is worth the time and money to invest in training for higher-paying jobs in industries that seem to offer a bright future over the remaining span of their careers.

Some CGE models allow factors to be ***partially mobile***. This assumption implies that transition costs are large enough to discourage some workers or equipment from changing employment unless pay differences are sufficient to compensate them for the cost of moving to other employment. Wages and rents can therefore diverge across production activities and, given identical shocks, factor movements are usually smaller with partially mobile factors than in a CGE model that assumes full factor mobility.

Text Box 6.1. The Economic Impacts of Global Labor Migration
Global Economic Prospects 2006, World Bank, Washington D.C.

What is the research question? The United Nations estimates that international migrants account for about 3 percent of the world's population. International labor migration can generate substantial welfare gains for migrants, their countries of origin and the countries to which they migrate but may also lead to social and political stresses. What is the estimated size of the economic welfare effect of global labor migration?

What is the CGE model innovation? The authors modify the World Bank's recursive dynamic CGE model, Linkage (van der Mensbrugge, 2005), to work with their comprehensive global database on labor migration, which differentiates between migrant and native workers and tracks remittance income sent by migrants to their countries of origin. They also adapt their welfare measure to account for the effects of cross-country differences in the cost of living on the spending power of migrant wages and remittances.

What is the model experiment? Migration flows from developing to high-income countries are assumed to increase at a rate sufficient to increase the labor force of high-income countries by 3 percent over the period 2001–25. The assumed increase, roughly one-eighth of a percentage point per year, is close to that observed over the 1970–2000 time period.

What are the key findings? Migration yields large increases in welfare for both high- and low-income countries. Migrants, natives, and households in countries of origin all experience gains in income, although income falls for migrants already living in host countries. There is a small decline in average wages in destination countries but migration's effect on the long-run growth in wages is almost imperceptible. Both the costs and the benefits of migration depend, in part, on the investment climate.

CGE models that allow partial factor mobility use a factor supply function for each partially mobile factor. This concave function is identical to the export transformation function described in Chapter 5, so we do not replicate it here. Using labor as an example, the function describes how the labor force can be transformed into different types of workers, such as agricultural or manufacturing workers. A ***factor mobility elasticity***, σ_F, defines the percentage change in the share of the labor force employed in sector X given a percentage change in the ratio of the economy-wide average wage to its industry wage. For example, if the wage in sector X rises relative to the average wage, then the share of the work force employed in sector X will rise. The factor mobility parameter value ranges between close to zero, which is an immobile factor, to minus 1, which is a fully mobile factor. The higher is this elasticity (in absolute value), the larger are the employment shifts in response to changes in wages and rents across industries. CGE

Table 6.2. *Capital Rents (pfe) by Sector with a 5 Percent Subsidy on Private Household Consumption of Domestic Manufactures, Under Alternative Capital Mobility Assumptions*

	Agriculture	Manufacturing	Services
Fully mobile capital	1.1	1.1	1.1
Partially mobile capital	1.4	3.9	0.2
Sector-specific capital	3.4	4.4	0.0

Note: Fully mobile capital has a factor mobility elasticity (etrae) of minus 1, partially mobile capital has an elasticity of minus .2 and sector-specific capital has an elasticity of minus .0001.
Source: GTAP model, GTAP v.7.0 US 3x3 database.

models that describe factor mobility in this way may assume a Constant Elasticity of Transformation (CET) factor supply function, so that parameter σ_F is the same for all ratios of factor employment and at all levels of aggregate factor supply.[1]

In the short run, some factors may be immobile, also called ***sector-specific***. That is, factors do not move from the production activity in which they originally are employed, regardless of the size of changes in relative wages or rents across industries. This assumption is often made in the case of capital because existing equipment and machinery are typically hard to transform for use in different industries. Similar to the case of partially mobile factors, the wage or rent of the sector-specific factor can differ across industries in the model – perhaps significantly so, because no amount of wage or rent premium can be enough to attract factors that are stuck in their current employment, or low enough to motivate them to quit.

A practical implication of the factor mobility assumption is that it influences the slope of industry supply curves. All else equal, the more mobile are factors, the flatter is the supply curve and the larger is the supply response to any type of economic shock. One way to think about it is that a producer who can easily attract more factors with a small wage or rent increase is better able to increase output while holding down production costs, so his supply curve is more elastic.

We explore the effects of alternative factor market assumptions in a CGE model by using the GTAP model and the U.S. 3x3 database to run an experiment that introduces a 5 percent subsidy to private households in the United States on their purchases of domestically produced manufactured goods. The subsidy stimulates demand for manufactures, so producers try to increase their output by hiring more labor and capital. The results reported in Table 6.2 describe the subsidy's effects on each industry's capital rents in

[1] See the section on export supply in Chapter 5 for a more detailed discussion of CET functions.

models with three different capital mobility assumptions – fully mobile, partially mobile, and sector-specific. When capital is fully mobile, it moves across industries until capital rents equalize, so the capital rents increase by the same rate in every industry. In this case, manufacturing output increases 3.7 percent. When capital is only partially mobile, intersectoral differences in rental rate emerge. Manufacturing's capital rents are higher and its output expands by slightly less, 3.5 percent. The capital rent in U.S. manufacturing rises most when capital is assumed to be sector-specific, and manufacturing output increases least in this model, by 3.4 percent.

Factor mobility assumptions are a useful way to categorize CGE model results as describing ***short-run***, ***medium-run***, or ***long-run*** adjustments to economic shocks. In the short run, some factors – usually capital – are immobile, and the economy's production response is therefore limited. In the medium run, factors are partially, or even fully, mobile. In this case, the adjustment period is long enough that existing stocks of capital and labor can be retooled or replaced, and workers can shift employment among industries in response to changes in wages and rents. Production therefore becomes more responsive to economic shocks. Analyses of long-run adjustment assume that all factors are fully mobile and, in addition, long-run changes in factor supply and productivity occur. The standard, static CGE models that we are studying can describe short- and medium-run adjustments, depending on their factor mobility assumptions. Dynamic CGE models that are capable of describing factor accumulation and productivity growth are needed to describe long-run adjustments to economic shocks.

Factor Endowment Change

A standard assumption in static CGE models is that a nation's factor endowments are in fixed supply. CGE modelers analyze shocks to factor endowments as model experiments. These shocks can occur for many reasons, such as immigration (increases the labor supply), foreign direct investment (increases the capital supply), or war (decreases both labor and capital supplies). A change in factor endowments can be a significant shock because it changes the productive capacity of an economy. Often more important from a public policy perspective, are the resulting distributional effects when a change in a factor endowment leads to increased wages or rents earned by some factors, but lower earnings by others.

An increase in the supply of a factor will cause its wage or rent to fall (unless demand for the factor is perfectly elastic). As an example, Figure 6.1 illustrates the effect of an increase in the supply of labor, from S_L^1 to S_L^2, on employment and wages. The national labor supply curve is a vertical line because we assume, as in a standard CGE model, that there is a fixed supply

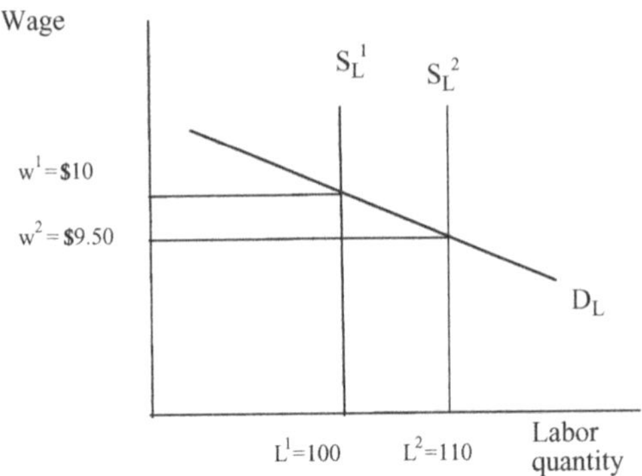

Figure 6.1. Effect of an increase in labor endowment on employment and wages

of workers and all of them are employed. D_L is the labor demand curve. In our example, there are initially 100 workers earning an equilibrium wage, w^1, of $10 per worker. An increase in the labor supply to 110 workers causes the market-clearing wage to fall to $9.50.

We observe the effects on aggregate output and the own-price of a factor endowment change in a CGE model by using the GTAP CGE model and the U.S. 3x3 database to run an experiment that increases the U.S. labor supply by 10 percent. The result is a 2 percent decline in the U.S. wage and a 7 percent increase in U.S. real GDP.

Factors as Complements and Substitutes

A change in the endowment of one factor can also affect the demand for and prices of other factors of production. For example, an increase in the supply of labor – perhaps due to immigration – will affect the wage in the host country, and the demand for and price of capital that is used in combination with labor to produce goods and services. However, we cannot say for sure how immigration will affect capital. Whether the quantity of capital demanded and capital rents will rise or fall depends on whether labor and capital are substitutes or complements in the production process.

We have already studied factor substitutability and complementarity in our description of producers' demand for value-added in Chapter 5. To reiterate briefly, the firm's technology determines the ability of producers to substitute labor for capital in the production of a given level of output. We depicted the flexibility of technology with a ***factor substitution elasticity***, σ_F, which defines the percentage change in the ratio of capital to labor given a percentage change in the ratio of wages to rents. If the parameter has a large value, the two factors are close ***substitutes***. The increase in the labor supply is more likely to cause rents to fall because firms will shift toward labor, the cheaper

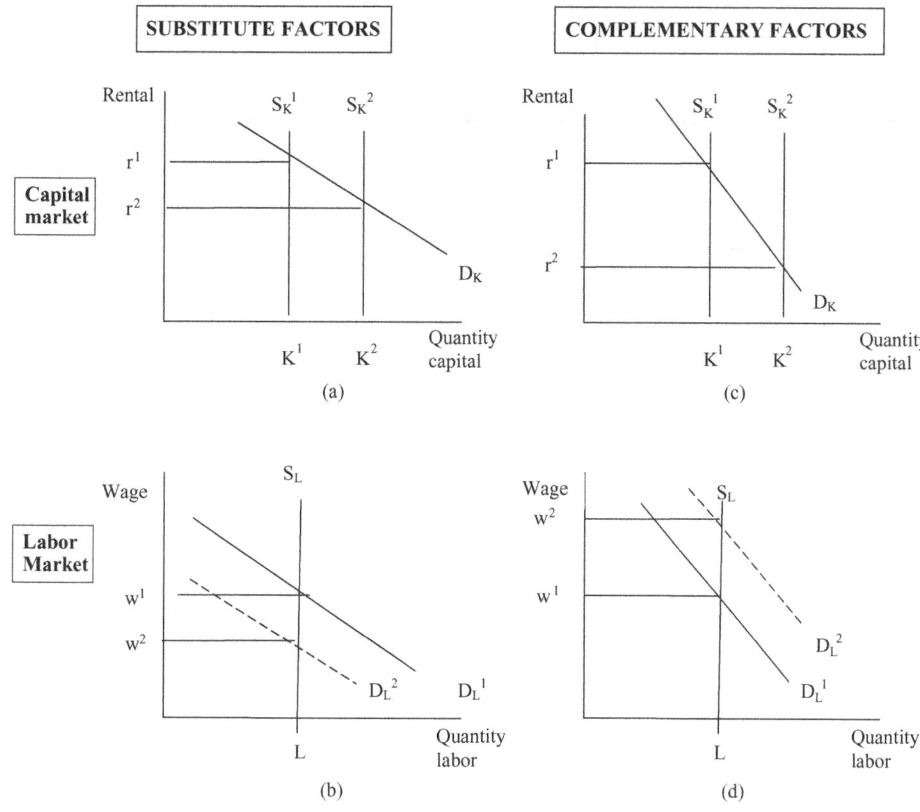

Figures 6.2a–d. Labor and capital as substitutes and complements

factor, and demand less capital for use in their production processes. If the elasticity has a small value, then the two factors are close ***complements***. In this case, the increase in the labor supply is likely to increase capital rents as firms hire demand more capital equipment to use with their new workers.

As another example, consider the case of a country that receives foreign aid in the form of capital equipment and machinery. Will this increase in its capital stock raise or lower its wages – will it help or harm its labor force? Figure 6.2 presents a four-quadrant graph that illustrates the effects of the increased supply of capital goods on the country's capital and labor markets under the alternative assumptions that capital and labor are substitutes or complements. Figures 6.2a and 6.2b describe the markets for capital and labor when the two factors are highly substitutable. Figures 6.2c and 6.2d describe the markets for capital and labor when the two factors are more complementary. Notice that the factor supply curves for both factors are shown as vertical lines, reflecting our CGE model assumptions of fixed factor endowments and full employment. In both capital market figures, an increase in the capital stock shifts the supply curve for capital to the right, from S^1_K to S^2_K. In the two labor market figures, the increase in capital stock shifts the demand curve for labor in opposite directions, from D^1_L to D^1_L.

First, we assume that capital and labor are strong substitutes. Perhaps in this country, industries can easily produce goods using either machinery or workers, so the demand for capital, D_K, is elastic (and drawn with a relatively flat slope) and the initial capital rent is r^1. An increase in the capital stock, from S^1_K to S^2_K, in Figure 6.2a, causes the price of capital to fall so producers substitute toward more cost-saving, capital-intensive production processes. In the new equilibrium, the quantity of capital demanded has increased from Q^1_K to Q^2_K and the capital rent has fallen to r^2.

The effect of the increase in capital on the labor market is shown in Figure 6.2b by the direction of the shift in the demand curve for labor. A shift to more capital-intensive processes is shown as a decline in the economy's demand for labor, from D^1_L to D^2_L. As the adoption of more capital-intensive production technologies reduces the demand for the fixed supply of workers, the wage falls from w^1 to w^2.

Contrast this outcome with the case of factors as strong complements. For example, perhaps capital equipment requires workers to operate it. The demand curve for capital equipment is thus relatively inelastic, with the steep slope shown by D_K in Figure 6.2c. The effect of capital stock growth on the demand for complementary labor is shown in Figure 6.2d as a rightward shift in the labor demand curve, from D^1_L to D^2_L. In this case, the demand for labor increases, causing the wage to rise from w^1 to w^2.

We study the role of the factor substitution elasticity in a CGE model by using the GTAP model to carry out an experiment that increases the U.S. capital stock by 10 percent. We compare the factor price results from two versions of the model. We first define capital and labor as strong substitutes and then as strong complements by changing the factor substitution elasticity parameters for all three production activities in the model.

Model results, reported in Table 6.3, show the key role of the factor substitutability assumption in determining whether a change in the supply of one factor raises or lowers the price of the other factor. When factors are strong substitutes, an increase in the U.S. capital stock lowers U.S. wages by .45 percent. If factors are assumed to be strong complements, an increase in the capital stock raises wages by 1.84 percent. In both cases, an increase in the capital stock lowers the price of capital.

Factor Productivity Change

Factor productivity describes the level of output per unit of factor input. An increase in factor productivity means that the same quantity of a factor can

Table 6.3. *Effects of 10 Percent Capital Stock Growth on Wages and Rents in the U.S. 3x3 Model When Factors are Substitutes or Complements (% change from base)*

% Change	Substitutes	Complements
Wage (pfe_L)	−.45	1.84
Rent (pfe_K)	−.52	−5.29

Note: Substitutes case specifies factor substitution elasticities for all production activities of 125. Complements case uses default GTAP elasticities. The model closure fixes the U.S. trade balance, DTBALr.
Source: GTAP model and GTAP v.7.0 U.S. 3x3 database.

produce more goods and services. New training, for example, may enable an autoworker to produce twice as many vehicles as previously whereas bad weather may cause an acre of land to yield only half the usual quantity of wheat. Productivity gains and losses can occur for a single factor (such as the labor productivity losses described in Text Box 6.2) or for a subset of factors, and in one or more industries. A change of equal proportions in the productivity of all factors of production in an industry or in an economy is called a change in ***total factor productivity*** (TFP).

A change in a factor's productivity changes the ***effective factor endowment***. Effective factor endowments take into account both the quantity and the efficiency of a factor. For example, suppose that an initial labor supply of 100 workers can now do the work of 110 workers (a 10 percent gain in their productivity), then the effective labor endowment is now 110 workers, although the actual number of workers remains at 100.

An increase in productivity tends to lower the wage per effective worker. This point is illustrated in Figure 6.3. Note carefully that its axes and curves refer to the quantity of and wage per effective worker, not actual workers, where EL is the quantity of effective workers. The demand curve for effective labor is D_L and S_L^1 describes its supply. In the initial equilibrium, the economy employs 100 workers at a wage of $10. An increase in labor productivity shifts the supply of effective workers to S_L^2. Given the labor demand curve, the new equilibrium has 110 effective workers at a wage per effective worker (the ***effective wage***) of $9.50. It may seem surprising that a factor's productivity gain could lead to a lower wage or rent, but remember that this is the price of an effective factor. Because 110 effective workers equal 100 actual workers, the wage per actual worker has *increased* to $10.45.[2]

[2] The actual wage is derived by calculating the total wage bill as the product of effective workers times the effective wage (110 * $9.50 = $1,045) and dividing it by the number of actual workers ($1,045/100 = $10.45).

Text Box 6.2. HIV/AIDS – Disease and Labor Productivity in Mozambique
"HIV/AIDS and Macroeconomic Prospects for Mozambique: An Initial Assessment." (Arndt, 2002).

What is the research question? As in other countries in the southern Africa region, a human development catastrophe is unfolding in Mozambique, where HIV prevalence rates among the adult population in 2000 are around 12 percent, and life expectancy is projected to decline to about 36 years. Due to the magnitude of the HIV/AIDS pandemic, it has overrun the bounds of a pure health issue and become a top priority development issue. What is the scope of its potential macroeconomic impact?

What is the CGE model innovation? The author develops a recursive dynamic CGE model, based on the IFPRI standard CGE model that updates sectoral productivity, the labor force (by skill category), and the physical capital stock to analyze the effects of HIV/AIDS over time.

What is the model experiment? There are three channels through which the HIV/AIDS pandemic is assumed to affect economic growth: (1) productivity growth effects for labor and other factors, (2) population, labor, and human capital stock accumulation effects, and (3) physical capital accumulation effects. Based on these channels, the author defines four scenarios. An AIDS scenario reduces all factors' productivity and endowments based on available estimates; a "less-effect" scenario reduces most of the HIV/AIDS impacts by about one-half. An education scenario combines the AIDS scenario with a strong effort to maintain school enrollments and the growth of the skilled labor supply. A No-Mega scenario combines the AIDS scenario with the assumption that large scale, donor-financed investment projects are curtailed.

What are the key findings? The differences in growth rates in the four scenarios cumulate into large differences in GDP over time. GDP is between 16 and 23 percent smaller than it would be in the absence of the pandemic. The major impacts on GDP are decomposed into the three channels. Although all are important, the decline in factor productivity is the largest source of the potential decline in Mozambique's GDP.

Similar to an endowment change, when the effective endowment of one factor changes, it may affect the demand for and prices of other factors. In Chapter 5, we showed how a change in one input price could lead to substitution and output effects on the demand for both factors. In the case of a change in the effective price, we decompose three effects. The first two are the same substitution and output effects that we have already studied. For example, if labor productivity increases, a fall in the effective wage motivates producers to become more labor-intensive and use less capital for any given output level, to the extent that their technology allows it. Automakers, for

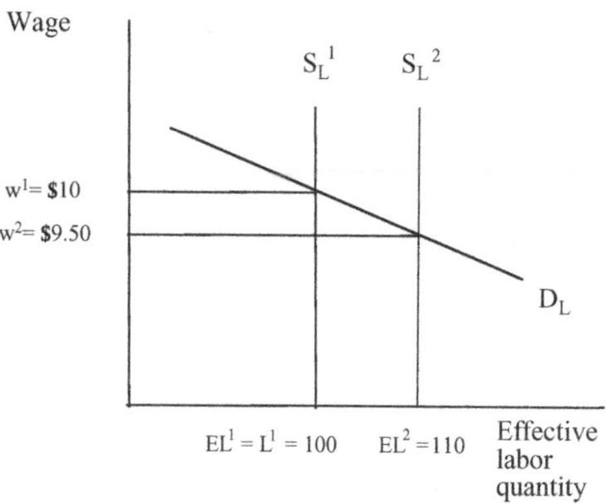

Figure 6.3. Effect of an increase in labor productivity on employment and wages.

instance, will want to use more of the newly trained autoworkers and less equipment to produce their current output quantity because the cost of labor per auto has fallen relative to the cost of capital. This is the substitution effect of productivity changes on the demand for actual workers and for capital. Second, given the competitive markets assumed in standard CGE models, a fall in production costs due to increased productivity is passed on to consumers through lower product prices, which in turn leads to higher demand and production levels. The output effect describes an increase in demand for all factors by the same proportion as the change in output, holding relative factor prices constant. The third, additional, effect is the impact of a factor's productivity change on demand for that factor, for a given output level. Automakers, for example, will need fewer workers to produce the same number of cars when labor productivity increases. The net effect of a factor's productivity change on demand for all factors in the economy is the sum of the substitution, output and productivity effects.

We illustrate these three effects in a CGE model using the GTAP model with the U.S. 3x3 SAM. Our experiment assumes a 10 percent increase in the productivity of the total U.S. labor force; for brevity, we report results only for the capital and labor markets. The factor substitution effect leads to a substitution toward labor and away from capital in all three industries as the effective wage falls (Table 6.4). The output effect in each industry is identical for both factors and is the same as their percent growth in output. The 10 percent increase in labor productivity also leads to a reduction of an equal proportion in firms' demand for workers. Notice that there is no productivity effect on capital demand because its productivity is unchanged in this experiment. On net, the resulting changes in factor demand cause the effective wage to fall by 4.2 percent, the actual wage to rise by 5.8 percent, and capital rents to increase by 3.3 percent.

Table 6.4. *Effects of a 10 Percent Increase in Economywide U.S. Labor Productivity on Demand for Labor and Capital (% change from base)*

	Agriculture	Manufactures	Services
Labor demand (*qfe*)	−7.4	−1.7	0.4
Factor substitution effect (*qfe-qo-afe*)	1.2	2.6	2.8
Output effect (*qo*)	1.4	5.7	7.7
Productivity effect (*afe*)	−10.0	−10.0	−10.0
Capital demand (*qfe*)	1.0	−1.0	0.2
Factor substitution effect (*qfe-qo-afe*)	−0.4	−6.7	−7.5
Output effect (*qo*)	1.4	5.7	7.7
Productivity effect (*afe*)	0.0	0.0	0.00

Note: We use the Johansen solution method.
Source: GTAP model, GTAP v.7.0 U.S. 3x3 database.

Factor Unemployment

In some countries, unemployment is a serious problem, and the common CGE model assumption of full employment of all factors may not realistically describe an economy. Unemployment can be depicted in a CGE model by changing the factor market closure. Recall from our discussion in Chapter 2 that model closure is the modeler's decision as to which variables adjust to re-equilibrate markets following an economic shock. With a full employment model closure, a shock to an economy causes wages and rents to adjust until the fixed supply of each factor is again fully employed. In a model with an ***unemployment*** closure, the wage or rent is assumed to be fixed, and economic shocks can lead to a change in the factor supply – that is, the size of the labor force or the stock of capital will adjust until factor supply and demand are again equal at the initial wage or rental rate.

In a model that allows unemployment, a decline in the size of the labor force, for example, means that some proportion of workers is now unemployed, so part of the nation's productive capacity is now idled. An increase in the size of the labor force means that previously unemployed workers have now found employment, so the economy's productivity capacity expands. In this case, industries are able to hire as many workers or as much equipment as they need following an economic shock, without bidding up wages or capital rents. As you might expect, experiments in a model that allows factor unemployment can result in very large changes in a nation's productive capacity and real GDP.

We explore the implications of the factor market closure assumption in a CGE model by comparing the effects of the same experiment in model versions with different labor market closures. We use the GTAP model and the U.S. 3x3 database to run an experiment that provides a 10 percent output

Table 6.5. *Effects of a 10 Percent Output Subsidy in U.S. Manufacturing Under Full Employment and Unemployment Labor Market Closures (% change from base)*

	Labor Unemployment Closure	Full Employment Closure
Manufacturing employment (*qfe*)	15.1	5.2
Manufacturing output (*qo*)	44.3	5.3
Wage (*pfe*)	0.0	13.4
Labor Supply (*qo*)	60.1	0.0
Real GDP (*qgdp*)	41.4	0.1

Source: GTAP model, GTAP v.7.0 U.S. 3x3 database.

subsidy in U.S. manufacturing. Model results show that the alternative factor market closures depict very different adjustments by the U.S. economy to the same economic shock (Table 6.5). Notably, when we assume an unemployment closure, there is a large expansion of manufacturing employment and output because the total U.S. labor supply increases by 60.1 percent. However, if labor is assumed to be fully employed, then manufacturers must compete for workers with other industries in order to expand production. This competition drives up wages and increases manufacturers' cost of production – costs that must be passed on to consumers through higher prices. Manufacturing production therefore does not grow as much in the full employment scenario compared to the unemployment scenario. In addition, real GDP growth is far larger (41 percent) if previously unemployed workers can be added to the nation's stock of productive resources, compared to only .1 percent growth in real GDP when factors are already fully employed.

Factors and Structural Change

The industry structure of an economy describes the share of each industry in total national output. For example, from Table 3.3, the structure table for the United States, we know that agriculture accounts for 2 percent of U.S. GDP and services accounts for 81 percent of GDP. Industry structure is linked to factor markets in two ways. First, all else equal, an increase (decrease) in the endowment of a factor causes an increase (decrease) in the relative size of industries that are most intensive in the use of that factor. Second, a change in industry structure affects relative factor prices and factor intensities. The relative price of the factor used most intensively in expanding industries rises, and the relative price of the factor used most intensively in declining industries falls, motivating both types of firms to substitute toward the cheaper factor.

Table 6.6. *Effects of 10 Percent Increase in the Capital Endowment on the Structure of U.S. Production*

	Capital Share in Total Factor Cost	Percent Change in Output
Agriculture	54	5.7
Manufacturing	27	5.4
Services	27	2.1

Source: GTAP model with v.7.0 U.S. 3x3 database.

Let's consider the first linkage in more detail. An industry is intensive in the use of the factor that accounts for the largest share of its total factor costs. Because the increase in the supply of a factor usually lowers its price, the cost savings will be greatest for those firms that use the factor most intensively. For example, a lower capital rental rate in the U.S. economy would most benefit U.S. agriculture – the most capital-intensive sector in the United States. In the competitive economy that we assume in our CGE model, farmers can therefore lower their sales price by proportionately more than other firms can. These price changes will tend to cause demand for and production of food to increase relative to other goods, depending on consumer preferences.

We can observe this linkage in a CGE model by using the GTAP model and the U.S. 3x3 database to carry out an experiment that increases the U.S. capital supply by 10 percent. This causes the capital rental rate in the United States to decline by almost 7 percent. The greatest cost savings occur in U.S. agriculture, in which capital costs account for more than half of its total factor payments. Lower capital rents cause output to increase in all three sectors but it increases by proportionately more in agriculture than in other industries (Table 6.6).

Next, we consider the link between ***structural change*** and factor returns. The structure of a nation's output can change for many reasons. For example, over time, services have become a larger part of the U.S. economy and the role of manufacturing has diminished. Trade shocks, such as a foreign embargo on a home country's exports, or a boom in export demand, can also cause structural change in an economy's output. Government programs, such as subsidies and taxes targeted at specific industries, can cause structural change, too. Factor prices change when industries that are expanding and contracting have different factor intensities in their production technologies.

To understand why, consider a simple, two-industry country, in which the capital-intensive sector (agriculture) is expanding. The agricultural production process uses one worker and three units of capital per unit of output. The other industry (services) is labor-intensive; it uses three workers and

Table 6.7. *Effects of a 10 Percent Production Subsidy to U.S. Manufacturing and Agriculture on Factor Prices and Factor Intensities (% change from base)*

	10% Production Subsidy to:	
	Manufacturing	Agriculture
Wage (pfe_L)	13.44	0.18
Capital rent (pfe_K)	13.05	0.23
Capital/labor input ratio ($qfe_K - qfe_L$)		
Agriculture	0.06	−0.01
Manufacturing	0.45	−0.07
Services	0.47	−0.08

Source: GTAP model, GTAP v.7.0 U.S. 3x3 database.

only one unit of capital for every unit of output. If agricultural production expands by one unit, it needs to hire three new units of capital and one new worker. However, when three units of capital leave the services industry, nine workers also become available for hire. There is now an excess supply of labor in the economy, which will cause wages to fall relative to rents. As labor become cheaper than capital, the agricultural industry has an incentive to become more labor intensive by using more workers per machine (assuming its production technology allows some factor substitution). As the services industry's capital is bid away by agriculture, and with wages falling, service producers have the same incentive to become more labor intensive (assuming their technology allows it). In the new equilibrium, if all workers and capital are re-employed (the full employment assumption), then wages will have fallen relative to rents, and both industries will have become more labor intensive than they were initially.

We can observe the effects of structural change on factor returns and factor intensities in a CGE model by comparing results from two separate experiments that change the structure of U.S. production in different ways. We use the GTAP model with the U.S. 3x3 database to introduce (1) a 10 percent production subsidy to U.S. manufacturing, a labor-intensive activity, and (2) a 10 percent production subsidy to U.S. agriculture, a capital-intensive activity. For brevity, we discuss only labor and capital markets and omit discussion of the land factor.

Results, reported in Table 6.7, describe the effects of the two experiments on wages and capital rents, and on the factor intensity of production activities. Structural change that favors the labor-intensive, manufacturing industry causes the wage to rise slightly relative to capital rents, and all three production activities to become more capital intensive. Structural change that favors the capital-intensive, agriculture industry causes capital rents to rise relative to wages and all three production activities to become more labor intensive.

The impacts are far smaller in magnitude in the case of agriculture because it accounts for only a small share of U.S. economic activity.

Summary

This chapter examined several important aspects of factor market behavior in a CGE model. We first described the factor market data in the SAM, which reports the sources of factor income and factor expenditure on taxes, depreciation and the regional household account. In the CGE model, factor mobility assumptions govern the readiness of factors to change their employment in response to changing wages and rents across sectors. An economy's supply response is larger when factors are more mobile. Factor endowments are usually assumed to be in fixed supply in standard CGE models, and modelers may change factor endowments as an experiment. We learned that an increase (decrease) in the supply of a factor usually causes its price to fall (rise), but that the effect on demand for and prices of other factors depends on whether the factors are substitutes or complements in the production process. Full employment of all factors is a common assumption in CGE models, but this may not be a realistic depiction of labor markets in many countries. We described the alternative model closures of full employment and unemployment and show how they depict different adjustments by an economy to economic shocks. Finally, we examined the links between economic structure and factor markets. When a change in factor endowments causes relative factor prices to change, it changes the costs of production for industries, and leads to an expansion (contraction) in the output of industries whose costs have fallen (increased) most relative to other industries. A change in the industry structure of an economy, perhaps due to changing demand or government policies, can lead to changes in the demands for and prices of inputs when the factor intensities of industries differ.

Key Terms

Complementary factors
Effective factor endowment
Effective factor price
Elasticity of factor mobility, σ_F
Factor endowment
Factor mobility
Factor price
Factor productivity
Factor unemployment
Immobile (sector-specific) factors

Long run
Medium run
Mobile factors
Partially mobile factors
Short run
Structural change
Substitute factors
Total factor productivity

PRACTICE AND REVIEW

1. Provide real life examples of an industry with a fully mobile factor and an industry with an immobile factor. In a graph, describe and compare their supply curves and the effects of an increase in demand for their products on their output price and quantity.
2. Assume that you are an industry analyst for manufacturers who build the capital equipment used in the manufacture of computer chips. You have been asked to develop and represent an industry viewpoint on a government-funded training program for engineers who can design and produce the chips using your equipment. Explain whether the engineers and your equipment are substitutes or complements in the production of computer chips. Prepare a graph that describes the effects of the training program on the output and price of your computer chip equipment and write a short paragraph explaining your industry's position.
3. Referring to the U.S. 3x3 structure table (Table 3.4), which industries are most labor-intensive? What are the shares of each production activity in the employment of labor? Based on this information, how do you think that an increase in the production of services in the United States will affect wages and the labor/capital ratios in the three production activities?

7

Trade in a CGE Model

In this chapter, we present the building blocks for trade policy analysis using a computable general equilibrium (CGE) model. We begin by reviewing the trade data in the Social Accounting Matrix (SAM). Next, we introduce two concepts, the real exchange rate and terms of trade, and explain how they are represented in standard CGE models. We then focus on trade theory as we simulate and interpret the results of two types of shocks: A change in endowment that changes comparative advantage, and a change in world prices that changes industry structure, trade and factor returns. We study an example of "Dutch Disease," a problem that illustrates the links between a change in world prices, the real exchange rate, and industry structure. We conclude with an explanation of the role of trade and transport costs in international trade.

Since David Ricardo first developed the theory of comparative advantage, showing that nations gain from specializing in the goods that they produce at relatively lower cost, most students of economics have learned that all countries can gain from trade. Yet, many countries are reluctant to move too far or too fast toward free trade. Their reasoning is not inconsistent with Ricardo's theory. Trade and specialization lead to changes in a country's industry's structure and, in turn, to changes in the wages and rents of factors used in production. Therefore, although trade confers broad benefits on a country, it can also create winners and losers. Protecting, compensating, or managing the social and economic transition of those who lose, has led many countries to qualify or delay their commitment to global free trade.

Since the early 1990s, CGE models have been widely used to analyze trade policy issues including unilateral trade liberalization, multilateral tariff reforms through the World Trade Organization (WTO), and regional free trade agreements such as the North American Free Trade Agreement (NAFTA) and the European Union's expansion. The contributions made by CGE models rest on their ability to identify which industries will grow or could contract with freer trade, to quantify the effects on economywide employment and factor returns, and, perhaps most important, to measure

Table 7.1. *Import Data in the SAM ($U.S. billions)*

	Commodity–Import Variety			
	Agriculture	Manufacturing	Services	Total
Tax–imports	1	24	0	25
Trade margin–imports	9	47	0	56
Rest-of-world	167	1,203	230	1,601
Total	177	1,274	230	1,682

Source: GTAP v.7.0 U.S. 3x3 database.

welfare effects, which summarize the overall effects of changing trade policies on an economy's well-being.

In this chapter, we present the building blocks for trade policy analysis using a CGE model. Our objective is to show, through discussion and example, how to use trade theory to understand and interpret the economic behavior observed in a CGE model. We begin by reviewing the trade data in the SAM, which separately reports exports, imports, tariffs and export taxes, and trade margins. Next, we define two concepts, the real exchange rate and terms of trade, and demonstrate how they behave in standard CGE models. We build on these two concepts as we study two types of shocks: a change in factor endowments that changes a country's production and terms of trade, and a change in world prices that affects production and factor returns. We also study the trade and transportation costs incurred in shipping goods from the exporter to the importer, and learn how changes in these costs can influence world trade flows.

Trade Data in a SAM

Import data are reported in the SAM as an expenditure by the import variety of each commodity column account. The import data separately report spending on import tariffs, trade margin costs, and the cost of the imports (valued in foreign *fob* export prices). For example, the United States spends a total of $177 billion on imported agricultural goods (Table 7.1). Of this amount, $1 billion is spent on import tariffs, $9 billion is spent on the trade and transport margins that brought the goods from foreign ports to the United States, and $167 billion is the amount paid to agricultural exporters in the rest of the world. The United States spends a total of $1,682 on imports, of which $1,601 is paid to exporters and the remainder is spent on U.S. import tariffs and trade margin costs.

The SAM decomposes export data into spending on export taxes, the value of exported trade margin services, and the value of all other types of exported goods and services. (Table 7.2). The SAM's domestic commodity

Table 7.2. *Export Data in the SAM $U.S. billions)*

Commodity–Domestic Variety	Mfg. Commodity Domestic Variety	Trade Margin–Export	Rest-of-World
Agriculture	0	0	50
Manufacturing	0	0	756
Services	0	24	259
Savings–investment	0	32	536
Export taxes	2	0	0
Total	–	56	1,601

Source: GTAP v.7.0 U.S. 3x3 database.

column accounts pay export taxes. In the United States, only manufacturing pays export taxes, which total $2 billion. The column account for export trade margins reports the export of U.S. services to the global trade and transport industry ($24 billion). The rest-of-world column account reports foreign purchases of U.S.-produced goods and services. These total $1,065 billion ($50 + $756 + $259 billion), valued in U.S. *fob* world export prices.

The balance of trade in trade margins is a deficit of $32 billion (the difference between $56 billion spent on import margins and $24 billion of exported margin services). The trade balance in goods and services, also a deficit, is the value of exports minus the value of imports, valued in world *fob* prices: $1,065 – $1,601 = –$536 billion. Both deficits are reported as positive payments by the trade margin and rest-of-world accounts to the savings-investment row of the SAM because these are inflows of foreign savings to the United States. The total U.S. trade deficit is the sum of the two trade deficits: $568 billion.

Exchange Rates

CGE models differ in their treatment of the exchange rate. Some have a ***nominal exchange rate*** variable that describes the rate at which currencies can be exchanged for one another. Usually, it is expressed as units of domestic currency per unit of foreign currency. For example, the exchange rate (EXR) of the U.S. dollar (the domestic currency) relative to the euro (the foreign currency) is defined as the number of dollars that can be exchanged for one euro:

$$\text{EXR} = \$/\text{euro}.$$

When this type of CGE model includes country SAMs that are denominated in different currencies, the initial value of the exchange rate is the market rate that prevailed in the year corresponding to the SAM database. For example, the U.S. exchange rate would be 1.30 in a CGE model of the U.S. and the European Union with a 2010 database. More often, all SAMs in a CGE model are denominated in dollars, or the CGE model has a single country. In these cases, the modeler defines the initial value of the exchange rate as one. Model results then report the percent change in the nominal exchange rate relative to the base period.

A rise in a country's exchange rate signals home currency depreciation because more domestic currency is required in exchange for the same quantity of foreign currency. For example, a rise in the exchange rate from \$1.00/euro to \$1.30/euro means that the U.S. dollar has depreciated relative to the euro. Conversely, a fall in the exchange rate signals home currency appreciation.

This nominal exchange rate may seem like a financial variable, but remember that a standard, real CGE model does not account for financial assets or describe financial markets. Instead, the nominal exchange rate is a model variable that determines the ***real exchange rate***, which is the relative price of traded to non-traded goods.[1] Traded goods are products that are imported or exported. Non-traded goods are products that are produced by, and sold to, the domestic market.

Let's first consider the import side. Recall from our discussion of import demand in Chapter 4 that consumers buy a composite commodity, such as autos, composed of the imported and domestically produced (nontraded) varieties. A change in the nominal exchange rate variable, EXR, affects the consumer's import price, PM, of good *i*:

$$PM_i = EXR * PXW_i$$

where PXW is the global price. For clarity, we assume there are no import taxes. Since the price of the domestically produced variety, PD, does not change, a change in the exchange rate will change the price ratio PD/PM. Let's assume that EXR rises (i.e., a depreciation), then, depending on the size of the Armington import substitution elasticity, the quantity ratio of the imported to the nontraded varieties in the consumption bundle will fall.

As an example, assume that Mexico is a small country in the world market for its auto imports, facing a fixed world import price that is denominated in U.S. dollars or a basket of foreign currencies. Assume, too, that the Mexican peso depreciates. Mexican consumers now must pay more in pesos for the same number of imported autos. As imports become relatively expensive, Mexican demand will shift toward domestic models, subject to consumer preferences as described by the import substitution elasticity. Conversely, if the peso appreciates, then the cost of imported autos in terms of pesos will fall and consumption will shift toward imports.

[1] See Robinson (2006) for a more detailed discussion of the role of a nominal exchange rate variable in a standard CGE model.

Table 7.3. *Causes and Effects of a Change in the Nominal Exchange Rate Variable on Traded Quantities When the Current Account Balance is Fixed*

Cause	Change in Nominal Exchange Rate Variable	Effect on Opposite Trade Flow
Imports rise	Depreciation	Exports rise
Imports fall	Appreciation	Exports fall
Exports rise	Appreciation	Imports rise
Exports fall	Depreciation	Imports fall

Likewise, recall from our discussion of export supply in chapter 5 that some CGE models describe producers' decisions to allocate production between domestic and export sales. A change in the nominal exchange rate variable will change the *fob* export price of good *i*:

$$PE_i = EXR * PXW_i$$

For clarity, we assume there are no export taxes. For example, a rise in the nominal exchange rate variable will decrease the price ratio PD/PE. Depending on the size of the export transformation elasticity, the share of nontraded to exported varieties in the production mix will increase.

Let's assume that Mexico is small in the world market for its exports, too, and faces fixed world export prices that are denominated in foreign currency. A depreciation of the peso will therefore generate more pesos for any given quantity of exports. Mexican producers will shift their sales toward the export market, subject to technological feasibility. Conversely, exchange rate appreciation would cause a fall in peso earnings from any given quantity of exports, so producers will shift their sales toward the domestic market.

The nominal exchange rate variable may be either flexible or fixed in value, depending on the model is macro closure. In practice, modelers often assume a closure in which a flexible exchange rate variable adjusts to maintain a fixed current account balance. The current account balance is the trade balance (the *fob* value of exports minus imports) plus other international monetary flows. One reason that modelers choose this closure is because changes in the current account balance are determined in part by macroeconomic and financial forces that lie outside the scope of real CGE models. It is therefore straightforward and transparent simply to fix the current account balance at the level observed in the initial equilibrium. A second reason is that most countries today have floating exchange rates; however, this is not always the case, and this closure decision offers the modeler the ability to explore alternative exchange rate regimes.

Table 7.3 describes how a flexible exchange rate variable adjusts to equilibrate a fixed current account balance. Suppose, for example, that a country's imports increase, perhaps because the country has removed its import tariffs. Its current account balance will worsen as the value of imports grows relative to exports. The exchange rate variable will therefore depreciate, both causing export quantities to rise and dampening the increase in import quantities, until the initial current account balance is restored.

The nominal exchange rate is a macroeconomic variable because it affects the relative prices of all traded and nontraded goods by the same proportion. For example, an exchange rate depreciation of 10 percent would increase the import price of steel, autos, books, and all other imported goods by 10 percent relative to domestically-produced steel, autos, books, etc. (and assuming a fixed world price.)

Some CGE models do not have an explicit, nominal exchange rate, but they nevertheless describe a real exchange rate mechanism. In the GTAP model, for example, a change in relative factor prices across countries, variable *pfactor*, reflects changes in the relative prices of goods that are similar in effect to a change in the real exchange rate. The *pfactor* variable describes the percent change in an index of a country's factor prices relative to the world average factor price, which is the model numeraire. An increase (decrease) in the variable is similar to a real exchange rate appreciation (depreciation). For example, consider two countries (A and B) that both produce apparel. A shock that lowers economy-wide wages in country A causes its world export price of apparel to fall relative to the world export price of apparel from the higher-wage, country B. Indeed, all goods produced in country A using labor become cheaper in the world market than similar goods from country B. This will stimulate A's consumers to shift from imports toward domestic goods in their consumption, and will lead country B's consumers to shift toward imports from domestic goods. Thus, a change in this factor price exchange rate leads to adjustments that are similar to those of a nominal exchange rate depreciation by A.

Terms of Trade

Terms of trade measure the import purchasing power of a country's exports. Any change in the terms of trade therefore affects an economy's well-being, or welfare, by changing its consumption possibilities. Terms of trade are calculated as the ratio of the price of a country's export good to the price of its import good. Prices are compared in *fob* prices, exclusive of trade margins, otherwise, a change in shipping costs would appear to change the relative prices of the two goods. Import tariffs are also excluded.

As an example, consider a two-country, two-good world in which the home country (country A) exports corn to its trade partner (country B), and B exports oil to A. Country A's terms of trade is the ratio of A's *fob* export

Table 7.4. *A Two-country Example of Terms of Trade Changes*

	% Change from Base			
	A's *fob* World Export Price of Corn	B's *fob* World Export Price of Oil	A's Terms of Trade	B's Terms of Trade
Scenario 1	25	−10	35	−35
Scenario 2	−2	8	−10	10

price of corn to B's *fob* export price of oil, and vice versa. A terms-of-trade improvement for A means that the price for its corn export has increased relative to the price of its oil import. The corn price may have increased or the oil price may have fallen, or both may have changed, as long as the corn price rose relative to the oil price. A's terms-of-trade improvement means that the export earnings from each unit of its corn exports now has more import-purchasing power for oil imports.

Table 7.4 presents two numerical examples to illustrate this concept. Because the price data are reported in percentage change terms, the percentage change in a country's export price minus the percentage change in its import price measures the percentage change in its terms of trade. In scenario 1, country A experiences a terms-of-trade gain, because its export price rises relative to B's export price; but A experiences a terms-of-trade loss in scenario 2. Notice, too, that A's terms-of-trade gain is exactly equal to country B's terms-of-trade loss, so globally, the terms of trade changes sum to zero.

Countries usually export and import many types of goods with many trade partners. A global CGE model that tracks bilateral trade flows and includes the Armington assumption that goods are differentiated by origin, has as many bilateral export prices as there are countries and commodities in the model. In this case, a country's terms of trade can be calculated as a price index that is defined for either an industry or for total imports and exports. Either index is calculated as a trade-weighted sum of the home country's bilateral (*fob*) export prices relative to a trade-weighted sum of the *fob* prices of its imports. The trade weights on the export side are the quantity shares of each trade partner in the home country's export market. The weights on the import side are the quantity shares of each source country in the home country's imports.[2] Terms-of-trade changes can vary widely among countries even though, globally, the terms-of-trade changes for all countries sum to zero.

A "small" country does not experience terms-of-trade effects because its world market shares are too small for changes in its export and import quantities to affect global prices. Single-country CGE models often, but not necessarily, include the assumption that a country is small in world markets and

[2] See Chapter 2 for an example of how to calculate a trade-weighted price index.

that its world export and import prices are fixed. However, in multicountry CGE models with Armington import aggregation functions, every country is potentially "large" to some extent – even countries that we ordinarily think of as small. Therefore, all countries in a multicountry model can experience terms-of-trade changes.

An important, practical implication of the use of Armington functions in multicountry CGE models is that terms-of-trade effects are usually due to larger changes in countries' world export prices than in their import prices. This insight was developed by Brown (1987), who studied terms-of-trade effects in the multicountry Michigan Model of international trade. To understand why this is so, consider what might happen if a very small country like Israel imposes a tariff on its orange imports, causing its consumers to reduce their import quantity and consume more domestically produced oranges. Israel's bilateral world import prices for oranges will likely fall, but not by much, since Israel is only one of many customers in each of its suppliers' markets, and probably only a small one at that. However, even a small country like Israel is large in its export market because the Armington assumption, that products are differentiated by source country, implies that Israel is the monopoly supplier of Israeli oranges. Increased domestic demand reduces the supply of Israeli oranges available for export. When the quantity of Israeli orange exports declines, its world export price will rise, perhaps by a lot if its foreign customers are unwilling to substitute their domestic good for the Israeli variety. (i.e., they have a low Armington import substitution elasticity)

We explore these concepts in a CGE model by using the GTAP CGE model and the U.S. 3x3 database to run an experiment that increases the U.S. manufacturing import tariff from 1.9 percent to 15 percent. We compare the terms-of-trade results for the United States' manufacturing sector when import substitution elasticities in manufacturing for all countries are assumed to have a relatively low value of three versus a high value of ten.[3]

Experiment results related to imports show that the tariff increases the price paid by U.S. consumers for manufactured imports from the rest-of-world, and causes the U.S. import demand quantity to fall (Table 7.5). The higher the import substitution elasticity, the greater is the fall in the U.S. import quantity. The United States is a large enough customer that a decline in its import demand causes the rest-of-world's bilateral export price to fall, which contributes to a terms-of-trade gain on the U.S. import side.

[3] Note that the GTAP model includes a third stage in the consumer decision that, for a given quantity of imports, describes the sourcing of imports from among suppliers. We define identical import substitution elasticities for both levels of the model's import aggregation functions: import versus domestic, and import sourcing.

Table 7.5. *Terms of Trade Effects on U.S. Manufacturing from a 15% U.S. Tariff on Manufactured Imports (% change from base values)*

Import Substitution Elasticities	Mfg. Import Quantity (*qiw*)	Mfg. Export Quantity (*qxw*)	Bilateral ROW Mfg. Export Price to United States ($pfob_{ROW}$)	Bilateral U.S. Mfg. Export Price to ROW ($pfob_{US}$)	U.S. Terms of. Trade in Mfg. ($pfob_{US}$) – ($pfob_{FOW}$)
3	−20.82	−26.11	−0.83	3.32	4.15
10	−45.91	−46.65	−1.71	5.02	6.73

Source: GTAP model, GTAP v.7.0 U.S. 3x3 database.

On the export side, the shift in U.S. demand toward consumption of the domestic variety causes the quantity of U.S. manufacturing available for export to fall. The higher the U.S. import substitution elasticity, the larger the decline in the U.S. export quantity. The decreased availability of U.S. exports drives up the world price of U.S. manufacturing exports and leads to a U.S. terms-of-trade gain that becomes larger as the import substitution elasticities become larger.[4] On net, most of the U.S. terms-of-trade gain is attributable to an increase in the U.S. export price.

Terms-of-trade effects can be an important outcome of any type of shock to an open economy. Many CGE analyses of trade liberalization find that the terms-of-trade effects are quite large and can even dominate efficiency gains in determining the welfare effects of trade policy reform. However, even when the modeler makes the small-country assumption and fixes the terms of trade, this variable remains a relevant subject of CGE analysis because exogenous changes in the world import or export price can be introduced as an experiment. As an example, the modeler could explore the effects of an increase in the world price of a natural resource export on a small, resource-exporting country, as we do later in this chapter in our discussion of Dutch Disease.

Trade Theory in CGE Models

Economists Eli Heckscher and Bertil Ohlin developed a simple, two-good, two-factor, and two-country model to explain the relationship between countries' relative factor endowments and the composition of their trade. In their

[4] In the GTAP model, the import substitution elasticities may differ by commodity but are identical for all countries. Increasing the import demand elasticity for the U.S. contributes to a larger U.S. terms of trade gain in its export price; but the simultaneous increase in the ROW import demand elasticity also tends to reduce that terms of trade gain. A higher elasticity value makes foreign consumers more willing to substitute away from the U.S. product as the U.S. export price rises. See Brown (1987) for a discussion of terms of trade effects in the case where import demand elasticities for the same commodity differ by trade partner.

stylized model, the two countries differ only in their relative factor endowments – one has a larger endowment of labor relative to capital, and the other has a larger endowment of capital relative to labor. The ***Heckscher-Ohlin theorem*** posits that both countries will export goods that are intensive in the factors of production that are in relatively abundant supply, and import goods that are intensive in the factors of production that are in relatively scarce supply.

This powerful insight into why countries trade has yielded additional theorems about trade. Two theorems that derive from the Heckscher-Ohlin model describe the effects of changes in factor endowments on industry structure (the ***Rybczynski theorem***) and the terms-of-trade; and the effects of changes in world prices on factor returns and income distribution (the ***Stolper-Samuelson theorem***). Because both theorems focus attention on the effects of changing market conditions on economic structure and factor income, they are of special interest to CGE modelers because these are the outcomes that we largely focus on in our studies.

However, the two theorems rest on very specific assumptions that are not usually met in the more realistic, applied CGE models that we are studying. For example, in our U.S. 3x3 model, the two regions both export and import the same type of good, and their production technologies differ. In many applied CGE models, there are more factors, more industries, and (in multicountry models) more countries than in the stylized theoretical models that yield these theorems. Nevertheless, grounding our interpretation of CGE model results in these theorems remains useful. In the following sections, we show how the theorems help us to identify which model results are most relevant to consider, and how they provide us with insights that help us understand and explain our results. Results tend to be consistent with, although they do not necessarily follow directly from, the stylized models of international trade.

Factor Endowment Changes, Trade, and Terms of Trade

A country's factor endowments can change for many reasons. Over the long term, economies grow because of the gradual accumulation of factor supplies, as savings augment the capital stock and population growth increases the labor supply. Economic shocks also affect factor supplies, such as labor immigration, capital inflows, and war and disease. And, as we learned in Chapter 6, a change in productivity changes the effective endowment of a factor. Education and training, for example, increase the effective number of workers, even if the actual number of workers remains the same.

A change in factor endowments can change a country's comparative advantage and lead to changes in the types of goods that it produces and trades.

Table 7.6. *Endowment Growth and Rybczynski Effects*

Endowment Growth	Exportable Output	Importable Output	Terms of Trade
Factor used intensively in exportable	+	−	−
Factor used intensively in importable	−	+	+

In turn, changes in a country's export supply and import demand can lead to changes in its terms of trade. These ideas were developed formally by the economist Tadeusz Rybczynski (1955). He posited that a change in the endowment of one factor has two effects. First, an increase in the quantity of one factor leads to an absolute increase in the production of the good that uses that factor intensively, and an absolute decrease in production of the good that does not use it intensively, holding world prices constant (Table 7.6). This observation is known as the Rybczynski theorem. Second, if the country engages in trade and if the quantity of the endowment used intensively in its export good increases, then its export supply and import demand will increase, and its terms of trade will deteriorate. On the other hand, if the endowment used intensively in the importable good increases, then the country's imports and exports will decline, and its terms of trade will improve.

Figure 7.1 illustrates the producer's efficiency-maximizing behavior that drives the Rybczynski theorem. First, assume that there are two sectors in the economy; one that produces exportable goods and one that produces importable goods. We also assume that the exportable sector is labor intensive and the importable sector is capital intensive. The figure includes a product transformation curve, QO^1, drawn concave to the origin. It represents all possible combinations of outputs of the exportable, QE, and importable, QE, goods that can be produced with a given factor endowment. Recall from Chapter 5 that the slope of any point on a transformation curve describes the marginal rate of transformation (MRT), which is equal to the ratios of the marginal costs of the importable to the exportable: MC_M/MC_E. As the producer moves down the transformation curve and relatively more of the importable good is produced, the prices of the importable's inputs are bid up, and the ratio MC_M/MC_E increases. The lines in the figure define the relative global prices of the country's export (PXW_E) and its import (PXW_M). For now, we assume that world prices are fixed, and the country is small in world markets, so both price lines have the same slope $-PXW_M/PXW_E$. In the initial equilibrium, output is at quantity ratio QM^1/QE^1. At this tangency, the ratios $MC_M/MC_E = PXW_M/PXW_E$. Rearranging, $MC_M/PXW_M{}^1 = MC_E/PXW_E{}^1$. This means that the producer optimizes when the marginal cost per dollar earned from the sale of both goods are equal.

Text Box 7.1. Rybczynski Effects in a Global CGE Model of East Asia
"Historical Analysis of Growth and Trade Patterns in the Pacific Rim: An Evaluation of the GTAP Framework." (Gehlhar, 1997).

What is the research question? A CGE model's validity is often tested by scrutinizing assumptions about behavioral equations and their elasticity parameters. This analysis proposes a more rigorous test by asking whether the GTAP model is capable of explaining and reproducing historical trade flows.

What is the CGE model innovation? The author performs an exercise in "backcasting" (as opposed to "forecasting") by seeing whether the GTAP model can replicate historical, bilateral trade flows. Because the GTAP model is based on standard, neoclassical theory, the author chooses a backcasting exercise that the theory is capable of explaining – the link between factor endowments and the commodity composition of trade. In general, East Asian countries are observed to have had faster growth in their human and physical capital stocks over 1982–92 than developed countries and the composition of their exports has consequently shifted from labor intensive to skill and capital intensive products. The author uses the CGE model to reverse East Asia's factor endowment growth and observe model results for Rybczynski-type effects on industry structure and trade.

What is the experiment? For each country/region, four types of endowments are reduced from their 1992 levels to 1982 levels: population, labor force, human capital, and physical capital. The same experiment is carried out with (1) the default import substitution elasticities; (2) a 20 percent increase in all import elasticities; (3) a database that disaggregates the labor force into skilled and unskilled workers and (4) a combination of the human capital split and higher import substitution elasticity parameters.

What are the key findings? There is a strong correlation between countries' actual 1982 shares in world trade by commodities and the trade shares simulated by the model. The correlation is strongest when trade elasticities are relatively large and labor is divided into skilled and unskilled workers. The comparison of correlations across the four scenarios demonstrates that elasticities and labor market disaggregation by skill level are critical assumptions in terms of the model's predictive ability.

In the figure, the convex curves are consumer indifference curves that describe all possible combinations of the exportable and importable good that yield equal utility to domestic consumers. Notice that the country's utility-maximizing consumption basket is different from its optimal production mix. In this country, international trade gives consumers the opportunity to consume a larger ratio of importable to exportable goods than it produces.

An increase in the country's labor endowment shifts its export transformation curve outward to QO^2 because now more of both goods can be produced. The increase in the labor supply drives down wages, which is most cost saving

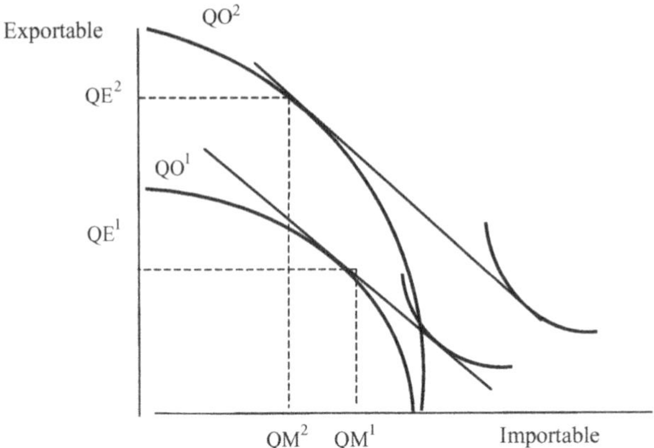

Figure 7.1. Exportable-expanding factor growth

for the exportable sector, which is relatively labor intensive. That is why the curve shifts out further on the exportable axis than on the importable axis. The fall in the wage causes MC_E to fall relative to MC_M at the initial product ratio of $Q_M{}^1$ and $Q_E{}^1$. Producers adjust by shifting toward production of the labor-intensive exportable, which drives wages back up until the marginal cost per dollar earned from exportables is again equal to that from importable production. At given world prices, the optimal production mix is now QE^2 and QM^2.

The increase in supply of exportables leads to an increase in export supply, and the decline in importable production leads to higher import demand. If we now assume that the country is large enough in world markets to affect world prices, then the world price of its exportable will fall, and the world price of its importable will rise. That is, the country's terms of trade will decline.

The effect of an increase in the capital stock, used intensively in the importable good, is analyzed in a similar fashion. In this case, production of the importable increases and import demand falls. Production of the exportable falls and export supply falls. The changes in the country's trade will lead to an improvement in its terms of trade.

This is the theoretical context for understanding the trade, and terms-of-trade, effects of CGE model experiments that increase the endowment of one factor. However, before we can explore Rybczynski effects in our CGE model, we first need to examine the U.S. 3x3 data to compare factor intensities across sectors and to identify which sectors are exportable or importable.

Based on data from the U.S. structure table (Table 3.4) on labor and capital shares in factor costs, we know that agriculture is the most capital intensive U.S. sector, and that manufacturing and services are equally labor intensive. Commodities are more exportable as the export share in production increases, and more importable as the import share of consumption increases. According to data from the U.S. structure table, manufacturing is a relatively exportable product compared to agriculture, and agriculture is relatively importable compared to manufacturing. Services are close to being a nontraded good, a possibility not considered in Rybczynski's stylized two-sector model and another example of how our applied model diverges from the strict assumptions of theory.

With this grounding in theory and in our model data, we can use the GTAP model with the U.S. 3x3 database to analyze a change in a factor endowment used intensively in the exportable sector. Our experiment is a 10-percent increase in the U.S. labor supply. The shock causes U.S. wages to fall by 1.62 percent, and capital rents to rise by 0.79 percent. On net, the U.S. experiences a real depreciation because its factor price index falls 0.91 percent relative to those in the rest of the world. Other results, reported in Table 7.7, are consistent with the Rybczynski effects. Production increases by more in the exportable sector (manufactures) than in the importable sector (agriculture) although output in both sectors increases because growth in the U.S. labor supply increases the productive capacity of its economy. Exports increase by more in the exportable than in the importable sector, but exports by both sectors increase. Imports increase by more in the importable than in the exportable sector, but imports increase in both.

Price results, too, are consistent with Rybczynski effects. The U.S. world export price declines most in the exportable sector and its import price increases most in agriculture. The Rybczynski prediction that the overall terms of trade will decline is also supported by our model.

World Price Changes and Factor Income Distribution

What happens to a country's wages and capital rents when world prices change? The Stolper-Samuelson theorem predicts that in a two-good economy, a change in the relative prices of goods will lead to a change in relative factor prices and the distribution of national income. The price of the factor used intensively in the production of the good whose relative price has risen will increase. The price of the factor used intensively in the production of the good whose relative price has decreased will fall.

The reasoning is as follows: An increase in the world price of one good will cause an economy's production to shift toward increased production of that good and away from production of the other good. If each industry employs a different mix of factors, then the composition of the economywide demand for factors will shift, leading to a change in relative factor prices.

Table 7.7. *Effects of a 10 Percent Increase in the U.S. Labor Supply (% change from base values)*

	Base Data: Initial Labor Share in Factor Costs	Output (qo)	Exports (qxw)	Imports (qiw)	World Price of U.S.: Export ($pfob_{US}$)	World Price of U.S.: Imports ($pfob_{ROW}$)	World Price of U.S.: Terms of Trade ($pfob_{us} - pfob_{row}$)
Agriculture	.32	7.18	5.73	5.51	−.26	.39	−.65
Manufacturing	.73	7.32	6.82	3.57	−.70	.35	−1.05
Services	.73	7.06	4.38	4.71	−.90	.38	−1.28

Note: Elasticity of factor substitution is four in all sectors.
Source: GTAP model, U.S. GTAP v.7.0 3x3 database.

Text Box 7.2. Stolper-Samuelson vs. Migration Effects in NAFTA
"Wage Changes in a U.S.-Mexico Free Trade Area: Migration versus Stolper-Samuelson Effects." Burfisher, Robinson, Thierfelder (1994).

What is the research question? Much of the debate over NAFTA reflected concerns about potential wage changes as described by the Stolper-Samuelson theorem (SST). The theorem suggests that NAFTA will lower unskilled wages in the United States and raise those in Mexico as free trade causes the exports and prices of Mexico's unskilled labor intensive exports to increase, and the production and price of these goods in the United States to fall. However, wages in both countries are also influenced by the impact of NAFTA in increasing labor migration flows within Mexico and between Mexico and the United States. Could an applied CGE model of a free trade agreement between the United States and Mexico predict the wage effects from both SST effects and migration?

What is the CGE model innovation? The authors develop a CGE model of the United States and Mexico that allows labor migration between the two countries in response to changes in relative wages. The model also includes tariffs, and domestic taxes and subsidies that are not directly affected by the NAFTA accord and which create a second-best environment that violates many of the assumptions of the SST.

What is the experiment? The model experiments describe tariff elimination between the United States and Mexico in (1) a realistic model with tax distortions and (2) a distortion-free model that replicates some (but not all) of the assumptions of the SST. A trade liberalization experiment is run in the model without migration to explore SST effects, and in the model with labor migration to describe combined SST and factor endowment effects.

What are the key findings? The SST effects are found to be empirically very small, and labor migration has the dominant influence on wages in the free trade area, in some cases reversing the wage changes that would be expected based on the SST alone.

As an example, let's assume that the world price of agriculture (a capital-intensive good) has increased relative to the world price of manufactures (a labor-intensive good). To expand agricultural output, farmers must hire capital and labor from the manufacturing industry. As the manufacturing industry contracts, it releases both labor and capital, but the proportion of labor is too high and the proportion of capital is too low relative to the demands of agriculture. Given its scarcity, the increased demand for capital will push capital rents up while the surplus of labor will push wages down.

We depict these changes in the economywide demand for capital and labor in Figures 7.2a and 7.2b. In the figures, K describes the economy's supply of

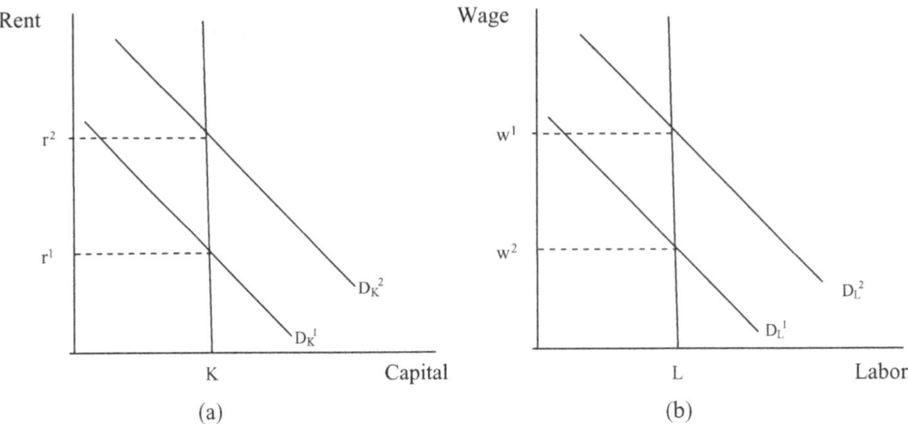

Figure 7.2. (a) Increase in economywide demand for capital due to an increase in the world price of the capital-intensive good. (b) Decrease in economywide demand for labor due to an increase in the world price of the capital-intensive good

capital, and L describes its supply of labor. Both supply curves are vertical because we assume fixed endowment quantities that are fully employed. In the initial equilibrium in Figure 7.2a, $D_K{}^1$ is the demand for capital and r^1 is the initial equilibrium rental rate. A shift in industry structure toward the capital-intensive industry increases the economywide demand for capital to $D_K{}^2$, causing the rental rate to increase to r^2. In the initial equilibrium in Figure 7.2b, $D_L{}^1$ is the demand for labor and w^1 is the equilibrium wage The shift in the country's industry structure toward the capital-intensive good causes the economywide demand for labor to fall to $D_L{}^2$ and the wage to decline to w^2.

We can use the Stolper-Samuelson theorem to understand the results of CGE model experiments that change world prices. As an example, we use the GTAP model with the U.S. 3x3 database to run an experiment that increases the world price of manufacturing by 10 percent. Based on our structure table in Chapter 3, we already know that U.S. manufacturing is relatively labor intensive. We might therefore expect that the increased world price of the manufactured good will lead to an increase in the U.S. wage relative to land or capital rents.

In our experiment, we find that that the production mix in the United States shifts toward manufacturing. Its output quantity increases 4.3 percent. Production of both agriculture and services decline. The shift toward production of a labor intensive product causes the U.S. wage to increase 7.7 percent, returns to capital to increase 7.5 percent, and the rental rate on land to decline 25.6 percent. The difference in impacts between wages and capital rents are very small but they are consistent with the predictions of the Stolper-Samuelson theorem.

Text Box 7.3. "Dutch Disease" in Cameroon
"The 'Dutch' Disease in a Developing Country: Oil Reserves in Cameroon."
(Benjamin, Devarajan, and Weiner, 1989)

What is the research question? Rising oil and gas prices confer substantial wealth on exporters of natural resources but these revenues can be a mixed blessing because they have the potential to cause deindustrialization, an unwelcome structural change known as "Dutch Disease." Most analyses of Dutch Disease have studied developed countries; how might a booming natural resource sector affect a developing country?

What is the CGE model innovation? The authors use a single-country CGE model of Cameroon that captures three key features of its economy: (1) agriculture, rather than manufacturing, is the traditional export sector (2) manufactured imports are imperfect substitutes for domestic varieties (i.e., they assume an Armington import aggregation function); and (3) the oil sector is an enclave so that, except for generating income, it has weak links to the rest of the Cameroonian economy.

What is the experiment? A boom in Cameroon's oil export industry is simulated as a $500 million inflow of foreign savings; an amount equal to its foreign oil export earnings in 1982.

What are the key findings? Similar to the experience of developed countries, Cameroon's economy experiences a structural change when its oil sector booms. Because the oil sector is an enclave, structural change is due mostly to the spending effect, as higher oil revenues increase incomes and demand, instead of the resource movement effect that pulls resources into oil production. However, instead of the deindustrialization that characterizes Dutch Disease, it is Cameroon's traditional agricultural sector that contracts.

Booming Sector, Dutch Disease

An increase in the world price of a country's export good would seem to offer it windfall benefits, but it can also lead to "deindustrialization," a problem that has received a great deal of attention from economists. This type of change in the production structure of an economy following an export boom has become known as ***Dutch Disease***, a reference to the deindustrialization that occurred in the Netherlands following its discovery of natural gas. The process was described more generally by Corden and Neary (1982) as the effects of a booming sector on the rest of the economy. Their analysis of an increase in the world price of a country's export is of interest to CGE modelers because it illustrates both the effects of a terms-of-trade shock on the country's industry structure as well as macroeconomic feedback through real exchange rate appreciation. Both are general equilibrium effects that CGE models are well-suited to analyze. (See Text Box 7.3.)

The Cordon-Neary model assumes a country with three sectors, capital that is fixed in each industry, and a labor force that is mobile among all three industries. Two sectors are traded – we'll call one of them oil (the booming sector) and call the other sector manufacturing. The third sector is services (including products like haircuts and lawn care), which are not traded. The country is small, so the prices of its oil and manufacturing are set by world markets. The price of its services is determined by domestic supply and demand.

A boom in the price of its oil export has two effects. The ***resource movement effect*** describes the reallocation of productive resources toward the booming sector. The increase in the export price enables the export sector to attract labor from manufacturing and services by paying higher wages. The country's industry structure then changes as the booming sector expands and output of services and manufacturing falls. Hence, the country begins to deindustrialize.

The ***spending effect*** results from the income growth due to higher export earnings. Higher income causes consumer demand for both services and manufactured goods to increase. Demand growth for manufactures can be met by increasing imports at the fixed world price but increased demand for services, which are not traded, can only be met by increasing domestic production. The spending effect therefore leads to further deindustrialization due to competition by the expanding services' sector for the resources used in manufacturing.

Both the resource movement effect and the spending effect lead to real exchange rate appreciation. The real exchange rate is the price of domestic services (a nontraded good) relative to manufactures (a traded good with a fixed world price). The fall in the supply of services in the resource movement effect creates a scarcity that causes the price of services to rise relative to the price of manufacturing. The spending effect leads to increased demand for services and an additional increase in the price of services relative to manufacturing. Because exchange rate appreciation makes imports more affordable, the appreciation linked to the spending and resource effects also contributes to increased imports and the decline in production of manufacturing.

To explore the Dutch Disease effects of a change in world prices in a CGE model, we use the GTAP CGE model with the U.S. 3x3 database to simulate a 10 percent increase in the world price of U.S. manufacturing (the booming sector). Our CGE model does not conform to all of the assumptions in the stylized model developed by Cordon and Neary. For example, our model includes intermediate demand and there is two-way trade in all three goods. Yet, the Dutch Disease framework remains useful because it informs us that the key effects of a boom (or bust) in world export prices are observed in changes in a country's industry structure, its real exchange rate, and trade.

Table 7.8. *Dutch Disease: 10 Percent Increase in the Rest-of-World Price of Manufacturing (% change from base values)*

	Production (*qo*)	Imports (*qiw*)	Exports (*qwx*)
Agriculture	−6.8	15.7	−34.5
Manufacturing	4.3	−4.8	15.6
Services	−0.7	14.4	−21.6

Source: GTAP model, U.S. GTAP v.7.0 3x3 database.

Based on the Dutch Disease model, we offer this prognosis for the U.S. economy: Output of U.S. manufacturing (the booming sector) will increase and agricultural output will decrease. However, the effect on output of services is ambiguous because the spending effect will tend to increase its output, but the resource movement and exchange rate appreciation will tend to decrease its output. We also expect that the U.S. real exchange rate will appreciate, causing foreign demand for all U.S. exports to fall, and U.S. demand for all imports to rise.

Results, reported in Table 7.8, show evidence of "disease" – the structural change that crowds out production in the nonbooming sectors. Output in the booming U.S. manufacturing sector increases, but output falls in both agriculture and services. The factor price exchange rate appreciates of almost 8 percent. U.S. import demand therefore increases for agriculture and services, but note that manufacturing imports fall. This is because the higher world price causes U.S. consumers to shift their demand toward the cheaper, domestic variety of manufactured goods. Exports of both agriculture and services fall because lower domestic production reduces the supply available for exports, and because exchange rate appreciation reduces foreign demand.

Trade and Transportation Margins in International Trade

Many multicountry CGE models and their underlying SAM databases explicitly account for the trade and transportation margin costs incurred in international trade. These costs include land, air, and sea freight costs, plus insurance and any other handling charges that are required to ship goods from the exporter's port to that of the importer. Trade and transport margins drive a wedge between the price received by the exporter and the price paid by the importer, and therefore can affect the quantity of trade. For example, the substantial decline in shipping costs since the 1950s is considered to be an important factor in explaining the rapid expansion of global trade over the

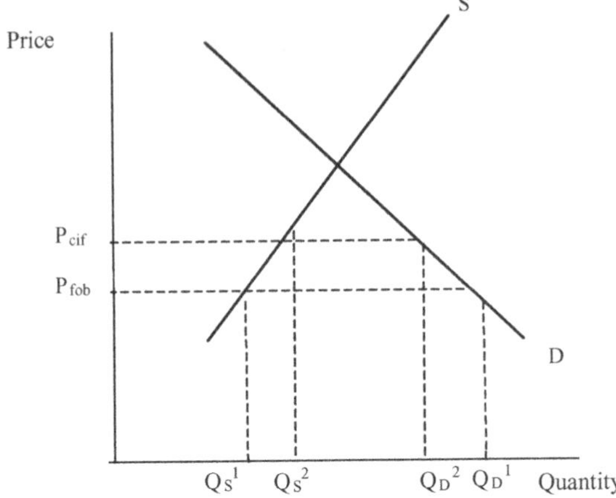

Figure 7.3. Import demand with trade and transport costs

past several decades.[5] There also can be shocks to shipping costs, which multi-country CGE models are well-suited to analyze. For example, Sullivan (2010) studied the effects of piracy off the East African coast that raised insurance and shipping costs for some commodities traded between certain partners. Jabara, Burfisher, and Ingersoll (2008) analyzed the bilateral trade effects of U.S. restrictions on the use of wood pallets to prevent the transoceanic introduction of invasive pests.

The effects of trade and transport margins on the quantity and prices of traded goods are illustrated in Figure 7.3, which describes a country's domestic supply and demand for good Q. In the figure, S is the small country's supply curve for the domestic production of Q, and D is its demand curve for the composite good, Q. Absent any margin costs, the country would produce Q_S^1 and import quantity $Q_D^1 - Q_S^1$ at a world price of P_{fob}. However, the inclusion of trade and transport margins increases the import price to P_{cif}, reducing the import quantity to $Q_D^2 - Q_S^2$ and causing domestic production to increase to Q_S^2. A shock that causes a change in margin costs would change the size of the trade margin cost per unit, $P_{cif} - P_{fob}$, and thus affect production and import quantities.

We explore the role of trade and transport margins in a CGE model by using the GTAP CGE model and the U.S. 3x3 database to run an experiment that reduces the margin costs on all U.S. imports. First, consider the initial import margin costs reported in the U.S. 3x3 SAM and replicated in Table 7.9. Margin services increase the cost of agricultural imports by 5.4 percent relative to their *fob* cost, and increase the cost of manufactured imports

[5] Hummels (2007), for example, found that U.S. air shipping costs declined by over 90 percent between 1955 and 2004, and ocean transport costs fell from 10 percent to 6 percent of import values over the past 30 years.

Table 7.9. *Effects of a Decline in Trade Margin Costs on U.S. Imports*

	Agriculture	Manufacturing
Base data		
Imports at *fob* price	167	1,203
Imports at *cif* price	176	1,250
Trade and transport margin	9	47
Trade margin rate	5.4	3.90
50% increase in productivity in trade margins (*atd*)		
U.S. import price *pcif* (% change)	−1.66	−1.25
U.S. import quantity *qiw* (% change)	2.61	2.66
U.S. production quantity *qo* (% change)	−0.79	−0.28
ROW export price *pfob* (% change)	0.06	0.01

Note: Trade margin rate is the trade margin cost as a percent of the *fob* value of imports.
Source: GTAP model, GTAP v.7.0 U.S. 3x3 database.

by 3.9 percent. Margin services are only required for trade in goods, not in services.

We model a reduction in the cost of margins as a 50-percent increase in productivity in trade margin services used for U.S. imports. This lowers the U.S. *cif* import prices for both goods, causing their import quantities to increase and their domestic production to fall. Notice that in our multicountry CGE model, the exporters' *fob* prices increase as a result of higher U.S. import demand, so U.S. *cif* import prices do not fall by the full amount of the reduction in margin costs. The benefits from the fall in margin costs therefore are split between the importer (the United States) and the exporter. The division of benefits of lower margin costs (or the burden of higher margin costs) between exporters and importers depends on the relative elasticities of the exporter's supply and the importer's demand.

Summary

Trade data in the SAM report trade valued in *fob* prices, import tariffs, export taxes, and the costs of trade and transport margins used in the international shipment of goods. Our discussion of trade behavior in a CGE model began by defining two concepts: the exchange rate and the terms of trade. The treatment of exchange rates differs among CGE models. The terms of trade measure a country's export prices relative to its import prices and describe the purchasing power of a country's export earnings. Terms of trade are thus a component in measuring changes in a nation's welfare. We used trade theory to ground our analyses of trade shocks in our CGE model. First, we relied on the Rybczynski theorem to explain the effects of an increase in a factor endowment on the commodity composition of trade and the subsequent effects on the terms of trade. The Stolper-Samuelson theorem informed our analysis of the effects of a change in world prices on a country's industry structure and factor prices. Our study of Dutch Disease explored a common problem in the world economy, in which a country experiences a change in its terms of trade (a boom or a bust for its main export) that causes changes in its industry structure. Finally, we explained how trade and transport margin costs affect trade volumes and world prices.

Key Terms

Dutch Disease
Heckscher-Ohlin theorem
Nominal exchange rate
Real exchange rate
Resource movement effect
Rybczynski theorem
Terms of trade
Spending effect
Stolper-Samuelson theorem

PRACTICE AND REVIEW

1. Suppose that technological innovation increases a country's capital productivity. It has two industries with the characteristics shown in Table 7.10:
   a. Which sector is capital intensive and which is labor intensive?
   b. How will the production of each sector be affected by an increase in capital productivity? Explain why.
   c. Which sector is exportable and which is importable?
   d. How do you expect imports and exports to be affected by the increase in capital productivity? How will this change in trade be likely to affect the terms of trade?
2. Venezuela is a developing country that derives much of its export earnings from oil. Use the Dutch Disease framework to explain the possible effects on production and trade of its nonoil industries following of a sudden hike in oil prices,

Table 7.10. *Industry Characteristics*

Industry	Capital Quantity	Labor Quantity	Production Quantity	Export Share of Production	Import Share of Consumption
Wine	142	1220	100	.50	.10
Televisions	97	25	100	.25	.40

Table 7.11. *Terms of Trade Exercises*

	U.S. Corn Exports		U.S. Oil Imports	
	Brazil	China	Saudi Arabia	Canada
Percent change in price	6	4	4	1
Market share	.6	.4	.8	.2

similar to that seen in summer 2008. What are the public policy issues that your analysis raises for Venezuelan policy makers?

3. Assume that a shock in world markets results in the price changes described in the Table 7.11. Using the information on market shares, calculate (1) the trade-weighted U.S. world export price (2) the trade-weighted U.S. world (*fob*) import price and (3) its terms-of-trade. Has the U.S. terms of trade improved or deteriorated?

8

Taxes in a CGE Model

This chapter examines the treatment of trade and domestic taxes in a computable general equilibrium (CGE) model. Trade taxes are imposed on imports and exports of goods and services. Domestic taxes are taxes paid by production activities on output and factor use and by purchasers on sales of intermediate and retail goods, and income taxes. We trace the tax data in a Social Accounting Matrix (SAM) to describe the agent and the economic activity on which the tax is levied and the amount of revenue generated by each tax; we also show how to use the SAM's data to calculate tax rates. Simple partial equilibrium diagrams then illustrate the theoretical effects of taxes on economic activity and economic efficiency. The results of tax policy experiments using a CGE model support the theoretical predictions and offer additional insight into their economywide effects.

The large federal deficit in the United States in 2011 has spurred intense debate on whether the sizeable tax cuts enacted by the previous administration should be maintained or allowed to lapse. Taxes influence the behavior of an economy's consumers and producers in important ways. CGE models have proven to be a valuable tool for researchers in empirically and comprehensively analyzing how taxes affect households' and firms' economic decisions, and therefore the economy as a whole.

Governments impose taxes for many reasons. Foremost is the need to raise revenue to support the provision of public goods such as national defense and education. Governments sometimes use taxes to redress market failures such as externalities. For example, the government may impose carbon taxes to reduce the harm to public health that is associated with air pollution by private industry. Governments may impose "sin taxes" on goods or activities such as alcohol, tobacco, and gambling to discourage private behaviors deemed to be socially offensive or costly. Most governments tax imports to protect or promote selected industries, and sometimes they tax exports. Governments also use taxes to achieve societal goals, such as income equality. In this case, governments redistribute income by imposing high taxes on high-income households while giving tax credits or income transfers to low-income households.

Taxes impose burdens on the private sector. The ***direct burden*** of a tax is the amount of tax revenue that it generates. A 5 percent sales tax on groceries, for example, imposes a direct burden of five cents for every dollar spent on groceries. The direct burden of taxation is not a loss to the economy because each tax dollar is a transfer of spending power from the tax payer to the government, absent any administrative costs.

Taxes deserve special scrutiny because they often lead to an ***excess burden***, which is the loss in economic efficiency when producers and consumers change the quantities that they produce or consume in order to avoid paying a tax. For example, the 5 percent sales tax on groceries may cause consumers to buy fewer groceries and more of other, untaxed goods that they enjoy less. The change in their consumption bundle is inefficient, given the nation's productive resources and consumer preferences. Tax-distorted consumption and production are an excess burden of taxes that is above and beyond the direct burden of paying the tax. Economists call these inefficiencies a ***deadweight loss*** because these foregone opportunities are not recouped elsewhere in the economy.

CGE models are especially useful for tax policy analysis because they can quantify both the direct (tax revenue) and excess (efficiency effects) burdens of taxes. Because the models are economywide, they also capture potential interactions among all taxes in an economy. This is important because governments typically impose many types and levels of taxes at the same time. Sometimes a tax or subsidy is actually beneficial, in the sense that it offsets the inefficiencies caused by another tax. For example, the introduction of a production subsidy to manufacturers may offset efficiency losses that result from a sales tax on their purchases of inputs. Of course, the overall impact of taxes on an economy also depends on the gains to society from the government spending that is funded by the tax. Keep in mind that societal gains, such as national security or cleaner air, are not readily monetized or generally accounted for in a typical CGE model, unless the economist adapts the model for that purpose.

We categorize taxes into five broad types for the discussion that follows:

- *Trade taxes* are levied on imports and exports.
- *Production taxes* are paid by production activities based on their output.
- *Sales taxes* are paid by domestic firms on their intermediate input purchases, and by consumers and investors on their purchases of final goods and services.
- *Factor use taxes* are paid by production activities based on their factor inputs.
- *Income taxes* are paid by factors or households based on income earned from wages and rents.

The first four taxes are ***indirect taxes*** because they are levied on the production or purchase of goods or factors. By comparison, ***direct taxes***, primarily income taxes, are levied on factors or individuals. Indirect taxes are also distinguished from direct taxes because their burden potentially can be shifted onto someone else, which is not possible with direct taxes. ***Tax incidence*** describes how the burden of paying for indirect taxes is shared among buyers and sellers after prices and wages adjust. For example, when a firm pays a tax to the government based on the value or quantity of its output (a production tax), the tax burden may be shifted, in whole or in part, to consumers, by charging higher retail prices. Individuals cannot similarly shift their income tax burden to others.

For each of the five taxes, we first trace the relevant data in the SAM. A review of the tax data is a useful starting point for any CGE-based tax analysis because the SAM identifies the agent in the model who pays the tax and the production or consumption decision on which the tax is assumed to be levied. For example, a tax on land use that is reported in agriculture's production activity column is paid by the producer and it increases farmers' costs of production. Raising or lowering that tax will directly affect producers' level of output (shifting their supply curve left or right). However, if that same land tax is instead recorded as an expense in the land factor's column, then it is a direct tax, much the same as Social Security or other transfer payments. Raising or lowering the tax will affect households' after-tax income and consumer demand. Placement of tax data in the SAM therefore reveals a great deal about how the tax is assumed to affect economic activity in the CGE model. Economists sometimes have stiff debates over how to represent a particular tax in a CGE model because this decision, similar to model closure rules, predetermines model outcomes.

We focus next on the economic analysis of taxes in a CGE model. We begin by developing simple partial equilibrium theories on taxation that help us to formulate our expectations about the effect of each tax in our general equilibrium model. Graphical analyses of trade taxes include their terms-of-trade effects but analyses of other taxes assume closed or small economies, with no terms-of-trade changes. These graphical analyses emphasize the direct burden (i.e., tax revenues) and the excess burden (i.e., the efficiency losses) associated with most taxes. The excess burdens appear in the graphs as "Harberger triangles," named after the economist, Alfred Harberger (1964), who refined this approach to measuring the efficiency waste caused by taxes.

With this foundation in data and theory, we are equipped to explore the effects of each type of tax in a CGE model. We start by creating a distortion-free version of the U.S. 3x3 CGE model, to provide a baseline or benchmark

Text Box 8.1. Welfare Decomposition in the GTAP Model

Decomposing Welfare Changes in the GTAP Model. (Huff and Hertel, 2000; McDougall, 2006).

The GTAP model contains a utility developed by Huff and Hertel (2000) and McDougall (2003) that decomposes the sources of the total, equivalent variation welfare effect of model experiments. The welfare effect is a money metric measure of the value of the effects of price changes on real consumption and savings in a region. Its decomposition allows a researcher to identify welfare contributions by commodity, factor, and tax type, and to account for second-best effects. The decomposition describes these six components:

- *allocative efficiency effect* – the excess burden of each tax;
- *endowment effect* – due to changes in quantities of factors of production (e.g., labor and capital), which change an economy's productive capacity;
- *technology effect* – due to changes in the productivity of factors and/or intermediate inputs, which change an economy's effective endowments and productive capacity;
- *commodity terms of-trade effect* – due to changes in the economy's world (*fob*) prices of exported goods and services relative to its world (*fob*) prices of imported goods and services;
- *investment-savings terms-of-trade effect* – due to a change in the price of domestically produced capital investment goods relative to the price of savings in the global bank; and
- *preference change effect* – due to changes in the shares of private consumption, government, and savings in national spending.

for our analysis. A distortion-free base model allows us to isolate the effects of each tax without the complexities that its interactions with other taxes in the economy can introduce. We then introduce each individual tax as a shock to this model and compare the model results to our theoretical predictions. Our discussion of model results focuses first on those variables that we highlight in our partial equilibrium analyses. Then, we consider selected general equilibrium results. Although these differ somewhat for each tax, we generally emphasize changes in the commodity composition of consumer baskets, industry output and trade flows, and in the terms of trade and national welfare (see Text Box 8.1).

Last, we return to our original U.S. 3x3 database and CGE model, in which there are many existing tax distortions. Tax experiments using this more realistic model allow us to explore how taxes interact and lead to second best outcomes. We also study the welfare effects of a small change in a complex tax system.

Table 8.1. *Import Tariffs and Imports From The U.S. 3x3 SAM*

Data in $U.S. Billion or Percent	Agriculture	Manufactures	Services
Import tariff revenue	1	24	0
Imports (value in *fob* prices)	167	1203	230
Import trade margins	9	47	0
Import tariff rate	0.5	1.9	0.0

Source: GTAP v.7.0 U.S. 3x3 SAM.

Trade Taxes

Import Tariffs

Import tariffs are taxes that are levied on the quantity or value of imported goods and services. Import tariffs are levied in one of two ways. ***Specific*** tariffs are paid per unit of import, such as $1 dollar per barrel of oil. Specific tariff payments grow in proportion to quantity, so that the import tariff on two barrels would cost $2 dollars and the tariff on three barrels would cost $3 dollars, and so on. Specific tariff payments do not change when prices change; for example, the importer pays $1 dollar per barrel regardless of whether oil costs $25 or $125.

Ad valorem tariffs are levied as a percentage of the *cif* import value (which includes trade margin costs). For example, a 5 percent *ad valorem* import tariff on a handkerchief with an import value of $1 increases its cost to $1.05. If the hanky's *cif* import value increases to $2, its cost, including the tariff, would be $2.10. In this case, tariff revenue for the single handkerchief increases from five cents to ten cents following the change in its price.

Import tariffs are paid by the import varieties of the commodity columns of the SAM to the import tariff row account. The tariff increases the cost of imported goods so all categories of intermediate and final demand that consume imports ultimately pay the tariff. Table 8.1 reports the import tariff revenue and the value of imports from the U.S. 3x3 SAM. We calculate *ad valorem* import tariff rates as:

import tariff revenue/*cif* value of imports * 100.

The U.S. *ad valorem* tariff rate on agriculture is therefore:

$$\$1 \text{ billion}/(\$167 \text{ billion} + \$9 \text{ billion}) * 100$$
$$= 0.5 \text{ percent (adjusted for rounding)}$$

The U.S. tariff rate is highest on imports of manufactured goods (1.9 percent) and lowest on services (approximately zero).

Figure 8.1 illustrates the economic effects an *ad valorem* import tariff on a large economy. In the figure, S describes the foreign supply of the imported

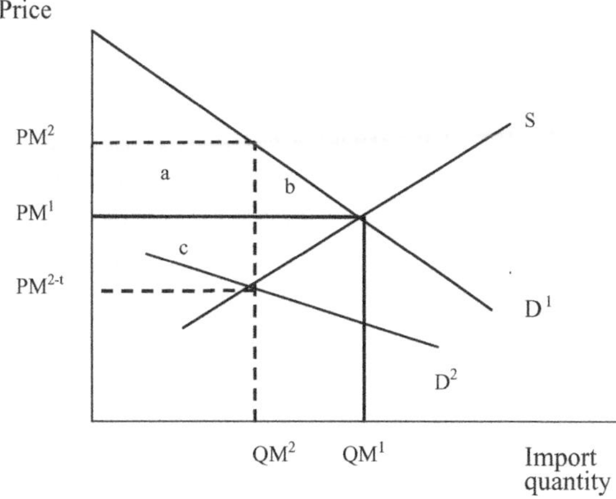

Figure 8.1. Effects of an import tariff on the importer

good. Given the Armington assumption that goods are differentiated by country of origin, there is no domestic production of the imported variety. D^1 is a compensated demand curve that describes the duty-free demand for imports by domestic consumers.[1] In the initial market equilibrium, the *cif* price of imports is PM^1 and the import quantity is QM^1.

The introduction of an import tariff adds an additional cost, *t*, to the import price, which shifts the demand curve downward to D^2. In the new equilibrium, consumers pay a higher domestic price of PM^2, which is the *cif* world import price plus the tariff, *t;* the import quantity declines to QM^2; and the import price net of the tariff falls to PM^{2-t}.

The tariff has three effects on the importing country. The direct burden of the tariff, shown as area $a + c$, is the amount of tariff revenue paid by consumers to the government on imports of quantity QM^2. Tariff revenue redistributes purchasing power from consumers to the government, so this area is not a loss to the economy.

The second effect is the excess burden on the importer, shown as area *b*. It represents a consumption inefficiency because consumers who would have been willing to purchase QM^1-QM^2 imports at the free market price no longer can do so. The difference between the price that consumers are willing to pay and the market price is the consumer's "surplus." For example,

[1] This type of demand curve implies that the government compensates consumers dollar for dollar for their tariff expenditure, either through a lump-sum transfer of income or other mechanism. This compensation assumption is common in tax policy analysis. It allows economists to attribute all quantity changes to the substitution effect (which is the excess burden) because the compensation cancels any income effects of the tax. In other words, this approach keeps the consumer on the same indifference curve by holding income constant and describes only the substitution along the curve when the tax changes relative prices. See Ballard and Fullerton (1992) for a survey of this approach in the economics literature and Technical Appendix 8.1 for more details.

at QM^2, a consumer who would have been willing to pay PM^2 actually paid only PM^1 at free trade prices, and so gained a surplus on that unit of $PM^2 - PM^1$. The sum of the surpluses enjoyed by consumers on all units up to QM^1, purchased at free trade prices, is the triangular area between PM^1 and D^1. The trapezoid formed by areas *a* plus *b* is the sum of the consumer surplus that is lost when consumers reduce their import consumption to QM^2 and pay the higher price of PM^2. Because the foregone surplus shown by area *a* is transferred to the government as a part of the tax revenue, the remaining area, *b*, is the loss in consumer surplus that is not recouped elsewhere in the economy.

For large countries, there may also be terms-of-trade effects as described by area *c*. Our example in Figure 8.1 shows a terms-of-trade gain for the importer because the decline in its import demand causes the import price, excluding the tariff, to fall from PM^1 to PM^{2-t}. The size of its terms-of-trade gain depends on the slope of the import supply curve. In general, the lower the foreign export supply elasticity (i.e., the steeper is the slope of the import supply curve), the larger the importer's terms-of-trade gain from a tariff. If the importing country is too small in the exporter's market to affect its export price, then the foreign supply curve is horizontal. In this case, the import price remains at PM^1 and there is no terms-of-trade effect.

The terms-of-trade effect, like the direct burden, redistributes purchasing power. In this case, purchasing power is redistributed from foreigners to domestic consumers. In effect, the lower price accepted by foreigners compensates consumers for area *c* of their tariff payment to the government so the domestic price increases by less than the full amount of the tariff. The terms-of-trade gain to the importer, area *c*, is a loss of import purchasing power by the exporting country.

Because tax revenue simply redistributes national income, the change in national welfare includes only the excess burden, or efficiency effect, of the tariff plus its terms-of-trade effect. Therefore, the net effect on the importer's welfare depends on whether its consumption efficiency loss, shown by area *b*, is greater than its terms-of-trade gain, area *c*. The effect on the exporter's welfare is unambiguously a loss, shown by its terms-of-trade decline, area *c*.

The figure also illustrates how tariffs diminish global welfare. The loss in global welfare is the sum of countries' efficiency losses, shown in our case as the importer's area *b*. Terms-of-trade effects are not included in a measure of global welfare. Because one country's terms-of-trade loss is equal to its partner's terms-of-trade gain, this price effect just redistributes purchasing power among countries, similar to the domestic redistribution of tariff revenue. Redistribution does not affect global welfare as long as we assume – as we do in standard CGE models – that income has the same value, regardless of its distribution among consumers, governments or countries. In a more sophisticated analysis, we might choose to relax this assumption to reflect

Table 8.2. *Effects of 15 Percent Import Tariff on Manufacturing Imports to the United States*

U.S. manufacturing	
Tariff revenue ($U.S. billion) (NETAXES)	134.7
Import quantity (*qiw*) (% change)	−20.1
Bilateral import price from ROW (% change) ($pfob_{ROW}$)	−1.3
Terms of trade (% change) ($pfob_{US}-pfob_{ROW}$)	5.6
Domestic market price of import (% change) (*pim*)	13.6
Efficiency effect. (U.S. $billion)	−15.6
Welfare ($U.S. billion)	
U.S. welfare	54.9
Rest-of-world welfare	−73.1
World welfare	−18.2
Selected general equilibrium effects in United States (% change)	
Bilateral export price of mfg, to ROW ($pfob_{US}$)	4.3
Factor price exchange rate (*pfactor*)	3.5
Exports of agriculture (*qxw*)	−22.5
Exports of manufactures (*qxw*)	−29.6
Exports of services (*qxw*)	−15.8

Source: GTAP model, U.S. 3x3 v.7.0 with taxes removed to create a distortion-free base model.

different valuations across market participants, depending, for example, on their initial levels of income. Arguably, another dollar might mean more to consumers in countries with very few dollars to start with than it does to someone who has a great many.

By studying the theory of import tariffs before we carry out a CGE model experiment, we can identify the results that are most relevant to consider and to report in our discussion, and we can develop expectations about their direction of change. With this foundation, we are ready to study a CGE analysis of the introduction of an import tariff in one industry. Our experiment is the introduction of a 15 percent import tariff by the United States on imports of manufactures. For this and most other tax experiments, we use the Global Trade Analysis Project (GTAP) model with a distortion-free U.S. 3x3 database.[2]

Results of the import tariff experiment, reported in Table 8.2, are consistent with the qualitative results shown in Figure 8.1. A contribution of our CGE model analysis is that it enables us to quantify these impacts. The tariff's direct burden is the import tariff revenue for the U.S. government of $135 billion. The quantity of U.S. manufacturing imports fall by 20 percent, contributing to a terms-of-trade gain for the United States as its import price falls by 1.3 percent. As a result, the domestic price of imports increases by less than

[2] We create a distortion-free base model using GTAP's Altertax utility to update all U.S. taxes and subsidies in the U.S. 3x3 model to zero.

the full amount of the tariff. The excess burden, or deadweight efficiency loss, related to manufacturing totals $15.6 billion dollars.

Our CGE analysis also takes into account general equilibrium effects that lie outside the scope of our theoretical, partial equilibrium model. First, we consider the manufacturing terms-of-trade effect. Recall from our discussion in Chapter 6 that the terms of trade depends on changes in both the import and export price. Our CGE-based analysis finds that the U.S. import tariff increases domestic demand for the U.S. variety and causes U.S. manufactured exports to fall by almost 30 percent. This results in a 4.3 percent increase in the U.S. *fob* world export price for manufactures. Thus, changes in *both* the U.S. import and export prices account for the nearly 6 percent improvement in the U.S. terms of trade in manufactures.

The import tariff on manufactured goods affects U.S. industry structure because an expanding manufacturing sector competes with other industries for productive resources. This competition causes U.S. wages and rents to rise relative to those in the rest-of-world. This is similar to a real exchange rate appreciation and it makes all U.S. goods relatively expensive on world markets. Both resource competition and real appreciation contribute to a decline in U.S. production and exports of agriculture and services, and an increase in U.S. imports of these goods. These changes in trade flows, too, contribute to an aggregate U.S. terms-of-trade gain and a total U.S. welfare gain of $55 billion. World welfare, which measures the efficiency losses due to the tariff, declines by more than $18 billion.

Export Taxes

Export taxes lower the price received by the producer on sales to the world market. Countries sometimes impose export taxes to ensure that adequate supplies of vital goods, such as foodstuffs or strategic minerals, remain available for the home market. For example, if a producer sells wheat for $1 per bushel in both the domestic market and foreign markets, a 10 percent export tax will lower his export price to ninety cents. An export tax therefore encourages producers to shift their sales from the export market to the domestic market – or to shift into the production of other goods and services.

Export taxes are reported in the SAM as an expenditure from the domestic variety of the commodity column account to the export tax row. Exports in *fob* prices, which include export taxes, are reported in the rest-of-world column account as a purchase from the domestic commodity account row. Data in the U.S. 3x3 SAM report an export tax of $2 billion on U.S. manufacturing exports of $756 billion.

We calculate the export tax or subsidy rate as:

Export tax revenue/value of export in world *fob* price * 100

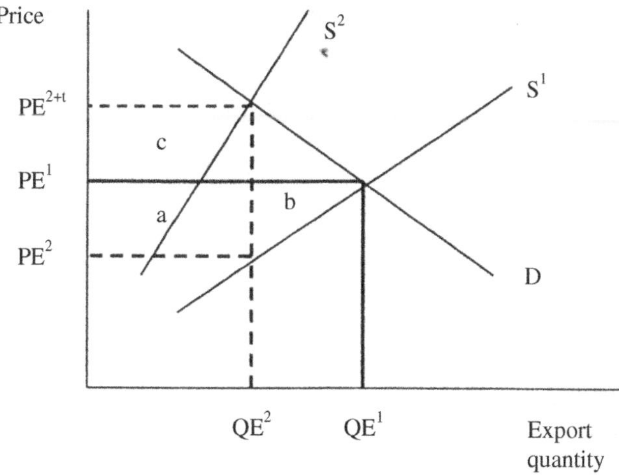

Figure 8.2. Effects of an export tax on the exporter

For example, the export tax rate on U.S. manufacturing exports is:

$$\$2/\$756 \text{ billion} * 100 = 0.3 \text{ percent}$$

Figure 8.2 illustrates the market effects of an *ad valorem* export tax. Although the graph looks similar to Figure 8.1, note carefully that the definitions of the supply and demand curves are different. In this case, S^1 describes the home country's supply of exports to the world market. Because we assume that products are differentiated by country of destination, there is no domestic demand for the export variety. D describes foreign demand for the home country's exports, QE. In the initial equilibrium, quantity QE^1 is exported at the *fob* export price of PE^1. The introduction of an export tax lowers the producer price to PE^2, and shifts the export supply curve backward to S^2. In the new equilibrium, export sales decline to QE^2 and foreign buyers pay price PE^{2+t}.

Similar to import tariffs, export taxes have three effects on the exporting country. The direct burden is the amount of export tax revenue that is transferred from producers to the government, shown as area $a + c$. The excess burden, or efficiency effect, in the exporting country is described by area b. Production is inefficient because the marginal cost of producing the foregone output $QE^1 - QE^2$, shown by the pretax supply curve, is less than the price that foreigners are willing to pay. Another way to think about it is that, before the tax, the marginal cost to produce QE^2 was PE^2 but producers sold it for PE^1, gaining a producer "surplus" for that unit of $PE^1 - PE^2$. The sum of these surpluses over all units of production up to QE^1 is total producer surplus, shown by the triangular area between PE^1 and S^1. The tax causes producers to lose producer surplus described by the trapezoid area of $a + b$. Area a is transferred to the government as tax revenue but area b is a deadweight loss, in excess of the tax burden, that is not recouped elsewhere in the economy.

Table 8.3. *Effects of 15 Percent Export Tax on U.S. Manufactures*

U.S. Manufacturing	
Tariff revenue ($U.S. billion) (NETAXES)	67.6
Efficiency effect (U.S. $billion)	−26.1
Export quantity (*qxw*) (% change)	−44.8
Producer price (*ps*) (% change)	−4.4
Production (*qo*) (% change)	−4.8
World export price ($pfob_{US}$) (% change)	12.7
Terms of trade (% change) ($pfob_{US} - pfob_{ROW}$)	13.9
Welfare ($U.S. billion)	
U.S. welfare	−22.6
Rest-of-world welfare	−1.9
World welfare	−24.5
Selected general equilibrium effects in the United States (% change)	
World (*fob*) import price ($pfob_{ROW}$) (% change)	−1.3
Import quantity of manufacturing (*qiw*)	−18.0
Export quantity of agriculture (*qxw*)	42.6
Exports quantity of services (*qxw*)	29.4
Factor price exchange rate (*pfactor*)	−5.7

Source: GTAP model, U.S. 3x3 v.7.0 with taxes removed to create a distortion-free base model.

The third effect is the terms-of-trade gain, area *c*, which measures the redistribution of purchasing power from foreigners to domestic producers because the reduction in export supply causes the export price to rise from PE^1 to PE^{2+t}. This transfer compensates producers for part of their revenue transfer to the government; in effect, producers have passed on part of the export tax burden to foreign importers through an increase in their export price. In this case, we assume a large country exporter, consistent with the Armington assumption that every country is large country in its export market. A small country (as in many single-country CGE models) would face a horizontal world demand curve, and the producer's price would fall by the full amount of the export tax.

The net effect on the exporter's welfare depends on whether its efficiency loss, area *b,* is larger than its terms-of-trade gain, area *c*. The effect on the importing country's welfare is unambiguously a loss, shown by area *c.* The loss in global welfare, too, is unambiguously negative; it is the sum of all countries' efficiency losses, which in this case is area *b.*

To explore the effects of an export tax on one industry in a CGE model, we use the GTAP model with the distortion-free U.S. 3x3 database to run an experiment that introduces a 15 percent export tax on U.S. manufacturing. We find a direct burden, the export tax revenue, of $67.6 billion and an excess burden, the efficiency loss in manufacturing, of $26.1 billion (Table 8.3). The

Table 8.4. *Production Taxes in The U.S. 3x3 SAM ($U.S. billions)*

	Agriculture	Manufactures	Services
Production tax	4	42	423
Gross value of production	434	5,227	14,974
Production tax rate	1.0	0.8	2.8

Source: GTAP v.7.0 U.S. 3x3 database.

U.S. export quantity falls almost 45 percent, but this yields a U.S. terms-of-trade gain in manufacturing. The U.S. world export price increases nearly 13 percent, so the producer price falls by only 4.4 percent

Our general equilibrium model yields additional insights into the effect of the tax. Because most are the mirror image of the effects of the import tariff, we leave it as an exercise for you to explain the effects of a decline in U.S. manufacturing production and exports on industry structure, trade flows, U.S. terms of trade, and U.S. and world welfare.

Production Taxes

Producers pay production taxes on the basis of the value or quantity of their output. These taxes are a part of their costs of production. For example, U.S. companies engaged in oil and natural gas production pay a wide variety of production-based taxes to state, federal, and local governments. These taxes raise their production costs. Production taxes can also be negative (i.e., subsidies). For example, many countries provide tax credits or direct subsidies based on the production of agricultural products.

In the SAM, the production activities' column accounts pay these taxes to the production tax row account. Table 8.4 displays these row and column accounts from the U.S. 3x3 SAM.

We calculate production tax rates (or subsidies) as:

$$\text{Production tax/gross value of production} * 100.$$

For example, the production tax rate for U.S. services is:

$$423/14{,}974 * 100 = 2.8.\ \text{percent}$$

Figure 8.3a illustrates the market effects of an *ad valorem* production tax. In the figure, the initial market supply curve, S_1, describes domestic production and the compensated demand curve, D, describes consumer demand. P^1 and QO^1 are the initial market equilibrium price and quantity, respectively. The introduction of a production tax shifts the industry supply curve inward to S^2. This results in a higher market equilibrium price P^{2+t} for consumers, a

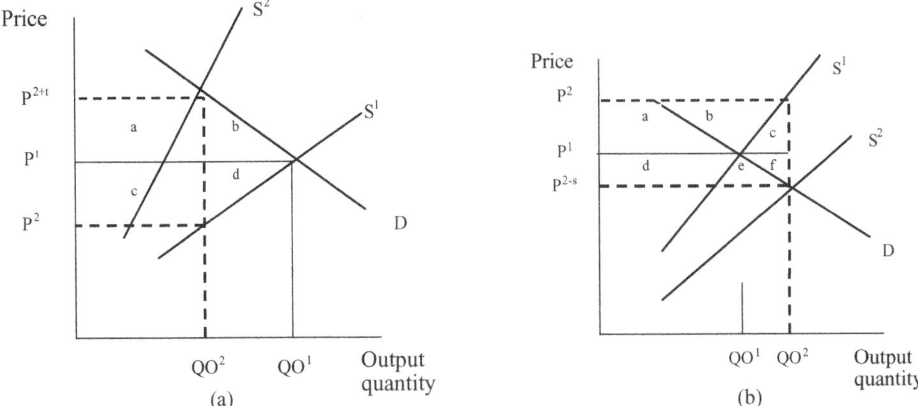

Figure 8.3.(a) Market effects of a production tax. (b) Market effects of a production subsidy

lower after-tax price for producers, P^2, and a fall in the equilibrium quantity of supply and demand to QO^2.

The direct burden of the production tax is area $a + c$, which is the tax revenue paid by producers to the government. Areas $a + b$ are the loss of consumer surplus and areas $c + d$ are the loss of producer surplus due to the tax. Because areas $a + c$ are recouped by the government as tax revenue, the excess burden is the combined loss in consumption efficiency, area *b*, and production efficiency, area *d*.

Areas *a* and *c* also describe the incidence of the production tax. The figure illustrates that, although producers actually pay the tax, the burden of paying for it is shared with consumers because producers have been able to raise their (gross of tax) sales price from P^1 to P^{2+t}. As you can see from the figure, the size of the tax revenue and its incidence are determined by the slopes of the supply and demand curves, which in turn are determined by the elasticities of supply and demand. If demand is perfectly elastic (a horizontal demand curve), then the consumer price would remain at P^1 and producers would absorb the full cost of the tax. If supply is perfectly elastic (a horizontal supply curve), then consumers would absorb the full cost of the tax.

Many countries subsidize rather than tax their producers. The analysis of a production subsidy differs in some respects from the analysis of a tax. In Figure 8.3b, the introduction of an *ad valorem* output subsidy shifts the supply curve outward to S^2. The new equilibrium output increases to QO^2, the consumer price falls to P^{2-s}, and the price received by producers increases to P^2.

In the case of a subsidy, the direct burden falls on the government because the subsidy is a transfer from the government to producers and consumers, instead of tax revenue for the government. In the figure, government spending is the sum of areas $a + b + c + d + e + f$. However, the subsidy increases

Table 8.5. *Effects of a 15 Percent Production Tax on U.S. Manufactures*

Manufacturing (% change from base)	
Production tax revenue (NETAXES)	655.0
Efficiency losses in mfg.	60.2
Production quantity (*qo*)	−15.0
Private household demand (*qpd*)	−19.0
Producer price (*ps*)	−3.2
Private household consumer price (*ppd*)	12.9
Selected general equilibrium results (% change from base)	
Manufacturing export quantity (*qxw*)	−32.1
Manufacturing import quantity (*qiw*)	6.4
Terms of trade in manufacturing ($pfob_{US} - pfob_{ROW}$)	6.7
Wages (*pfe*)	−15.4
Capital Rents (*pfe*)	−15.1
Agricultural production (*qo*)	13.2
Services production (*qo*)	2.7
Welfare ($U.S. billion) (EV)	−121.3

Source: GTAP model, U.S. 3x3 v.7.0 with taxes removed to create a distortion-free base model.

consumer surplus only by areas $d + e$ and increases producer surplus only by areas $a + b$. The increased quantity of production and consumption is inefficient because at quantities that exceed QO^1, the marginal benefit to consumers of each additional unit is less than the marginal cost of its production. This inefficiency is described by areas $c + f$, which is the excess burden of the subsidy.

With these insights from our partial equilibrium models, we turn to an examination of the effects of a production tax in one industry in a CGE model. Our experiment is the introduction of a 15 percent production tax on U.S. manufacturing output. We find that the direct burden is the manufacturing production tax revenue of $655 billion and the excess burden is a $60 billion loss in efficiency due to a 15 percent decline in manufacturing output and a 19 percent decline in consumer demand (Table 8.5). The 3.2 percent fall in the producer price and the 13 percent increase in the consumer price tell us that the tax burden has been shared between U.S. producers and consumers, but that most has been passed on to consumers.

Our CGE model also describes the general equilibrium effects of the tax. In the manufacturing sector, lower domestic production reduces its demand for inputs and causes economywide wages and rents to fall. Lower factor prices encourage agricultural and services production and exports to increase. Manufactured exports decline sharply, causing the manufacturing terms of trade improve. The total U.S. welfare effect, which combines efficiency loss and all terms-of-trade effects is a loss of $121 billion.

Table 8.6. *Sales Taxes on Household Purchases of Domestically Produced Variety*

	Household
Purchases ($U.S. billion)	
Agriculture	60
Manufactures	1,104
Services	6,392
Sales tax ($U.S. billion)	
Agriculture	2
Manufactures	115
Services	41
Sales tax rate (%)	
Agriculture	4
Manufactures	10
Services	1

Source: GTAP v.7.0 U.S. 3x3 database.

Sales (and Intermediate Input) Taxes

Sales taxes are paid by domestic final demand (households, investment, and sometimes government) on purchases of commodities used for consumption or investment. Production activities pay sales taxes on their purchases of intermediate inputs. The sales taxes are a part of their cost of production. Foreigners do not pay other countries' sales taxes, so a country's exports do not generate sales tax revenue.

In many countries, sales tax rates vary by commodity and type of buyer. In the United States, for example, consumers usually pay sizeable sales taxes on their purchases of autos but often pay little or no sales tax on their grocery purchases. Private household consumers pay sales taxes on many products while sales taxes on these same goods are waived for entities like churches and other nonprofit organizations. Negative sales taxes, like other negative taxes in the SAM, denote subsidies. They reduce the cost of a purchase. Some common examples of subsidies are food stamps, which low-income households can apply to their food purchases, or rebates on farmers' purchases of intermediate inputs, like fertilizer.

The SAM reports sales taxes as a payment from the column account of the purchaser to the sales tax row account for each purchased good. As an example, Table 8.6 reports data from the U.S. 3x3 SAM on private households' sales taxes on their purchase of the domestically produced variety of each commodity. These total $158 billion ($2 billion + $115 billion + $41 billion) on purchases of agriculture, manufactures, and services.

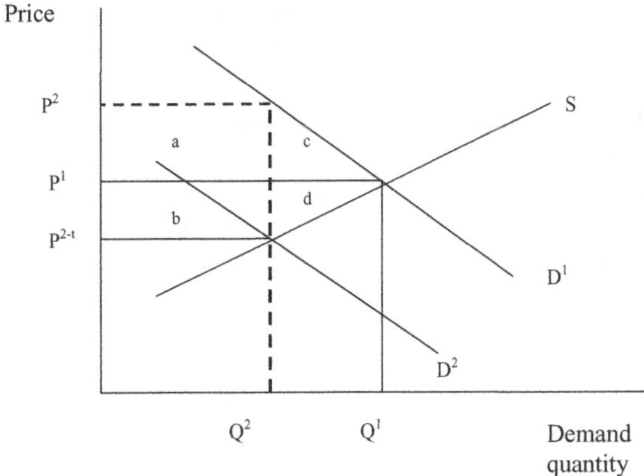

Figure 8.4. Effects of a sales tax on the domestic market

Sales tax rates are calculated as the ratio of the tax to the pretax value of the sale:

commodity sales tax/pretax value of commodity purchase ∗ 100.

For example, the tax rate on households' purchases of domestic manufactured goods is calculated as:

$$115/1{,}104 * 100 = 10.4 \text{ percent.}$$

Firms' payment of a sales tax or their receipt of a subsidy on purchases of intermediate inputs are called an intermediate input tax or subsidy. The effects of input taxes or subsidies on the output of a firm are identical to those of a production tax or subsidy, shown in Figures 8.3a and 8.3b, so we do not reproduce that analysis here.[3]

Figure 8.4 describes the effect of a specific (per unit) sales tax on the domestic supply and compensated demand for a final good, Q. In the figure, D^1 is the initial compensated demand curve and S is the supply curve for the domestic production of Q that is sold in the domestic market. Q^1 is the initial market equilibrium quantity, and P^1 is the initial market equilibrium price. The sales tax shifts the demand curve inward to D^2. The new market equilibrium is at quantity Q^2 where consumers pay the tax-inclusive sales price of P^2 and producers receive price P^{2-t}.

The direct burden of the tax is shown by area *a* + *b,* which is the amount of sales tax revenue collected by the government on sales of Q^2. Although the tax is paid by consumers, the figure shows that the burden is shared with producers due to the decline in the producer price from P^1 to P^{2-t}. The excess burden of the tax, described by areas *c* + *d,* measures the loss in

[3] The effects are identical if we assume fixed Leontief intermediate input-output coefficients, which is a common assumption in CGE models.

Table 8.7. *Effects of 15 Percent Sales Tax Rate on Household Purchases of the Domestic Manufacturing Commodity*

U.S. Manufacturing	
Sales tax revenue ($U.S. billion)	122.6
Efficiency loss ($U.S. billion)	12.9
Household consumption (*qpd*) (% change)	–17.9
Production quantity (*qo*) (% change)	–2.8
Consumer price (*pd*) (% change)	14.1
Producer price (*ps*) (% change)	–0.8
Selected general equilibrium effects	
Agriculture domestic sales (% change) (*qpd*)	0.5
Manufacturing domestic sales (% change) (*qpd*)	–4.7
Services domestic sales (% change) (*qpd*)	0.8
Agricultural production (*qo*)	0.6
Services production (*qo*)	0.6
Manufacturing export quantity (*qxw*)	7.5
Manufacturing import quantity (*qiw*)	5.6
U.S. welfare ($U.S. billion)	–29.7

Source: GTAP model, GTAP v.7.0 U.S. 3x3 database with taxes removed to create a distortion-free base model.

consumer and producer surplus as the market equilibrium quantity falls by $Q^1 - Q^2$. The decline in consumption and production is inefficient because the marginal benefit to consumers of each additional unit between $Q^1 - Q^2$ exceeds its marginal cost of production.

To explore the effects of a sales tax on one commodity in a CGE model, we carry out an experiment that imposes a 15 percent sales tax on households' purchases of the domestic variety of the manufactured commodity. We use the GTAP CGE model with the distortion-free U.S. 3x3 database. We find that the direct burden of the sales tax is a tax revenue of $123 billion (Table 8.7). Its excess burden is an efficiency loss in manufacturing of nearly $13 billion as both the quantity of household demand and production fall. The consumer price increases by nearly the full amount of the tax but the producer price declines only slightly – indicating that U.S. consumers bear most of the burden of the tax.

Once again, we also consider selected general equilibrium effects of the tax. For this tax, we focus on the role of demand shifts in influencing industry structure. The sales tax changes the relative prices of consumer goods, causing private households to change the commodity composition of their baskets. When they reduce their consumption of domestic manufactures, they increase their consumption of domestically produced agriculture and services. Production in these two sectors therefore increases as manufacturing output falls.

Table 8.8. *Factor Use Taxes in the United States in Agriculture and Manufacturing*

	Agriculture	Manufacturing
Factor payment ($U.S. billion)		
Land	34	0
Labor	68	1,109
Capital	122	467
Factor use tax ($U.S. billion)		
Land	−3	0
Labor	5	166
Capital	−1	15
Factor use tax rate (%)		
Land.	−9	0
Labor	7	15
Capital	−1	3

Source: GTAP v.7.0 U.S. 3x3 database.

Trade flows are also an important part of this tax's impacts. On the import side, the sales tax on the domestic variety causes the imported variety to become relatively cheaper, which increases the quantity of manufactured imports demanded by U.S. households. On the export side, the fall in U.S. demand for the domestic supply increases the quantity available for export; causing exports to rise. The changes in both trade flows contribute to a decline in the U.S. terms of trade in manufacturing. U.S. terms of trade in the other two sectors also fall as their production and export supply increase. Total terms-of-trade losses, combined with efficiency losses, cause U.S. welfare to decline by $30 billion due to the sales tax.

Factor Use Taxes

Producers pay taxes or receive subsidies based on the quantity of factors (e.g., labor, capital, and land) that they employ in their production process, or on the value of their factor payments. Data on factor use taxes are reported in the production activity column of the SAM as a payment to the factor use tax row. Factor tax rates are calculated for each factor in each industry as:

$$\text{factor tax/pretax factor payment} * 100.$$

We report these data for the agricultural and manufacturing activities from the U.S. SAM in Table 8.8. For example, in the U.S. 3x3 SAM, the factor tax rate for land used in agriculture is:

$$-3/34 * 100 = -9 \text{ percent.}$$

Note that the rate is negative, which means that U.S. farmers receive a subsidy on land use.

It is not unusual for different governmental entities within the same country to impose simultaneous factor use taxes and subsidies on the same factor. For example, landowners may pay a real estate tax to their state or local government and, if they are farmers using the land for agricultural purposes, they may also receive an acreage-based subsidy, based on the very same parcel of land, from the federal government. Thus, factor use tax data may report the combined costs of different tax programs.

Sometimes factor use taxes are uniform across industries, such as the Social Security tax that is paid as a percentage of wages by all employers in the United States. Uniform factor use taxes or subsidies do not influence the distribution of factor employment across industries. However, it is often the case that factor taxes differ among industries or by use, such as different real estate tax rates for commercial and residential zones. In the U.S. SAM, for example, the 7 percent tax rate on labor used in agriculture, reported in Table 8.8, is lower than the 15 percent tax rate on labor employed in manufacturing. In this case, the factor use tax changes the relative costs of production in the two industries, discouraging employment and production in the industry with the higher tax.

Factor use taxes also typically differ by factor. For example, an industry's corporate tax rate on capital services may be quite high relative to its payroll tax. Tax rates on land, labor, and capital in U.S. agriculture, reported in Table 8.8, illustrate this point. Agriculture's land and capital inputs are subsidized, but its use of labor is taxed. When factor use tax rates differ by factor then – if the production technology allows it – this, too, can lead to a misallocation of factors. Those factors whose employment is taxed will be under-used and those factors that are subsidized will be over-used relative to their most efficient level of employment in each industry.

The effect of a factor use tax on industry output is similar to that of a production tax, as already shown in Figures 8.3a and 8.3b, so we do not replicate that analysis here.[4] Instead, we direct our attention to a general equilibrium analysis of a factor use tax on one factor in one industry on factor use and output in all industries. Figure 8.5 describes the effects of a factor tax – in this case a tax on labor – on the allocation of the workforce in a two-factor, two-sector model. The economy's two sectors are agriculture and manufacturing, and its two factors are labor and capital. In this beaker diagram, a rightward movement from the left origin on the horizontal axis indicates an

[4] Like a production tax, a factor tax increases the cost of production and shifts the supply curve inward. However, a factor use tax can have a smaller impact on production costs than an equivalently-sized production tax if producers can substitute away from the taxed factor within the value-added bundle.

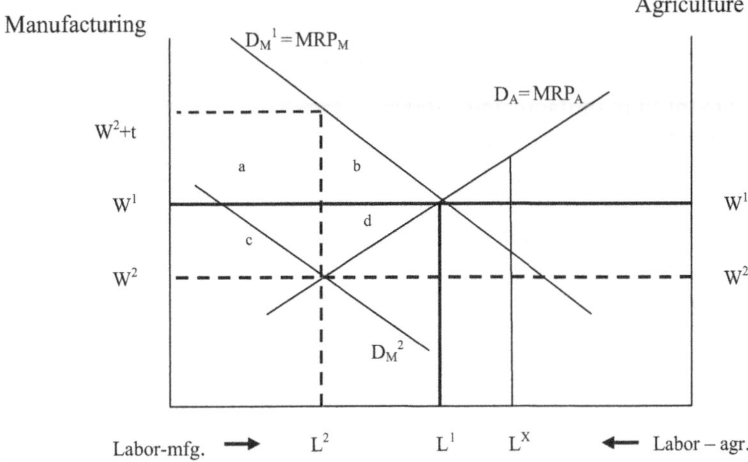

Figure 8.5. Effects of a factor tax on the economywide labor market

increase in the employment of labor in manufacturing and a leftward movement from the right origin describes an increase in the employment of labor in agriculture. Employment in the two sectors sums to L, the total labor force.

An assumption of the model is that labor is fully mobile across the two sectors, but that capital is fixed in each industry at its initial quantity. This assumption means that the theoretical model describes adjustment over a shorter time frame than in the CGE models with fully mobile factors that we mostly have usually used for demonstration. The industry demand curves for labor by the manufacturing (D_M^1), and agricultural (D_A) sectors are downward sloping. This reflects the assumption that the marginal revenue product (MRP) of labor (the additional revenue earned from the addition of one more worker) declines in both industries as the quantity of labor increases relative to the fixed quantity of capital. The MRP of each industry describes the wage that a firm is willing to pay. For example, as the ratio of farm workers to a fixed number of tractors increases from zero to L, moving leftward on the horizontal axis, the marginal revenue product and wage of each additional farm worker in agriculture gradually falls.

In the initial equilibrium, employment is allocated across the two industries at L^1. This allocation of labor equalizes the wage across the two industries at w^1, the economywide wage. Suppose the economy were not at equilibrium, and instead had a labor allocation such as L^X. At this point, the MRP of labor in agriculture, which is the vertical height of the intersection of L^X and D_A exceeds that in manufacturing. Agriculture's higher wage will attract labor into agriculture. The decline in the ratio of workers to capital in manufacturing will cause an increase in labor's MRP in manufacturing sector and the higher labor-capital ratio in agriculture relative will lower the MRP

Table 8.9. *Effects of a 15 Percent Tax on Labor Used in U.S. Manufacturing*

Effects on Industries (% change from base)	
Employment in manufacturing (*qfe*)	−4.7
Employment in agriculture (*qfe*)	1.8
Employment in services (*qfe*)	0.9
Economywide wage (*ps*)	−5.2
Wage (including tax) in manufacturing (*pfe*)	2.9
Agricultural production (*qo*)	0.6
Manufacturing production (*qo*)	−3.4
Services production (*qo*)	0.7
Government revenue ($U.S. billion) (NETAXES)	159.1
Efficiency loss ($U.S. billion)	−3.4
Welfare (EV) ($U.S. billion)	−24.7

Source: GTAP model, GTAP v.7.0 U.S. 3x3 database with fixed capital stocks and taxes removed to create a distortion-free base model.

of farm labor until the MRP of labor in both industries equalize at L^1 and wage w^1.

The introduction of a specific (per worker) labor use tax in manufacturing shifts manufacturers' after-tax labor demand curve downward, to $D_M{}^2$. As the manufacturing wage falls, labor moves from manufacturing into agricultural employment. At the new equilibrium, the employment allocation is L^2, the economywide wage falls to w^2, and manufacturers pay a wage plus tax of w^{2+t}. The wage is now lower in manufacturing because the tax reduces its demand for labor, and it is lower in agriculture because the increase in its labor force causes the MRP of its workers to decline.

The direct burden of the factor use tax is the sum of rectangles $a + c$, which is the amount of tax revenue generated by the employment of L^2 workers in manufacturing. The excess burden of the tax related to manufacturing is the sum of triangles $b + d$. Labor employment in manufacturing is now inefficiently low because the marginal product of each additional worker between L^2 and L^1 exceeds its marginal cost, measured by curve D_A.

We simulate a factor use tax in one sector in a CGE model by conducting an experiment that introduces a 15 percent tax on labor employed in U.S. manufacturing. We use the GTAP model with the distortion-free U.S. 3x3 database. We assume that the capital stock employed in each industry is fixed, but that labor is fully mobile among sectors. Our CGE model differs from our theoretical model because it has a third factor of production, land. Similar to capital, we assume that a fixed quantity of land is employed in agriculture. For brevity, we do not include land in our discussion of results.

Consistent with our theoretical model, the labor tax raises employers' cost per worker in manufacturing and reduces their labor demand (Table 8.9). In the new equilibrium, manufacturing employment falls by 5 percent. Higher agricultural and services employment, with declining labor productivity in those two industries, also contribute to a decline in the economy-wide wage of more than 5 percent. Yet, manufacturers pay an after-tax wage that is 2.9 percent higher. Increased agricultural and services employment also contribute to a change in the industrial structure of the economy. Agriculture and services output increase while manufacturing output declines.

Our CGE model quantifies the direct and excess burdens illustrated in Figure 8.5. The direct burden of the tax is $159.1 billion. The excess burden, or efficiency effect, in manufacturing is a loss of nearly $4 billion. The national welfare effect includes both the efficiency loss and a deterioration in the U.S. terms of trade, resulting in a total U.S. welfare loss of nearly $25 billion.

Income Taxes

Income taxes, also called direct taxes in CGE models, are paid by factors of production or by households, usually as a percentage of their income from land rents, wages, and capital returns. Income taxes differ in an important respect from the indirect taxes discussed previously. Because they are not imposed directly on goods and services, they do not alter relative market prices. They do not make textiles and apparel more or less expensive than food, for example. Because they do not directly influence relative prices, they therefore are generally less distorting of production and consumption decisions, and therefore of economic efficiency, than indirect taxes.

Income taxes do affect things like after-tax, or net, wage. When income taxes lower net wages, some people may choose to work less and spend more time on leisure activities. A decline in net wages can also motivate some people to work more hours, instead of less, if they need the additional earnings to compensate for the fall in their after-tax income. Income taxes, in addition, affect the rate of return on savings and may cause households to change their allocation of income between consumption and savings. This is an intertemporal distortion because it changes the timing and amount of consumption over a lifetime and the availability of savings for investments in future production. Income taxes also can influence households' investment allocations if tax rates differ among asset classes as they do in the case of interest income and capital gains. For these reasons, income taxes are likely to distort some household decisions.

These impacts of income taxes on labor supply, and on savings and investment decisions, though very important, are not accounted for in the standard CGE model that we are studying. Dynamic, multiperiod CGE models are needed to analyze the intertemporal effects of income taxes, and a labor-supply response must be incorporated to analyze the tax's effects on

Text Box 8.2. U.S. Tax Reform in a Dynamic Overlapping-Generations CGE Model
"Simulating the Dynamic Macroeconomic and Microeconomic Effects of the FAIR Tax." (Jokisch and Kotlikoff, 2005).

What is the research question? The Fair Tax is a proposal to replace the U.S. federal payroll tax, personal income tax, corporate income tax, and estate tax with a progressive federal retail sales tax on consumption. Given the aging of America's aging population, which will lead to growing health and pension costs, could adoption of the FAIR Tax Act preclude the need for higher taxes to fund these liabilities, and even lead to welfare gains?

What is the model innovation? The authors' dynamic, overlapping generations, CGE model captures detailed demographic characteristics of the U.S. economy, including age- and year-specific projections for three income classes of households within each generation (e.g., mortality rates, pension benefits, health costs). The model also includes year-specific projections of government revenue and expenditure.

What is the experiment? The authors model the Fair Tax as the replacement of most federal taxes by a progressive federal retail sales tax on consumption of 23 percent (i.e., it increases a sales price of $1 to $1.23). The plan includes a tax rebate whose size depends on households' characteristics and an increase in Social Security benefits to maintain their real purchasing power. Their tax plan reduces non-Social Security federal expenditures to help pay for the Fair Tax rebate.

What are the key findings? The Fair Tax almost doubles the U.S. capital stock by the end of the century and raise long-run real wages by 19 percent compared to the base case alternative. The winners from this reform are primarily those who are least well off, and large welfare gains accrue to future generations.

individuals' labor-leisure trade-off. A prominent example of a CGE model with both of these features was developed by Auerbach and Kotlikoff (1987) and used to analyze U.S. tax policies. A subsequent version of this model, developed by Jokisch and Kotlikoff (2005) and summarized in Text Box 8.2, was used to analyze the FAIR Act. (The FAIR Act is a plan to replace most types of U.S. taxes with a single sales tax on consumers.) Equity considerations of income taxes and income subsidies are other dimensions not typically addressed in a standard CGE model. Nevertheless, standard CGE models must still account for income taxes, even if in a rather simplified way, because they are a part of the flow of national income and spending.

However, even among standard, static CGE models, the presentation of income tax data in a SAM, and its treatment in the corresponding CGE model, may differ in meaningful ways. For this tax in particular, it is important to study your SAM in order to understand how the tax is assumed to affect

Table 8.10. *Income Tax Data in a U.S. SAM with a Regional Household ($U.S. billion)*

	Land	Labor	Capital	Income tax
Income tax	3	1,446	244	–
Regional household	31	5,397	1,632	1,693
Total factor income	34	6,844	2,921	–
Income tax rate	8.4	21.1	8.4	–

Source: GTAP v7.0 U.S. 3x3 database.

behavior in the model. Let's first consider how income tax is described in the U.S. 3x3 SAM, which includes a regional household. In the U.S. SAM, income taxes are paid directly from the column accounts of the factors of production to the income tax row account (Table 8.10). Factors pay the remaining, after-tax income directly to the regional household row account. Then, the income tax column account pays the tax revenue to the regional household row account. Therefore, all income in the economy – which is the sum of income taxes plus after-tax income – is ultimately paid to the regional household.

The income tax rate for each factor is calculated as:

$$\text{Income tax/total factor income} * 100.$$

As an example, the income tax rate for labor is:

$$1{,}446/6{,}844 * 100 = 21.1 \text{ percent}$$

In the U.S. SAM, the tax rate on wage income is quite high relative to the tax rates on land-based income and capital income – which are both 8.4 percent.

Recall from Chapter 3 that a regional household is a macroeconomic account similar to GDP that describes the sources of national income and the composition of aggregate demand. In a CGE model with this structure, a change in the income tax typically has no effect on the economy. To explain why, consider the income tax on labor in Table 8.10. Labor ultimately pays a total of $6.8 trillion to the regional household, composed of income taxes of $1.4 trillion plus after-tax income of $5.4 trillion. If the labor income tax rate should fall to zero, labor would still pay $6.8 trillion to the regional household, now composed entirely of after-tax income. Thus, a change in the income tax does not change regional household income or the the shares of households, government, and savings in national spending.

In some static CGE models without a regional household, an income tax has structural effects on an economy if it shifts spending power among the categories of final demand. CGE models without a regional household generally link income directly to each component of aggregate demand. For example, households spend their after-tax income and governments spend their tax revenue, so an increase in an income tax lowers household spending and increases government spending. Depending on the closure in these models, income taxes also may affect investment by changing households' after-tax savings or the government surplus or deficit (which is public savings). If households, governments, and investors differ in the type of goods that they demand, then a change in income taxes and the composition of final demand will lead to changes in the industrial structure of the economy.

Second-Best Efficiency Effects

So far, we have used a distortion-free model of the United States to study the direct and excess burdens of one type of tax at a time. In more realistic CGE models, and in real life, governments usually impose many taxes at the same time, and usually in many industries simultaneously. Policy changes therefore entail introducing or changing a tax in the presence of many preexisting tax distortions.

This tax setting raises an important question: Does the excess burden of a tax depend on the preexisting taxes in an economy? To answer this, we draw on the theory of the second best developed by the economists Richard Lipsey and Kelvin Lancaster (1956). According to this theory, a free market equilibrium in one market may not lead to the most efficient, economywide outcome if there is already a distortion in another market due to a tax, a market failure, or other type of economic constraint. For example, suppose there is already a production subsidy in the services industry that has caused its output to exceed the economically efficient level. The government now may be considering the introduction of a production subsidy to the manufacturing industry. In this distorted setting, the manufacturing subsidy could actually improve economic efficiency in the services sector by drawing away some of its productive resources. In this case, a new, distorting manufacturing subsidy may cancel out at least part of another subsidy's distortionary effect. Of course, there are circumstances where a new tax or subsidy can exacerbate the effects of existing tax distortions.

Let's explore a case of second-best in our GTAP model with the distortion-free U.S. 3x3 database. Our experiment is the introduction of a 10 percent production subsidy on U.S. manufacturing. First, we assume that there are no other distortions in the economy. The subsidy causes manufacturing output to increase by 8.57 percent, an oversupply relative to the free market level (Table 8.11). The excess burden in manufacturing of $18.5 billion corresponds to the efficiency triangles of $c + f$ in Figure 8.3b. The increased use of the economy's resources by manufacturing also causes the production of agriculture and services to decline.

Table 8.11. *Second-Best Effects of a Production Subsidy in U.S. Manufacturing With/Without a Pre-Existing Production Subsidy in U.S. Services*

	Base Production Subsidy	New Production Subsidy	% Change in Production (*qo*)	Excess Burden ($US million)
Base equilibrium with no pre-existing tax distortions				
Agriculture	0	0	−8.5	0
Manufacturing	0	10	8.6	18,521
Services	0	0	−1.6	0
Base equilibrium with a pre-existing subsidy				
Agriculture	0	0	−8.6	0
Manufacturing	0	10	8.7	18,396
Services	5	5	−1.6	−9,555

Source: GTAP model with GTAP v7.0 U.S. 3x3 database.

Now, we assume that the economy has a preexisting, 5 percent subsidy on the production of services. In this setting, there is already an oversupply of services relative to the free market level. The introduction of the manufacturing production subsidy increases manufacturing output (8.7 percent) and leads to an efficiency loss in the industry of $18.4 billion. However, in this case, manufacturing's expansion corrects for part of the inefficient oversupply of services. Its competition for the economy's productive resources causes services output to decline and yields a reduction of nearly $9.6 billion in the excess burden associated with service's production subsidy. The new distortion in the manufacturing sector therefore corrects for part of a preexisting distortion in the services sector.

Our simple example analyzes just two taxes. A CGE model with a more realistic SAM is likely to have a large number of taxes. The welfare effect of a change in any one tax is therefore the sum of its own excess burden plus its, second-best effects in correcting or exacerbating the excess burdens associated with every other tax in the model.

Marginal Welfare Burden of a Tax

The marginal welfare burden of a tax is the change in national welfare due to a very small – a marginal – change in an existing tax. The change in welfare, divided by the change in tax revenue, describes the marginal welfare burden per dollar of additional tax revenue. This per dollar concept, developed by Edgar Browning (1976), has had practical use as a yardstick for determining whether a government project is worthwhile if its funding requires raising additional tax revenue. This is a realistic and important analytical problem because policymakers are typically seeking ideas for designing modest tax hikes or tax cuts from an already-distorted tax base.

The yardstick builds on the idea that every additional dollar of tax revenue incurs both a direct tax burden, which is a transfer of tax revenue from private expenditure to the government, and an excess tax burden, which is the tax's deadweight efficiency cost to the economy. Browning studied the marginal excess burden of the U.S. labor income tax, finding that raising an additional dollar of tax revenue would generate an excess burden of nine to sixteen cents, depending on how the tax increase is structured. He concluded that the return on a government project funded by this additional tax revenue would have to be 9 to 16 percent greater than the private expenditure that it displaced, or national welfare would decline.

Browning used a partial equilibrium model for his study of the labor income tax but CGE models have proven to be well-suited for this type of analysis. One reason is that CGE models offer a comprehensive measure of the welfare effects of a change in one tax. The model takes into account not only the excess burden of the tax that changes, but also any second-best efficiency effects linked to other existing taxes. In addition, a CGE model's welfare measure includes any terms-of-trade effects due to the tax change, which may be important when the country is large in world markets.

CGE models also provide a comprehensive measure of the direct burden of a tax because they account for the impacts of a change in one tax on the revenue generated by all taxes in an economy. For example, an increase in the sales tax on cigarettes may cause employment and output in the tobacco industry to fall. Payroll and production taxes paid by the tobacco industry may then fall, and perhaps sales tax revenue from other goods will rise as consumers readjust their spending. Thus, the total change in tax revenue will likely include changes in revenue from many types of taxes in addition to the tobacco sales tax.

Ballard, Shoven, and Whalley (1985) developed a pioneering CGE-based analysis of the marginal welfare cost of the entire U.S. tax system. They found that, depending on the elasticities assumed in the model, the marginal welfare cost per dollar of additional U.S. labor income tax revenue was between twelve and twenty-three cents – substantially higher than Browning's partial equilibrium estimate. For the U.S. tax system as a whole, they calculated a marginal welfare burden of seventeen to fifty-six cents per dollar of additional tax revenue. For example, a ratio of 17 percent indicates that for a dollar of additional tax revenue, there is an additional deadweight efficiency loss to the economy of seventeen cents. In this case, a government project must yield a marginal return of at least 117 percent if it is to be worth its cost to the economy in terms of tax dollars spent plus lost efficiency. (You will replicate the Ballard, Shoven, and Whalley analysis in Model Exercise 8.) Devarajan,

Text Box 8.3. Marginal Welfare Burden of Taxes in Developing Countries
"The Marginal Cost of Public Funds in Developing Countries." (Devarajan, Thierfelder, and Suthiwart-Narueput, 2001).

What is the research question? The notion that raising a dollar of taxes could cost society more than a dollar is one of the most powerful ideas in economics. By causing agents to alter their behavior in inefficient ways as a result of the tax, the marginal cost of raising a dollar of public funds is higher than a dollar. Despite the importance of this idea, few estimates are available on the marginal welfare cost of funds in developing countries. What are the estimated costs of funds in three developing countries – Cameroon, Bangladesh, and Indonesia?

What is the CGE model innovation? A standard, static, single-country CGE model is used for each country. Their macroclosure rules fix investment, real government spending, and the current account balance. These closure rules imply that an increase in tax revenue causes a government budget surplus (i.e., public savings rise); but because investment spending is fixed, households' savings falls and their consumption rises by the full amount of the tax revenue. In effect, households are compensated in a lump-sum fashion for higher taxes so that model results measure only the excess burden of the taxes.

What is the experiment? There are four tax experiments for each country: (1) an increase in the production tax by sector; (2) a uniform increase in all production taxes, (3) an increase in individual tariff rates, and (4) a uniform tariff rate increase. Additional factor market distortions are introduced one-by-one into the Cameroon model to illustrate second-best effects.

What are the key findings? The marginal costs of funds in the three countries are quite low, ranging between 0.5 and 2.0, which refutes the conventional wisdom that the marginal costs of funds in developing countries are likely to be high due to their relatively high tax rates. Experiments in which taxes are increased by sector confirm that the marginal cost of funds is highest in sectors where distortions are large. Policies that increase the lowest tax rates tend to reduce the marginal cost of funds because the tax structure becomes more uniform.

Thierfelder, and Suthiwart-Narueput (2001) carried out a similar CGE-based analysis of the marginal costs of taxes in three developing countries, described in Text Box 8.3. Their study is of special interest because most studies of marginal welfare burdens focus on developed countries.

The concept of the marginal welfare burden is illustrated in the partial-equilibrium model shown in Figure 8.6. The figure describes changes in direct and excess burdens due to marginal increases in a production tax. In the figure, S^1 is the tax-free supply curve and, to simplify our analysis, D describes a perfectly elastic compensated demand curve. In the absence of the tax, P^1 and QO^1 are the equilibrium price and quantity. Now, assume that a specific (per unit) production tax of t^1, shown as the distance between $P^1 - P^2$,

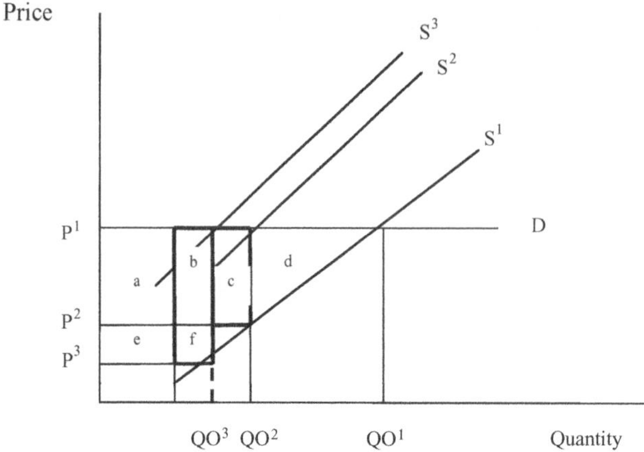

Figure 8.6. Marginal excess burden of a production tax

is already present in our initial equilibrium. The tax-inclusive supply curve corresponding to t^1 is S^2. In this tax-distorted equilibrium, consumers pay price P for quantity QO^2 and producers receive price P^2. The total loss in producer surplus is the combined area of $a + b + c + d$; but of this total, area $a + b + c$ is transferred to the government as tax revenue so it is not a loss to the economy. The excess burden of the tax is the area of triangle *d*.

Next, assume a marginal increase in the production tax to t^2, shown in the figure by the distance P^2-P^3. The increased tax raises producers' costs of production and shifts the new tax-inclusive supply curve to S^3. In the new equilibrium, consumers still pay price P^1, but producers receive only price P^3 and the equilibrium quantity declines to QO^3. Producers lose the additional producer surplus areas of $e + f$. (The small triangular area to their right can be ignored for small changes in the tax.) The government gains new tax revenue of area $e + f$ but loses tax revenue of area *c*. Area *c* becomes an addition to area *d*, the excess burden of the tax, as the tax increases from t^1 to t^2.

The marginal excess burden of the tax per dollar of additional government revenue is the ratio of the change in the excess burden to the change in tax revenue. In Figure 8.6, the ratio is described as areas $c/(e + f - c)$ for the tax increase from t^1 to t^2.

Our partial equilibrium model shown in Figure 8.6 describes only the change in excess burden in the taxed sector. Recall from our study of the theory of the second best that, in an economywide framework, a change in one tax rate may cause the excess burdens associated with other taxes in the economy to change also. In a general equilibrium model, therefore, measurement of the marginal welfare effect will include the marginal excess burden associated with all taxes in the economy, as well as any changes in

Table 8.12. *Marginal Welfare Effect of a 1 Percent Increase in The U.S. Production Tax on Services*

Excess Burden by Tax	
Total excess burden	−18.9
Import tax	−10.6
Export tax	2.5
Production tax	−15.3
Sales tax on intermediate inputs	−7.7
Sales tax on final demand	16.3
Factor use tax	−4.1
Terms of trade	−140.3
Total welfare effect	−159.2

Source: GTAP model, U.S. 3x3 v.7.0 database.

the terms of trade. Changes in tax revenue, too, are the sum of changes in revenue from all tax sources.

To illustrate these points, we use the GTAP model with the distorted U.S. 3x3 database to analyze the welfare effect of a marginal, 1 percent increase in the initial 2.8 percent tax on U.S production of services. Our model results indicate that the increase in the tax on services increases the total excess burden, or efficiency loss, by $18.9 million and causes welfare to decline by $159.2 million (Table 8.12). The efficiency losses are associated with production, import, and factor use taxes, whereas other types of taxes generate second-best efficiency gains. Total U.S. tax revenue increases by $3.492 billion. Thus, the marginal welfare burden of the additional tax revenue is:

$$\text{Change in welfare/Change in tax revenue} * 100$$
$$-159/3,492 * 100 = -4.6 \text{ percent.}$$

This means that an additional tax dollar costs 4.6 cents in efficiency losses. The government project should be undertaken only if its marginal benefit will be at least 4.6 percent greater than the amount of the additional producer tax revenue required to finance it. Otherwise, its cost to the economy in terms of tax dollars spent plus related efficiency losses will be greater than its benefit.

In an already distorted economy, it is also possible that the tax increase could lead to marginal welfare gains. In this case, the ratio is positive. If, for example, the ratio is 10 percent, then a public project could generate a marginal benefit that is as little as 90 percent of its cost in taxpayer funding and still be worthwhile because the tax increase corrects other distortions in the economy. This scenario may not be too far-fetched; our model results in table 8.12 showed that a marginal increase in a U.S. production tax yielded second-best welfare gains associated with some pre-existing U.S. taxes.

Summary

Our study of tax policy analysis in a CGE model began with an examination of the tax data in the SAM, because the SAM describes the agent who pays the tax, the production or consumption decision on which the tax is assumed to be levied and tax revenues. We studied five types of taxes: trade taxes on exports and imports, and taxes on production, sales, factor use, and incomes. Our study of each tax began with a simple, partial equilibrium, theoretical model that illustrated how taxes distort production and consumption decisions and result in a direct burden (the tax revenue that it generates) and an excess burden (the loss in production and consumption inefficiency). Our theoretical approaches helped us to formulate expectations about the effects of taxes on the economy under study, identify key results, and recognize the consistency of CGE model results with theoretical models of taxation. We then progressed from analyzing single taxes in partial equilibrium frameworks to analyzing taxes in general equilibrium, culminating in applied examples of second-best effects and the marginal burden of a tax system.

Key Terms

Ad valorem tariff or tax
Direct burden
Direct tax
Excess burden
Export tax
Factor use tax
Import tariff
Income tax
Indirect tax
Marginal welfare burden
Output tax
Tax incidence
Sales tax
Second-best effects
Specific tariff or tax

PRACTICE AND REVIEW

1. Suppose the government is considering the introduction of an import tariff on one of two products – one product exhibits a high own-price elasticity of demand

and the other has a low elasticity. In a graph, compare the effects of a tariff on the excess burden for the two goods. Label the axes, curves, and initial market equilibrium. On which type of good do you recommend that the tariff be imposed? Explain why.

2. Use data from the U.S. 3x3 SAM to calculate the factor use tax (or subsidy) rate for labor and capital used in the production of manufactures and of services. How do these factor use taxes distort the allocation of capital and labor between the manufacturing and service sectors? How do they distort the ratios of labor to capital within each industry?
3. Assume that a country introduces a 25 percent sales tax on the purchase of gasoline. Draw a graph of the effects of the sales tax on the supply and demand for gas. Label the axes and curves, and explain your assumptions about the elasticities of supply and demand that define the slopes of your curves. Identify the direct tax burden, the excess burden, and changes in the market equilibrium price and quantity.
4. Suppose that the government increases retail sales taxes on students' purchases of selected items in the university bookstore. Government analysts project a $1 million increase in sales tax revenue that will fund a reduction in student tuition, and a marginal welfare loss of $200,000.
   a. What is the marginal welfare cost of the tax increase, per dollar of additional tax revenue?
   b. What is the minimum return that the government must make on its investment in the university to ensure that national welfare does not decline?
   c. How do you think the marginal welfare cost per dollar might change if the government increases the sales tax on a good for which student demand is relatively price inelastic, such as food? What if the government increases the sales tax on a good for which demand is relatively price sensitive, such as novelty items with the school logo?
   d. Assume a preexisting production subsidy in the industry that supplies the university bookstore with taxed items, such as textbooks. In a short paragraph, explain the possible second-best effect of the new tax.

Technical Appendix 8.1: Compensated Demand and Welfare Effects

In this chapter, we mostly use partial equilibrium models to illustrate the effect of a tax on the supply and demand for a single good. Similar to our study in Chapter 4 of consumer demand for two goods, we can decompose the consumer's response to a tax-induced price change for one good into income and substitution effects. If the good is normal, which is the case in standard CGE models, the income effect on demand for a good is always positive (negative) when its price declines (increases). The substitution effect describes the change in consumer demand for a good when its price changes, holding purchasing power constant. In CGE models, the substitution effect is always positive (negative) when the price of a good declines (increases).

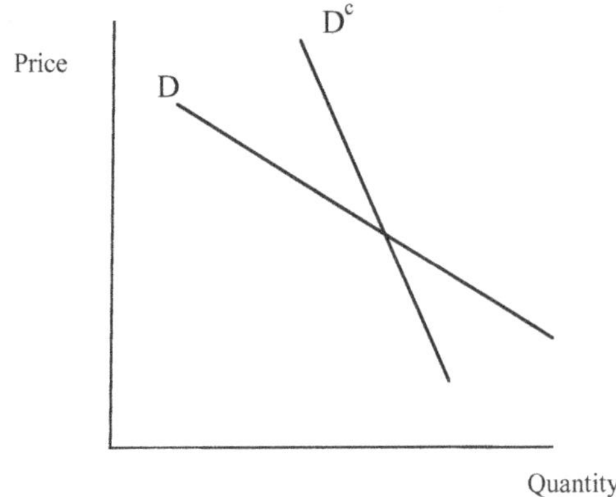

Figure 8.7. Compensated and uncompensated demand curves

To measure the welfare effects of a tax, we want to be able to describe only its substitution effect (its excess burden), since the income effect is a transfer of purchasing power from the consumer to the government and is not a loss to the economy as whole.

Economists use compensated demand curves to describe the substitution effects of a price change, exclusive of income effects. These curves describe the consumer's budget allocation, assuming that he is fully compensated for the effect of the tax on his purchasing power. In Figure 8.7, we plot both an uncompensated demand curve, D, and a compensated demand curve, D^c. The uncompensated curve is a usual (Marshallian) demand curve that includes both the income and substitution effects of a price change. The compensated (Hicksian) demand curve describes only the substitution effect. The two curves intersect at the initial market equilibrium. When the price increases, the consumer is given additional income to compensate for the loss in purchasing power, so compensated demand exceeds uncompensated demand, and vice versa. Notice, too, that the compensated curve is relatively inelastic. The consumer response is smaller because this measure includes only the price effect.

Figure 8.8 illustrates the welfare effect of a tax that increases the price of a good from P^1 to P^2. In the figure, D is the uncompensated demand curve and D^{c1} is the initial compensated demand curve. Both demand curves pass through Point A, depicting the initial equilibrium quantity, Q^1, and price P^1. An increase in price due to a sales tax causes the consumer to move upward along the uncompensated demand curve, and the quantity demanded declines to Q^2 at price P^2, at point B. We draw a second compensated demand curve, D^{c2}, consistent with this new, lower level of purchasing power. Both D and D^{c2} pass through point B.

The welfare effect of the tax is the loss in consumer surplus associated with the compensated demand curves. The figure illustrates that, because there

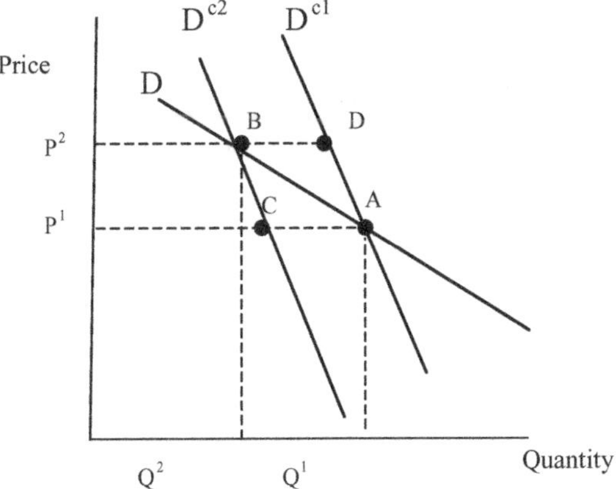

Figure 8.8. Equivalent and compensated variation welfare effects

are two compensated demand curves associated with the pre- and post-shock equilibria. We can measure the welfare effect in two alternative ways. One approach is to assume that the consumer remains on the initial compensated demand curve, as we do in our partial equilibrium diagrams in Chapter 8. In this case, the loss in consumer surplus is described by area P^2DAP^1. This area is the compensated variation measure of welfare; it quantifies the minimum amount that consumers would be willing accept as compensation to leave them as well off as before the price increase. The alternative is to measure the change in surplus based on the new level of utility associated with D^{c2}, which is described by area P^2BCP^1. This is the equivalent variation measure of welfare. It is equivalent to the maximum amount of income consumers would be willing to pay to return to the old price level. Our modeling examples in Chapter 8 report the equivalent variation measure of the welfare effects of various taxes.

9

Conclusion: Frontiers in CGE Modeling

Computable general equilibrium (CGE) models are sometimes criticized for being "black boxes" in which everything is moving at once. By deconstructing a standard CGE model with the aid of basic principles of economics, we hope to have dispelled some of their mystery and made them more comprehensible and useful to students and professional economists alike. Such an introductory study seems especially timely given the increased accessibility of CGE models and CGE model databases.

In this book, we studied the main components of a CGE model. We learned that producers in the model are assumed to maximize efficiency, and consumers are assumed to maximize utility. Their microeconomic behavior adds up to the macroeconomic performance of the economy. Our study of each component of the model – supply, demand, factor markets, trade, and taxes – emphasized the model's underlying economic theory and supplied practical examples from small-scale CGE models to illustrate these concepts.

We studied a "standard" CGE model that assumes a representative household consumer, a representative producer of each type of product, and uniquely determined solution values for prices and quantities. It is a static, or single-period, model that provides a before and after comparison of an economy after a shock, such as a tax, but it does not describe the economy's adjustment path from the old to the new equilibrium. All of these features of our CGE model can at times represent shortcomings or constraints. The aggregation of all households, in their rich diversity in incomes, tastes, ages, and wealth, into one representative household consumer is quite a strong assumption. Producers, too, may be diverse in ways that are important to an analysis, perhaps producing the same product using different types of technologies or facing very different transportation costs in different regions of a country. In addition, our world is characterized by some amount of randomness, like weather variability, and this stochasticity is not reflected in our deterministic CGE model. Static models also may not fully address the concerns of policymakers about the transition process, when there can be high unemployment or other types of dislocation as an economy adapts to shocks. Economists working in more sophisticated and frontier areas of CGE modeling have extended the models' capabilities in all of these dimensions. Your foundation in working with a standard CGE model now leaves you well prepared to appreciate the significance of these advances.

CGE modelers have addressed the problem of how to disaggregate representative households in two different ways. On approach is to decompose the single household account in the Social Accounting Matrix (SAM) and in the CGE model into multiple accounts, in which sources of factor income and the baskets of goods purchased by each household type differ. In this way, a shock such as the decline in one industry's employment will directly affect only households whose income derives from that sector. Likewise, a tax on capital income would affect households with significant dividend income more than households with mainly wage income.

A second approach is to link the CGE model with a "micromodel" that may contain thousands of households. The micromodel includes estimated behavioral equations, usually based on national household survey data, which describe how households' hours of work and quantities of consumption respond to changes in wages, prices, and income. The endogenous price and income results of the CGE model, the "macromodel," are then incorporated into the micromodel as exogenous shocks, which results in responses at the household level. With this approach, the distribution of macro effects across households does not feed back to influence production, employment, or other variables in the CGE model. Macro-micro models have made important contributions to the analysis of the distributional effects of policies on household income and poverty [e.g., Bourguignon, Robilliard, and Robinson (2003, summarized in Text Box 4.2); Hertel, et al. (2004); and Verma and Hertel (2009, summarized in Text Box 9.1)].

Extensions of CGE models to describe diversity among producers are similar in many respects to the disaggregation of the representative household. One approach is to differentiate industries by adding additional industry accounts to the SAM, as in Block et al., 2006 and Diao, et al., 2008. For example, agricultural production of each commodity could be differentiated by region, so that the SAM has row and column activity accounts for two vegetable industries – one in the north and one in the south of the country, or perhaps one of the two vegetable industries uses irrigation and one does not. A second approach is to allocate the national-level results of a CGE analysis across production activities using a routine that is separate from the CGE model. The USAGE-ITC model, for example, uses this "top down" approach. It includes an "add-in" that allocates endogenous national impacts from the CGE model across state-level industries and employment (see Text Box 3.2). Perhaps the state of Michigan will receive 10 percent of

Text Box 9.1. An Intertemporal Dynamic CGE Model of the United States
"***Trade Liberalization in General Equilibrium: Intertemporal and Inter-Industry Effects.***" (Goulder and Eichengreen (1989)).

What is the research question? Most CGE analyses of trade liberalization have studied its effects on trade in goods and services. How might trade liberalization impact the U.S. economy if its effects on the international flow of investment capital are also considered?

What is the CGE model innovation? The authors develop an intertemporal, dynamic CGE model of the United States and an aggregate, rest-of-world region. The model assumes forward-looking behavior by U.S. and foreign firms, who pursue investment strategies over time that maximize their current and future profits. Forward-looking U.S. and foreign households maximize their lifetime utility by deciding how much to save or consume in each period and how to allocate their savings to domestic or foreign investments. The model is first solved to produce a baseline, steady-state equilibrium. After the policy shock, the model solves for a time path of temporary equilibria that converge to a new steady-state equilibrium. In each period of the time path, supply and demand for goods and factors are equal, and savings equals investment, but capital returns can diverge across industries and portfolio returns can diverge between countries. Over time, firms adjust their investments, and households adjust their savings and portfolio choices, until capital and portfolio returns equalize in a new steady-state equilibrium.

What is the model experiment? The authors assume permanent, unilateral cuts of 50 percent in U.S. tariffs and voluntary export quotas.

What are the key findings? The welfare gain to the United States is larger when international capital flows are taken into account because inflows of foreign investment increase U.S. household consumption in the near term, although this lowers U.S. consumption in the long run because the foreign debt must be repaid.

the change in national U.S. consumer demand for good X. As in the macro-micro model of households, this approach does not allow feedback from changes in state-level production and employment back to the national CGE model.

Stochastic models are an innovative, frontier area of CGE modeling that is poised to make major contributions to the analysis of long-term climate change. Stochastic models stand in contrast to the deterministic CGE model that we have studied in this book. In a deterministic model, the solution value of every variable is uniquely determined by the equations, base data, parameter values, and shock. For example, an experiment may be a 10 percent change in wheat productivity, which results in a 10 percent change in the quantity of wheat production. Stochastic models account for the randomness that may be present in an economic environment. Perhaps year-to-year output of wheat is variable, and is expected to become increasingly variable due to climate change. A stochastic CGE model would describe the baseline output of wheat in terms of a mean value and probability distribution and the effects of a climate change shock as a change in the mean and distribution of wheat output. CGE modelers have taken different approaches to describing stochastic behavior in a CGE models. See for example, Block, et al.'s (2006) study of droughts and floods in Ethiopia, summarized in Text Box 5.2, and contrast it with Verma and Hertel's (2009) study of the effects of world food price volatility on caloric consumption in Bangladesh, summarized in Text Box 9.1.

Dynamic CGE models essentially capture the notion that an economy's reaction to a shock, such as a new tax, changes its long run growth trajectory. First, the models trace a baseline time path (usually a series of annual observations for specified time period), over which the supply and productivity of an economy's stock of capital and labor grows in the absence of a shock. A shock to the economy leads to changes in its growth trajectory by changing the timing and level of capital accumulation. Capital stock growth is altered when the experiment changes the rate of return to capital, which changes savings and investment behavior. Instead of static before and after snapshots, the results of a dynamic CGE model thus describe the difference between the baseline time path and the time path with the economic shock.[1]

Broadly speaking, there are two types of dynamic models. A recursive dynamic CGE model traces out a time path by sequentially solving a static model, one period at a time. First, the model solves for one period after the shock, similar to a static model. Then, all of the solution values are used as the variables' initial values for the next period and the model is re-solved, and so on. The capital stock grows over time because the change in savings that occurs in one period becomes an addition (minus depreciation) to the productive capital stock in the next time period. The modeler may also include time trends for labor force and productivity growth as the model is solved over the time path. Producers and consumers are assumed to be myopic. They minimize their costs or maximize their utility only for the current period, and they are assumed to believe that current economic conditions will prevail at all periods in the future.

Recursive dynamic CGE models are used by many governmental and international institutions to analyze important public policy problems. Prominent examples of these models are the World Bank's multicountry Linkage model (van der Mennsbrugghe, 2005) the single-country MONASH model of Australia (Dixon and Rimmer, 2002) and its descendant, the USAGE-ITC model of the United States (Koopman, et al. 2002) and the World Bank's

[1] See Devarajan and Go (1998) for an introduction to dynamic CGE models.

Text Box 9.2. A Stochastic CGE Model: Caloric Intake in Bangladesh
"Commodity Price Volatility and Nutrition Vulnerability." Verma and Hertel (2009).

What is the research question? Agricultural production can be highly variable due to stochastic, or random, changes in weather. Production volatility in turn leads to volatility in food prices and food consumption. The authors examine how food price volatility leads to variability in caloric intake in Bangladesh. Could a special safeguard mechanism, which limits imports whenever their quantities surge, lead to increased average caloric intake or a reduction in its variability?

What is the CGE model innovation? The authors use a macro-micro model that links the GTAP CGE model with a microsimulation model of the caloric intake of Bangladeshi households. Macroeconomic results from the CGE model are used as inputs into the micromodel of Bangladeshi households' food purchases. The authors define a stochastic shock to the total input productivity of grains and oilseeds production in the CGE model. This step creates baseline means and probability distributions for commodity prices and households' caloric intake. They validate their CGE model by testing that results from their stochastic productivity shock reproduces historical crop price volatility.

What is the experiment? The authors introduce their stochastic productivity shock with and without an offsetting special safeguard mechanism on imports.

What are the key findings? Differences among households in distributions of caloric intake, with and without import safeguards, are very small because Bangladesh does not import much of its food. The general lesson is that special safeguard policies raise food prices so they are likely to affect countries adversely, particularly their poor households.

MAMS model (Gottschalk, et al. 2009). Recursive dynamic models have also begun to assume an important role in the analysis of long-term global climate change. Recursive dynamic climate models include CIM-EARTH, an open CGE model available at www.CIM-earth.org (Elliott, et al., 2010a), and the MIT-EPPA model (Paltsev, et al., 2005).

The second type of dynamic CGE model is intertemporal. It assumes that producers and consumers have rational expectations, which means that they anticipate and take into account prices and income in all time periods as they make their current decisions. Producers minimize the present value of all of their costs over the full time period of the analysis, and consumers maximize their total utility over that period. Like the recursive model, an intertemporal CGE model describes two growth paths – with and without the economic shock. The models differ because the intertemporal type solves for prices and quantities in all time periods simultaneously. The time dimension adds many variables to the model. For example, the output of a single industry over a thirty year time path equals thirty variables. Researchers therefore make a trade-off between the time dimension and the number of countries, industries, or consumer types in the model, so that these models usually offer very aggregated and stylized representations of an economy. As a result, this type of model is not typically maintained as a core analytical tool of institutions like the U.S. government. Nevertheless, intertemporal dynamic CGE models offer important insights and have provided the underpinnings for many influential studies of trade and tax policies [e.g., Goulder and Eichengreen (1989 – see Text Box 9.2), Jokisch and Kotlikoff (2005), Rutherford and Tarr (2003), and Diao, Somaru, and Roe (2001)].

As we conclude our study of CGE models with this brief summary of its extended and frontier applications, it is a good idea to now think back to the simple bicycle model of Chapter 1, and to remind ourselves that, whether we use our simple model of supply and demand or whether we advance to the frontiers of CGE modeling, we are always trying to distill a simplified representation of a complex world.

Model Exercises

Introduction

The objective of these eight model exercises, and an additional challenge exercise, is to provide you with step-by-step guidance in building a model, designing experiments, identifying relevant results, and interpreting findings.

The exercises are intended to:

- Engage your interest by showing the breadth of real world problems that can be analyzed using a CGE model.
- Illustrate how to use economic theory to make predictions about and to interpret model results.
- Demonstrate how the design of model experiments is grounded in economic theory and background research.
- Introduce a broad sampling of methodological tools, including how to change elasticities and model closure, decompose shocks into subtotals, and run sensitivity analyses of assumptions about elasticity parameter values and shock sizes.

The case studies are suitable for use with many types of CGE models. However, the detailed instructions provided in the model exercises are designed for use with the Global Trade Analysis Project (GTAP) CGE model. The model, developed by Thomas Hertel and colleagues at Purdue University, is documented in Hertel and Tsigas, 1997. Its friendly, menu-driven interface, RunGTAP, was developed by Mark Horridge (2001) and is ideal for use by novice modelers.

Model exercises 1–3 show you how to create a small, three-sector, three-factor database for the United States and an aggregated, rest-of-world region from the GTAP global database (Table 1 ME introduction 1). The instructions also guide you in setting up, running, and learning about the GTAP CGE model. You should complete these three exercises sequentially before doing the subsequent case studies. You can also use the model developed in these exercises to replicate the modeling results reported throughout the textbook chapters.

Table ME Introduction 1. *Skill Development in Model Exercises*

Exercise	Case Study	Economic Concepts	Modeling Skill
1. Set up the GTAP model and database			Download GTAP model, develop a database and SAM, run the model
2. Explore the GTAP model and database			Locate elements of model: sets, parameters, variables, equations, closure, and market-clearing constraints
3. Run the GTAP model			Define and run experiments, change elasticities and closure, read results, use GTAP utilities for welfare decomposition,and systematic sensitivity analysis
4. Soaring food prices and the U.S. economy	Trostle (2008), Sachs (2008), Cline (2008), Collier (2008)	Comparison of utility functions. Armington import demand, small country assumption	Change income and substitution demand elasticities, small country (fixed world price) closure
5. Food fight: Agricultural production subsidies	Samuelson (2005)	Production function, production subsidies	Use GTAP SUBTOTAL utility, change factor substitution elasticity
6. How immigration can raise wages	Borjas (2004), Ottaviano and Peri (2006)	Factors as substitutes and complements, factor endowment changes and factor prices	Change factor endowments and factor substitution elasticity
7. The Doha Development Agenda	Anderson and Martin (2005)	Input, output and export subsidies, import tariffs, welfare analysis	Use GTAP SUBTOTAL and welfare decomposition utilities, compare models

Exercise	Case Study	Economic Concepts	Modeling Skill
8. The marginal welfare burden of the U.S. tax system	Ballard, Shoven and Whalley (1985)	Taxation, tax burdens, welfare analysis	Use GTAP welfare decomposition and systematic sensitivity analysis utilities
9. Challenge exercise: Successful Quitters: the Economic Effects of Growing Anti-Smoking Attitudes	Goel and Nelson, 2004.	Utility functions, changes in consumer preferences, parameter uncertainty	Update model with macroeconomic projections, use GTAP systematic sensitivity analysis utility

Model Exercises 4–8 provide case studies that complement and reinforce the concepts learned in the related chapters of the textbook. You can do all, or any one, of these exercises, and in any sequence. Model Exercise 9 presents more challenging techniques for the advanced student. Model Exercises 4-9 are ideal for use as small, collaborative group projects. Each exercise poses questions about model results that can serve as a starting point for your exploration and study of your findings.

An important caveat about the model exercises is that they are only a teaching tool. Although the exercises introduce real-life problems and the practical modeling skills used in their analysis, the results from your small-dimensioned, toy CGE model should not be relied upon as realistic.

Model Exercise 1: Set Up the GTAP Model and Database

Concepts: Download GTAP model, develop a model database, create a SAM, create model version, run GTAP model

In this exercise, you will learn how to (1) build a CGE model database and (2) set up and run a version of the GTAP model to use with your database.[1] In the first step, you will download the GTAP global database aggregator from the GTAP Web site. You will learn how to use the database aggregator to create a two-region, three-sector and three-factor database that we use for examples throughout the book and in the model exercises. The two regions are the United States (USA) and the rest of the world (ROW); the three sectors are agriculture, manufacturing, and services; and the three factors are land, labor, and capital. We use the GTAP 7.0 database, released 21 November 2008. You may carry out the model exercises with versions 5 and higher of the GTAP database but model results will differ from those reported in the answer key.

In the second step, you will download the RunGTAP model and learn how to create a "version" of the model to run with your 3x3 database. At the end of this exercise, your CGE model and database will be ready to use for analysis or to replicate modeling examples in Chapters 1–8.

A. Create a Folder on Your Computer for Your Project

Ccreate a folder on your computer in which you will save your database and all of the other files that you will create for your research project. Name the directory "MyLastName" or something else that is easy to remember.

B. Download the Database Aggregator and Create a Model Database

The GTAP model can be used interchangeably with any aggregation of the GTAP database. You will create a three-sector, three-factor aggregation that describes the United States and an aggregated rest-of-world region. We refer to it as the U.S. 3x3 database throughout this book. You can follow these same steps to create a database for your individual research project. Instead of the United States and rest of world, you may choose to study different aggregations of countries, industries, and factors of production. We encourage you to limit yourself to no more than ten industries and four factors of production. (Without a GTAP license, you are restricted to three

[1] For students with some experience in GEMPACK, Pearson and Horridge (2003) provide a detailed introduction to the GEMPACK software and its use in the GTAP model. Also, see Horridge (2008a and 2008b) on use of the GTAP aggregation utility.

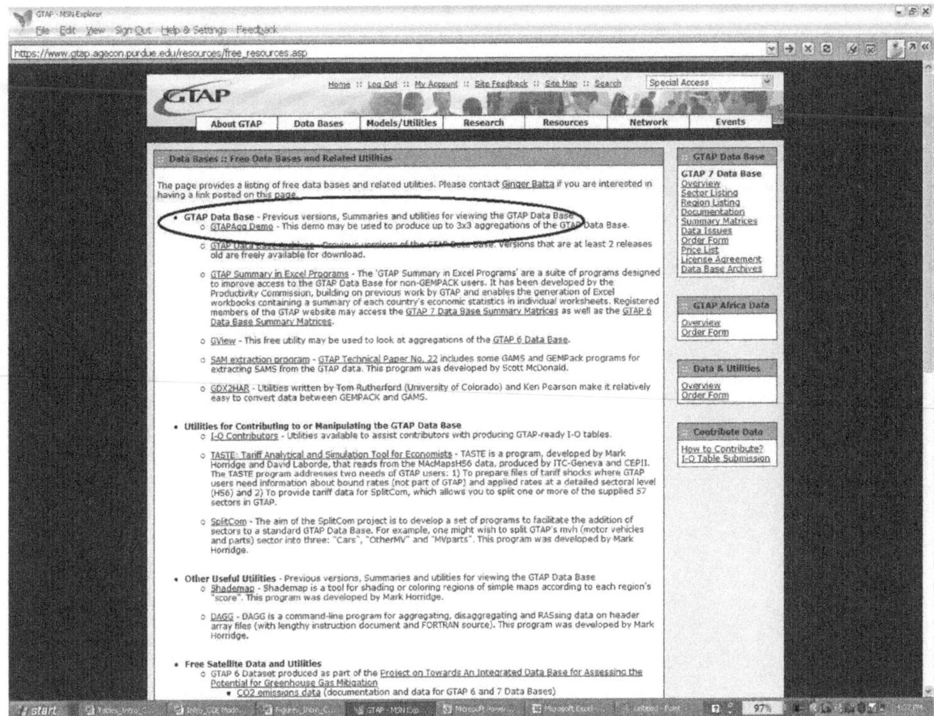

Figure ME 1.1. Download GTAP-Agg demo

countries and three sectors.) Otherwise, it becomes difficult to distill key results and major findings, especially as a beginning modeler.

The instructions below are consistent with the GTAP website as of October 2010. You may need to adapt these instructions if the GTAP website changes over time.

1. go to www.GTAP.org
2. Become a member of GTAP. Select "My Account" from the top menu bar and register as a new member. If you are a member already, log in.
3. From the main menu:
   > Select Databases
   > Select Free Databases from the drop down menu
   > Select GTAP-Agg Demo (see Figure ME 1.1).
   > Click on GTAPAgg7 Demo, from the "Attachments" section at the bottom of the page.
4. Download the GTAP-Agg demo file and select "Unzip and Install." Then select "set-up" program. It will prompt you to install the program to your hard disk in directory "C:/GTPAg7." You may instead specify any drive in which you prefer to install the program. (If this installation process is not an option on your computer, save the zip file to your temp directory. You can continue the set-up process from there, first by clicking on the zipped file, labeled "4144," and then by clicking on the "set-up" computer icon within it.)

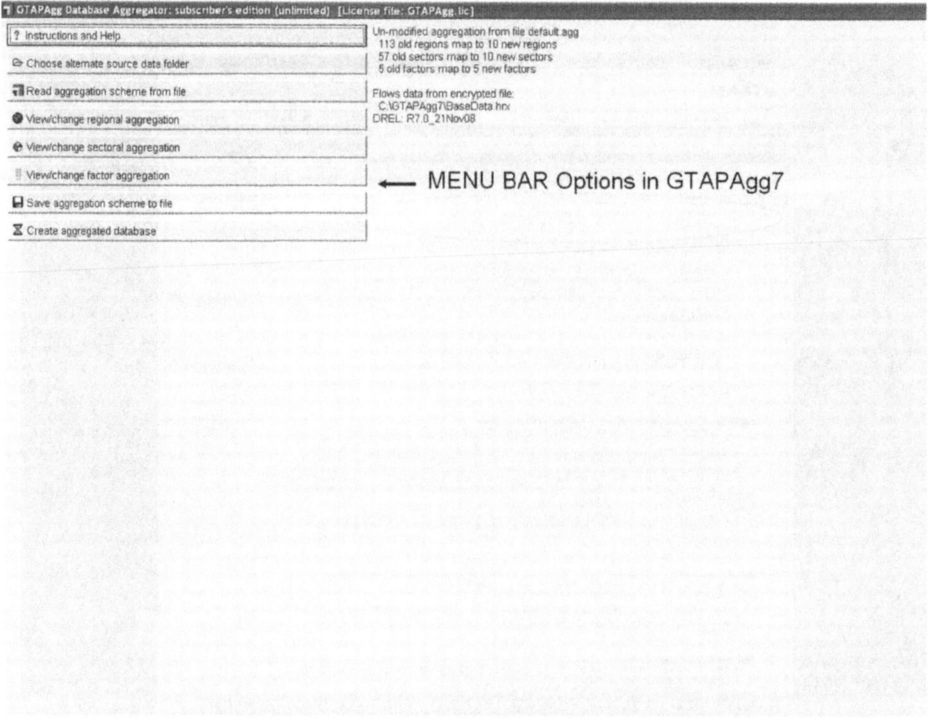

Figure ME 1.2. GTAPAgg7 menu bar options

5. As of this writing (November 2010) a patch to the GTAPAgg7 program is required to enable it to generate a Social Accounting Matrix, the format used to organize and display the databases used in CGE models. Download the patch from the following Web site, and *follow the installation directions for the patch*:
   > go to http://www.monash.edu.au/policy/aggpatch.htm
   > Open the GTAPAgg7 program. (Either click on GTAPAgg7 icon on the desktop or go to "Start," and select "All Programs," then select "GTAPAgg7."). The GTAPAgg7 program will open and display the menu bar options shown in Figure ME 1.2.
   > Check that you have updated the GTAPAgg7 program by clicking on the globe in the lower right corner. The version should be 7.10 or higher.
6. Define the country aggregation.
   > From the menu bar options, select "View/change regional aggregation"
   > In the table at the bottom of the page (shown in Figure ME 1.3), define two regions by right-clicking on rows and deleting all but two.
   > In the left column of the table, "New region code," re-label the rows "USA" and "ROW"
   > In the right column of the table, "New region description," enter "United States" and "Rest of World" to match the new region codes
7. Map all countries into a two-region aggregation
   > Go the mapping table in the upper right quadrant of the page.

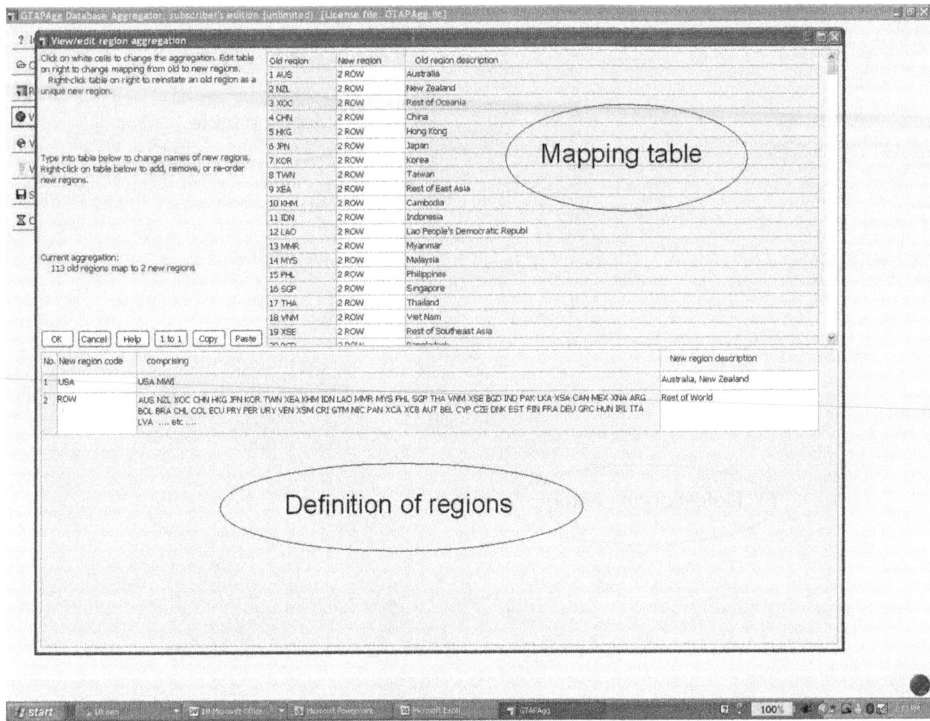

Figure ME 1.3. Mapping regions in GTAPAgg7

> Click on the first row (Australia), and the center column (New region) and pull down the menu, which should list "USA" and "ROW."
> Map each country in the mapping table to one of the two regions. When you are finished, only "USA" should occupy the "comprising" column in the table at the bottom of the page for the newly defined "USA" region. All other regions should be mapped to "ROW."
> Click OK (this saves your regional aggregation)

8. Define the sector aggregation.
   > From the menu bar, select "View/change sectoral aggregation." This opens a mapping page similar to that used to create the regional aggregation (shown in Figure ME 1.4).
   > In the table at the bottom of the page, right-click to remove all but three sector rows.
   > In the left column of the table, "New sector code," re-label the rows "AGR," "MFG," and "SER"
   > In the right column, "New sector descriptions," describe these sectors as Agriculture Natural Resources, Manufacturing, and Services.
9. Map sectors to a three-sector aggregation
   > In the mapping table in the upper right quadrant of the page, click on the first row (paddy rice) and the center column (New sector) and pull down the menu, which should list "AGR," "MFG," and "SER."

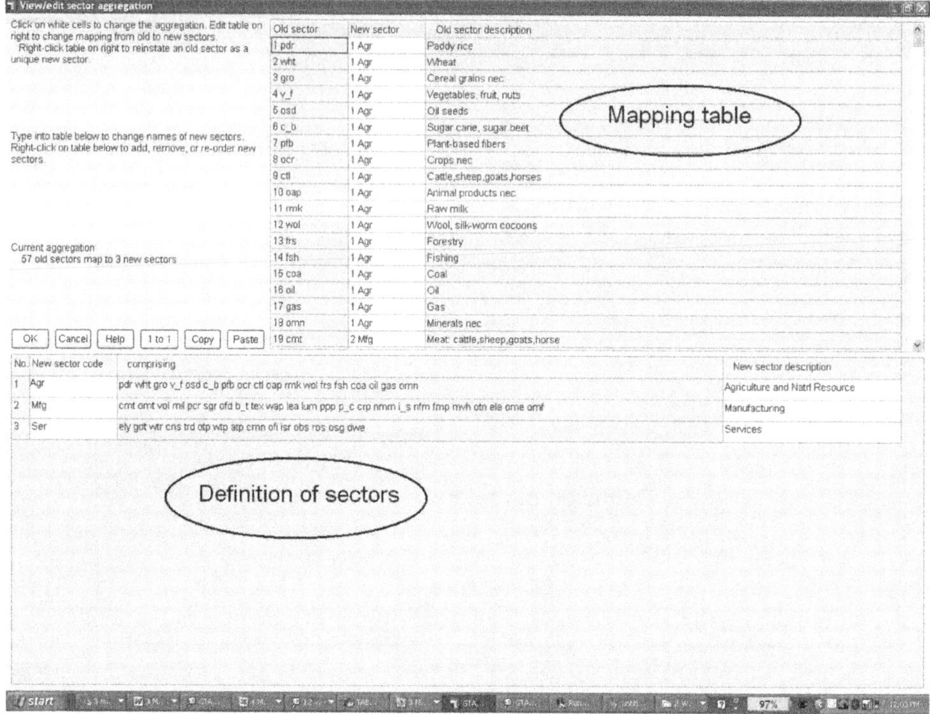

Figure ME 1.4. Mapping sectors in GTAPAgg7

> Map sectors 1–18 into AGR; sectors 19–42 into MFG; sectors 43–57 into SER.
> OK (this saves your sector definitions)

10. Define the factor aggregation
    > From the menu bar, select "View/change factor aggregation." This opens a mapping page similar to that used to create the regional aggregation (shown in Figure ME 1.5).
    > In the table at the bottom of the page, right-click to remove all but three factor rows.
    > In the left column, type "Land," "Labor," and "Capital," putting one factor in each row .
    > In the column labeled "Comprising," type "Land," "Labor," and "Capital" in the appropriate row.
11. Define factor mobility assumptions
    > The column labeled "ETRAE or mobile" describes the model's factor mobility assumptions. We study factor mobility assumptions in detail in Chapter 6. For now, simply change all factor mobility assumptions in this column to "mobile."
12. Map factors into three-factor aggregation
    > In the mapping table in the upper right quadrant, click on the center column, "New factor," and pull down the mapping menu.
    > Map: land to LAND; skilled and unskilled labor to LABOR; and capital and natural resources to CAPITAL.
    > OK

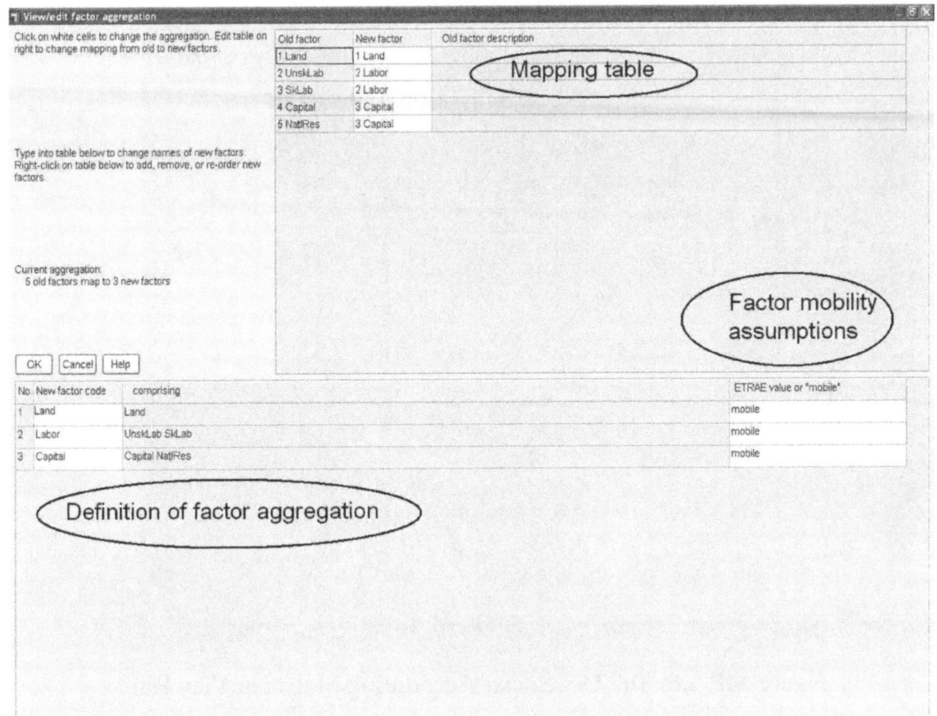

Figure ME 1.5. Mapping factors in GTAPAgg7

13. Save your data aggregation file
    > From the menu bar, select "Save aggregation scheme to file." (GTAP provides a default name, "gtp3_2," which you can change to something more descriptive, like US3x3.
    > Save this aggregation file in the folder that you created for your research project.
14. Create the aggregated database.
    > From the menu bar, select "Create aggregated database." This creates a zip file with the aggregated database. Give it the same name as your aggregation scheme (e.g., US3x3.zip), and save it in your project folder.
    Your database is now saved in Header Array (HAR) files that are ready to use in your CGE model.
15. Create a Social Accounting Matrix (SAM) in EXCEL
    > From the menu bar, select "View Output files."
    > Select GTAPSAM.har (this opens a list of HAR, or header array, files)
    > Click on ASAM – Aggregated Social Accounting Matrix. This will open a file in ViewHar, the software that is used to view HAR files.
16. Display the U.S. SAM
    A HAR file often contains data of more than two dimensions. To display the data of interest to you, select the dimensions, or elements, of the database in the upper right corner of the file (shown in Figure ME 1.6). To display all SAM accounts for the United States, select these dimensions:
    ALL ASAMAC, ALL ASAMAC, USA

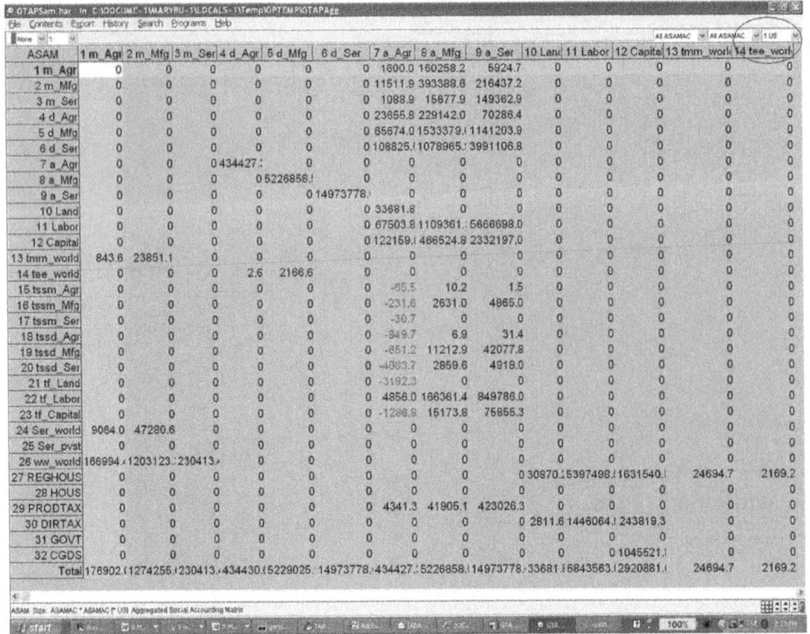

ASAM	1 m_Agr	2 m_Mfg	3 m_Ser	4 d_Agr	5 d_Mfg	6 d_Ser	7 a_Agr	8 a_Mfg	9 a_Ser	10 Land	11 Labor	12 Capital	13 tmm_world	14 tee_world
1 m_Agr	0	0	0	0	0	0	1600.0	160258.2	5924.7	0	0	0	0	0
2 m_Mfg	0	0	0	0	0	0	11511.9	393388.6	216437.2	0	0	0	0	0
3 m_Ser	0	0	0	0	0	0	1088.9	15677.9	149362.9	0	0	0	0	0
4 d_Agr	0	0	0	0	0	0	23655.8	229142.0	70286.4	0	0	0	0	0
5 d_Mfg	0	0	0	0	0	0	65674.0	1533379.	1141203.9	0	0	0	0	0
6 d_Ser	0	0	0	0	0	0	108825.	1078965.	3991106.8	0	0	0	0	0
7 a_Agr	0	0	0	434427.	0	0	0	0	0	0	0	0	0	0
8 a_Mfg	0	0	0	0	5226858.	0	0	0	0	0	0	0	0	0
9 a_Ser	0	0	0	0	0	14973778.	0	0	0	0	0	0	0	0
10 Land	0	0	0	0	0	0	33681.8	0	0	0	0	0	0	0
11 Labor	0	0	0	0	0	0	67503.8	1109361.	5666698.0	0	0	0	0	0
12 Capital	0	0	0	0	0	0	122159.	466524.8	2332197.0	0	0	0	0	0
13 tmm_world	843.6	23851.1	0	0	0	0	0	0	0	0	0	0	0	0
14 tee_world	0	0	0	2.6	2166.6	0	0	0	0	0	0	0	0	0
15 tssm_Agr	0	0	0	0	0	0	-65.5	10.2	1.5	0	0	0	0	0
16 tssm_Mfg	0	0	0	0	0	0	-231.6	2631.0	4865.0	0	0	0	0	0
17 tssm_Ser	0	0	0	0	0	0	-30.7	0	0	0	0	0	0	0
18 tssd_Agr	0	0	0	0	0	0	-949.7	6.9	31.4	0	0	0	0	0
19 tssd_Mfg	0	0	0	0	0	0	-851.2	11212.9	42077.8	0	0	0	0	0
20 tssd_Ser	0	0	0	0	0	0	-4083.7	2859.6	4918.0	0	0	0	0	0
21 tf_Land	0	0	0	0	0	0	-3192.3	0	0	0	0	0	0	0
22 tf_Labor	0	0	0	0	0	0	4856.0	166361.4	849786.0	0	0	0	0	0
23 tf_Capital	0	0	0	0	0	0	-1286.9	15173.8	75855.3	0	0	0	0	0
24 Ser_world	9064.0	47280.6	0	0	0	0	0	0	0	0	0	0	0	0
25 Ser_pvst	0	0	0	0	0	0	0	0	0	0	0	0	0	0
26 ww_world	166994.	1203123.	230413.	0	0	0	0	0	0	0	0	0	0	0
27 REGHOUS	0	0	0	0	0	0	0	0	0	30870.	5397498.	1631540.	24694.7	2169.2
28 HOUS	0	0	0	0	0	0	0	0	0	0	0	0	0	0
29 PRODTAX	0	0	0	0	0	0	4341.3	41905.1	423026.3	0	0	0	0	0
30 DIRTAX	0	0	0	0	0	0	0	0	0	2811.6	1446064.	243819.3	0	0
31 GOVT	0	0	0	0	0	0	0	0	0	0	0	0	0	0
32 CGDS	0	0	0	0	0	0	0	0	0	0	0	1045521.	0	0
Total	176902.	1274255.	230413.	434430.	5229025.	14973778.	434427.	5226858.	14973778.	33681.	6843563.	2920881.	24694.7	2169.2

Figure ME 1.6. The U.S. Social Accounting Matrix in ViewHar

17. Export the U.S. SAM database to Excel
    > From the menu bar on the ViewHar page, select "Export"
    > Select "Copy Screen to Clipboard" from dropdown menu
    > Open Excel
    > Paste SAM into an Excel file and save it as US3x3.xls.
    > Verify that your SAM's column sums match those displayed in Figure ME 1.6. If they do not, reopen your aggregation file and check your definitions of regions, sectors, and factors, for errors. Correct them and re-create the aggregated database.

C. Download the GTAP Model

These directions for downloading, unzipping, and installing the GTAP model are quite general. Your computer and browser may present a slightly different set of choices for how to do this. The important thing is that you download the model, unzip it and locate the SETUP.exe file, and run the installation program. The installation will create a directory on your hard drive, RunGTAP5, in which the model will be placed.

1. Go to www.GTAP.org
2. From the main menu bar:
    > Select Models/Utilities
    > Select RunGTAP, from the Models/Utilities dropdown menu
    > Select Download RunGTAP, from the RunGTAP downloads section.

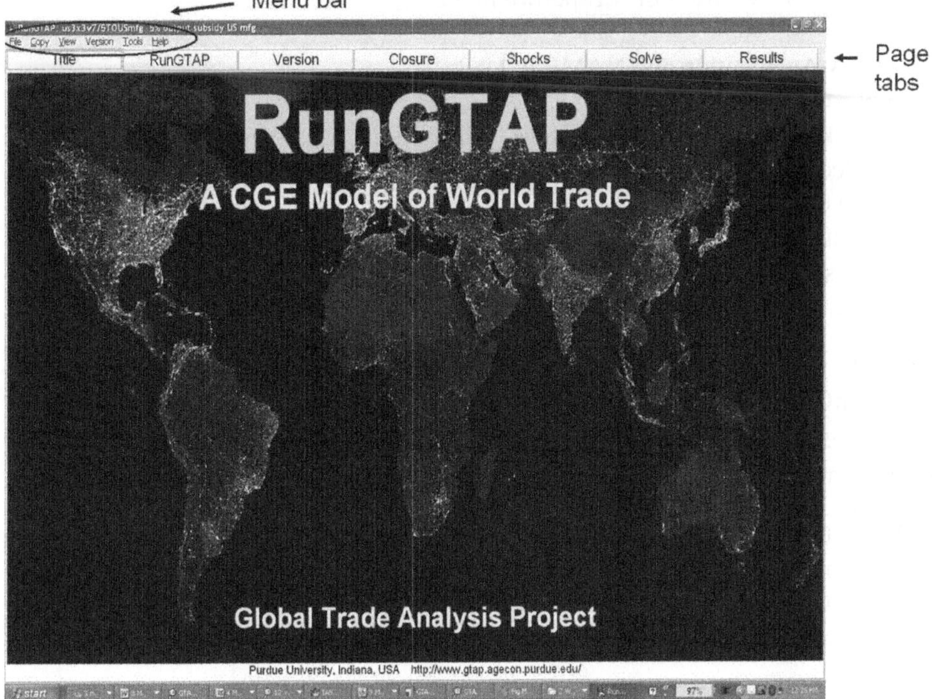

Figure ME 1.7. GTAP model

3. Download the file and select "Unzip and Install." Then select "Set-up" and the program will prompt you to install the program to your hard disk. The default directory is C, but you may choose to install it in a different directory. (Another option is to download and save the file to your temp directory and install it from there, first by clicking on the zipped RunGTAP file and then by clicking on the "set-up" computer icon inside it.)

D. Create a Version of the GTAP Model for the US3x3 Database

The GTAP model is expressed in general functional notation so that it can be used with any database. In this exercise, you will create a "version" of the GTAP model that uses the U.S. 3x3 database. The model version will be called, "US3x3." You can follow these same steps to create a version of the GTAP model that works with any database that you choose to aggregate.

1. Open the RunGTAP model by clicking on the Windows icon for RunGTAP or open it from your start menu. The title page includes a menu bar at the top, and page tabs below the menu bar (Figure ME 1.7). The first time you open it, there may be a warning that an SLI file is missing or obsolete. If so, select "OK."
2. Create a U.S. 3x3 version of your model. In RunGTAP:
   > Select "Version" from the menu bar.

> Select "New" from the dropdown menu
> Next
> New Aggregation and NAME it: US3x3
> Next
> Click on "Locate the Zip archive" (the bottom "locate button"
> Select the US3x3 zip file in the folder that you created for your research project, and click on "Open"
> Next
> Finish
> OK

There is now a folder with the name of your version (i.e. US3x3) saved in the RunGTAP5 directory. GTAP software automatically runs a test of the model version using your data. When this is completed, your U.S. 3x3 model is calibrated and ready to use for experiments.

3. Describe the version of your model
> From the menu bar in the RunGTAP model, select "Tools"
> Select "Options"
> Check the "Developer mode" box
> OK
> Select Version from the page tabs (not from the menu bar above)
> Delete all the text on this page and write your own brief description of your USA 3x3 model; for example, "USA 3x3 model has two regions (U.S. and Rest of World), three factors (Land, Labor, and Capital), and three sectors (Agriculture, Manufacturing, and Services).
> From the menu bar, select Developer
> Select "Save Version.txt" from the dropdown menu
> OK
> From the menu bar, select Tools
> From the dropdown menu, select "Options"
> Uncheck the "Developer mode" box
> Select "OK"

When you open the GTAP model, it always opens the last version that you worked on. If you want to work with a different version, or if you want to change versions as you are working, select "Version" from the menu bar (at the top of the page), and you will find a list of model versions, including the U.S. 3x3 and any other versions that you have created. Select the version that you want to open.

E. Change to Uncondensed Version of the Model

In this course, we will use the "uncondensed" version of the GTAP model, which includes more tax and productivity parameters than the default, condensed version. To switch to the uncondensed version:

1. Change the model version.
   > Select "Version" from the menu bar
   > Select "Modules" from the dropdown menu
   > In the Main model row, click on GTAP in the center (Tab file) column
   > Select GTAPU.TAB from the menu box
   > Click on OK
   > OK
   > OK
2. Run a test simulation:
   > Select "Tools" from the menu bar
   > Run test simulation from the dropdown menu
   > Continue to select OK if there are bad closure warnings, even if there are several.

The GTAP program will now use the uncondensed GTAP model for any model version that you open.

Model Exercise 2: Explore the GTAP Model and Database

Concepts: Locate elements of model – sets, parameters, variables, equations, closure and market-clearing constraints.

The objective of this model exercise is to give you an orientation to the main components of the CGE model and its database. You will learn how to open and search the CGE model's program code, and you will locate and identify your model's sets, parameters, variables, closure, and market clearing constraints.

A. Open the Version of the GTAP Model with U.S. 3x3 Database

1. Open "RunGTAP"
2. On the menu bar, choose "Version"
   > Change
   > Select US3x3
   > OK

B. Explore the Sets in the Database.

1. Open the sets file
   > On the menu bar, select "View"
   > From the dropdown menu, select "Sets"

This opens a HAR file that lists all sets in the model (Figure ME 2.1).
Identify the regions in the model database

> Double click on Set REG (in row 2).
> Write the elements of REG (regions in model):

____

3. Identify the sectors in the model (they are called traded commodities)
   > Click anywhere in the matrix to return to the previous menu
   > Double click on Set TRADE_COMM (in row 3).
   > Write the elements of TRAD_COMM (traded commodities):

____

4. Identify the factors in the model

> Click anywhere in the matrix to return to the previous menu.
> Double click on Set ENDW_COMM (in row 4).
> Write the elements of ENDW_COMM (factors of production):

____

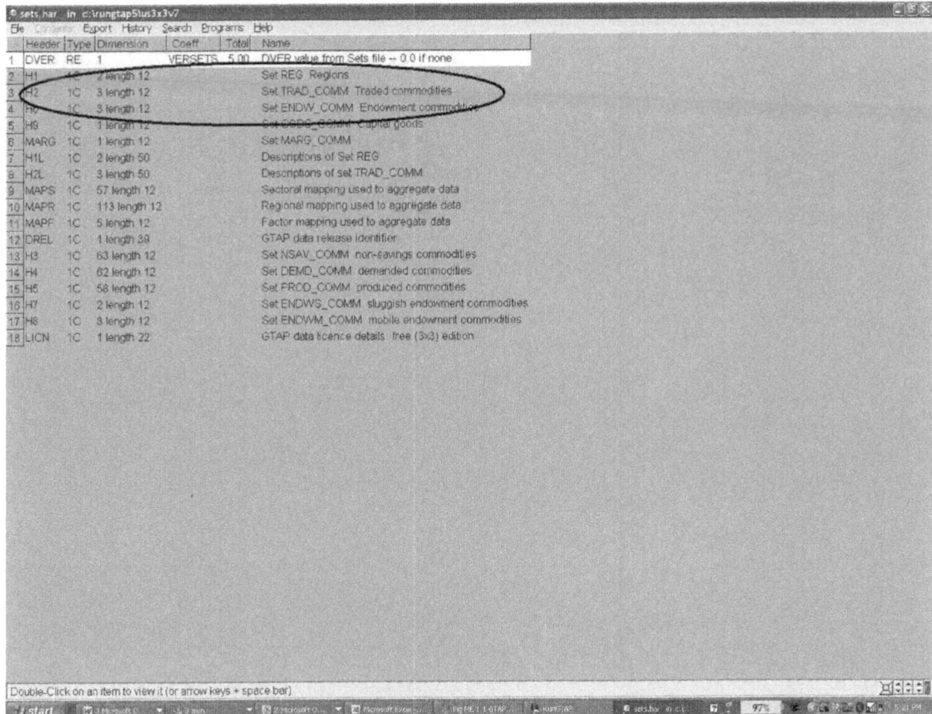

Figure ME 2.1. View set elements

> Close the sets.har file by clinking on the red x in the upper right corner of the HAR file.

C. Explore Table Dimensions of a HAR File

Tables have only two dimensions, rows and columns, yet many variables in the CGE model have more than two dimensions. For example, in the GTAP model, parameter rTMS(TRAD_COMM, s, r) is the import tariff rate on traded goods imported by country *r* from country *s*. The parameter has three dimensions: It is defined for the set of traded goods (TRAD_COMM); the set of source countries, *s;* and the set of destination countries, *r*. To explore variables like this one, you will need to learn how to view variables and parameters of three or more dimensions in a two-dimensional table.

Data used in the GTAP model are contained in header array (HAR) files. You select which dimensions to display in the HAR file by selecting set elements from the dropdown boxes in the upper right corner of the file (Figure ME 2.2). There is one drop down box for each dimension of the variable. In the case of import tariffs, for example, there are three dropdown boxes: TRADE_COMM, countries *s*, and countries *r*. (If the variable has only two dimensions, only two dropdown boxes appear in the upper right

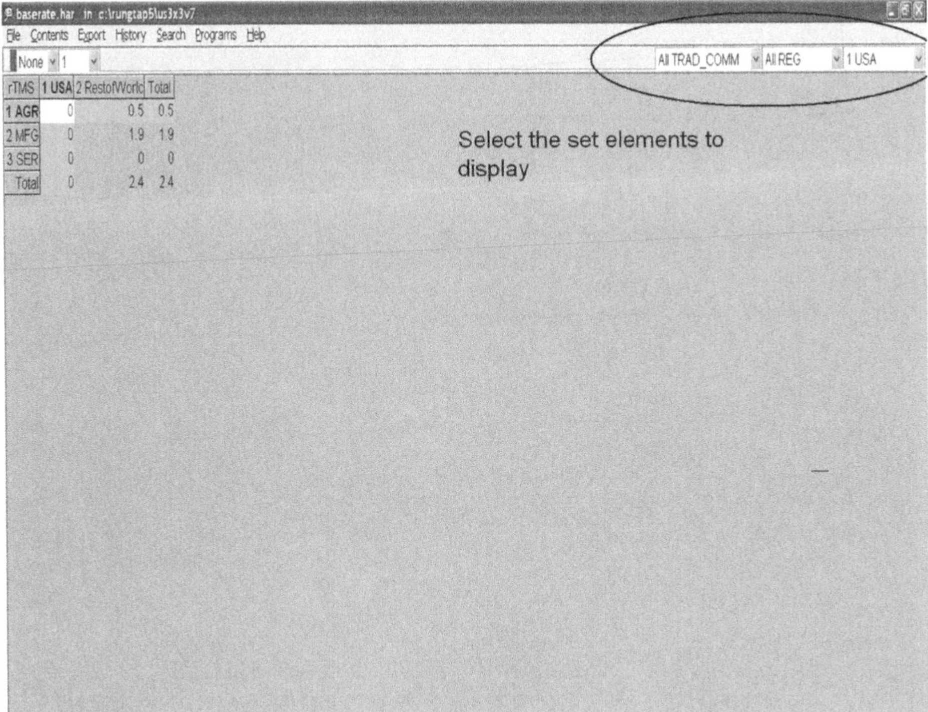

Figure ME 2.2. Select the set elements to display

corner of the file.) Note the set name convention in the GTAP model – country *s,* usually the first country in a variable name, is always the exporter, or source country, of a traded good; and country *r,* usually the second country in the variable name, is always the importing, or destination, country of a traded good.

In the steps below, we show how to view in a table the U.S. import tariff rates on each commodity from each of its trade partners. In this case, we want to display data for all traded goods (TRAD_COMM) and all source countries, s. We will display data for only one importing country, *r*, which is the United States.

In RunGTAP:

> Select "View" from the menu bar
> Select "Base data" from the dropdown menu
> Select "Tax rates" from the dropdown menu
> Select "rTMS" (the last row), which reports import tariff rates

> In the upper right corner of the HAR file, the left side box is ALL TRAD_COMM. Its dropdown box displays all elements of this set: AGR, MFG and SER. Select "All TRAD_Comm." This selection means that data for every traded commodity will be reported in the table.

> In the upper right corner of the HAR file, the center box is ALL_REG. Its drop down box displays all elements of set *s*, the source country for imports. In our model, the set *s* includes the USA and ROW. Select "ALL_REG." This selection means that all source regions will be reported in the table.
> In the upper right corner of the HAR file, the right side box is Sum REG. Its drop down box displays all elements of set r, the destination country for imports. Select "USA." This selection means that data for only one element of set *r* will be displayed.
> Experiment with selecting other elements of set *r*, in the right hand drop down menu. What happens if you select "ALL REG"?
> Close the base rate HAR file by clicking on the red X in the upper right corner.

D. Explore the Elasticity Parameters

In RunGTAP:

> Select "View" from the menu bar.
> Select "Parameters" from the dropdown menu. This har file contains all of the elasticities used in model equations.
> Select INCPAR (row 3).
> What is the INCPAR parameter for U.S. services?
> INCPAR("USA", "SER") = ________
> Double click anywhere in the file to return to the list of parameters.
> Report the elasticities for U.S. agriculture in Table ME 2.1.
> Close the default.prm file by clicking on the red X in the upper right corner.

E. Explore the Tax Rate Parameters

In RunGTAP:

> Select "View" from the menu bar.
> Select "Base data" from the dropdown menu.

Table ME 2.1. *Elasticity Parameters for U.S. Agriculture*

Elasticity	Value
Supply parameters	
Factor substitution (ESUBVA)	0.2
Intermediate input substitution (ESUBT)	
Demand parameters	
Consumer income (INCPAR)	
Consumer substitution (SUBPAR)	
Import substitution (imports v. domestic good) (ESUBD)	
Import substitution (among trade partners) (ESUBM)	

Table ME 2.2. *Tax Rates for U.S. Agriculture*

Tax rate	Name	Value
rTO	% ad valorem output (or income) subsidy in region r	
rTF		
rTPD		
rTPI		
rTGD		
rTGI		
rTFD		
rTFI		
rTXS		
rTMS		

> Select "Tax rates" from the dropdown menu. This HAR file reports all of the tax rates in the GTAP model.
> Double-click on the rTO (first row) to display the output (or income) tax rate.
> In the Table 2.2, report the production tax rate for U.S. agriculture (a negative rate denotes a subsidy).
> Write the names of all of the other taxes in the GTAP model in Table 2.2.
> For each tax, report the tax rate for U.S. agriculture in Table 2.2.
> Be careful to check the dimensions in the upper right corner of the HAR files. In the case of export and import taxes, which are three dimensional parameters, report the export tax on agricultural goods shipped from the U.S. to ROW; and the import tariff on agricultural goods shipped from ROW to the United States.
> Close the base rates HAR file by clicking on the red x in the upper right corner of the file.

F. Explore Model Closure

Model closure defines which variables are endogenous and which variables are exogenous, or fixed.

1. Find the Variable Names and Definitions in the GTAP Model

In RunGTAP:

> Select "View" from the menu bar
> Select "Variables and subsets" from the dropdown menu
> Select "Variables" from the folder tabs in the information file.

Write the definition of the following variables:

pm ________________________________
pop ________________________________
ps ________________________________
qfe ________________________________

qiw ______________________________

qxw ______________________________

> Close the information HAR file by clicking on the red x in the upper rifht corner of the file.

2. Find the Model Closure Statement and Identify the Endogenous and Exogenous Variables

The GTAP model assumes that all model variables are endogenous unless they are explicitly defined to be exogenous. To see which variables are defined as exogenous:

In RunGTAP:

> Select "Closure" from the page tabs.

Which of the variables listed in F.1 above are exogenous? Which are endogenous?

Exogenous: ______________________________

Endogenous: ______________________________

G. Explore the Equations in the GTAP Model

You will become more familiar with the equations of the GTAP model as you gain experience in running the model and analyzing your results. For now, just open the GTAP model's underlying programming code and find the roadmap that describes how equations are organized into blocks of model code:

In RunGTAP, select:

> "View" from the menu bar
> "Tab files" from the dropdown menu
> "Main model" (this command displays the programming code of the main GTAP model.)

Search for the term "Overview of the GTAP.TAB Structure," by selecting:

> Search
> Find
> Enter the search term in the search box.

This section of the model describes the organization of the modeling code in the GTAP model into preliminaries, modules with economic equations, and the calculation of welfare effects using model results.

H. Explore Market-Clearing Constraints

Still in the GTAP.tab file, search for an identity equation that is an example of a market-clearing constraint that ensures that the model's results describe an economic equilibrium in supply and demand. In the search box, enter the term:

"MKTCLDOM"

This equation imposes the constraint that, in each country, the total domestically produced supply of each good is equal to the sum of demand for that good by firms, households, and government.

Model Exercise 3: Run the GTAP Model

Concepts: Define and run experiments, change elasticity parameters and model closure, read model results, use GTAP utilities for welfare decomposition and systematic sensitivity analysis

In this exercise, you will learn to define and run a model experiment (called a "shock"), and to search for and report model results. You will learn how to change an elasticity parameter, change a model closure, and export and compare results. This exercise also shows you how to use GTAP utilities for welfare decomposition and for a systematic sensitivity analysis with respect to elasticity parameters. Model Exercise 3 is designed to serve as a reference that you can turn back to for basic directions as you carry out exercises 4–8. In this exercise, we focus only on the mechanics of using and controlling the GTAP model; we study the economic behavior in the model in exercises 4–9.

A. Open GTAP Model with U.S. 3x3 Database

This step opens the "version" of the GTAP model that uses the U.S. 3x3 database. You created this version of the model in Exercise 1.

1. Open RunGTAP
2. On the upper menu bar, choose Version
   > Select "Change" from the dropdown menu. This opens a list of model versions.
   > Select US3x3
   > OK (this changes the database, or version, used in the GTAP model.)

B. Prepare Your Model to Define and Run an Experiment

The following housekeeping steps may not always be necessary but, like a pilot's preflight check list, it is a good practice to follow them before defining or running any model shock.

1. Prepare your model to define an experiment – check closure
   > Select the Closure page tab.

Check that no closure changes are lingering there. The closure should end with "Rest Endogenous." If not, erase all text below that line.

2. Prepare your model to define an experiment – check shocks
   > Select Shocks page tab
   > Clear shock list

This check ensures that there are no shocks lingering in your experiment file other than those you want to introduce.

3. Check the elasticity parameter file
   > Select Solve page tab
   > Check that the parameter file named in the upper right corner is your preferred file (in this exercise, let it remain as the default parameter file).
4. Check model solution method
   > Select Solve page tab
   > Solution Method (in the upper right corner of the page): select "Change"
   > Choose "Gragg" solution method. (Your choice of solution method may vary; this is the method we use for this exercise. It divides the shock into smaller shocks which the model solves sequentially.)
   > OK (this selects the new solution method)

C. Define a Model Experiment Using the "Shocks" Page

In this exercise, you will introduce a 5 percent output subsidy to U.S. manufacturing. Experiments are defined on the "Shocks" page (see Figure ME 3.1).

1. Select the "Shocks" page tab
   > Select from the "Variable to Shock" dropdown menu: *to*
   > Select from the "Elements to Shock" dropdown menu: MFG
   > Select from the Region dropdown menu: USA

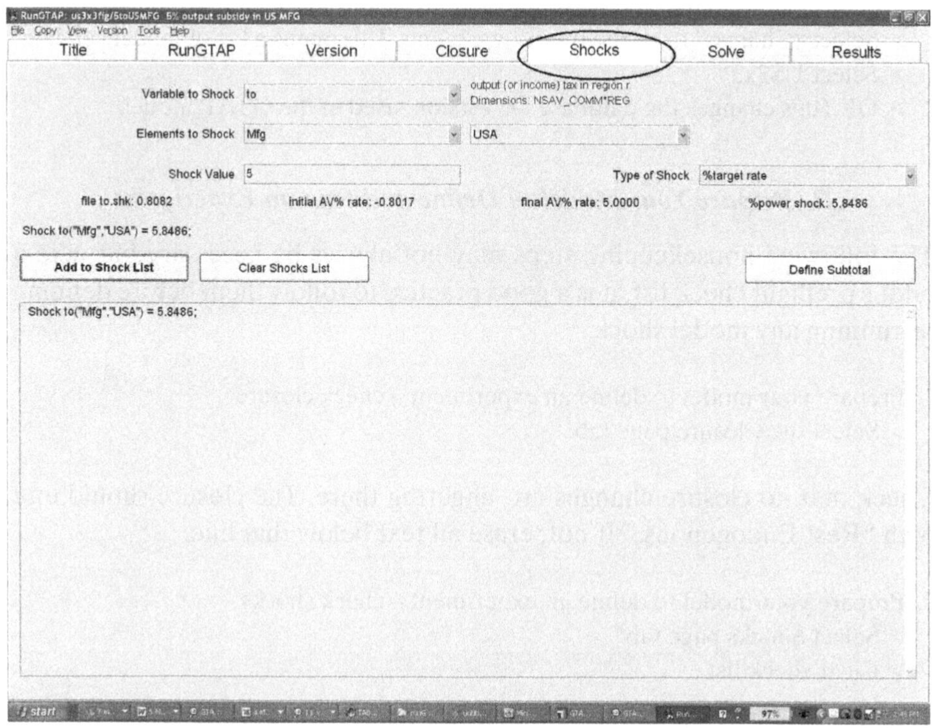

Figure ME 3.1. Shocks page

> For “Shock Value” enter: 5 (positive value is a subsidy, negative is a tax)
> Select from the “Type of Shock” dropdown menu: % target rate
> Click on “Add to shock list.”
> Verify that the shock to the U.S. production tax is the only shock in the shocks list

2. What is the definition of “to”? ____________________
3. What is the initial *ad valorem* (AV) tax rate of “to” in U.S. manufacturing? ________
4. Is the initial rate of “to” a subsidy or a tax? ________________

D. Save a Model Experiment and Solve the Model

Select the “Solve” page tab:

1. Save the experiment file
   > Check solution method. It should be Gragg 2-4-6. If it is not, click on “Change,” select Gragg and then click on “OK”
   > Check parameter file. It should be “Default.” If it is not, click on “Change,” select “Default” from the box and click on “OK”
   > Click on “Save experiment”
   > Name the experiment: 5toUSMFG (see Figure ME 3.2)
   > Description: “5% output subsidy in U.S. MFG”
   > OK (this saves the experiment file)

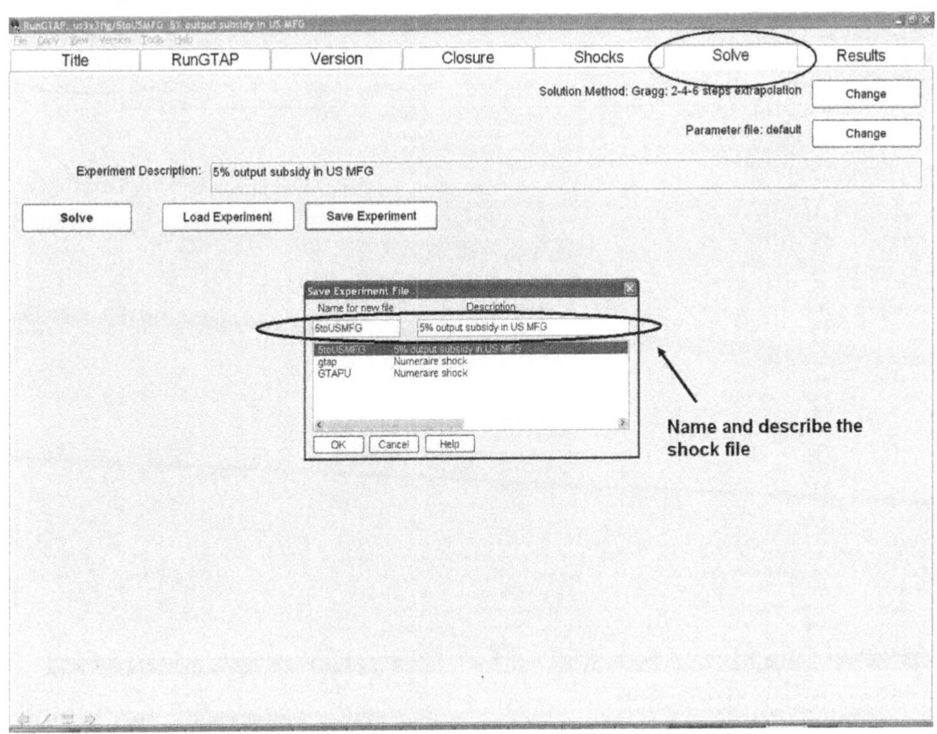

Figure ME 3.2. Solve page

2. Solve the model
   > Still on the Solve page, click on the “Solve” button
   > OK (this closes the accuracy summary report box)
   > OK (this closes a solution information box)
3. Verify that your tax shock was what you think it is. Select:
   > “View” from the menu bar
   > “Updated data” from the dropdown menu
   > Updated tax rates
   > Click on the first row, rTO, to view the rTO matrix and then check the entry for column “USA” and row “MFG”
   > Confirm that rTO for USA MFG is now 5.0. (Note that in this display, a negative value is a tax and a positive value is a subsidy.)
   > Close the file by clicking on the red X in the upper right corner

E. Find and Report Experiment Results

Model results for most variables in the model are reported on the Result page, which is opened by clicking on the Results page tab (Figure ME 3.3). GTAP’s naming convention is to use lower case letters to denote a variable reported as a percentage change from base values, and upper case to denote

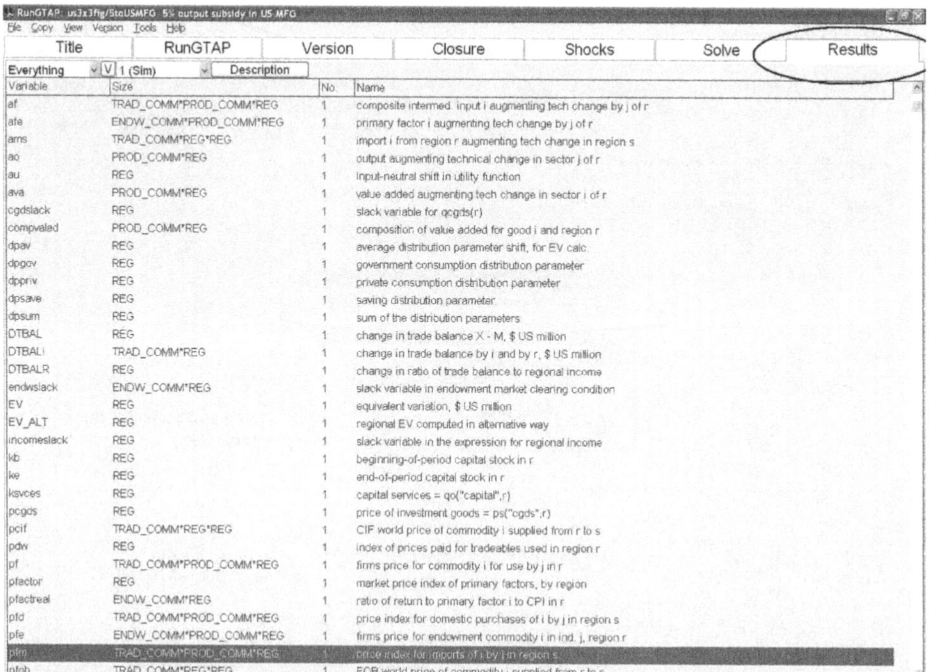

RunGTAP: us3x3fig/5toUSMFG 5% output subsidy in US MFG

File Copy View Version Tools Help

Title | RunGTAP | Version | Closure | Shocks | Solve | Results

Everything | V | 1 (Sim) | Description

Variable	Size	No.	Name
af	TRAD_COMM*PROD_COMM*REG	1	composite intermed. input i augmenting tech change by j of r
afe	ENDW_COMM*PROD_COMM*REG	1	primary factor i augmenting tech change by j of r
ams	TRAD_COMM*REG*REG	1	import i from region r augmenting tech change in region s
ao	PROD_COMM*REG	1	output augmenting technical change in sector j of r
au	REG	1	input-neutral shift in utility function
ava	PROD_COMM*REG	1	value added augmenting tech change in sector i of r
cgdslack	REG	1	slack variable for qcgds(r)
compvalad	PROD_COMM*REG	1	composition of value added for good i and region r
dpav	REG	1	average distribution parameter shift, for EV calc.
dpgov	REG	1	government consumption distribution parameter
dppriv	REG	1	private consumption distribution parameter
dpsave	REG	1	saving distribution parameter
dpsum	REG	1	sum of the distribution parameters
DTBAL	REG	1	change in trade balance X - M, $ US million
DTBALi	TRAD_COMM*REG	1	change in trade balance by i and by r, $ US million
DTBALR	REG	1	change in ratio of trade balance to regional income
endwslack	ENDW_COMM*REG	1	slack variable in endowment market clearing condition
EV	REG	1	equivalent variation, $ US million
EV_ALT	REG	1	regional EV computed in alternative way
incomeslack	REG	1	slack variable in the expression for regional income
kb	REG	1	beginning-of-period capital stock in r
ke	REG	1	end-of-period capital stock in r
ksvces	REG	1	capital services = qo("capital",r)
pcgds	REG	1	price of investment goods = ps("cgds",r)
pcif	TRAD_COMM*REG*REG	1	CIF world price of commodity i supplied from r to s
pdw	REG	1	index of prices paid for tradeables used in region r
pf	TRAD_COMM*PROD_COMM*REG	1	firms price for commodity i for use by j in r
pfactor	REG	1	market price index of primary factors, by region
pfactreal	ENDW_COMM*REG	1	ratio of return to primary factor i to CPI in r
pfd	TRAD_COMM*PROD_COMM*REG	1	price index for domestic purchases of i by j in region s
pfe	ENDW_COMM*PROD_COMM*REG	1	firms price for endowment commodity i in ind. j, region r
pfm	TRAD_COMM*PROD_COMM*REG	1	price index for imports of i by j in region s
pfob	TRAD_COMM*REG*REG	1	FOB world price of commodity i supplied from r to s

Double click on an item to view it (or arrow keys + spacebar)

Figure ME 3.3. Results page

Table ME 3.1. *Results of a 5 Percent Production Subsidy in U.S. Manufacturing, with Different Elasticities and Closures*

	Definition of Variable	Base Results	High Substitution Elasticity	Unemployment Closure
qo("MFG", "USA")				
qo("MFG", "ROW")				
qfe("LABOR", "MFG", "USA")				

Source: GTAP model, GTAP v.7.0 U.S. 3x3 database.

a variable reported in levels. For example, variables in lower case, such as *ps* or *pm*, are the percentage changes in the supply price and market price of a good, respectively. The variable DTBAL is the change in a country's trade balance, reported in $U.S. millions.

1. Find a variable result on the "Results" page
   > Select the Results page tab. (Variables are listed in alphabetical order).
   > Write the definition of the variable *qo("MFG","USA")* in Table 3.1
   > Double-click on variable *qo*
   > Report the result for variable *qo("MFG","USA")* in the United States in the "base results" column of Table 3.1
   > Report the result for manufacturing output in ROW in the "Base results" column of Table 3.1
   > Double-click on data anywhere in the table to return to the variable list

2. Display results of variables with three dimensions using data filter

Tables are two-dimensional displays of data but some variables have more than two dimensions. For example, variable *qfe(i,j,r)* has three dimensions: the quantity of factor *i* used in industry *j* in country *r*. To display results for variable *qfe*, use the data filter in the upper left corner of the results page to select the dimensions to control and the dimensions to display (see Figure ME 3.4). In the example below, you will control dimension r by selecting "USA," so that the variable *qfe(i,j,"USA")* is displayed in a table with a dimension of *i* by *j*.

> Double-click on variable *qfe* – you'll get an error – "Sorry, you cannot view a 3-D matrix."
> From the dropdown menu on the upper left side, which says "Everything" choose "USA" – this controls set *r* so that sets *i* and *j* can be displayed
> Double-click on variable *qfe* and report results for labor demand in MFG for the USA in the "Base results" column of Table ME 3.1
> Double-click on data anywhere in the table to return to the variable list.

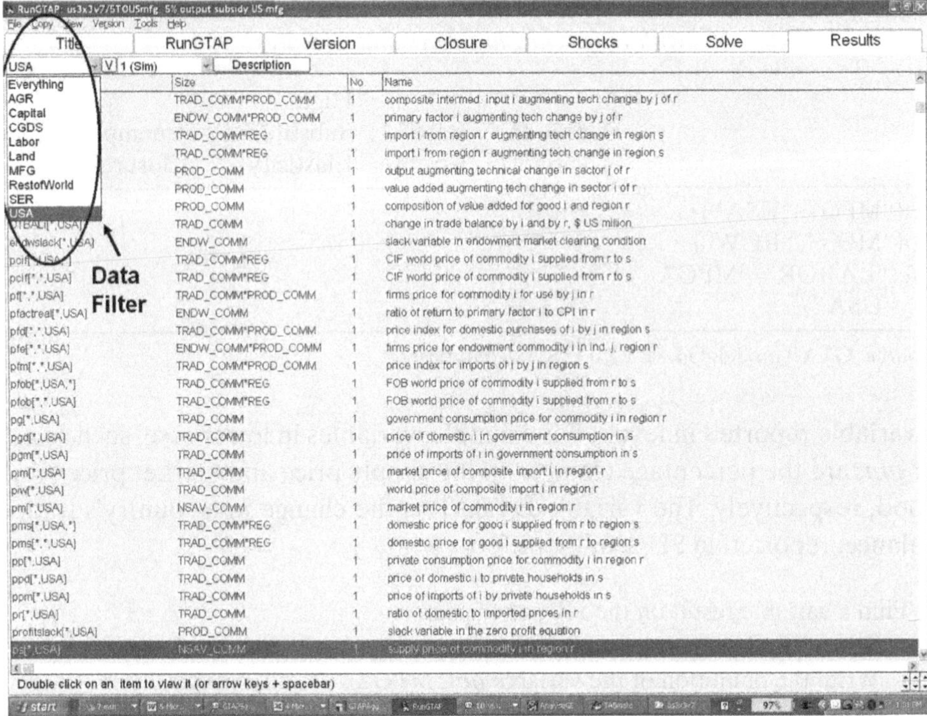

Figure ME 3.4. Data filter on the results page

F. Find and Report Welfare Decomposition Results

The GTAP model includes a utility that decomposes the equivalent variation (EV) welfare effect of an economic shock. We discuss welfare measures in detail in Chapter 6. The utility disaggregates the total welfare effect into six components: resource allocation (efficiency) effects (the excess burden of taxes), endowment effects due to changes in factor supplies, technical change due to productivity gains or losses, the effects of population growth, changes in terms of trade for goods and for savings and investment flows, and changes in preferences (the structure of aggregate demand). Welfare effects are reported in levels, in $ U.S. millions.

1. Open the GTAP welfare decomposition utility:
   > Select "View" from the menu bar
   > Select "Updated Data" from the dropdown menu
   > Select "Welfare Decomposition" from the dropdown menu

This page lists the full decomposition of EV (Figure ME 3.5).

2. View the summary of the welfare decomposition.
   > Double click on first row: EV Decomposition Summary.

Table ME 3.2. *Welfare Decomposition of a 5 Percent Production Subsidy in U.S. Agriculture*

Resource Allocation Effect	Endowment Effect	Technical Change	Population Growth	Terms of Trade	Investment-Savings Terms of Trade	Preference Change	Total
1 alloc_A1 7,399.7	2 endw_B1	3 tech_C1	4 pop_D1	5 tot_E1	6 IS_F1	7 pref_G1	

Source: GTAP model, GTAP v.7.0 U.S. 3x3 database.

> Report the welfare impacts of the 5 percent output subsidy in U.S. manufacturing in Table ME 3.2. As a check, the first element, "Resource allocation effect," is already reported in the table.

> Double click anywhere on the page to return to the main EV decomposition page.

3. View the detailed welfare decomposition

The main welfare decomposition page, shown in Figure ME 3.5, lists all available decompositions. For example, all of rows with headers names that begin with A list decompositions of allocative efficiency effects, by type of tax, and by commodity. All rows with a header name that starts with C

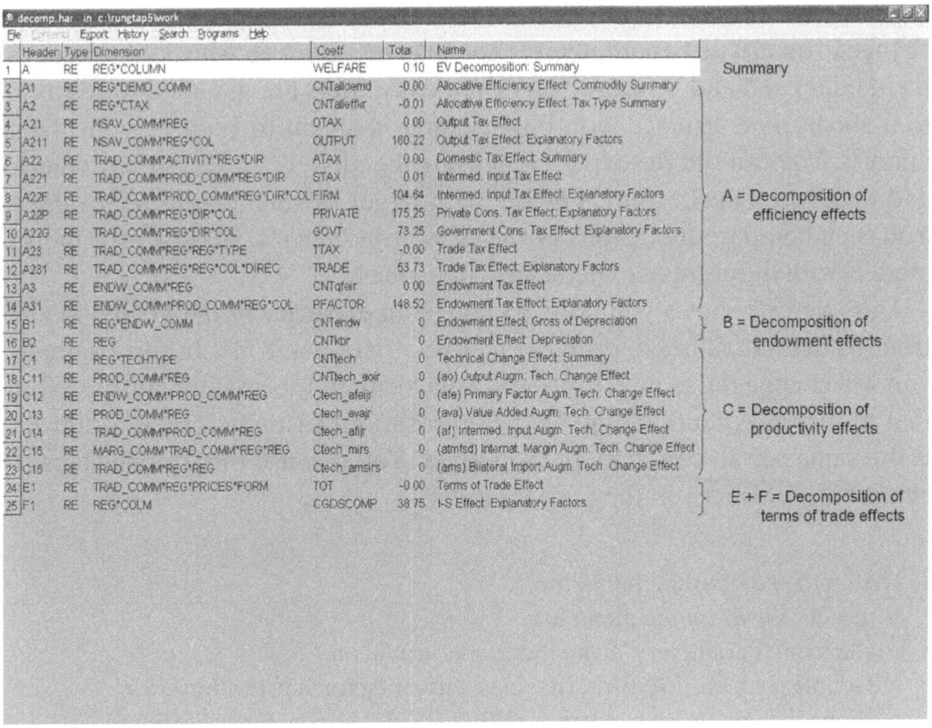

Figure ME 3.5. Welfare decomposition utility in the GTAP model

list decompositions of the productivity effect, and so on. You can view any decomposition in the list by clicking on it.

G. Export Model Results to Excel

You may want to compare the results of two experiments but the GTAP model only reports results for one experiment at a time. The easiest way to save and compare selected results is to export results, one variable at a time, to your clipboard and paste them into an Excel file that identifies the experiment that generated the results.

After running an experiment,

> Select the "Results" page tab
> Double click on the variable that you want to display
> Select "Copy" from the upper menu bar (this copies the results to your clipboard)
> Open Excel and paste your results into your file.
> Label the results with the name of your experiment.

H. View and Change an Elasticity Parameter

Elasticities are the exogenous parameters used in model equations to define the responsiveness of supply and demand to changes in prices or income. A change to an elasticity parameter is not an experiment or "shock." It changes the model itself and how producers and consumers are assumed to respond to a shock. For instance, you might define a shock to be a new tariff on imports. You can run the experiment using the model's base elasticity values, and then run it again using a model with larger or smaller elasticity values. You then compare the results of the *same experiment* across two (or more) models with different assumed elasticity values.

This exercise shows you how to change an elasticity in the GTAP model from its default values and save it in a new parameter file. In this example, you will change the factor substitution elasticity in U.S. manufacturing. Note that in the GTAP model, the factor substitution elasticity for each industry is the same for all countries in the model. You can use these same steps to change any elasticity in the GTAP model.

1. Define the new parameter values
> Select "View" on the menu bar
> Click on "Parameters" from the dropdown menu
> Double click on ESUBVA (the elasticity of factor substitution) row.
> Right click on the data entry for MFG ESBUVA (see Figure ME 3.6)
> Enter new ESUBVA value in manufacturing of "5"

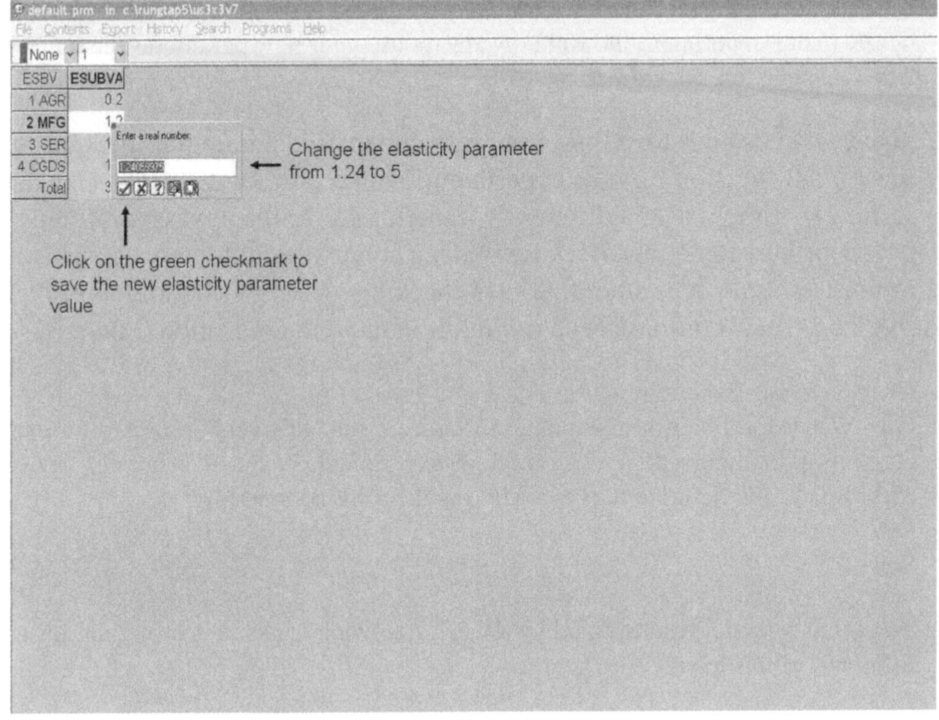

Figure ME 3.6. Changing an elasticity parameter

> Click on the green check mark to save the new elasticity parameter value on this sheet. But be careful, this does not save a new parameter file – see the next step (You may get an error message that "You modified the file but need a GEMPACK license." You may safely ignore the warning for this exercise.)

2. Save your new parameter file
   > Select "File" (in the ESUBVA window).
   > Close
   > Yes (answers the prompt, Save Changes?)
   > IMPORTANT do not overwrite your default parameter file. In the box, provide a new file name with a .prm suffix, such as "5vaMFG.prm"
   > Click on "Save." This step saves your new parameters in a file in your model version folder in the RunGTAP5 directory
   > OK
3. Re-solve the model with a new elasticity
   > Select "Solve" page tab.
   > Check that the experiment description box describes "5toMFG," which means that your experiment is loaded and ready to run
   > If a different experiment is described, select "Load Experiment" and click on "5toMFG" and then click on OK to load the experiment 5toMFG
   > Click on "Change" next to "Parameter file:Default" in the upper right corner of the page

> Select the name of your new parameter file: 5vaMFG
> OK (Your experiment file will now always use your new parameter file unless you change this selection.)

You have two options for saving your experiment and parameter file. One is to save a new version of your experiment, with a new name, which signals that this experiment uses a different parameter file. In the next several steps, we describe how to do this. Because this can create file clutter, an alternative is to reuse a single experiment, always checking to see which parameter file is specified. That is the approach we follow in the remaining model exercises.

> Click on "Save Experiment"
> Give your experiment a new name, to indicate that this version uses different elasticity parameters than your original experiment. Name it something like: "5toMFG2" and describe it as "5toMFG with 5 ESUBVA in Mfg"
> OK
> Solve

4. Report new model results in Table ME 3.1, following the same instructions as in section E of this model exercise.

I. Change Model Closure

Model closure statements define which variables adjust (i.e., which are endogenous) and which are fixed (i.e., which are exogenous). To modify the model's standard closure statements, you must "swap" an exogenous variable for an endogenous variable. This swap preserves the same number of endogenous variables that were originally in the model.

In this exercise section, you will modify the labor market closure. The default closure has an exogenous, fixed national supply of labor (*qo*) and an endogenous economywide wage (*ps*). You will change the closure to swap the labor supply variable with the wage variable . Note that we are changing the closure statement for one factor market (labor) in one country (USA), as shown in Figure ME 3.7.

1. Select the Solve page tab
   > Open the experiment file "5toMFG"
   > Click on the "Load Experiment" button
   > Select the experiment "5toMFG"
   > OK
2. Select the "Closure" page tab
   > Insert the bolded text below the final line of the closure instructions – "Rest Endogenous" (see Figure ME 3.7):
   > **swap qo("labor","USA") = ps("labor","USA");**

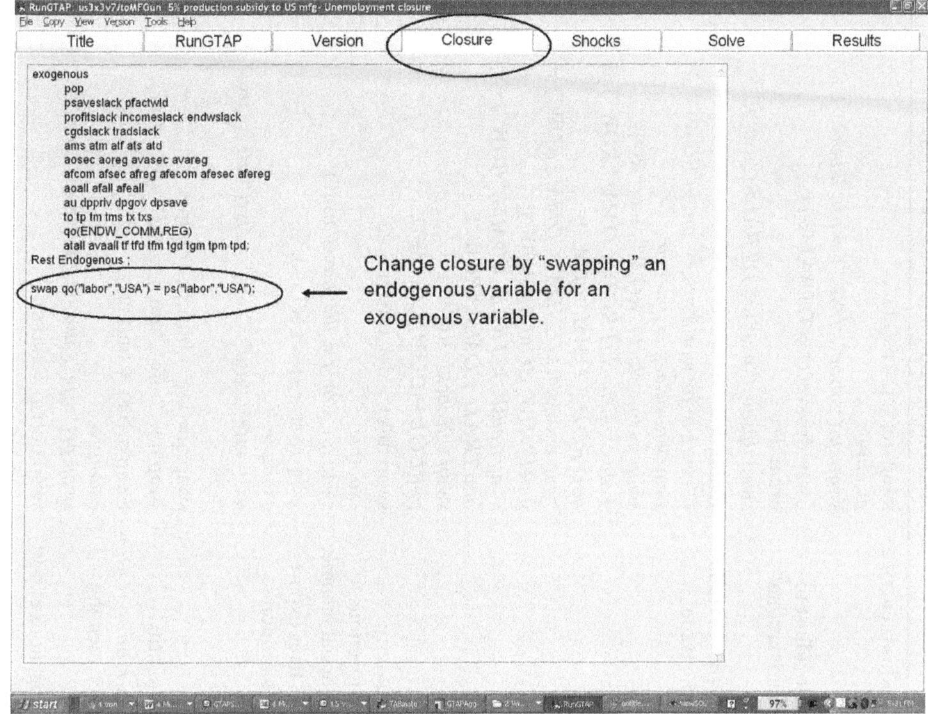

Figure ME 3.7. Changing the labor market closure

3. Select the "Solve" page tab
   > Save experiment
   > Name it "toMFGun" and describe it as "5% output subsidy to US MFG with unemployment." This step saves both the experiment and the new closure statement. You can now rerun this experiment at any time without having to respecify your new closure statement.
   > OK
   > Solve
   > OK
   > OK
   > Report new model results in Table ME 3.1.
4. Do results of your experiment change when the elasticity or model closure statement changes?

Table ME 3.3 lists commonly used closure modifications in the GTAP and their related swap statements.

J. Systematic Sensitivity Analysis and Stochastic Shocks

The GTAP model includes a utility developed by Arndt and Pearson (1998) that automates a systematic analysis of the sensitivity of model results to the assumed values of elasticity parameters or to the size of an experiment

Table ME 3.3. *Commonly Modified Closures in the GTAP Model*

Closure in GTAP Model	Explanation	Add this Model Code to Closure Statement
Factor unemployment	For a specified country *r* and factor *f*, allows the endowment of a factor to vary and fixes that factor's price.	swap qo(f,r) = ps(f,r); *example:* *swap qo("labor","USA") = ps("labor","USA");*
Fixed balance of trade	For a specified country *r*, allows domestic savings to adjust to maintain a fixed ratio between the trade balance and national income.	Swap dpsave(r) = DTBALR(r); *example:* *swap dpsave("usa") = DTBALR("usa");*
Fixed world import price (small country assumption for country r)	For a specified country *r*, fixes world import prices (*pm* in trade partner, *s*) by swapping several slack variables in the trade partner country.	*Example:* *Closure to fix world price – pm in ROW* *swap walraslack = pfactwld;* *swap incomeslack("ROW") = y("ROW");* *swap profitslack(PROD_COMM,"ROW") = qo(PROD_COMM,"ROW");* *swap endwslack(ENDW_COMM,"ROW") = pm(ENDW_COMM,"ROW");* *swap tradslack(TRAD_COMM,"ROW") = pm(TRAD_COMM,"ROW");* *swap cgdslack("ROW") = pm(CGDS_COMM,"ROW");*
Tax replacement or balanced government budget	For a specified country *r*, sales tax on private commodity consumption (imports plus domestic) becomes endogenous to maintain a fixed ratio of indirect tax revenue to national income.	swap tp(r) = del_ttaxr(r); *example:* *swap tp("usa") = del_ttaxr("usa");*
Export quantity control	For a specified commodity and bilateral trade flow, fixes export supply to partner; endogenous export tax measures economic rent to exporting country.	swap qxs(i,r,s) = txs(i,r,s); *example:* *qxs("mfg", "usa", "row") = txs("mfg", "usa", "row");*
Import quantity control	For a specified commodity *i* and importing country *r*, an endogenous import tariff maintains fixed import quantity.	swap qiw(i,s) = tm(i,s); *example:* *swap qiw("mfg","usa") = tm("mfg","usa");*
Variable import levy	For a specified commodity *i* and importing country *r*, an endogenous import tariff maintains a fixed ratio between the domestic market price and its world import price	Swap pr(i,r) = tm(i,r); *example:* *swap pr("mfg","usa") = tm("mfg","usa");*
Insulate domestic production levels from world market conditions	For a specified commodity *i* and country *r*, an endogenous export subsidy varies to maintain a fixed domestic production level.	swap qo(i,s) = tx(i,s); *example:* *swap qo("mfg","usa") = tx("mfg","usa");*

Text Box ME 3.1. Chebyshev's Theorem

At least the fraction $(1 - (1/k^2)$ of any set of observations lies within k standard deviations of the mean, therefore:

a. 75% of the observations are contained in the interval $\overline{x} \pm 2sd$
b. 88.9% of the observations are contained in the interval $\overline{x} \pm 3sd$
c. 95% of the observations are contained in the interval $\overline{x} \pm 4.47sd$
d. 99% of the observations are contained in the interval $\overline{x} \pm 10sd$

shock.[2] To test the sensitivity to elasticity values, the modeler chooses which elasticity parameter(s) to test and specifies the range of values over which each will be tested. For example, the modeler may have assumed a value of two for the import substitution elasticity, but wants to test the sensitivity of model results if its value ranges between 50 and 150 percent. The utility reports an estimate of the mean and standard deviation of results for every variable in the model as the elasticity value ranges between one and three.

A test of the sensitivity of model results to variability in model shocks is carried out in a similar way. In this case, the modeler defines a possible range for the parameter that is being shocked. For example, the modeler may be studying the effects of climate change on productivity in agricultural production, which he has described in the model as a negative 10 percent shock to total output productivity. If estimates of productivity losses vary widely in the literature, the modeler may want to test a range in productivity loss between 50 percent and 150 percent of the 10 percent decline. In this case, the sensitivity analysis would estimate the mean and standard deviation of model results for each variable, as the productivity shock ranges in value between minus 5 percent and minus 15 percent.

You can use the estimated means and standard deviations to calculate confidence intervals for your model result. We use Chebyshev's theorem for these calculations because it does not require us to assume anything about the shape of the probability distribution of the results for each variable (Text Box ME 3.1).

As an example, imagine that you carried out a model experiment for which you assumed an import substitution elasticity value of two, with the result that output of good Q increases 19.1 percent. You then carried out a systematic sensitivity analysis to a range of between 50 and 150 percent of that elasticity value. Suppose your sensitivity analysis reports that the percent change in output of good Q has an estimated mean of nineteen and standard deviation of one. Using Chebyshev's theorem, you can construct a 95 percent confidence interval. For example, the upper limit of a 95 percent

[2] A detailed and intuitive description of the Stochastic Sensitivity Analysis (SSA) utility is available after opening this utility in the GTAP model.

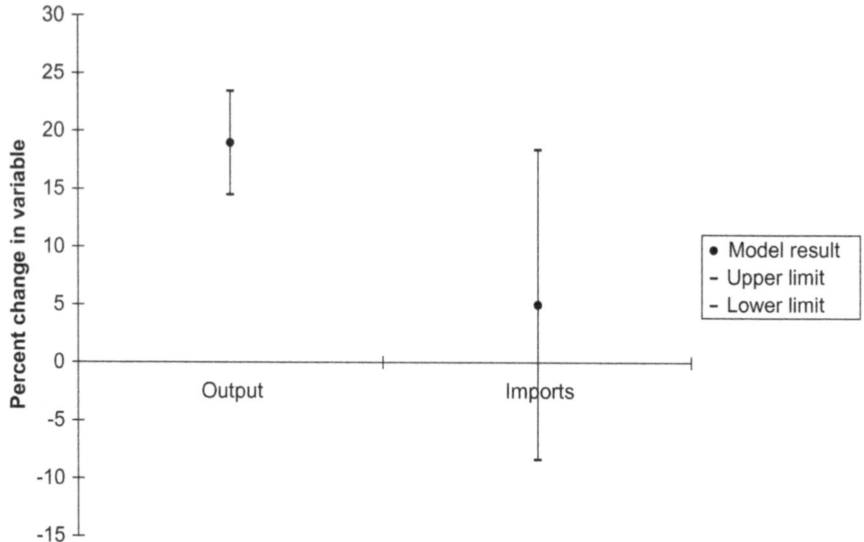

Figure ME 3.8. 95 percent confidence intervals for output and import quantities of good Q

confidence interval is twenty-four , because 19 + (4.47 * 1) = 24. The lower limit is fifteen, because 19 – (4.47 * 1) = 15. Similarly, you can report with 75 percent confidence that the result lies between twenty-one and seventeen, which is nineteen plus or minus two (two times the standard deviation of one), and so forth.

Figure ME 3.8 plots these results on a graph. It shows the point estimate for the percentage change in output, which is the result reported in your model. It also plots the upper and lower limits of the 95 percent confidence interval that we calculated. Plotting model results along with confidence intervals is an effective way to visually communicate information about model sensitivity. In this case, a positive output change is a robust model result over the range that you specified for the value of the import substitution elasticity.

On the other hand, let's assume that your analysis reports a percentage change in the import quantity of good Q of 5 percent, with a mean of five and a standard deviation of three. Using Chebyshev's theorem, you have a 95 percent level of confidence that the percentage change in imports lies between eighteen and minus eight, and a 75 percent level of confidence that the result lies between eleven and minus one. In this case, you cannot be 95 percent confident or even 75 percent confident that imports increase, instead of fall, over your specified range of alternative elasticity parameter values.

The following steps will guide you in carrying out an analysis of the sensitivity of model results to the elasticity of factor substitution. A sensitivity analysis with respect to the size of an experiment shock is analyzed in the same way, so we do not repeat the instructions for that case. Our example is a systematic sensitivity analysis of the results of a 5 percent output

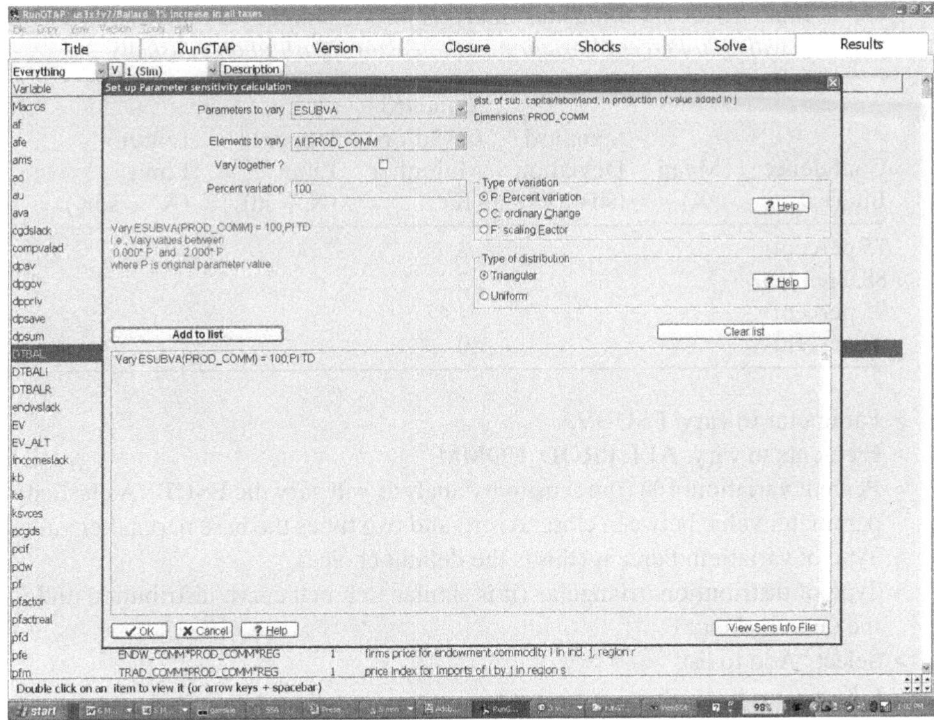

Figure ME 3.9. Systematic sensitivity analysis of an elasticity parameter

subsidy in U.S. manufacturing to the value of the import substitution (ESUBD) elasticity parameter.

1. In runGTAP, reload and rerun your experiment "5toUSMFG."
   > go the to "Solve" page tab
   > Click on "Load Experiment" button
   > Select "5toUSMFG" experiment
   > OK
   > Check that parameter file to be used is default.prm; if not, click on the "Change" button, select default.prm from the list, and click >OK.
   > Solve
   > OK
   > OK
2. Open the Systematic Sensitivity Analysis utility
   > Select "Tools" from the top menu bar
   > Select Sensitivity
   > Help on sensitivity (This provides documentation and explanation of this utility that you can use as a reference.)
   > Close the help document by clicking on the red X in the upper right corner of the file. This returns you to the GTAP model.
   > "Tools"
   > "Sensitivity"
   > "w.r.t. parameters" (the worksheet shown in Figure ME 3.9 will open)

Table ME 3.4. *Confidence Intervals for the Output Quantity Result with 100 Percent Variation in the Factor Substitution Elasticity*

Confidence Interval	Mean (X)	Standard Deviation (sd)	Standard deviation Multiplier (K)	Upper Limit (X + sdK)	Lower Limit (X − sdK)
75 percent			2		
88.9 percent			3		
95 percent			4.47		
99 percent			10		

> Parameter to vary: ESUBVA
> Elements to vary: ALL PROD_COMM
> Percent variation: 100 (the sensitivity analysis will vary the ESUBVA elasticity parameter value between close to zero and two times the base parameter value
> Type of variation: Percent (this is the default choice)
> Type of distribution: triangular (it is similar to a bell curve distribution and is the default choice)
> Select "Add to list"
> OK
> Select "Stroud" (this is the default choice. It defines the sampling of parameter values within the range that you specified.)
> OK (this starts the analysis)
> Yes (to the prompt, do you want to save the two solutions reporting means and deviations?)
> OK (to the prompt asking you to name the two report files)
> Replace the star in the file name with "5toUSMFG" – without the quotes. The files with the means and deviations will be named: 5toUSMFGm1.sl4 and 5toUSMFGsd.sl4.
> Yes (this opens ViewSol utility, used to view the files with the sensitivity analysis results)

3. Report results from the ViewSol file for U.S. manufacturing output, *qo*("MFG", "USA").
   a. Model result (reported in first column of data) ______________
   b. Mean (m1 – reported in second column of data) ______________
   c. Standard deviation (sd – reported in third column of data) ______________
4. Construct confidence intervals using Chebyshev's Theorem, following the example in the first row of the table. Report them in Table ME 3.4. What is your level of confidence that the effect on U.S. manufacturing output is positive?

Model Exercise 4: Soaring Food Prices and the U.S. Economy

Concepts: Utility function, Armington import demand, small-country closure

Background

In 2008, the prices of major agricultural commodities soared by more than 60 percent compared to their 2006 levels, after many years of relative price stability (Trostle, 2008). Prices abated when the global economy entered a recession, but some analysts view this price decline as temporary. They anticipate a long-term trend of rising food prices as future growth in global food demand outpaces growth in global supply.

Both short and long term factors were at play in the skyrocketing of prices during 2008, according to Jeffrey Sachs, a noted Harvard economist writing for *Scientific American*. On the demand side, rising world incomes have led to a steady increase in the demand for grains because increased affluence leads to higher demand for meat. More grain must be used as feed, and the grain-to-food conversion ratio for meat is lower than when grain is consumed directly in products such as bread. China's rapid economic growth and the rising share of meat in the Chinese diet has been a major factor in this trend. Rising demand for feed affects not only the food-feed trade-off for grains; it has also led farmers around the world to grow more of the other necessary livestock feedstuffs such as soybeans, instead of grains. On the supply side, short-term supply shocks that influenced prices in 2008 included Australia's deep drought and the U.S. policy to use corn for ethanol. In the longer term, climate change due to rising world temperatures is expected to change the suitability of land for its traditional agricultural uses, possibly leading to lower productivity in the supply of food.

Given the multiple causes of the potential imbalance between world supply and demand for food in the long term, economists have called for multipronged solutions (Cline, 2007; Collier, 2008). Their proposals include increasing research to raise agricultural productivity, particularly in developing countries where climate change is expected to have the most severe consequences for farming. Other recommendations are for policy change in the United States to end the diversion of corn into ethanol; an end to the European Union ban on imports of high-productivity, genetically modified food products; and global action on mitigating the long-term threat of climate change.

How will long-term rising food prices affect U.S. households' demand for food and the composition of their consumption basket? Will U.S. welfare rise or fall? How might this demand shift affect U.S. industry structure and trade? In this exercise, you will simulate a 50 percent increase in the world price of agricultural products imported to the United States and use your model results to answer these and other questions. You will also analyze the sensitivity of your results to alternative assumptions about U.S. consumer preferences.

Experiment Design

You will run a single model experiment – a 50 percent increase in the global price of agricultural products. This experiment will require you to change the GTAP model closure to fix market prices in the rest-of-world region. This closure implies that the United States is too small in the world markets to affect global price levels. The size of the price shock is slightly smaller than the 60 percent world price increase reported by Trostle (2008). We scale the price effect downward because our single agricultural sector includes commodities and natural resources not studied by Trostle; but for illustrative purposes, we still assume a relatively large price shock.

You will run the same model experiment when assuming two different utility functions. In the first experiment, scenario 1, you will use the GTAP model's, CDE demand system with the default consumer demand elasticity parameters in the U.S. 3x3 database. (INCPAR is the income parameter and SUBPAR is the compensated, own-price demand parameter.) In scenario 2, you will modify the consumer's utility function by changing the INCPAR and SUBPAR parameters to replicate those of a Cobb-Douglas utility function.

Instructions

1. Open GTAP model with U.S. 3x3 database

This step opens the "version" of the GTAP model that uses the U.S. 3x3 database. You created this version of the model in Model Exercise 1.

> Open RUNGTAP
> On the top menu bar, choose "Version"
> "Change"
> Select "US3x3"
> OK

2. Prepare your model to run an experiment – check closure
> Select the "Closure" page tab.

Check that no closure changes are lingering there. The closure should end with "Rest Endogenous." If not, erase all text below that line.

3. Prepare your model to run an experiment – check shocks
> Select "Shocks" page tab
> Clear shock list

Table ME 4.1. *Elasticities in Two Scenarios of a 50 Percent Increase in the World Agricultural Price*

	Scenario 1		Scenario 2	
Elasticities	INCPAR	SUBPAR	INCPAR	SUBPAR
Agriculture				
Manufacturing				
Services				

This check ensures that there are no shocks lingering in your experiment file other than those you want to introduce.

4. In Table ME 4.1, report your model's base parameter values for INCPAR and SUBPAR for the United States for scenario 1. (See Model Exercise 2 for instructions on exploring elasticity parameters.)
5. In Table ME 4.2, report base budget shares of each commodity in household expenditure.
   > Select "View" from the upper menu bar
   > "Base data" from the dropdown menu
   > "GTAPView Output"
   > "NVPA" (Row 16) this reports commodity composition of household consumption
   > Open the dropdown menu at top left, next to the box that says "None"
   > Select "COL" from the dropdown box This reports each cell as a percentage of the column total. In this case, the matrix now reports the shares of each commodity in total private household spending. Report the data for the U.S. household.
6. Change the model closure to fix the world price (*pm*) of AGR in the rest-of-world by adding these lines of code to the Closure page, following the final line "Rest Endogenous." (See Model Exercise 3 for instructions on changing model closure.)

```
swap walraslack = pfactwld;
swap incomeslack("ROW") = y("ROW");
swap profitslack(PROD_COMM,""ROW") = qo(PROD_COMM,"ROW");
swap endwslack(ENDW_COMM,"ROW") = pm(ENDW_COMM,
  "ROW");
swap tradslack(TRAD_COMM, "ROW") = pm(TRAD_COMM,"ROW");
swap cgdslack("ROW") = pm(CGDS_COMM,"ROW");
```

Table ME 4.2. *Household Budget Shares*

	Base	Scenario 1	Scenario 2
Agriculture	.009		
Manufacturing			
Services			

Table ME 4.3. *Effects of a 50 Percent Increase in the World Price of Imported Agriculture (% change from base)*

	Consumer Price	Consumer Commodity Quantity	Household Domestic Quantity	Household Import Quantity	Production Quantity	Household Expenditure	Welfare $U.S. Million
GTAP variable name	*pp*	*qp*	*qpd*	*qpm*	*qo*	*yp*	EV
Agr.							
Mfg.							
Services							
Cobb-Douglas							
Agr.							
Mfg.							
Services							

7. Define your model experiment: 50 percent increase in *pm*("AGR","ROW")
   > Select Shock page table
   > Variable to shock, : "*pm*"
   > Elements to shock: "AGR,""ROW")
   > % change shock: 50 percent
   > Add to shock list
8. Change solution method and save the experiment
   > Select the "Solve" page tab
   > On the solve page, the solution method should be Johansen. If it is not, click on "Change." Select Johansen and then click on "OK"
   > On the solve page, check that the parameter file is "Default." If it is not, click on "Change," select "Default" from the box and click on "OK"
   > Click on "Save" and name the shock "PWAgr", describe it as 50 percent increase in the U.S. AGR import price
9. Solve the model
   > Click on "Solve"
   > OK
   > OK
10. Report model results in Table ME 4.3.
11. Report your results for new budget shares:
   > Select "View" from the upper menu bar
   > "Updated data" from the dropdown menu
   > GTAPView Output
   > NVPA (Row 16) this reports the updated commodity composition of household consumption
   > Select the dropdown menu for the box at top left, that says "None"
   > Select "COL", this reports each cell as a share of the column sum. These are the updated shares of each commodity in total private household spending. Report the data for the U.S. household in Table ME 4.2

12. Change your utility function parameters to replicate a Cobb-Douglas function (see Model Exercise 3 for instructions on how to change elasticity values and save a new parameter file.)
    > Set all INCPAR for the United States and rest-of-world equal to exactly one
    > Set all SUBPAR for the United States and rest-of-world equal to exactly zero
    > Save your new parameter file as "CobbDoug.prm"
13. View, and report in Table ME 4.1, your model's new parameter values for INCPAR and SUBPAR for the United States for scenario 2.
14. Save your experiment and rerun the model with the new parameter values
    > Select the "Solve" page tab
    > Click on the "Change" button next to "Parameter file: default" in the upper right corner
    > Select "CobbDoug" from the list
    > OK
    > Save the shock under its original name "PWAgr" (this saves the shock's linkage to the new parameter file)
    > Click on "Solve"
    > OK
    > OK
15. Report your new model results in Table ME 4.3.

Interpret Model Results

1. Compare the assumptions of the two utility functions in your CGE analysis about own-price elasticities of demand for agriculture (Table 4.3). How do you anticipate that the price increase will affect the quantity of household demand for AGR in both scenarios? Is this expectation consistent with the results of your general equilibrium model for both scenarios?
2. Compare the income effects implied by the utility functions and their parameter values, used in each scenario. Are the functions homothetic? For each utility function, describe whether each of the three goods are a necessity or a luxury, or if its demand quantity changes by the same proportion as income.
3. The elasticity of substitution is calculated as the percentage change in the quantity ratio of X to Y, relative to the percentage change in the price ratio of Y to X. (Hint, recall Text Box 2.1 on how to calculate the percentage change in a ratio.) Use model results from the experiment with the Cobb-Douglas utility function to calculate the elasticities of substitution (σ_C) between AGR and MFG and between AGR and SER. How would you characterize the relative curvature of indifference curves between these two pairs of goods?
4. How do changes in budget shares spent on agriculture compare in the two scenarios? Explain why these results, using your knowledge of the two different utility functions.

5. Most discussion of the world agricultural price shock focuses on consumers. How will the world price shock affect producers and the industrial composition of the U.S. economy? Can you explain why?
6. What is the Armington assumption? What is the import substitution elasticity (ESUBD) for AGR in your model? Given this assumption and parameter value, how do you expect U.S. demand quantities for AGR imports will respond when the world price increases by 50 percent? Is this expectation borne out by model results in both scenarios?
7. Using the model's results for the percentage changes in quantities of private household demand for imported (*qpm*) and domestic varieties (*qpm*), calculate households' elasticity of import substitution between the domestic and imported varieties for both scenarios. For scenario one, the percentage changes in the household's prices of domestic and imported varieties are 21.8 percent and 47.42 percent respectively. For scenario two, the respective percentage price changes are 21.29 percent and 47.43 percent. Are model results consistent with the elasticity you reported in question 6?
8. What does it mean when a country experiences a change in an equivalent variation measure of its welfare? In this experiment, is the United States better or worse off after the shock? Is this result sensitive to your choice of utility function?
9. Compare the effects of the two scenarios on household incomes (*yp*). Is this result sensitive to your choice of utility function?

Model Exercise 5: Food Fight: Agricultural Production Subsidies

Concepts: Production function, production subsidy, SUBTOTAL, factor substitution elasticity

Background

"Farm subsidies have outlived their usefulness," according to Robert Samuelson, the economic columnist for the *Washington Post* and *Newsweek*. In a recent column, "*The Endless Foodfight*," Samuelson argued that the original goals of farm subsidy programs have been met in the United States and other high-income countries. In the United States, agricultural subsidies were introduced in the depths of the Great Depression in order to raise incomes in rural areas and keep food prices low. Although there have been some modifications in the subsidy program over the years, the United States still provides production subsidies to its agricultural producers. Yet, conditions for farmers today are much different than they were in the 1930s. U.S. farm households now earn as much or more than the average urban U.S. household, and food accounts for only a small share of the budget of the average American family. Some people may advocate subsidies as a strategy to ensure that the United States maintains its ability to feed itself and avoids dependence on food imports. However, growing food imports by the United States largely reflect Americans' rising standard of living. Imports provide U.S. consumers with specialized agricultural and food products, and year-round access to seasonal produce.

Subsidies are costly and governments pay for them by levying taxes on other parts of the economy. Agricultural subsidies in the United States and other high-income countries have an additional cost – they jeopardize the success of global negotiations on trade liberalization, sponsored by the World Trade Organization (WTO). The countries' use of agricultural subsidies is thought to distort global markets by increasing their farm production and lowering world agricultural prices, thereby creating unfair competition for farmers in other countries. As long as high-income countries' agricultural subsidies remain in place, many of their trade partners are unwilling to lower their tariffs and allow greater entry to these and other exports from high-income countries.. The stalemate over agricultural subsidies contributed to the breakdown of the WTO negotiations in 2008.

If farm subsidies have outlived their usefulness and are increasingly costly, why do the United States and other high-income countries continue to use them? In this model exercise, you will conduct an experiment in which you eliminate all U.S. agricultural subsidies, which include production subsidies, intermediate input subsidies, and land use subsidies. You will use SUBTOTAL, a GTAP utility that allows you to decompose the results of each component of a multi-part experiment. Experiment results will illustrate the costs and benefits of agricultural subsidies in the United States, and provide some insight as to why it is so hard to eliminate them.

Experiment Design

What is the effect of an existing tax or tariff on an economy? One way to measure its effect is to remove it. The difference between an economy with and without the tax or subsidy provides a measurement of its economic impact.

In this exercise, you will calculate the cost of U.S. agricultural taxes and subsidies by removing them in three steps:

1. Eliminate all production taxes/subsidies;
2. Eliminate all land-base factor use subsidies; and
3. Eliminate all subsidies on the purchase of intermediate inputs by agricultural producers.

Instructions

1. Open the GTAP model with U.S. 3x3 database

This step opens the "version" of the GTAP model that uses the U.S. 3x3 database. You created this version of the model in exercise 1.

> Open "RUNGTAP"
> On the top menu bar, choose "Version"
> Change
> Select "US3x3"
> OK

2. Prepare your model to run an experiment – check closure
   > Select the "Closure" page tab.

Check that no closure changes are lingering there. The closure should end with "Rest Endogenous." If not, erase all text below that line.

3. Prepare your model to run an experiment – check shocks
   > Select "Shocks" page tab
   > Clear shock list
   This check ensures that there are no shocks lingering in your experiment file other than those you want to introduce.

Table ME 5.1. *Base and Updated Subsidy Rates*

	Base Rate	Updated Rate
Production subsidy		
rto("AGR", "USA")		
(negative value = tax)		
Land subsidy		
rtf("LAND", "AGR", "USA")		
(negative value = subsidy)		
Intermediate input subsidy on domestic input		
rtfi("AGR", "AGR", "USA")		
(negative value = subsidy)		
Intermediate subsidy on imported input		
rtfi("AGR", "AGR", "USA")		
(negative value = subsidy)		

4. Eliminate output subsidies in U.S. agriculture (*to*, "AGR", "USA")
   > Choose "Shocks" page tab
   > From the dropdown menu "Variable to shock," choose variable "*to*"
   > Select these elements of *to*: AGR and USA.
   > Note the initial *ad valorem* (AV) percent rate. This is the percentage production tax rate on U.S. agriculture. Write it down in Table ME 5.1.
   > Set a shock value of zero
   > Select "target rate = 0"
   > Click on "Add to shocks list"

5. Define output subsidy elimination as a "Subtotal" in your results
   > Click on "Define subtotal" button

This opens a dialogue box, shown in Figure ME 5.1, where you define each subtotal. You can wait and define all of your subtotals after you have finished setting up your experiment file, or you can define each subtotal after selecting each part of your shock, as we do in these instructions.

> Select variable: *to*
> Select elements: "AGR" and "USA"
> Click on "Add variable to the subtotal"
> OK
> Name it "AGR output subsidy"
> OK

6. Eliminate the factor use subsidy on land, *tf*, used in AGR by setting *tf* for elements Land, AGR, USA to zero (target rate = 0). Note the initial AV percent tax rate for *tf* and write it in Table ME 5.1.
7. Define the elimination of the land use subsidy as a subtotal in your results, named "Land subsidy"

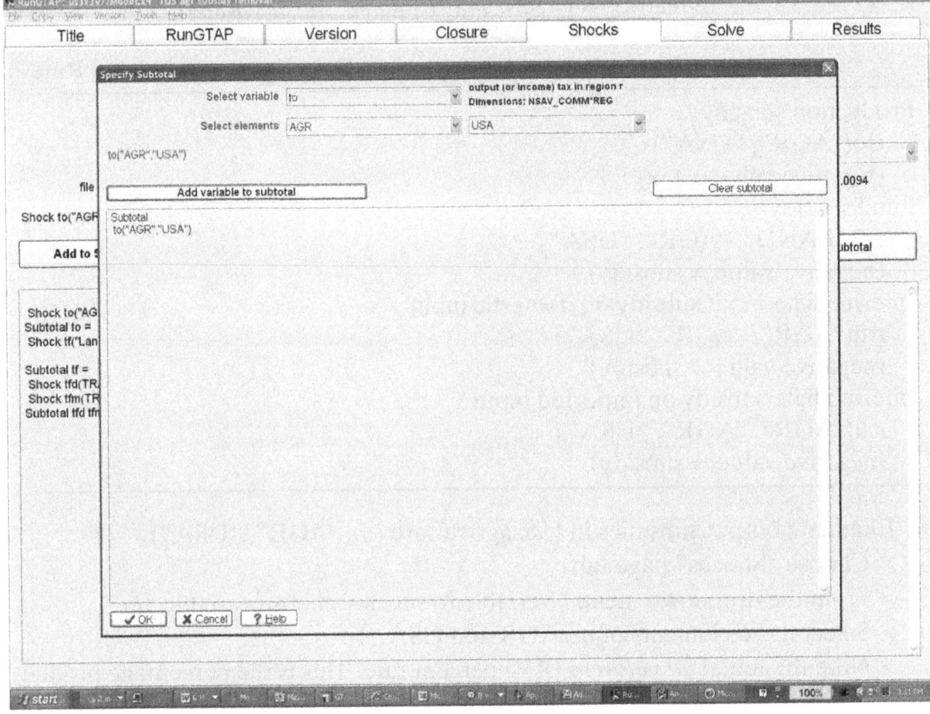

Figure ME 5.1. Define subtotals of a model shock

8. Eliminate input subsidies on domestically produced intermediate inputs, *tfd*, for elements All TRAD_COMM, AGR, USA by setting *tfd* to zero (target rate = 0).
9. Eliminate input subsidies on imported intermediate inputs, *tfm*, for elements All TRAD_COMM, AGR, USA by setting *tfm* to zero (target rate = 0)
10. Define the removal of both *tfd* and *tfm* as a subtotal in your results, named "Intermediate input subsidies"
11. Save the experiment
    > Select the "Solve" page tab
    > Check that the solution method is "Gragg 2-4-6." If it is not, click on "Change." Select Gragg and click on "OK"
    > Check that the parameter file is "Default." If it is not, click on "Change," select "Default" from the box and click on "OK"
    > Click on "Save" and name the shock "PWAgr", describe it as 50 percent increase in the U.S. AGR import price
12. Locate and view the base values for subsidies to U.S. agricultural firms on their purchases of domestic intermediate inputs
    > Click on "View" on the menu bar
    > Select "Base data" from the dropdown menu
    > Select tax rates from the dropdown menu
    > Select rTFD to display base *ad valorem* taxes to firms' purchases of domestic intermediate inputs

Figure ME 5.2. Select set elements to display for a tax with three dimensions tax

> Select elements: ALL_TRAD_COMM, AGR and USA in the upper right corner of the HAR file (Figure ME 5.2). In Table ME 5.1, report only the tax that is paid by agriculture on the agricultural input (rTFD("AGR","AGR", "USA")

13. Repeat these steps to report subsidies on U.S. AGR purchases of imported intermediate inputs (rTFI("AGR", "AGR, "USA") in Table ME 5.1.
14. Solve the model
    > Click on the "Solve" page tab
    > Click on the "Solve" button
    > OK
    > OK
15. Before viewing results, verify that your experiment has changed the tax rates as you expect by viewing the updated tax rates.
    > Click on "View" from the menu bar.
    > Select "Updated data" from the dropdown menu.
    > Select "Tax rates" from the dropdown menu.
    > Select "set elements" in the upper right corner that correspond to the dimensions for each tax listed in Table ME 5.1 Report the new tax rates in Table ME 5.1, for each of the four taxes in this experiment.
16. Report model results in Table ME 5.2 and in the first column of Table ME 5.3.

Table ME 5.2. *Effects of U.S. Agricultural Subsidy Elimination (% change from base)*

	Variable name in GTAP	Base ESUBVA Factor Substitution elasticity	ESUBVA = 2			
		Subtotals				
		Total	Production Tax/Subsidy Effect	Land Tax/Subsidy Effect	Intermediate Input Tax/ Subsidy Effect	TOTAL
Agricultural output quantity	*qo* (AGR,USA)					
Agricultural producer price	*ps*(AGR,USA)					
Land rent	*ps*(LAND,USA)					
Labor wage	*ps*(LABOR,USA)					
Capital rent	*ps*(CAPITAL,USA)					
Household consumption	*qp*[AGR,USA)					
Export quantity	*qxw*(AGR,USA)					

Table ME 5.3. *Change in Input-output Coefficients due to U.S. Agricultural Policy Reform (% change from base)*

Output and Inputs	Output and Input Quantities	Change in Input-Output Coefficients (*qfe-qo*) or (*qf-qo*)
AGR output (*qo*)	−0.37	Not applicable
Land (*qfe*)		
Labor(*qfe*)		
Capital(*qfe*)		
AGR intermediate (*qf*)		
MFG intermediate (*qf*)		
SER intermediate (*qf*)		

17. Follow the instructions in Model Exercise 3 to change the elasticity of factor substitution (ESUBVA) in all sectors to two. After changing your experiment to run with the new parameter file, re-solve the model and report only the total effects in Table ME 5.2.

Interpret Model Results

1. Draw a technology tree for U.S. agriculture in the U.S. 3x3 model. Identify the inputs in each nest and the values in your model for the elasticity parameters that govern substitutability within each nest and at the top level. Assume that σ_{AGG} equals zero.
2. Given the elasticity parameters in the AGR technology tree, explain how a change in relative input costs due to the policy reform could affect the ratios of intermediate and factor inputs used in U.S. agriculture.
3. In Table ME 5.3, calculate the percentage changes in input-output ratios for each input. Describe the changes in input intensities. Are these findings consistent with your depiction and discussion of the technology tree in the questions 1 and 2? Are they consistent with the changes in your factor price results reported in Table 5.2?
4. In the base elasticity case, how does the total effect of U.S. policy reform on AGR output compare with reforms of each separate component? If you were a policy maker, how might the availability of subtotaled results influence your thinking on the best way to phase in the reform program?
5. Compare the total effects of all reforms using the default versus the high factor substitution elasticity. Are they different? Why? Do you think that your model results are highly sensitive to the factor substitution value that you choose for your analysis?
6. Based on data in the U.S. structure table, in Chapter 3, what is the share of food in households' total expenditure on goods and services? Given that expenditure pattern, what might be the views of U.S. consumers on agricultural subsidy reform?

7. Farmland is mostly owned by farming households and land rents are an important source of farm household income. Based on the change in land rents in your results, how do you think rural U.S. households will view subsidy elimination?
8. In the our simple 3x3 model, land is employed only in agriculture while labor and capital are fully mobile across all three sectors; and all factors are fully employed. Given this assumption, why do you think there is no change in agricultural output in the subtotal in which only the land factor use subsidy is removed?
9. Based on your model results, what is your view of the concern of U.S. trade partners that U.S. farm programs increase output and exports, which depresses world prices?

Model Exercise 6: How Immigration can Raise Wages

Concepts: Factor endowment shocks, factors as complements and substitutes, factor substitution elasticity

Background

In 2008, there were 38 million immigrants living in the United States (U.S. Census Bureau, 2009). The United States is a nation of immigrants and historically has been a land of refuge and opportunity for foreigners. But with the number of immigrants now reaching more than 12 percent of the population, a contentious public debate has opened over the costs and benefits of the newcomers. On one hand, new workers add to the nation's stock of wealth, so the United States benefits from an increase in its productive capacity. On the other hand, new workers compete with native workers for jobs and may drive down wages – a key concern for U.S. labor. In addition, there are costs associated with the public services needed by immigrants that may not be sufficiently offset by the taxes that they pay.

The growing body of economic research on immigration offers conflicting results on their net impact on the U.S. economy and, in particular, its labor force. In a 2003 study, Dr. George Borjas concluded that immigration to the United States in the 1980s and 1990s reduced the average annual earnings of native-born workers by an estimated $1,700 or roughly 4 percent. Wages fell because employers can easily substitute immigrant labor for native U.S. workers in the same skill class. An immigrant auto mechanic, for example, can be substituted easily for a native-born auto mechanic. Dr. Borjas also accounted for the "cross-price effects" of immigration across skill classes. An increased number of auto mechanics, for example, leads to increased demand for native-born workers with complementary skills, such as dentists and teachers for the immigrants' children. But he found these cross-price wage benefits to be small. In a supply and demand framework, he concluded that the main effect of immigration has been to shift the labor *supply* curve outward for each skill class, causing the wages of native workers to fall.

Gianmarco Ottaviano and Giovanni Peri (2006) disagree with Borjas. In their study of immigration to the United States since the 1990s, they found that immigration has increased the average U.S. wage by 1.8 percent and the average wage of American-born workers by 2.7 percent. Two factors are at work. First, they argue that immigrant and native-born workers are relatively poor substitutes in the workplace. Even when they have similar educations, they tend to choose different occupations and have different types of skills. For example, an immigrant auto mechanic is a poor substitute for a native-born health technician. As a result, immigration mainly depresses the wages of earlier immigrants. Moreover, they found that cross-price effects are large, so that the increased number of immigrant auto workers has led to increased demand and higher wages for workers with complementary skills, like dentists and teachers. In a supply and demand framework, they argue that the dominant effect of immigration is to shift out the *demand* curve for native workers of all education levels.

A second factor, they argue, is that firms take advantage of the growing labor market by increasing their investment. In turn, new investment leads to increased demand for labor, a complementary factor to capital. In a supply and demand framework, an increase in the capital stock causes an outward shift in the demand for all labor types, which also helps boost wages.

Experiment Design

A key contribution made by the two studies was their authors' use of a general equilibrium framework to analyze the wage effects of immigration. Their studies took into account how wages in each type of labor market depended on its interaction with other types of workers and, in the Ottaviano and Peri study, with increased capital investment. This exercise is designed to help you to control and manipulate your CGE model in order to deconstruct and replicate the underlying assumptions made in these two influential and competing views on the economic effects of U.S. labor immigration.

In this model exercise, you will carry out a simulation of the general equilibrium effects of immigration on the United States. Your analysis is comparatively limited because your CGE model will have only two labor markets, skilled and unskilled labor, and will not differentiate between native and immigrant workers. In addition, your experiments rest on the simplifying assumption that labor migration occurs only in the unskilled labor category, although both skilled and unskilled workers immigrate to the United States. In the exercise, you will:

(1) Create a U.S. 3x3 model aggregation and model version that includes unskilled labor, skilled labor, and capital,
(2) Develop small theoretical models to illustrate the assumptions about labor supply and demand underlying your analysis.
(3) Carry out three experiments:

BORJAS simulates a 10 percent increase in the unskilled labor supply, assuming that factors are highly substitutable;
OTTA1 simulates the BORJAS experiment but assumes that factors are relatively complementary;
OTTA2 adds to OTTA1 a 6 percent increase in the U.S. capital stock.

Instructions

1. Open GTAPAgg7
2. From the menu bar, select "Read Aggregation Scheme from File."
   > Select the US3x3 aggregation file. This is a shortcut to creating a new 3x3 model, because regions and sectors in your database for this exercise remain the same as in the US3x3 database. If you did not create a U.S. 3x3 model, follow instructions in Model Exercise 1 to create a U.S. 3x3 database, and replicate the steps for "Define the country aggregation" and "Define the sector aggregation."
3. Define the factor aggregation.
   > From the menu bar, select "View/change factor aggregation"
   > In the table at the bottom of the page, right-click to remove all but three factor rows.
   > In the left column, type "UNSKILLED," "SKILLED," and "CAPITAL"
4. Define all factors as "mobile" in the column headed "ETRAE value or mobile"
5. Map factors into three-factor aggregation
   > Click on the "New factor" column of the mapping table in the upper right quadrant and pull down the mapping menu
   > Map: land to CAPITAL; unskilled labor to UNSKILLED, skilled labor to SKILLED LABOR; and capital and natural resources to CAPITAL
   > OK
6. Save your data aggregation file
   > From the menu bar, select on "Save aggregation scheme to file." (GTAP provides a default name, "gtp3_2.agg," which you can change to something descriptive, like "Imm.agg"
   > Save this aggregation file in the folder that you created for your research project
7. Create the aggregated database
   > From the menu bar, select "Create aggregated database." This creates a zip file with the aggregated database. Give it the same name as your aggregation scheme (e.g., Imm.zip), and save it in your project folder.
   > Close GTAPAgg7
   > Your database is now saved in zipped Header Array (HAR) files that are ready to use in your CGE model
8. Create a GTAP model version for the immigration exercise following the instructions in Model Exercise 1. Give your model version the same name as your aggregation scheme and database, (e.g. IMM).
9. The GTAP model will run a test simulation. It may fail if you are using the uncondensed version of the GTAP model. If so, click on "Tools" on the menu bar, and select "Run test simulation" from the dropdown box, and it will again run a test simulation.

10. Prepare your model to run an experiment – check closure
    > Select the "Closure" page tab
    Check that no closure changes are lingering there. The closure should end with "Rest Endogenous." If not, erase all text below that line.
11. Prepare your model to run an experiment – check shocks
    > Select "Shocks" page tab
    > Clear shock list
    > This check ensures that there are no shocks lingering in your experiment file other than those you want to introduce.
12. In the BORJAS scenario, you assume that factors can be substituted for each other relatively easily by changing the factor substitution elasticity to twelve for all industries (ESUBVA = 12). Follow instructions in Model Exercise 3 on how to change an elasticity parameter and save it in a new parameter file, named BORJAS.prm
13. Define the BORJAS model experiment:
    > Variable to shock: "*qo*"
    > Elements to shock: "UNSKILLED,""USA"
    > % change shock: 10 percent
    > Select: Add to shock list
14. Save the experiment file
    > Select the "Solve" page tab
    > Check that the solution method is Gragg 2-4-6. If it is not, click on "Change," select Gragg from the box and then click on "OK"
    > Change your parameter file by clicking on "Change" next to "Parameter file: default," and select your new parameter file name, Borjas.prm
    > OK (this closes your parameter file dialogue box)
    > Click on "Save experiment," name the shock BORJAS, describe and it as 10% increase in unskilled labor
15. Solve the model
    > Click on "Solve"
    > OK
    > OK
    Report your results in Table ME 6.1 and Table ME 6.2.
16. Create a new parameter file for OTTA1 and OTTA2 that describes factors as complementary by reducing the elasticities of substitution to:

    AGR = 0.2; MFG = 0.5; SER = 0.5 (the CGDS elasticity is irrelevant because this sector does not employ factors of production)
    Follow instructions in Model Exercise 3 on how to change an elasticity and save a new parameter file, named Otta.prm.

17. Create the OTTA1 experiment file
    > Adapt the BORJAS experiment file to use the Otta.prm parameter file. On the Solve page, click on the "change" button next to "Parameter file." Select Otta.prm.

Table ME 6.1. *Effects of 10 Percent Increase in the U.S. Supply of Unskilled Labor*

			Demand for Labor (*qfe*)		
Factor	Factor Price (*pfe*)	Industry	Unskilled	Skilled	Output (*qo*)
BORJAS – 10 percent increase in unskilled labor supply, high factor substitution					
Unskilled labor		Agriculture			
Skilled labor		Manufactures			
Capital		Services			
OTTA1 – 10 percent increase in unskilled labor supply, low factor substitution					
Unskilled labor		Agriculture			
Skilled labor		Manufactures			
Capital		Service			
OTTA2 – 10 percent increase in unkilled labor, 6 percent increase in capital, low factor substitution					
Unskilled labor		Agriculture			
Skilled labor		Manufactures			
Capital		Services			

> OK
> save the Borjas experiment as OTTA1
> Select the "Solve" button, solve the model, and report your results in Tables ME 6.1 and ME 6.2.

18. Define OTTA2 experiment by adding capital stock growth to the OTTA1 experiment:
    > Variable to shock: "*qo*"
    > Elements to shock: "CAPITAL," "USA"
    > % change shock: 6 percent
    > Select the "Solve" page tab
    > Save the model experiment and name it OTTA2
    > Select the "Solve" button, solve the model, and report your results in Tables ME 6.1 and ME 6.2.

Table ME 6.2. *Real GDP Effects of a 10 Percent Increase in U.S. Unskilled Labor Supply*

Scenario	% Change in Real GDP (*qgdp*)
BORJAS	
OTTA1	
OTTA2	

Interpret Model Results

1. Develop a theoretical model to describe the Borjas argument. Draw a graph for each labor market, identifying the supply and demand curves and the initial equilibrium quantities and wages. In the graph of the unskilled labor market, show the effects of unskilled labor immigration on wages and employment. Which curve shifts? In the graph of the skilled labor market, show the effect of the increased supply of unskilled workers. Which curve shifts? In which direction will it shift if the two types of labor are substitutes, as argued by Borjas?
2. How did you change the CGE model to represent factors as substitutes or as complements? What does a larger parameter value signify?
3. Are the wage results of the BORJAS experiment consistent with those of your theoretical model? Why are the effects of immigration on skilled wages and capital rents negative when factors are good substitutes?
4. Develop a theoretical model to describe the Ottaviano and Peri argument. Draw a graph for each labor market, identifying the supply and demand curves, and the initial equilibrium quantities and wages. In the graph of the unskilled labor market, show the effects of unskilled immigration on wages and employment. Which curve shifts? In the graph of the skilled labor market, show the effect of the increased supply of unskilled workers. Which curve shifts? In which direction will it shift if the two types of labor are relatively complementary, as argued by Ottaviano and Peri?
5. Are the wage results of the OTTA1 experiment consistent with those of your theoretical model? Why are the effects of immigration on skilled wages and capital rents positive when factors are relatively complementary?
6. Using your theoretical model describing the Ottaviano and Peri argument, add the effects of capital stock growth. Which curve shifts in each graph? In which direction will they shift if all factors relatively complementary, as argued by Ottaviano and Peri?
7. Are the wage results of the OTTA2 experiment consistent with those of your theoretical model? What happens in your model to the price of capital? Can you explain why?
8. How does the effect on agricultural output differ between the OTTA1 and OTTA2 scenarios. Can you explain why, using your knowledge of factor cost shares from the U.S. structure table?
9. Why does real GDP increase in all three scenarios? Why is real GDP growth higher in the BORJAS scenario compared to OTTA1?
10. What conclusions about modeling and the choice of elasticity parameters do you draw from your study of the two competing models of labor immigration?

Model Exercise 7: The Doha Development Agenda

Concepts: Import tariffs; export, production and input subsidies; SUBTOTAL and welfare decomposition

Background

The United States has participated in global trade negotiations under the General Agreement on Tariffs and Trade (GATT) – now named the World Trade Organization (WTO) – since shortly after the end of World War II. Consecutive rounds of trade negotiations have led to a reduction of global tariffs and other trade barriers, which has helped facilitate growth in global trade over the past six decades. Agriculture was generally excluded from the trade liberalization process until the Uruguay Round negotiations, which lasted from 1986–94. These talks placed limits on agricultural trade barriers and production and export subsidies. The WTO-sponsored trade negotiations continue today in the Doha Development Agenda Round, so-called because this round of negotiations was initiated in Doha, Qatar, in 2000 and is intended to benefit developing countries in particular.

There is much at stake for the global economy in the Doha Round, particularly for low-income countries, according to Kym Anderson and Will Martin, two prominent economists who studied the potential gains from the negotiations. Current trade barriers are high: high-income and low-income countries impose average tariffs of 16 percent and 18 percent tariff, respectively, on their agricultural imports (Table ME 7.1). Their average tariffs on manufactures average 1 percent and 8 percent, respectively. Agricultural subsidies continue to be provided, mostly by high-income countries.

To analyze the potential gains from eliminating these taxes and subsidies, Anderson and Martin used the World Bank LINKAGE model, a recursive dynamic global CGE model, to conduct their analysis (van der Mensbrugghe, 2005). The LINKAGE model is solved sequentially for a period of several years. The time path of solution values account for population growth over

Table ME 7.1. *World* ad valorem *Import Tariff Rates in Anderson and Martin (2005)*

	High-income Importers	Low-income Importers
Agriculture	16	18
Textiles	8	17
Other manufacturing	1	8
Total	3	10

Source: GTAP v6, 2001 database, as reported in Anderson and Martin.

the time period and the role of savings and investment in capital stock and productivity growth. Their version of the LINKAGE model uses the GTAP 2001 (v6) database.

Anderson and Martin concluded that the full removal of all import tariffs, export subsidies, and domestic agricultural subsidies would boost global welfare by nearly $300 billion annually. They then decomposed this welfare impact by high- versus low-income countries and by type of policy (Table ME 7.2). They concluded that agriculture is the key to the success of the negotiations because global liberalization of agricultural tariffs and subsidies would contribute nearly two-thirds of the potential global welfare gains, mostly through developed countries' reforms. Low-income countries also have a role in the reform process. Their removal of nonagricultural import tariffs would account for most of their contribution to world welfare gains from Doha. Anderson and Martin argue that it is important that the Doha Round address the full range of policies and industries because that approach offers possibilities for trade-offs, such as concessions on agricultural policies in exchange for concessions on nonagricultural policies.

Experiment Design

In this exercise, you will replicate Anderson and Martin's analysis of a global elimination of tariffs and agricultural subsidies using your U.S. 3x3 CGE model. Note some important differences between your model and theirs that make your results not directly comparable: (1) Their model uses a different, older version of the GTAP data, generally with higher tariffs and higher agricultural subsidy rates than in the v.7.0 data base used in this exercise. (2) Their model, LINKAGE, is a recursive dynamic CGE model that allows economies to grow in size, implying that their welfare effects of the same proportionate size to the economy will be larger than welfare results from your static CGE model. (3) The most important difference is that their model contains more country and industry disaggregation than the toy 3x3 CGE model used

Table ME 7.2. *Effects on Economic Welfare of Full Trade Liberalization from Different Groups of Countries and Products, 2015 (Total welfare effect = $U.S. 287 billion)*

	Agriculture	Textiles and Clothing	Other Manufactures	All Goods
High-income country policies	46	6	3	55
Low-income country policies	17	8	20	45
Total	63	14	23	100

Source: Anderson and Martin (2005).

in this exercise. The large aggregation of the rest-of-world economy in our toy CGE model results in very large terms-of-trade effects and substantial distortions remain in within-region trade in the rest-of-world. Both factors skew our welfare effects. Despite these model differences and caveats, this exercise remains useful for teaching you the modeling skills used to study multilateral trade liberalization, which has been an important application of CGE models.

In your experiment, you will use the GTAP SUBTOTAL facility (see directions in Model Exercise 5) to decompose global trade reform into four components:

1. U.S. Agricultural Policy Reform: eliminate U.S. agricultural tariffs, export subsidies, and production subsidies.
2. U.S. Nonagricultural Policy Reform: eliminate U.S. nonagricultural tariffs and export subsidies.
3. Rest-of-world (ROW) Agricultural Policy Reform: reduce ROW agricultural tariffs and export subsidies on trade with the U.S. by 50 percent, and eliminate agricultural production subsidies.
4. ROW Nonagricultural Policy Reform: reduce ROW nonagricultural tariffs and export subsidies on trade with the U.S. by 50 percent.

Instructions

1. Open the GTAP model with U.S. 3x3 database

This step opens the version of the GTAP model that uses the U.S. 3x3 database. You created this version of the model in Model Exercise 1.

> Open RunGTAP
> On the top menu bar, choose "Version"
> Change
> Select US3x3
> OK

2. Prepare your model to run an experiment – check closure
   > Select the "Closure" page tab.

Check that no closure changes are lingering there. The closure should end with "Rest Endogenous." If not, erase all text below that line.

3. Prepare your model to run an experiment – check shocks
   > Select "Shocks" page tab
   > Clear shock list

This check ensures that there are no shocks lingering in your experiment file other than those you want to introduce.

Table ME 7.3. *Base Tax Rates in U.S. 3x3 Model*

	United States (USA)			Rest-of-World (ROW)		
Tax Type	Agr.	Mfg.	Services	Agr.	Mfg.	Services
Subsidies on domestic intermediate inputs used in agricultural production (rTFD)						
Subsidies on imported intermediate inputs used in agricultural production (rTFI)						
Export subsidies (rTXS)						
Import tariffs (rTMS)						

Source: GTAP v.7.0.

4. Report selected base tax rates in Table ME 7.3.
   > Select "View" from the menu bar
   > Select "Base data" from the dropdown menu
   > Select "Tax rates" from the dropdown menu

For each tax, select the appropriate set elements to display from the boxes in the upper right corner. For export taxes and import tariffs, report the bilateral rates on U.S. and ROW exports to and imports from each other.

5. Define the first part of the experiment: U.S. Agricultural Policy Reform
   > Select the "Shocks" page tab
   > Set each of the variables listed below to a zero target rate (See directions on defining experiments in Model Exercise 3):
   tfd (tax on domestic intermediate inputs):
   elements All TRAD_COMM, "AGR", "USA"
   tfm (tax on imported intermediate inputs):
   elements All TRAD_COMM, "AGR", "USA"
   tms (import tariff): elements "AGR", "All REG," "USA"
   txs(export tax): elements: "AGR","USA," "All REG"
6. Define these shocks as the subtotal "US Ag Policy Reform" following the directions on defining subtotals in Model Exercise 5. Be careful to select the elements for each variable on the SubTotals page to match the set elements on the shocks page.
7. Define the second part of the experiment: U.S. Nonagricultural Policy Reform
   > Set each of the variables listed below to a zero target rate:
   tms (import tariff): elements("MFG","ROW","USA")
   txs (export tax): elements("MFG","USA","ROW")

Because tariffs and taxes on trade in services are zero in the GTAP database, we do not need to remove them in our experiment.

8. Define the two shocks in the step above as the subtotal "US NonAg Policy Reform."
9. Define the third part of the experiment: Rest-of-World Agricultural Policy Reform
   > Select the "Shocks" page tab
   > Set each of the variables listed below to a zero target rate:
   tfd (tax on domestic intermediate inputs):
   elements All TRAD_COMM, "AGR","ROW"
   tfm (tax on imported intermediate inputs):
   elements All TRAD_COMM, "AGR", "ROW"
   > Set each of the variables listed below to minus 50 percent change in the tax rates
   tms (import tariff): elements "AGR", All "USA","ROW"
   txs(export taxes): elements: "AGR","ROW", "USA"
10. Define these shocks as the subtotal "ROW Ag Policy Reform"
11. Define the fourth part of the experiment: ROW Nonagricultural Policy Reform
    > Set each of the variables listed below to minus 50 percent change in the tax rates.
    tms (import tariff): elements("MFG","USA","ROW")
    txs (export taxes): elements("MFG","USA","ROW")
    Because tariffs and taxes on trade in services are zero in the GTAP database, we do not need to remove them in our experiment.
12. Define these shocks as the subtotal "ROW NonAg Policy Reform."
13. Check that your shock page looks like Figure ME 7.1.
14. Save the experiment file
    > Select the "Solve" page tab
    > Check that the solution method is Gragg 2-4-6. If it is not, click on "Change," select Gragg from the box and then click on "OK"
    > Check that the parameter file is "Default". If it is not, click on "Change," select default.prm from the box and click OK.
    > Click on "Save experiment," name the shock DOHA, and describe it as Doha Development Agenda
15. Solve the model
    > Select "Solve" page tab
    > Save experiment
    > Name the experiment "Doha"
    > >OK
    > Solve
16. After running the experiment, check that the updated tax rates are what you expect them to be. This is a good habit to practice, especially when carrying

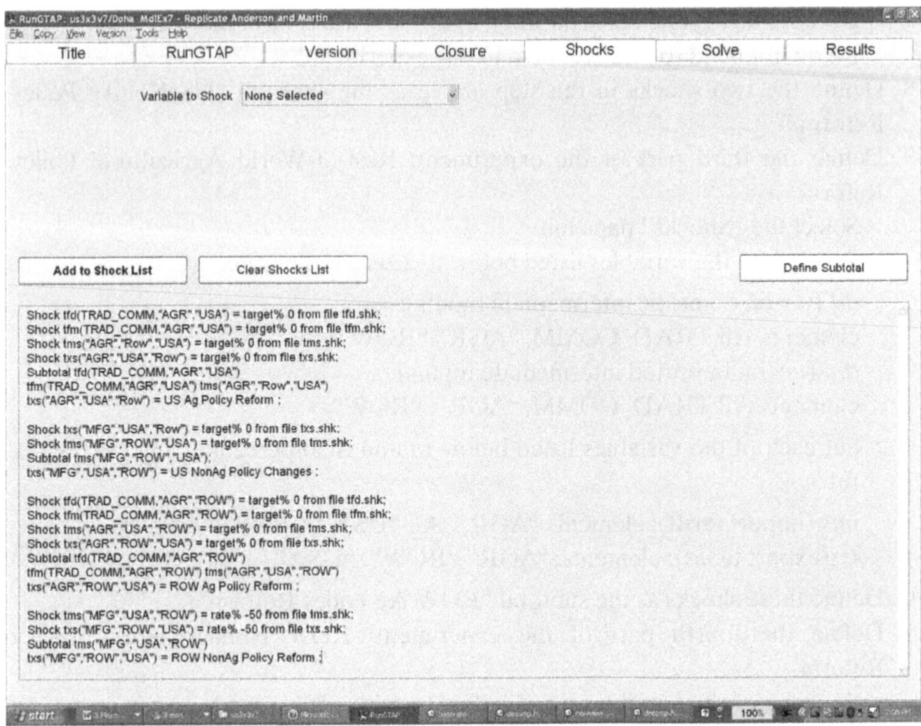

Figure ME 7.1. Shocks page for Doha Development Agenda experiment

out complex tax experiments such as this. For example, check that the input subsidies used by the agricultural sectors in the U.S. and rest-of-world are now zero:

> Select "View" from the menu bar
> Updated data (from the dropdown menu)
> Tax rates (from the dropdown menu)
> rTFD – the *ad valorem* tax rate on firms' domestic purchases
> Select set elements to display (in the upper right corner of the tax display page):
ALL TRAD_COMM, AGR, ALL REG. All should have a value of zero.
> Select and view each of the taxes that you have changed in this experiment.

17. From the results page, report model results for the equivalent variation welfare effect, EV, in Table ME 7.4.
18. Report the decomposition of the total welfare effect, reported in the GTAP welfare decomposition utility in Table ME 7.5.
> Select "View" from the menu bar
> Select "Updated data" from the dropdown menu
> Select "Welfare decomposition"
> Click on "EV decomposition summary" (in row 1)
19. From the results page, report changes in export quantities, *qxw*, in Table ME 7.6.

Table ME 7.4. *Welfare Effects of Trade Liberalizationby Region and by Policy, $U.S. Millions*

	Total	U.S. Agricultural Policy Reform	U.S. Nonagricultural Policy Reform	Rest-of-World Agricultural Policy Reform	Rest-of-World Non-agricultural Policy Reform
United States					
ROW					
World					

Note: Welfare is an equivalent variation measure.
Source: GTAP model, GTAP v.7.0 U.S. 3x3 database.

Interpret Model Results

1. Is the total world welfare effect of global trade reforms positive or negative? Explain what a change in the equivalent variation measure of welfare means.
2. Which elements of the global reform contribute most to increasing or decreasing global welfare? Based on these findings, what advice would you give to policy makers on the best win-win strategy for participants in this negotiation?
3. Comment on the changes in export quantities. Can you explain these changes based on the initial import tariffs in your model?
4. Consider your welfare decomposition results. The allocative efficiency effect measures the efficiency gains to each economy when distorting taxes are reduced or removed. How important are these efficiency gains to both regions?
5. Consider your welfare decomposition results. What does the terms of trade effect measure? How important is this effect in your model results? Explain why the terms of trade gains and losses to each region offset each other in your 3x3 model.
6. Which elasticity parameter in your CGE model most directly influences the terms of trade results in your model? Explain why.

Table ME 7.5. *Decomposition of the Total Welfare Effect, $U.S. Millions*

	Total	Allocative Efficiency	Terms of Trade in Goods and Services	Terms of Trade in Savings-Investment
United States				
ROW				
World				

Note: Welfare is an equivalent variation measure.
Source: GTAP model, GTAP v.7.0 U.S. 3x3 database.

Table ME 7.6. *Effect of Trade Liberalization on Exports (% change from base)*

	U.S.	Rest-of-World
Agriculture (*qxw*)		
Manufacturing (*qxw*)		
Services (*qxw*)		

7. How does your total world welfare result compare with that of Anderson and Martin? What are the differences between your CGE model and theirs that might explain some of the differences in your results?
8. Compare your tariff data with that of Anderson and Martin. How do your tariff data and your model experiment differ from theirs? Explain how these might lead to differences in your model results.

Model Exercise 8: The Marginal Welfare Burden of the U.S. Tax System

Concepts: Taxation; direct, excess and marginal welfare burden of taxes, welfare decomposition, systematic sensitivity analysis

Background

The United States tax system was the subject of some of the earliest applications of CGE models. An influential contributor to this body of research was the economist team of Charles Ballard, John Shoven, and John Whalley. They developed a recursive dynamic CGE model that supported several analyses of U.S. taxes, including Ballard, Shoven, and Whalley (1985). Their CGE model of the United States was based on a 1973 database with nineteen industries, twelve household types and eight types of taxes. Their model solved first for a baseline time path of the economy's growth. Their experiments then introduced changes in U.S. tax rates. The results of their model experiments plotted alternative time paths of U.S. economic growth, with and without the tax changes.

In their 1985 study, the team used their CGE model to analyze the combined marginal excess burden – the deadweight efficiency losses – of all taxes in the U.S. economy. The marginal tax rates in their model, reported as the average across industries and commodities, are presented in Table ME 8.1. Their tax rates are reported as the rate paid on net-of-tax income or net-of-tax expenditure. For example, if the tax paid on $1 of dividend income was 50 cents, then the individual would retain fifty cents in net-of-tax income. In this case, the tax rate would be 100 percent of net income (which is close to the rate of .97 reported in Ballard, et al.'s model).

Their experiments were a 1 percent increase in every tax rate in the U.S. economy simultaneously and a 1 percent increase in each tax rate at a time. In this dynamic model, tax changes influenced households' savings rates and therefore the accumulation of capital and investment in the economy. Tax changes also influenced households' decision about how many hours to work. And, as in our standard, static CGE model, taxes led consumers and producers to change the quantities that they produced and consumed as taxes changed relative prices of goods and services. Together, changes in investment and the supply of labor, and resource reallocation, altered the growth path of the economy. The authors also explored the sensitivity of their results to alternative elasticity parameter values for labor supply and household savings.

The team found that, depending on the elasticities, the marginal excess burden of the U.S. tax system ranged between seventeen cents and fifty-six cents per dollar of additional tax revenue (Table ME 8.2). This meant

Table ME 8.1. *Level and Dispersion of Tax Rates in the Model*

	Average Marginal Tax Rates
Capital and property taxes	.97
Labor (factor use) taxes	.101
Consumer sales taxes	.067
Output and excise taxes	.008
Motor vehicle taxes	.052
Personal income taxes	.239

Source: Ballard, Shoven, and Whalley, 1985.

Table ME 8.2. *Marginal Excess Burden per Additional Dollar of Revenue for U.S. Taxes*

	Saving Elasticity		
Labor supply elasticity	0.0	0.4	0.8
0.0	.170	.206	.238
0.15	.274	.332	.383
0.30	.391	.477	.559

Source: Ballard, Shoven, and Whalley, 1985.

that government projects to be funded by the tax increase would have had to yield benefits at least 17 percent greater than the amount of the additional tax revenue. After changing one tax at a time, they concluded that the consumer sales tax was the most distorting of the U.S. taxes (Table ME 8.3).

Based on their findings, Ballard, et al., argued that plans for public spending on projects or on income transfers, such as welfare payments, needed to take into account the efficiency losses incurred by raising additional tax revenue. They also argued that the large marginal excess burden of additional

Table ME 8.3. *Marginal Excess Burden per Dollar of Additional Revenue from Specific Portions of the Tax System*

Uncompensated saving elasticity	0.0	0.4	0.0	0.4
Uncompensated labor supply elasticity	0.0	0.0	.15	.15
All taxes	.17	.206	.274	.332
Capital taxes	.181	.379	.217	.463
Labor taxes	.121	.112	.234	.230
Consumer sales tax	.256	.251	.384	.388
Sales tax on commodities other than alcohol, tobacco, gas,	.035	.026	.119	.115
Income taxes	.163	.179	.282	.314
Production taxes	.147	.163	.248	.279

Source: Ballard, Shoven, and Whalley, 1985.

taxes conversely offered opportunities, because there could be large marginal efficiency gains from small reforms in taxes.

Experiment Design

In this exercise, you will replicate the Ballard, Shoven, and Whaley (1985) study using the GTAP model with the U.S. 3x3 database. There are differences between your models that are likely to lead to differences in your results. Your model has a 2004 database and you will be asked to see how its tax rates differ from the 1973 rates described in the Ballard, et al., analysis. Note that almost all tax rates reported in your CGE model are calculated gross of tax, so they will be lower. That is, if the tax paid on $1 of dividend income was 50 cents, then the tax rate would be 50 percent of gross income. Your model is aggregated to three industries and a single household so there is less scope for distortions in the relative prices of goods, and the efficiency losses from tax increases could therefore be smaller. Also, Ballard, et al., use a recursive dynamic CGE model while yours is a static CGE model with a fixed supply of capital and labor. Therefore, by assumption, your model will not account for taxes' effects on the supply of savings and investment. In addition, income taxes influence labor supply in their model, whereas the labor supply is fixed in your model. On the other hand, your model has capabilities that theirs did not. Because it is a multicountry model, your measure of the welfare effects of tax reform includes not only the excess burden of taxes but also their terms of trade effects. Also, the welfare decomposition utility of the GTAP model allows you to decompose the contributions of each type of tax to the total excess burden, instead of running separate experiments. Finally, the systematic sensitivity analysis utility allows you to describe confidence intervals around your results as you test for sensitivity to one parameter, the factor substitution elasticity.

In this exercise, you will:

1. Change selected elasticity parameters.
2. Define and run an experiment that increases all U.S. taxes by 1 percent.
3. Use the GTAP welfare decomposition facility to decompose the contribution of each tax to the excess burden of the tax increase.
4. Carry out a systematic analysis of the sensitivity of welfare results to alternative assumptions about the factor substitution elasticity.

Instructions

1. Open GTAP model with U.S. 3x3 database
   This step opens the version of the GTAP model that uses the U.S. 3x3 database. You created this version of the model in exercise 1.

> Open RUNGTAP
> On the top menu bar, choose "Version"
> Change
> Select "US3x3"
> OK

2. Prepare your model to run an experiment – check closure
   > Select the "Closure" page tab.
   Check that no closure changes are lingering there. The closure should end with "Rest Endogenous." If not, erase all text below that line.
3. Prepare your model to run an experiment – check shocks
   > Select "Shocks" page tab
   > Clear shock list
   This check ensures that there are no shocks lingering in your experiment file other than those you want to introduce.
4. Change these elasticity parameters and save a new parameter file (see instructions in Model Exercise 3):
   > ESUBVA (factor substitution elasticity) = 2 in all production activities
   > ESUBD (demand substitution between imported and domestic) = 6 for all commodities
   > ESUBM (demand substitution among imported varieties) = 10 for all commodities
   > RORFLEX parameters = 1 (this reduces the effect of investment changes on the rate of return to investment)
   > Save the new parameter file and name it "Ballard.prm"
5. Define your experiment:
   > Select, sequentially, each of these tax rates: *tf*, *tfd*, *tfm*, *tgd*, *tgm*, *to*, *tm*, *tp*, *tx*
   > Select all elements for each tax for the U. S. region only
   > Define shock value for each tax as 1
   > Define type of shock as "% change rate"
6. Your experiment page should look like Figure ME 8.1.
7. Save the experiment file
   > Select the "Solve" page tab
   > Check that the solution method is Gragg 2-4-6. If it is not, click on "Change," select Gragg from the box and then click on "OK"
   > Change your parameter file by clicking on "Change" next to "Parameter file: default," and select your new parameter file name, Ballard.prm
   > OK (this closes your parameter file dialogue box)
   > Click on "Save experiment," name the shock "Ballard," describe and it as 1% increase in all taxes
8. Solve the model
   > Click on Solve
   > OK
   > OK

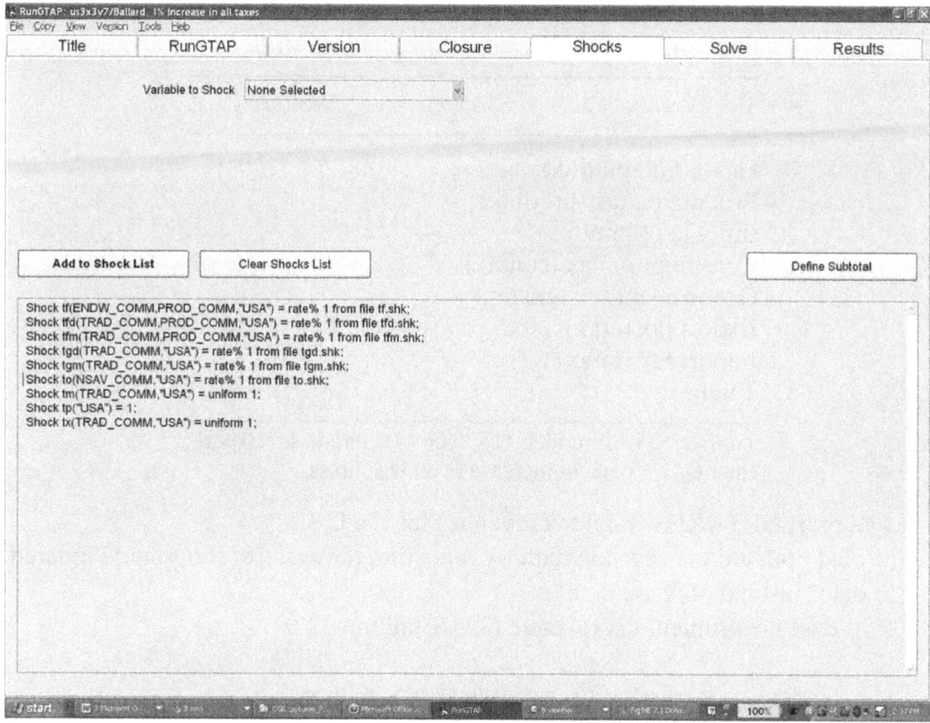

Figure ME 8.1. Shocks page in marginal welfare burden experiment

9. Report results from the welfare decomposition utility in Tables 8.4 and 8.5.
   > Select "View" from the menu bar
   > Updated data
   > Welfare decomposition
   > Select "EV Decomposition Summary" (row 1) for Table ME 8.4 results
   > Return to main menu of decomposition by double-clicking on data anywhere in the matrix
   > Select "Allocative efficiency by tax type" (row 3) for Table ME 8.5 results
10. Calculate the change in total government tax revenue by comparing the pre- and post-experiment tax revenues. Find the base tax revenue value by selecting from the top menu bar:
    > Select "View" from the menu bar
    > Base data
    > GtapView Output
    > GDPSCR (GDP from the income sources side)

Table ME 8.4. *Welfare Effects of a 1 Percent Increase in U.S. Taxes ($U.S. Million)*

Allocative efficiency	Endowment	Technology	Population	Terms of trade in goods and services	Terms of trade in investment-savings	Preference	Total welfare cost	Change in government tax revenue	Welfare cost per dollar of revenue

Source: GTAP model, U.S. 3x3 v.7.0 database.

Table ME 8.5. *Welfare Decomposition of the Allocative Efficiency Effect ($U.S. Million)*

Tax Type	Welfare Cost
Factor tax (pfattax)	
Production tax (prodtax)	
Input tax (inputtax)	
Consumption tax (contax)	
Government tax (govtax)	
Export tax (etax)	
Import tax (mtax)	
Total	

Source: GTAP model, U.S. 3x3 v.7.0 database. Experiment is a 1 percent increase in all U.S. taxes.

> Report NETAXES (total tax revenue) for the U.S.
Find updated tax revenue data by repeating these steps, choosing "Updated data" instead of "base data":
a Base government tax revenue ($ U.S. millions)

____

b Updated government tax revenue ($ U.S. million)

____

c Change in government tax revenue ($ U.S. million)

____

11. Calculate the marginal welfare burden of the U.S. tax system. It is the welfare cost per additional dollar of tax revenue:

    Total welfare cost/Change in government tax revenue * 100 = Marginal welfare burden

12. Carry out a systematic sensitivity analysis (SSA) of model results to changes in the elasticity of factor substitution (ESUBVA) parameter. Follow the instructions in Model Exercise 3, and use the information below as your inputs to the SSA utility.
> Parameter to vary: ESUBVA
> Elements to vary: ALL PROD_COMM
> Percent variation: 100 (the sensitivity analysis will vary the ESUBVA elasticity parameter value between close to zero and two times the base parameter value, or 4)
> Type of variation: Percent (this is the default choice)
> Type of distribution: triangular (it is similar to a bell curve distribution and is the default choice)
> Name and save your two result files from the SSA by replacing the star in the file name with "Ballard" – without the quotes.
> Open and view the files with the sensitivity analysis results.

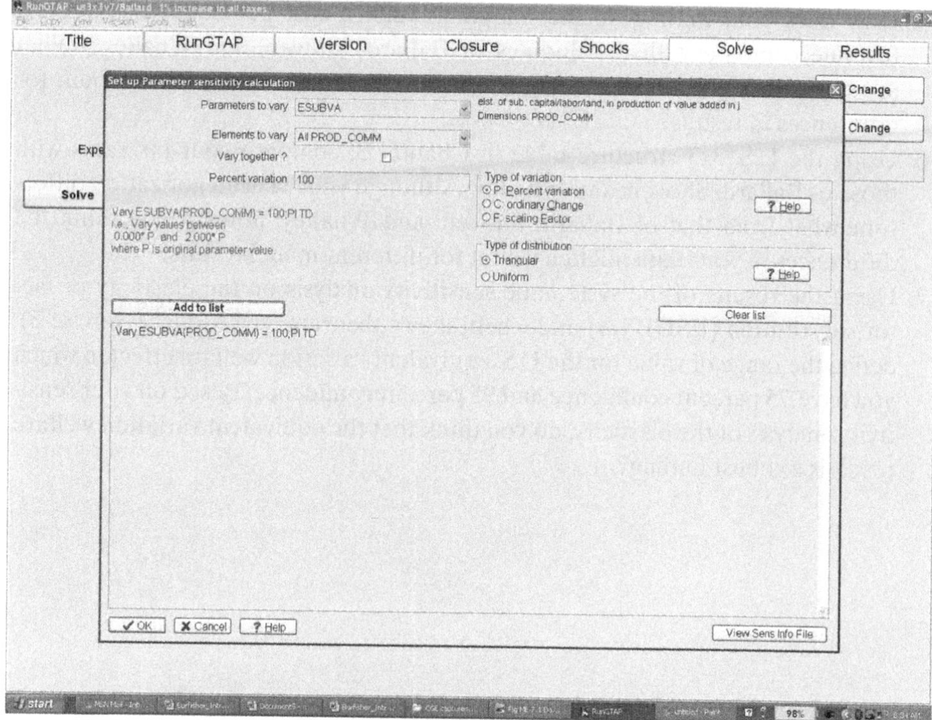

Figure ME 8.2. Systematic sensitivity analysis

13. Report results from the ViewSol file for U.S. equivalent variation measure of welfare (EV):

    EV ________________

    Mean ________________

    Standard deviation _______

Interpret Model Results

1. Based on your results, what is the direct burden of the marginal tax increase? What is its excess burden (allocative inefficiency)?
2. According to results reported in Table 8.5, which tax has the largest marginal welfare effect? The smallest? Use data from the U.S. 3x3 structure table and your knowledge of the excess burden of taxes to explain your results for these two taxes.
3. Based on your results in Table 8.4, what is the marginal welfare cost per dollar of additional revenue from the U.S. tax system? Explain how you would use this number to advise policy makers considering a tax increase to fund a government project.
4. How important is the terms of trade gain in goods and services in the welfare results? Explain what a change in the terms of trade means. Why is it included in the welfare measure?

5. How does your finding on the marginal welfare cost per dollar of marginal revenue compare with the findings of Ballard, Shoven, and Whalley? What are some of the differences between your CGE models that might account for differences in results?
6. Using the U.S. 3x3 structure table in Chapter 3, compare your tax rates with those of Ballard, Shoven, and Whalley. Although your tax categorization differs somewhat from that of Ballard, Shoven, and Whalley, how do you think the differences in your data might account for different model results?
7. Using the results of the systematic sensitivity analysis on the elasticity of factor substitution (ESUBVA) and Chebyshev's theorem (see Model Exercise 3), define the range of value for the U.S. equivalent variation welfare effect in which you have 75 percent confidence and 95 percent confidence. Based on your sensitivity analysis of the elasticity, do you think that the equivalent variation welfare result is a robust finding?

Model Exercise 9: Successful Quitters – The Economic Effects of Growing Antismoking Attitudes

Concepts: Changing consumer preferences, macroeconomic projections, systematic sensitivity analysis

Background

Cigarette smoking can have serious health consequences, not only for smokers but also for those around them who breathe in their second-hand smoke. As more becomes known about the negative effects of cigarettes on health, consumer attitudes toward smoking – at least in some countries – have begun to change. The days of glamorous movie stars puffing on cigarettes on the silver screen are long gone. Instead, smoking is increasingly viewed unfavorably, and there is growing social acceptance of (and even demands for) bans on smoking in public places like offices, restaurants, and airplanes.

Globally, cigarette consumption has declined since the 1990s, but this broad trend masks differences among categories of countries, according to Goel and Nelson (2004). Their international comparison of smoking trends found that declining cigarette consumption is correlated with a country's stage of development. Approximately one-half of the high and upper middle-income countries in their data set witnessed a decline in per capita cigarette consumption in excess of 20 percent since the 1990s. In contrast, cigarette consumption actually increased over that period in half of the low-income countries in their study. Goel and Nelson suggest a number of reasons why a country's stage of development may affect its national smoking habits. For example, wealthier nations have better resources to monitor and control tobacco use, and a more educated population might be more aware of the health risks posed by smoking. But the researchers also found many exceptions to this broad relationship between smoking and income. These variations probably reflect the significant differences across countries in antismoking policies, such as taxes and regulations on trade and advertising.

Changes in consumer attitudes toward particular products can have important consequences for an industry. Sometimes changing attitudes lead to a boom in consumer demand, such as the new popularity of organic foods. In other cases, consumers develop aversions, such as the avoidance of conflict diamonds because their proceeds may fund wars. When the affected industries are important in a national economy, changes in consumer preferences can also have significant economywide effects.

In this exercise, you will create a 3x3 database with a tobacco sector, to explore the effects of changing consumer attitudes about smoking as incomes grow. You will start by studying your SAM database, to understand the role of tobacco in the U.S. and ROW economies. Next, you will develop a model experiment that describes long-term income growth by incorporating macroprojections for endowment growth and productivity effects, following the methodology used by Arndt, et al. (1997). Then, you will simulate the effects of projected economic growth when (1) global consumer preferences remain unchanged, and (2) consumers in the rest-of-world become more averse to tobacco products as their incomes grow. You will select and examine model results that answer the question, "How will consumer attitudes toward smoking affect countries' tobacco industries and their national economies as global incomes rise over the next decade?" Given the uncertainty about the extent to which income growth may change consumer preferences, you will use the systematic sensitivity analysis utility with respect to the income parameter, INCPAR. This will allow you to describe model outcomes in terms of means, distributions, and confidence intervals.

Experiment Design

Your static CGE model describes an economy in equilibrium before and after a model shock. Defining 10 year macroprojections as a model shock essentially imposes a new macroeconomic equilibrium with higher levels of capital, labor, and productivity. Your model then solves for the consistent microeconomic structure. For example, if the economy's total capital stock (a macroeconomic parameter) is assumed to increase by 10 percent, your model results describe the microeconomic changes in capital stock in each industry, industry output, commodity demand, and so forth.

To define your experiment, you will need to know the *cumulative* growth in endowments and productivity over your projection time period of 2005–14. (We begin with 2005 because 2004 is the base year for our data.) For example, consider a three period case, in which capital stock growth between periods one and two (k_1) is 2.5 percent, and growth between periods two and three (k_2) is 1.3 percent. Assuming that the initial capital stock (K) in period one is fifty, we calculate the cumulative growth between periods one and three in two steps:

1. Calculate the size of the capital stock in the final period: $K * (1 + k_1/100) * (1 + k_2/100)$

$$50 * 1.025 * 1.013 = 51.92$$

2. Calculate the cumulative growth rate as the percent change between the base capital stock and the capital stock in the final period:

$$(51.92 - 50)/50 = .0384 * 100 = 3.84$$

Table ME 9.1. *Annual Growth Rates in Factor Endowments and Productivity*

	Base Quantity	2005	2006	2007	2008	2009	2010	2011	2012	2013	2014
Labor force Cumulative											
USA	1	0.4	1.6	1.7	1.6	1.6	1.6	1.6	1.6	1.6	1.6
ROW	1	1.6	1.5	1.5	1.5	1.4	1.4	1.4	1.4	1.4	1.4
Capital stock											
USA	1	4.1	4	4	3.9	3.9	3.8	3.8	3.7	3.7	3.7
ROW	1	3.9	3.9	3.9	3.9	3.9	3.9	3.9	3.9	3.8	3.8
Total factor productivity											
USA	1	1.2	1.2	1.2	1.2	1.2	1.2	1.2	1.2	1.2	1.2
ROW	1	2.4	2.4	2.4	2.4	2.4	2.4	2.4	2.4	2.4	2.4

Notes: We assume that Walmsley's data for North America describes growth rates for the United States and that the average of growth rates for all other regions describe growth rates for ROW. Productivity projections for the United States extrapolate the 2007–08 multifactor productivity growth reported for the U.S. by the BLS and ROW productivity growth is assumed to be twice the level of the United States.

Source: Endowment data from Walmsley (2006); productivity data from Bureau of Labor Statistics (2009) and author calculations.

Table ME 9.1 presents macroprojections reported in the literature. Use these data to calculate the cumulative growth rates in endowments and productivity for the U.S. and ROW during 2005–14, rounding up your answers to whole numbers. Report the cumulative growth rates Table ME 9.2. One answer is provided to help you to check your work. You will use the cumulative growth rates to define your model shock.

In the first scenario, you will run the growth experiment using the default parameters in the CDE consumer utility function assumed in the GTAP model. In this scenario, there are no changes in attitudes about smoking as incomes grow.

In the second scenario, you will assume that consumers in the rest-of-world develop stronger antismoking attitudes as their incomes grow. You describe this change in preferences in the GTAP model by reducing the value of the INCPAR parameter, which is similar to, but not exactly the same as, the income elasticity of demand. When this parameter is reduced, any given

Table ME 9.2. *Cumulative Growth Rates*

	Labor force
USA	16
ROW	
	Capital stock
USA	
ROW	
	TFP
USA	
ROW	

percentage increase in income will result in a smaller increase in consumers' tobacco purchases. You will reduce INCPAR to a value that reduces the quantity of tobacco demanded in ROW by about 20 percent compared to current preferences. This is about the same quantity reduction experienced in developed countries during the 1990s.

There are some limitations to our analysis. One is our simplifying assumption that "ROW" preferences describe developing countries. Our 3x3 aggregation scheme includes all countries except the United States, so at least some countries included in ROW have already experienced changes in attitudes about smoking. A second limitation is that the GTAP database combines beverages with tobacco, so demand and production of "tobacco" in our model is not completely accurate. Third, it is difficult to predict how economic growth will affect consumer preferences because these are not always fully explained by economic forces. The systematic sensitivity analysis with respect to the INCPAR parameter allows us to characterize the preference change as a range instead of a specific value, and to present our model results in terms of means and distributions.

Instructions

1. Open GTAPAgg7
2. From the menu bar, select "Read Aggregation Scheme from File."
   > Select the U.S. 3x3 aggregation file (This is a shortcut to creating a new 3x3 model, because regions and factors in your database for this exercise remain the same as in the U.S. 3x3 database. If you did not create a U.S. 3x3 model, follow instructions in Model Exercise 1 to create a U.S. 3x3 database, and replicate the steps for "Define the country aggregation" and "Define the factor aggregation.")
3. Define the sector aggregation.
   > From the menu bar, select "View/change sectoral aggregation."
   > Create these three sectors:

TOB – "tobacco"	comprised of sector 26 b_t
AGRMFG – "AGR and MFG"	comprised of sectors 1–25, 27–42
SER – "Services"	comprised of 43–57

   > OK (this saves your new sector aggregation)
4. Save your data aggregation file
   > From the menu bar, select on "Save aggregation scheme to file." (GTAP provides a default name, "gtpXX.agg," which you can change to something descriptive, like "TOB.agg.")
   > Save this aggregation file in the folder that you created for your research project.

Table ME 9.3. *Role of Tobacco in Economywide Production*

	USA	ROW
Share of tobacco in total activity output		

Source: GTAP v.7.0 3x3 tobacco database.

5. Create the aggregated database.
   > From the menu bar, select "Create aggregated database." This creates a zip file with the aggregated database. Give it the same name as your aggregation scheme, for example TOB.zip, and save it in your project folder.
   Your database is now saved in zipped Header Array (HAR) files that are ready to use in your CGE model.
6. Explore the SAM to learn about the role of the tobacco sector in the economy
   > Still in GTAPAgg7, click on "View output files" in the menu bar
   > Select "ASAM" (the top row)
   > On the upper right side, choose these set elements to display the ROW SAM:

   ALL SAMAC, ALL SAMAC, ROW

   Calculate the share of the gross value of tobacco output in total activity output in ROW, and report it in Table ME 9.3.
7. Repeat these steps to calculate and report the share of tobacco in activity output in the United States, after changing the set elements to display to:

   ALLSAMAC ALLSAMAC USA

8. Create a GTAP model version for the antismoking exercise following the instructions in Model Exercise 1. Give your model version the same name as your aggregation scheme and database, TOB.
9. The GTAP model will run a test simulation. It may fail if you are using the uncondensed version of the GTAP model. If so, click on tools on the menu bar, and select "Run test simulation" from the dropdown box, and it will again run a test simulation.
10. Prepare your model to run an experiment – check closure
    > Select the "Closure" page tab
    Check that no closure changes are lingering there. The closure should end with "Rest Endogenous." If not, erase all text below that line.
11. Prepare your model to run an experiment – check shocks
    > Select "Shocks" page tab
    > Clear shock list
    This check ensures that there are no shocks lingering in your experiment file other than those you want to introduce.
12. Report your model's base parameter values for INCPAR in Table ME 9.4.

Table 9.4. *Base and Updated INCPAR Parameter Values*

	Base Parameter Values		Updated Parameter Values
	USA	ROW	ROW only
Tobacco			0.4
Agr/Mfg			*No change*
Services			*No change*

13. Define the macroprojections experiment
    > Select "Shocks" page tab
    > Using your calculated cumulative growth rates, define the shock for each of these parameters, for each region:
    Labor endowment: *qo*("LABOR", r,)
    Capital endowment: *qo*("CAPITAL", r,)
    Total factor productivity: *afeall*(ENDOW_COMM, PROD_COMM, r)
    Your shocks page should look like Figure ME 9.1.

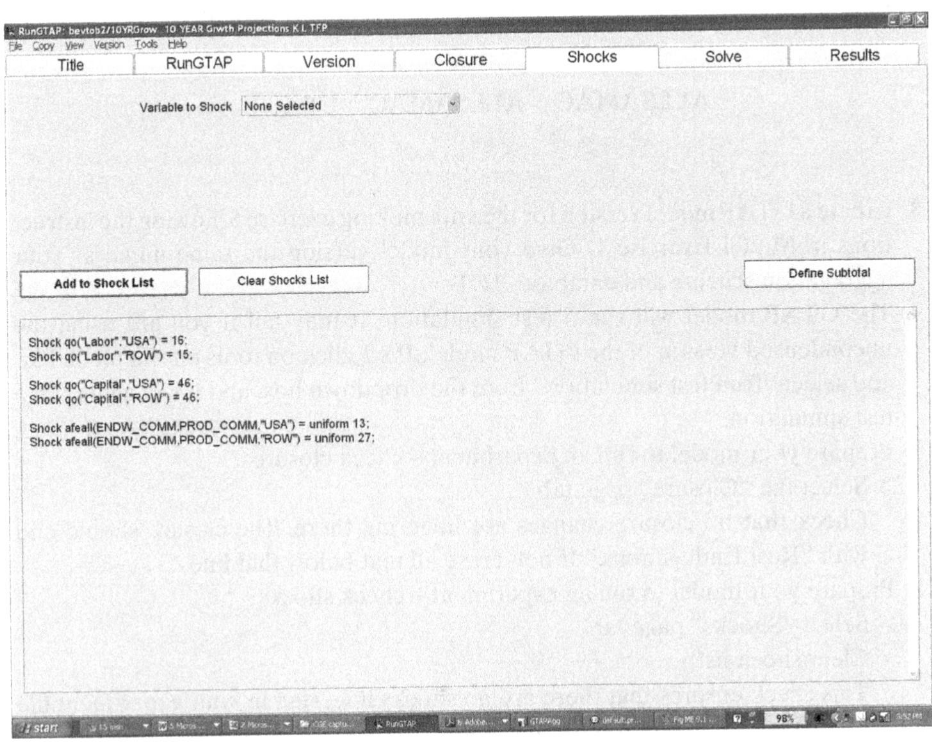

Figure ME 9.1. Shock page for the smoking preference experiment

Table 9.5. *Private Household Budget Shares Under Alternative Scenarios*

	Base		Income Growth		Income Growth with Row No-Smoking Preferences	
	USA	ROW	USA	ROW	USA	ROW
Tobacco	.013	.029				
Agr./Mfg.	.198	.387				
Services	.789	.584				
Total	1.000	1.00				

14. Save the experiment file
    > Select the "Solve" page tab
    > Check that the solution method is Gragg 2-4-6. If it is not, click on "Change," select Gragg from the box and then click on "OK"
    > Check that the parameter file is "Default". If it is not, click on "Change," select default.prm from the box and click OK.
    > Click on "Save experiment," name the shock MACRO, and describe it as "macroeconomic projections"
15. Solve the model
    > Click on "Solve"
    > OK
    > OK
16. Report model results in Tables ME 9.5, ME 9.6 and ME 9.7
    > To view budget share data:
    > Select "View" from the menu bar
    > Updated data
    > Updated GTAPView output
    > Double click on "Cost Structure of Consumption," or NPVA
    > Select "COL" in the menu box on the upper left hand corner of the page that says "None.". This calculates each cell as a ratio of the column total. In this case, the matrix displays budget shares of each commodity in total private household spending. Report your results to three decimal places.
17. Change consumer preferences for tobacco in ROW by changing the value of INCPAR. (For detailed instructions on changing an elasticity parameter and saving a new parameter file, see Model Exercise 3.)
    > Change INCPAR for tobacco in ROW to 0.4
    > Re-solve the model with the new parameter file and report results.
18. Carry out a systematic sensitivity analysis (SSA) of the degree of change in ROW attitudes about smoking as incomes grow (INCPAR). Follow the instructions in Model Exercise 3, and use the information below as your inputs to the SSA utility.
    > Parameter to vary: INCPAR in ROW
    > Percent variation: 100 percent (between close to zero and 0.8.)
    > Type of variation: Percent (this is the default choice)

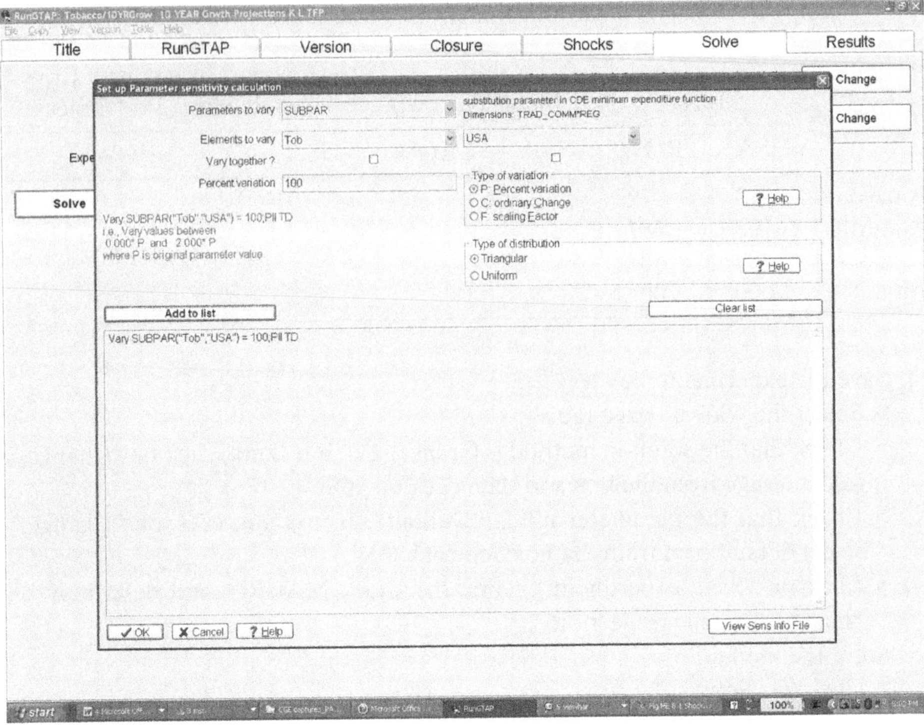

Figure ME 9.2. Systematic sensitivity analysis of INCPAR for tobacco in ROW

> Type of distribution: triangular (it is similar to a bell curve distribution and is the default choice)
> Name and save your two result files from the SSA by replacing the star in the file name with "Smoking" – without the quotes.
> Open and view the files with the sensitivity analysis results.

19. In Table ME 9.8, report the mean and standard deviation results for two variables: tobacco output, *qo*, in ROW and quantity of consumer demand, *qp*, for tobacco in ROW. Calculate the 95 percent confidence interval for both results, using Chebychev's theorem (see Text Box ME 3.1).

Table ME 9.6. *Change in Rest-of-World Household Budget Shares (% change from base)*

	Income Growth	Income Growth with ROW no-smoking Preference
Tobacco		
Agr./Mfg.		
Services		

Table ME 9.7. *Industry Output with and Without Changes in ROW Smoking Preferences (% change from base)*

	Income Growth		Income Growth with no-smoking Preferences	
	USA	ROW	USA	ROW
Tobacco				
Agr/Mfg				
Services				

Interpret Model Results

1. Provide an intuitive explanation of the INCPAR parameter and explain how the reduction in the value of INCPAR will affect ROW consumer demand as income grows.
2. Compare the base values for ROW's INCPARs for all three goods. Given these parameter values, how do you anticipate that growth in income will affect their relative budget shares in your base model scenario (with no preference change)? Are these expectations consistent with your model results?
3. Given the INCPAR parameters in the base model, how do you expect that income growth will affect industry structure? Are your results consistent with this expectation?
4. Develop your predictions for model results by drawing a graph that describes the market for tobacco in the ROW region. To keep it simple, ignore the effects of long-term economic growth on production.
   a. Draw a graph of the supply and demand for tobacco. Label the axes and curves, and label the initial market equilibrium, A.
   b. Draw the effect of an increase in income, assuming the base value of the INCPAR parameter, on the demand curve. Label the new market equilibrium, B.
   c. Draw the effect of an increase in income, assuming the new INCPAR parameter, on the demand curve. Label the new market equilibrium, C. How do the equilibrium quantities and price at C compare to those at equilibrium point B?
   d. Are the industry output results, *qo*, and price results, *ps*, from your two CGE model scenarios consistent with your simple theoretical model?

Table ME 9.8. *Systematic Sensitivity Analysis of Preference Changes on Tobacco Quantities in the Rest-of-World*

	Model Result	Mean	Standard Deviation	95 % Confidence Interval	
				Upper	Lower
Production (*qo*)					
Private consumption (*qp*)					

Source: GTAP CGE model and v.7.0 3x3 tobacco database.

5. Based on data from the SAMs for activity output in each country, how would you characterize the role of the tobacco sector in each economy? Based on these shares, how would you describe the likely size of economywide effects in each country of changes in tobacco preferences in ROW?
6. Write a short paragraph that describes your level of confidence in your model results for ROW's tobacco output, *qo*, and consumer demand for tobacco, *qp*. *Challenge:* present your results and your confidence interval in a graph, similar to that presented in Model Exercise 3.

Appendix

Social Accounting Matrix for the United States, 2004 $U.S. Billions

	Production Activity			Commodities: Imported Variety			Commodities: Domestic Variety			Factors of Production			Indirect Taxes: Trade Taxes		Indirect Taxes: Sales Tax on Imported Variety		
	AGR	MFG	SER	AGR	MFG	SER	AGR	MFG	SER	Land	Labor	Capital	Import Tariff	Export Tax	AGR	MFG	SER
Activity–AGR	0	0	0	0	0	0	434	0	0	0	0	0	0	0	0	0	0
Activity–MFG	0	0	0	0	0	0	0	5,227	0	0	0	0	0	0	0	0	0
Activity–SER	0	0	0	0	0	0	0	0	14,974	0	0	0	0	0	0	0	0
Import–AGR	2	160	6	0	0	0	0	0	0	0	0	0	0	0	0	0	0
Import–MFG	12	393	216	0	0	0	0	0	0	0	0	0	0	0	0	0	0
Import–SER	1	16	149	0	0	0	0	0	0	0	0	0	0	0	0	0	0
Domestic–AGR	24	229	70	0	0	0	0	0	0	0	0	0	0	0	0	0	0
Domestic–MFG	66	1,533	1,141	0	0	0	0	0	0	0	0	0	0	0	0	0	0
Domestic–SER	109	1,079	3,991	0	0	0	0	0	0	0	0	0	0	0	0	0	0
Land	34	0	0	0	0	0	0	0	0	0	0	0	0	0	0	0	0
Labor	68	1,109	5,667	0	0	0	0	0	0	0	0	0	0	0	0	0	0
Capital	122	467	2,332	0	0	0	0	0	0	0	0	0	0	0	0	0	0
Import tariff	0	0	0	1	24	0	0	0	0	0	0	0	0	0	0	0	0
Export tax	0	0	0	0	0	0	0	2	0	0	0	0	0	0	0	0	0
Sales tax–AGR import	0	0	0	0	0	0	0	0	0	0	0	0	0	0	0	0	0
Sales tax–MFG import	0	3	5	0	0	0	0	0	0	0	0	0	0	0	0	0	0
Sales tax–SER import	0	0	0	0	0	0	0	0	0	0	0	0	0	0	0	0	0
Sales tax–AGR dom.	–1	0	0	0	0	0	0	0	0	0	0	0	0	0	0	0	0
Sales tax–MFG dom.	–1	11	42	0	0	0	0	0	0	0	0	0	0	0	0	0	0
Sales tax–SER dom.	–4	3	5	0	0	0	0	0	0	0	0	0	0	0	0	0	0
Factor use tax–land	–3	0	0	0	0	0	0	0	0	0	0	0	0	0	0	0	0
Factor use tax–labor	5	166	850	0	0	0	0	0	0	0	0	0	0	0	0	0	0
Factor use tax–capital	–1	15	76	0	0	0	0	0	0	0	0	0	0	0	0	0	0
Production tax	4	42	423	0	0	0	0	0	0	0	0	0	0	0	0	0	0
Income tax	0	0	0	0	0	0	0	0	0	3	1,446	244	0	0	0	0	0
Regional household	0	0	0	0	0	0	0	0	0	31	5,397	1,632	25	2	1	47	0
Household	0	0	0	0	0	0	0	0	0	0	0	0	0	0	0	0	0
Government	0	0	0	0	0	0	0	0	0	0	0	0	0	0	0	0	0
Savings–investment	0	0	0	0	0	0	0	0	0	0	0	1046	0	0	0	0	0
Trade margin–import	0	0	0	9	47	0	0	0	0	0	0	0	0	0	0	0	0
Trade margin–export	0	0	0	0	0	0	0	0	0	0	0	0	0	0	0	0	0
Rest-of-world	0	0	0	167	1,203	230	0	0	0	0	0	0	0	0	0	0	0
Total	434	5,227	14,974	177	1,274	230	434	5,229	14,974	34	6,844	2,921	25	2	1	47	0

Social Accounting Matrix for the United States, 2004 $U.S. Billions, continued

	Indirect Taxes							Direct Tax	Final Demand							
	Sales Tax on Domestic Variety			Factor Use Taxes									Trade/Transport Margins			
	AGR	MFG	SER	Land	Labor	Capital	Production Tax	Income Tax	Regional House-Hold	Private House-Hold	Gov't.	Saving/ Investment	Import Margin	Export Margin	Rest-of-World	Total
Activity–AGR	0	0	0	0	0	0	0	0	0	0	0	0	0	0	0	434
Activity–MFG	0	0	0	0	0	0	0	0	0	0	0	0	0	0	0	5,227
Activity–SER	0	0	0	0	0	0	0	0	0	0	0	0	0	0	0	14,974
Import–AGR	0	0	0	0	0	0	0	0	0	9	0	0	0	0	0	177
Import–MFG	0	0	0	0	0	0	0	0	0	415	1	237	0	0	0	1,274
Import–SER	0	0	0	0	0	0	0	0	0	60	1	3	0	0	0	230
Domestic–AGR	0	0	0	0	0	0	0	0	0	60	1	0	0	0	50	434
Domestic–MFG	0	0	0	0	0	0	0	0	0	1,104	2	628	0	0	756	5,229
Domestic–SER	0	0	0	0	0	0	0	0	0	6,392	1,805	1,315	0	24	259	14,974
Land	0	0	0	0	0	0	0	0	0	0	0	0	0	0	0	34
Labor	0	0	0	0	0	0	0	0	0	0	0	0	0	0	0	6,844
Capital	0	0	0	0	0	0	0	0	0	0	0	0	0	0	0	2,921
Import tariff	0	0	0	0	0	0	0	0	0	0	0	0	0	0	0	25
Export tax	0	0	0	0	0	0	0	0	0	0	0	0	0	0	0	2
Sales tax–AGR import	0	0	0	0	0	0	0	0	0	1	0	0	0	0	0	1
Sales tax–MFG import	0	0	0	0	0	0	0	0	0	35	0	5	0	0	0	47
Sales tax–SER import	0	0	0	0	0	0	0	0	0	0	0	0	0	0	0	0
Sales tax–AGR dom.	0	0	0	0	0	0	0	0	0	2	0	0	0	0	0	2
Sales tax–MFG dom.	0	0	0	0	0	0	0	0	0	115	0	10	0	0	0	178
Sales tax–SER dom.	0	0	0	0	0	0	0	0	0	41	0	1	0	0	0	45
Factor use tax–land	0	0	0	0	0	0	0	0	0	0	0	0	0	0	0	–3
Factor use tax–labor	0	0	0	0	0	0	0	0	0	0	0	0	0	0	0	1,021
Factor use tax–capital	0	0	0	0	0	0	0	0	0	0	0	0	0	0	0	90
Production tax	0	0	0	0	0	0	0	0	0	0	0	0	0	0	0	469
Income tax	0	0	0	0	0	0	0	0	0	0	0	0	0	0	0	1693
Regional household	2	178	45	–3	1,021	90	469	1693	0	0	0	0	0	0	0	10,628
Household	0	0	0	0	0	0	0	0	8,233	0	0	0	0	0	0	8,233
Government	0	0	0	0	0	0	0	0	1,810	0	0	0	0	0	0	1,810
Savings–Investment	0	0	0	0	0	0	0	0	585	0	0	0	0	32	536	2,198
Trade margin–import	0	0	0	0	0	0	0	0	0	0	0	0	0	0	0	56
Trade margin–export	0	0	0	0	0	0	0	0	0	0	0	0	56	0	0	56
Rest-of-world	0	0	0	0	0	0	0	0	0	0	0	0	0	0	0	1,601
Total	2	178	45	–3	1,021	90	469	1,693	10,628	8,233	1,810	2,198	56	56	1,601	

Glossary

Activity is the domestic production of a good or service.

Agents include industries, factors of production (e.g., labor and capital), household consumers, the government, and the rest-of-world region, which supplies imports and demands exports.

Ad valorem tax is a tax levied as a percentage of value.

Backward linkage index is the sum of the input-output coefficients for all intermediate goods *i* used in industry *j*. It describes an industry's intensity in the use of intermediate inputs from upstream suppliers.

Behavioral equation see equation, behavioral.

Budget constraint is the amount of income received by an agent that is then allocated to consumption, savings and taxes.

Budget share is the value share of each good or service in total expenditure.

Calibration is a procedure that calculates the shift and share parameters used in the production and utility functions in the CGE model so that the solution to each model equation replicates the initial equilibrium as reported in the base data.

cif see cost, insurance, freight.

Circular flow of income and spending describes transactions in an economy: Firms buy inputs and pay wages and capital rents to factors used in the production of goods and services. Firm payments to factors are the income earned by households and spent on goods and services, government taxes, and savings. Taxes and savings lead to government and investment demand. Firms respond to demand by buying inputs and hiring labor and capital.

Closure defines whether a variable is endogenous or exogenous.

Commodity is a composite input or consumption good, composed of domestically produced and imported varieties; and, in some CGE models, it is a composite production good, composed of varieties produced for domestic and export sales.

Complements are inputs or consumption goods that are used together, so that a rise in the price of one input or good causes demand for the other to fall.

Computable general equilibrium (CGE) model describes an economy as a whole, and the interactions among its parts. It is solved to find the set of prices at which supply and demand is in equilibrium in all markets.

Consumer price is the price paid by consumers. It is the domestic producer price plus sales tax, or bilateral *cif* import price plus import tariff and sales tax

Cost-insurance-freight (*cif*) is the price of a good, including the trade and transportation margins service incurred in its international trade.

Deadweight loss is the loss in producer and consumer surplus that is not recouped by the government as tax revenue.

Deterministic CGE model provides unique solution values for each variable, given model equations, parameters, and base data.

Direct burden is the amount of tax paid to the government.

Direct tax is a tax that is levied on factors or individuals and whose burden cannot be passed on to other agents.

Downstream industries are the production activities that use the output of other, "upstream" industries as intermediate inputs into their production process.

Dutch Disease describes the deindustrialization of an economy when an increase in the world price of a natural resource export price leads to an expansion of the booming resource sector, higher incomes and spending, and real exchange rate appreciation.

Dynamic CGE model describes a country's long run growth path, with capital accumulation, and productivity growth.

Effective factor price is the wage or rental paid per unit of effective labor or capital.

Elasticity is an exogenous parameter in a CGE model that describes the responsiveness of supply or demand to a change in prices or income.

Elasticity, aggregate input substitution (σ_{AGG}) in the production of good i describes the percent change in the ratio of the value-added bundle to the intermediate input bundle in the final product, given a percent change in their inverse price ratio, holding final output constant.

Elasticity, cross-price describes the percent change in quantity demanded of commodity i demanded given a percent change in the price of commodity j.

Elasticity, export demand for commodity i describes the percent change in a country's world market share given a percent change in the ratio of the average global price to its *fob* export price.

Elasticity, export transformation (σ_E) in production of good i describes the percent change in the quantity ratio of exports to domestic sales given a percent change in the ratio of the domestic sales price to the *fob* world export price, holding output of i constant.

Elasticity, factor mobility (σ_F) for factor f describes the percent change in an industry's quantity share in total employment of a factor given a percent change in the ratio of the economywide average factor price to the industry's wage or rent.

Elasticity, factor substitution (σ_{VA}) for industry i, describes the percent change in the quantity ratio of a factor to total factor inputs given a percent change in the inverse ratio of the factor's price relative to the prices of other factors, holding the value-added bundle constant.

Elasticity, import substitution (Armington) (σ_M) for commodity i describes the percent change in the quantity ratio of imported to domestic varieties given a percent change in their inverse price ratio, holding consumption of i constant.

Elasticity, income for commodity i describes the percent change in quantity demanded given a percent change in income.

Elasticity, intermediate input substitution (σ_{INT}) for industry i describes the percent change in the quantity ratios of intermediate inputs given a percentage change in the inverse ratio of input prices, holding output of i constant.

Elasticity, own price for commodity i describes the percent change in quantity demanded given a percent change in its price.

Elasticity, substitution in consumption (σ_C) between commodities i and j describes the percent change in the quantity ratios in a given consumer basket, relative to a percent change in their inverse price ratio.

Endogenous variable has a value that is determined as the solution of a model equation.

Equation, behavioral describes the economic behavior of producers or consumers based on microeconomic theory.

Equation, identity defines a variable as a mathematical function (sum, product, etc.) of other variables. Closure rules specify which variable adjusts to maintain the identity.

Equilibrium occurs when the quantities of supply and demand are in balance at some set of prices.

Equivalent variation see welfare, equivalent variation.

Excess burden is the loss in economic efficiency when producers and consumers change the quantities that they produce or consume to avoid a tax.

Exchange rate, nominal measures the rate at which currencies are be exchanged for one another.

Exchange rate, real measures the relative price of traded to nontraded goods.

Exogenous parameters in a CGE model are tax and tariff rates, elasticities of supply and demand, and the calibrated shift and share coefficients used in supply and demand equations.

Exogenous variable is a variable whose value is taken as given and does not change when model equations are solved.

Factor is a primary productive resource, such as land, labor, or capital, that is combined with intermediate inputs to produce goods and services.

Factor endowments are the stocks of labor, capital, and other primary factors that constitute the productive resource base of an economy.

Factor endowment, effective is the stock of a factor that takes into account both the quantity and the efficiency of a factor.

Factor, immobile (sector-specific) does not move from the production activity in which it is originally employed, regardless of differences in relative wages or rents across production activities.

Factor intensity is measured by the relative size of factors' input-output coefficients. The comparison of coefficients can be made across factors within a production activity, or by comparing a factor's coefficient across industries or countries. An activity is intensive in a factor if the coefficient for that factor is higher than for other factors, higher for that factor compared to other activities, or higher for that factor compared to the same activity in other countries.

Factor, mobile moves across production activities within a country in response to changes in relative wages and rents, until wages and rents are equalized.

Factor mobility describes the ease with which labor, capital, and other factors can move to new employment within a country when wages and rents differ across production activities.

Factor, partially mobile is a factor for which transition costs are important enough to discourage it from changing its employment unless pay differences across industries are sufficient.

Factor price is the wage or rent paid to a factor by the production activity that employs it.

Factor price, effective is the wage or rent paid per unit of effective factor quantity.

Factor productivity describes the level of output per unit of factor input.

Factor unemployment describes factors that are not employed by any production activity and are not counted as part of the productive capacity of an economy.

Factors, complementary describe factors for which an increase (decrease) in the use of one factor in the production process requires an increase (decrease) in use of the other.

Factors, substitute describe factors that can replace one another in the production of a good or service.

Final demand is the demand for goods and services in their end-use; they are not further combined or processed into other goods and services.

Flow is the change in quantity of a stock over a period of time.

fob see free on board.

Forward linkage index is the share of sales used as intermediates inputs in an industry's total sales. It describes an industry's role in providing inputs for downstream industries.

Free-on-board (*fob*) is the value of the export good, including export taxes but excluding the *cif* costs paid by the importer.

Gross complement Two goods are gross complements if a decline in the price of one good causes the quantity demanded of the second good to rise.

Gross Domestic Product (GDP) from the income side reports the sources of total national income from the wages and rents earned by factors of production, taxes on economic activity, and depreciation.

Gross Domestic Product (GDP) from the expenditure side reports the allocation of national income across four categories of spending: private consumption (C), investment demand (I), government demand (G), and net exports (E-M).

Gross substitute Two goods are gross substitutes if a decline in the price of one good causes the quantity demanded of the second good to fall.

Gross value of output of a production activity is the sum of value-added plus the cost of intermediate inputs. It is the market value of industry output and reported as the sum total of the activity column in the SAM.

Hecksher-Ohlin theorem posits that countries will export goods that are intensive in the factors of production that are in relatively abundant supply, and import goods that are intensive in the factors of production that are in relatively scarce supply.

Homothetic utility function assumes an income elasticity of demand of one so that the percentage change in quantity demanded is the same as the percentage change in income.

Identity equation, see equation, identity.

Immobile factor (sector-specific) is a factor that remains fixed in its original sector of employment.

Import (Armington) aggregation function describes how imported and domestic varieties are combined to produce a commodity.

Independent goods or factors are items for which demand does not change when the prices of other goods or factors change. Their cross-price elasticity of demand is zero.

Indifference curve describes all possible combinations of commodities that yield the same level of utility or satisfaction to the consumer.

Inferior good is a good for which demand declines as income grows.

Input intensity is measured by the relative size of intermediate input-output coefficients. The comparison of coefficients can be made across intermediate inputs within a production activity, or by comparing an input's coefficient across industries or countries. An activity is intensive in an intermediate input if its input-output coefficient for that input is higher than for other intermediate inputs, higher for that input compared to other production activities, or higher for that input compared to the same activity in other countries.

Input-output coefficient describes the ratio of an intermediate or factor input per unit of output.

Input-output coefficient matrix displays the input-output coefficients of all inputs in every production activity. The matrix shows how industries are linked through their demand for intermediate inputs.

Intermediate input is a good that is combined with other inputs and factors to produce a final product.

Isocost describes all combinations of inputs that can be purchased for the same cost.

Isoquant describes all technologically feasible combinations of inputs that can be used to produce the same level of output.

Isorevenue line shows all combinations of outputs that generate the same amount of revenue for the producer.

Large country's world prices for its imports and exports are influenced by its export and import quantities.

Law of Demand states that demand for a good will rise (fall) when its price falls (rises).

Leontief fixed-proportions production function assumes that all inputs must be used in fixed proportions, to output.

Long run is a postshock adjustment period that is sufficiently long that factors are fully mobile across production activities, and factor endowments and factor productivity may change.

Luxury good has an income elasticity of demand that is greater than one.

Macro-micro model provides the endogenous, macroeconomic results from a CGE model (the macro model) as the exogenous inputs into a microeconomic model with large numbers of households or firms.

Marginal rate of substitution is the rate at which the consumer is willing to trade off one good for one unit of the other good.

Marginal product is the addition to output from an additional unit of an input, holding other inputs constant.

Marginal welfare burden is the change in national welfare due to a very small – a marginal – change in an existing tax.

Medium run is a postshock adjustment period sufficiently long that factors are fully mobile across production activities, but too short for long-run changes in factor accumulation or productivity to take place.

Model closure is the modeler's decision as to which variables are exogenous and which are endogenous.

Multicountry model contains two or more countries (or regions) whose economies and economic behavior are described in detail and which are linked through trade and, sometimes, capital and labor flows.

Necessity good has an income elasticity of demand that is less than one.

Nested production function, see production function, nested.

Net substitute Two goods are net substitutes if a decline (rise) in the price of X relative to Y causes an increase (decrease) in the quantity ratio of X toY, holding output or utility constant.

Nonhomothetic utility function assumes the income elasticity of demand does not equal one so that the percentage change in quantity demanded changes by less than (the income elasticity is less than one) or more than (the income elasticity exceeds one) the percentage change in income.

Normal good has a positive income elasticity of demand. Demand for a normal good increases when income rises.

Numeraire is a price that is fixed at its base value and serves as the standard of value against which all other prices in the model can be measured.

Output effect is the change in demand for all inputs by the same proportion as the change in output, holding input price ratios constant.

Parameters in a CGE model include elasticity parameters, calibrated shift and share parameters used in production and consumption functions, and calculated tax rates.

Partial equilibrium model is a system of mathematical equations that describe the economic motives and behaviors in the market for one good, or of one type of economic agent, such as consumers, holding prices and quantities in the rest of the economy constant.

Price, bilateral *(fob)* export for good *i* is the exporter's *fob* price to each export market; it includes the export tax.

Price, bilateral *(cif)* import for good *i* is the exporter's bilateral export price plus *cif* costs; it excludes the import tariff.

Price, consumer for good *i* is the producer price plus consumer sales tax for domestic varieties, and the *cif* import price plus import tariffs and consumer sales taxes for imported varieties.

Price, global for good *i* is the trade-weighted sum of the bilateral *fob* prices of all exporters.

Price, producer for good *i* is the producer's sales price; in a competitive market, it is equal to the costs of production and inclusive of production taxes and subsidies.

Price, world export for an exporter's sale of commodity *i* is the trade-weighted sum of its bilateral *fob* export prices.

Price, world import for an importer's purchase of commodity *i* is the trade-weighted sum of its bilateral *cif* import prices.

Product transformation curve plots all possible combinations of two goods that can be produced with a given quantity of productive resources.

Production function defines the technology, or physical production process, by which intermediate inputs are transformed by machinery and workers into a product.

Production function, nested separates the production process into smaller production processes that are "nested" within the larger process of producing the final product. Each nest has its own production function.

Quasi-homothetic preferences describe fixed minimum consumption requirements and homothetic preferences for discretionary consumption goods.

Rational expectations describe producers and consumers who anticipate and take into account prices and income in all time periods as they make their current decisions.

Real exchange rate, see exchange rate, real.

Regional household is a macroeconomic account that aggregates total national income from factor earnings and taxes, and allocates the income to private consumption, government, and savings.

Rybczynki theorem posits that an increase in the quantity of one factor will lead to an absolute increase in the production of the good that uses that factor intensively, and an absolute decrease in production of the good that does not use it intensively, holding world prices constant.

Second-best is the most efficient outcome attainable if there is an existing distortion in another market due to a tax, a market failure, or other type of economic constraint.

Sector-specific factor (see immobile factor).

Sets are the domains over which parameters, variables, and equations are defined.

Short run equilibrium describes a postshock adjustment period that is short enough that at least one factor of production, usually capital, remains immobile, and no long-term changes in factor endowments or productivity occur.

Single-country model describes only one country in detail and summarizes the rest-of-world economy.

Small country's world prices for its imports and exports are determined by world price levels and are independent of its export and import quantities.

Social Accounting Matrix is a square matrix whose columns and rows describe transactions among buyers and sellers in the circular flow of income and spending in an economy in a time period.

Static model describes an economy's equilibria before and after a shock, holding factor supplies constant, and does not depict the adjustment path.

Stochastic CGE model accounts for randomness in the economy and solves for the mean values and probability distributions of the endogenous variables.

Stock is the available quantity of a factor at a point in time.

Stolper-Samuelson theorem posits that an increase in the world price of a good leads to a rise in the price of the factor used intensively in its production, and a decline in the price of the other factor.

Structure refers to the economy's industrial composition, the commodity composition of demand and trade, shares of each factor in employment and earnings, and relative tax rates.

Structure table uses the microeconomic data in the SAM to describe the economy in terms of shares (e.g., shares of each commodity in households' consumption) and rates (e.g., import tariff rates or income tax rates).

Substitute goods or factors are items for which the producer or consumer is willing to trade-off more of one for less of the other as their relative prices change.

Substitution effect is the change in the ratio of inputs in production or in consumption as relative prices change, at constant output or utility levels.

Tax, *ad valorem* is levied as a percentage of the value of goods or services.

Tax, direct is levied on factors or individuals; its direct burden cannot be shifted to other agents.

Tax, export is levied on exports.

Tax, factor use is levied on producers based on their employment of factors of production.

Tax incidence describes how the direct burden of indirect taxes is shared among buyers and sellers after prices and quantities adjust.

Tax, income is a direct tax paid by factors or households on the basis of income earned.

Tax, indirect is levied on the production or purchase of goods or factors; its direct burden can be shifted from the entity that pays the tax onto someone else through a change in price of the good or factor.

Tax, lump sum is a fixed tax liability that does not depend on income, wealth, or level of consumption or production.

Tax, output is levied on producers based on their output.

Tax, sales is levied on purchases of goods and services used as intermediate inputs or in final demand.

Tax, specific is levied per quantity unit.

Tax structure table expresses tax flow data in the SAM as tax rates.

Technology tree (see nested production function).

Terms of trade is the ratio of the world (*fob*) price of a country's export good(s) relative to the *fob* price of its import good(s).

Total factor productivity (TFP) is the output level per unit of aggregate factor input.

Trade margins are the insurance, and freight charges incurred when goods are shipped by air, sea, or overland from the exporting country to the importing country.

Upstream industries are the production activities that produce goods that are used as intermediate inputs into other, "downstream" industries.

Utility function describes how commodities can be combined, according to the tastes and preferences of consumers, to generate consumer utility or satisfaction.

Value-added includes factor input costs and tax payments by activities in the production of goods and services.

Value-added production function describes the stage of the production process in which producers choose the most efficient ratios of factors in the value-added bundle.

Welfare, equivalent variation is a money-metric measure of the value to the consumer of the price changes due to a shock. It is calculated as the difference in income required to achieve the new versus the initial levels of utility when goods are valued at base year prices.

Welfare, real consumption is a money-metric measure of the value to the consumer of the price changes due to a shock. It is calculated as the difference in income required to buy the new basket of goods versus the initial basket of goods when both baskets are valued at base year prices.

World *cif* import price for good *i* is the trade-weighed sum of the bilateral *cif* import prices of commodities imported by destination country s from source country *r*. The price includes trade margins but excludes import tariffs in country s.

World *fob* export price for good *i* is the trade-weighed sum of the bilateral *fob* prices of commodities exported from source country *r* to destination country *s*. The price includes export taxes in country *r* but excludes trade margins costs.

Practice and Review Answer Key

Chapter 1

1. Pq = 4, Qs = Qd = 4.
2. Pq = 5, Qs = Qd = 6

Table 1.2. *Partial Versus General Equilibrium Analysis (answer key)*

	Bicycle Equilibrium Price is Higher/Lower than $1.50	Bicycle Supply/Demand Equilibrium is Greater/Less than 15	Which Curve Shifts and in which Direction?
Increase in price of rubber tires	**$1.50**	**15**	**Supply – upward/left**
Bicycle workers accept lower wages	lower	greater	*Supply shifts downward/right*
Consumer demand shifts to imported bicycles	lower	less than	*Demand shifts upward/left*
Decline in exports causes depreciation and higher imported input costs	higher	less than	*Supply shifts upward/left*
Bicycle seat price falls due to fall in demand from bicycle producers	lower	greater than	*Supply shifts downward/right*

Chapter 2

1. PP_c, $PP_{\text{“manufactures”}}$
2. Quantity of agricultural imports by Brazil from the United States.
3. The graph shows two different market outcomes: A in the case of an inelastic supply curve, and B in the case of an elastic supply curve. The supply curve is

more elastic when (1) factor substitution elasticities are larger and (2) factor mobility elasticities are larger in absolute value.

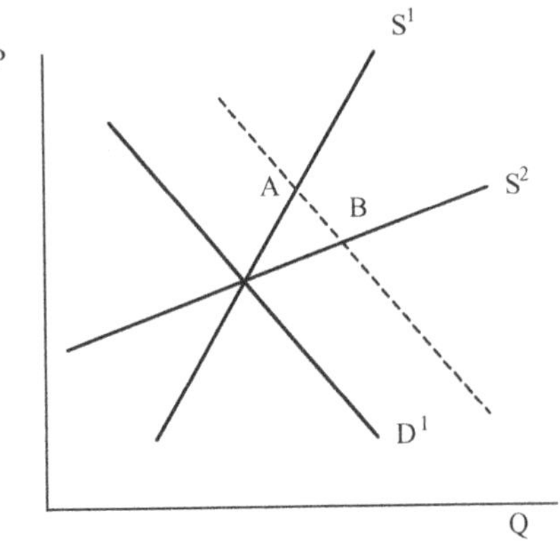

Chapter 2, Practice and review problem 3.

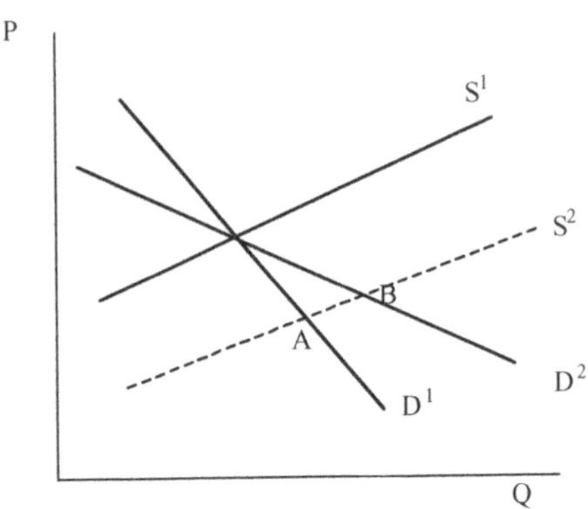

Chapter 2, Practice and review problem 4.

4. The graph shows two different market outcomes: A in the case of an inelastic demand curve, and B in the case of an elastic supply curve. Demand for the domestic good is more elastic when (1) own-price substitution elasticities are larger and (2) import substitution elasticities are larger.

Table 2.3. *Normalized Prices and Quantities of Apples (answer key)*

	Base Values			50% Change in Quantity			
	Price	Quantity	Value	Price	Quantity	Value	% Change in Value
Actual	4	6	24	4	9	36	50
Normalized	1	1.5	1.5	1	2.25	2.25	50

Table 2.4. *Calculating the U.S. World Import Price of Corn (answer key)*

	France	Germany	South Africa
Exporter's market share of U.S. corn imports	50	25	25
Exporter bilateral (*fob*) export price	$1.25	$0.85	$1.90
Trade margin	$0.25	$0.15	$0.10
U.S. bilateral import price	1.50	1.00	2.00
Trade-weighted import price	.5 * 1.50 = .75	.25 * 1.00 = .25	.25 * 2.00 = .50
U.S. world price	.75 + .25 + .50 = $1.50		

Chapter 3

1. a. $5,227 billion
   b. Manufacturing uses:
      Agric. intermediates plus sales taxes: $160 + $229 = $389
      Mfg. intermediates plus sales taxes: $393 + $1,533 + $3 + $11 = $1,940
      Services intermediates plus sales taxes: $16 + $1,079 + $3 = $1,098
      Total intermediate input costs = $3,427.
      Manufactured intermediates accounts for the largest share of input costs: 57 percent.
   c. $3 + $11 + $3 + $166 + $15 + $42 = $240 in tax payments. The largest tax payment is for labor use.
   d. Labor factor use tax is 15 percent.
2. a. imports = $1,274
   b. domestic variety = $5,229
   c. total supply = $6,503
3. a. The imported MFG variety is sold to production activities as an intermediate input ($12 + $393 + $216), to private households ($415), to government ($1), and to investment ($237). A total of $1,274 is sold.
   b. The domestic MFG variety is sold to production activities as an intermediate input ($66 + $1, 533 + $1, 141). There are also sales to private households ($1,104) to government ($2), to investment ($628), and to exports ($756). A total of $5,230 ($5,229 adjusted for rounding) is sold.
4. a. Labor has the largest factor cost share in U.S. services production:

      Factor cost for labor: $5,667 + $850 = $6,517
      Factor cost share for capital: $2,332 + $76 = $2,408
      Total factor cost: $8,925
      Labor cost share: $6,517/$8,925 = 73 percent

Capital cost share: \$2,408/\$8,925 = 27 percent
Labor has the highest cost share.

b. Services pays \$423 billion in output taxes.

Chapter 4

1. a. Agriculture: C = 60, I = 0, G = 1, E = 50
   b. Services: C = 6,392, I = 1,315, G = 1,805, E = 283
2. Agr = (60+2)/8,233 = .008; MFG = (1,104 + 115)/8,233 = .15; SER = (6,392 + 41)/8,233 = .78
3. A homothetic utility function assumes that consumers will change their demand for all goods and services by the same proportion as the change in income. A nonhomothetic utility function can describe goods as luxuries or necessities, for which growth in demand will not change by the same proportion as income. The main differences between the two utility functions in an analysis of economic growth is that the nonhomothetic function will lead to higher demand for luxury goods and lower demand for necessities relative to the change in income, which will cause a shift in production and trade toward luxury products. The homothetic function will lead to a more balanced growth in demand, production, and trade.
4. A large value for the Armington parameter describes in a flatter isoquant, becoming linear as the parameter value approaches infinity. When the parameter value becomes smaller, the isoquant becomes more curved. In the limit, the parameter value approaches zero and the curve is L-shaped. When the tariff is removed, a larger parameter causes a larger change in quantity ratios.

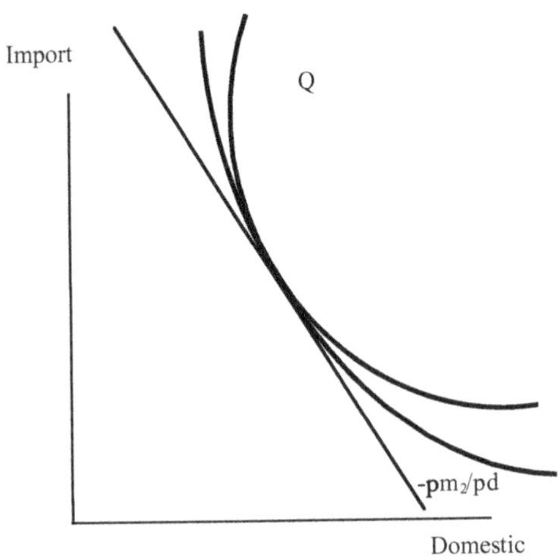

Chapter 4, Practice and review problem 4. Low versus high Armington import substitution elasticities (answer key)

5. The real consumption welfare change in welfare is \$6. The price changes have increased national welfare.

Table 4.8. *Practice and Review Calculation of the Real Consumption Welfare Measure (answer key)*

	Initial Price	Initial Quantity	New Quantity	Cost of Initial Quantity at Initial Prices	Cost of New Quantity at Initial Prices
Apples	$1.00	5	6	$5.00	$6.00
Oranges	$1.00	5	4	$5.00	$4.00
Candy bars	$1.00	2	8	$2.00	$8.00
Total	–	–	–	$12.00	$18.00

Chapter 5

1. Total intermediates: 5,574
   Total factor payments: 7,999
   Total taxes: $926 + 52 + 423 = 1401$
   Value-added: $14,974 - 5,574 = 9400$
   Gross output: 14,974 (with rounding)

Table 5.7. *Input-Output Coefficients (answer key)*

	Inputs into Production		Input-Output Coefficients	
	Manufacturing	Services	Mfg.	Services
Labor	12	12	.24	.10
Capital	8	18	.16	.18
Manufacturing	10	50	.20	.50
Services	20	20	.40	.20
Gross value of output	50	100	1.00	1.00

2. a. Mfg. is labor intensive.
   b. Services is capital intensive.
   c. Manufacturing is the most labor-intensive sector in the economy.
   d. Upstream role: manufacturing is an important input supplier of intermediate inputs services, accounting for 50 percent of its input requirements. Downstream role: manufacturing depends on services for a large share of its intermediate inputs – 40 percent of these input requirements.
3. Lower wage costs relative to the price of capital rotates the isocost curve from C1 to C2. The labor/capital ratio rises from L^1/K^1 to L^2/K^2 in the production of value-added bundle QVA^1.
4. This CGE model probably has a Leontief-fixed proportion production function because there is no substitution among intermediates, and demands for intermediate inputs change by the same proportion as output. The model has a value-added production function that allows substitution among factors because the factor input ratio changes. Because production becomes more labor intensive, wages must have fallen relative to rents.

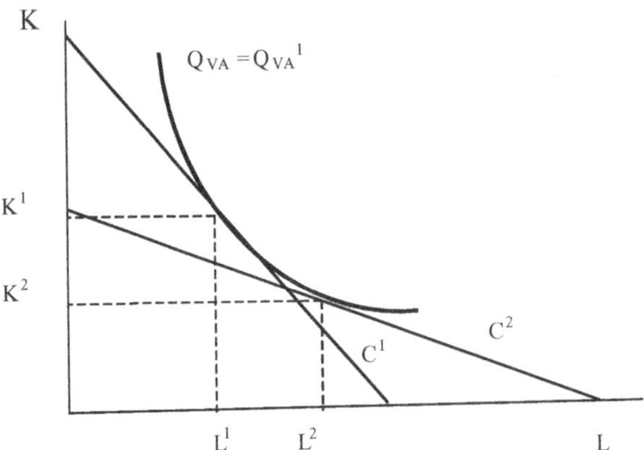

Chapter 5, Practice and review problem 3. A fall in wages in the industry (answer key)

Chapter 6

1. Figure 2.1 describes the relatively elastic supply curve of an industry with a mobile factor and the relatively inelastic supply curve of an industry with an immobile, sector-specific factor. A demand shock leads to a larger quantity effect and smaller price effect for an industry when factors are mobile compared to when factors are immobile.
2. Assuming that the equipment is a capital input that is complementary to engineering labor in the production of computer chips, an increase in the supply of engineers should increase demand for the equipment (see Problem 6.2 Figure). The increase in number of engineers shifts the demand curve for the capital good outward and results in a higher price and quantity for the equipment. You should advise the industry to support the training program.

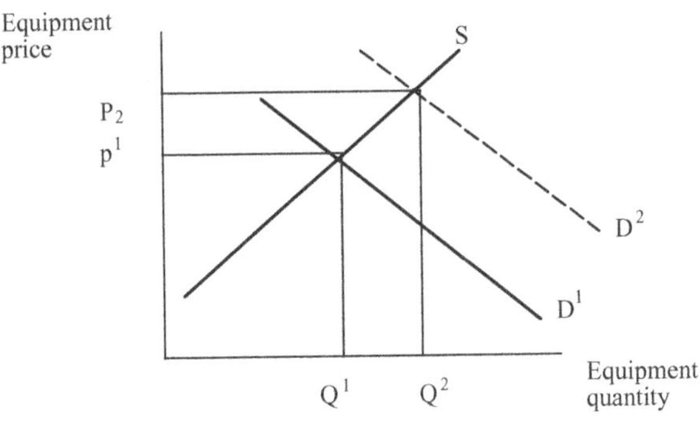

Chapter 6. Practice and review problem 2 (answer key)

3. Services is a large and labor-intensive sector in the U.S. economy. Its expansion is likely to increase the price of labor and cause all three sectors to become more capital intensive.

Chapter 7

1. a. Televisions are capital intensive, and wine is labor intensive.
   b. Capital costs will fall due to increased productivity, and this will lower the costs of production of televisions more than of wine.
   c. Wine is relatively exportable, and televisions are relatively importable.
   d. An increase in production of the importable will reduce the country's demand for imports, so the world import price is likely to fall. A decrease in production of the exportable will decrease its supply of exports, so its world export price is likely to rise. This country's terms of trade will likely improve because its world export price will increase relative to its world import price.
2. The Dutch Disease model describes (1) resource endowment effects and (2) spending effects. The resource endowment effect describes resource competition by the expanding oil sector, which causes output in other industries to fall. The spending effect describes the increased demand for goods and services as incomes grow. Both effects lead to real exchange rate appreciation and increased import competition for Venezuela's industrial sector, and the potential for deindustrialization.
3. % change in U.S. world export price = (.6 * 6) + (.4 * 4) = 5.2
   % change in U.S. world (fob) import price = (.8 * 4) + (.2 * 1) = 3.4
   % change in U.S. terms of trade = (5.2 – 3.4) = 1.8. The U.S. terms of trade improves.

Chapter 8

1. In the graph, the import with a more price-elastic demand is described by a flatter demand curve and a larger excess burden than the import with price-inelastic demand. The welfare cost of the tariff will be smaller for the less elastic import.
2. For both sectors, the factor use tax is 15 percent for labor and 3.25 for capital. Because the factor use taxes are the same in both industries, they do not distort factor allocation between them. The taxes make labor relatively cheaper than capital and create an incentive for both industries to become more capital intensive.
3. See Text Figure 8.4.
4. a. –$200,000/$1,000000 * 100 = 20
   b. The government must earn a return of 120 percent on its project, or the cost in terms of tax dollars spent and inefficiencies linked to the taxes will be greater than the project's benefits.
   c. The marginal excess burden will be smaller if the tax is levied on price-inelastic goods, because this will minimize distortions of the student's consumption basket.
   d. The subsidized textbook industry is likely producing quantities that are greater than is economically efficient, given the nation's resources and preferences. A sales tax in the bookstore will likely reduce demand for and output of textbooks, and reduce the inefficiency linked to the textbook subsidy.

Model Exercise Answer Key

Model Exercise 2

B.2 REG = US, ROW are the regions in the database
B.3 TRAD_COM = AGR, MFG, and SER are the sectors in the database
B.4 END_COM = land, labor, capital are the factors of production in the database
C. An error message: "You cannot view more than two dimensions."
D. INCPAR("USA", "SER") = 1.0.

Table ME 2.1. *Elasticity Parameters for U.S. Agriculture (answer key)*

Elasticity	Value
Supply parameters	
Factor substitution (ESUBVA)	0.2
Intermediate input substitution (ESUBT)	0.0
Demand parameters	
Consumer income (INCPAR)	0.3
Consumer substitution (SUBPAR)	0.7
Import substitution (imports v. domestic good) (ESUBD)	3.8
Import substitution (among trade partners) (ESUBM)	10.1

Table ME 2.2. *Tax Rates for U.S. Agriculture (answer key)*

Tax rate	Name	Value
rTO	% ad valorem rate, output (or income) tax in region r	−1.0
rTF	% ad valorem rate, taxes on primary factors	−9.5
rTPD	% ad valorem rate, private domestic consumption taxes	4.1
rTPI	% ad valorem rate, private import consumption taxes	6.4
rTGD	% ad valorem rate, government domestic purchases taxes	0.0
rTGI	% ad valorem rate, government import purchases taxes	0.0
rTFD	% ad valorem rate, taxes on firms' domestic purchases	−4.0
rTFI	% ad valorem rate, taxes on firms' import purchases	−4.1
rTXS	% ad valorem rate, export taxes by destination	−0.0
rTMS	% ad valorem rate, import taxes by source	0.5

F.1 Variable definitions:

pm = market price of commodity *i* in region *r*
pop = regional population
ps = supply price of commodity *i* in region *r*
qfe = demand for endowment *i* for use in industry j in region *r*
qiw = aggregate imports of *i* in region s, CIF weights
qxw = aggregate exports of *i* from region *r*, FOB weights

F.2 Population is exogenous and all the rest of the variables listed in F.1 are exogenous.

Model Exercise 3

C2. *to* is defined as the output or income tax in region r.
C3. −.8017
C4. a tax

Table ME 3.1. *Results of a 5 percent Production Subsidy to U.S. Manufacturing, with Different Elasticities and Closures (answer key)*

	Definition of Variable	Base Results	High Factor Substitution Elasticity in MFG	Unemployment Closure
qo("MFG","USA")	Industry output of MFG in USA	2.98	2.95	23.91
qo("MFG","ROW")	Industry output of MFG in ROW	−0.23	−0.22	0.42
qfe("LABOR", "MFG", "USA")	Demand for LABOR in MFG in USA	2.91	2.76	33.25

Source: GTAP model, GTAP v.7.0 U.S. 3x3 database.

Table ME 3.2. *Welfare Decomposition of a 5 percent Production Subsidy to U.S. Manufacturing (answer key)*

Resource Allocation Effect	Endowment Effect	Technical Change	Population Growth	Terms of Trade	Investment–Savings Terms of Trade	Preference Change	Total
1 alloc_A1	2 endw_B1	3 tech_C1	4 pop_D1	5 tot_E1	6 IS_F1	7 pref_G1	
7,399.7	0	0	0	23,477	27,055	0	57,932

Source: GTAP model, U.S. 3x3 v.7.0 database.

a. *qo*("MFG", "USA") = 2.98
b. Mean = 2.96
c. Standard deviation = 0.14

Table ME 3.4. *Confidence Intervals for the Output Quantity Result with a 100 percent Variation in the Factor Substitution Elasticity (answer key)*

Confidence Interval	Mean (X)	Standard Deviation (sd)	Standard Deviation Multiplier (K)	Upper Limit (X + sdK)	Lower Limit (X – sdK)
75 percent	2.96	0.14	2	3.24	2.68
88.9 percent	2.96	0.14	3	3.38	2.54
95 percent	2.96	0.14	4.47	3.59	2.33
99 percent	2.96	0.14	10	4.36	1.56

Model Exercise 4

Table ME 4.1. *Elasticities in Two Scenarios of a 50 percent Increase in the World Agricultural Price (answer key)*

	Scenario 1		Scenario 2	
Elasticities	INCPAR	SUBPAR	INCPAR	SUBPAR
Agriculture	0.25	0.74	1	0
Manufacturing	0.87	0.24	1	0
Services	1.04	0.22	1	0

Table ME 4.2. *Household Budget Shares (answer key)*

	Base	Scenario 1	Scenario 2
Agriculture	.009	.010	.009
Manufacturing	.203	.203	.203
Services	.789	.786	.789

Table ME 4.3. *Effects of a 50 percent Increase in the World Price of Imported Agriculture (% change from base) (answer key)*

	Consumer Price	Consumer Commodity Quantity	Household Domestic Quantity	Household Import Quantity	Production Quantity	Household Expenditure	Welfare $U.S. Million
GTAP variable name	*pp*	*qp*	*qpd*	*qpm*	*qo*	*yp*	*EV*
CDE utility							
Agric.	25.24	−6.95	5.93	90.16	53.92	−0.72	−70,651.7
Mfg.	1.87	−2.24	−4.52	−3.94	−5.66		
Services	−0.73	−0.29	−0.27	−1.70	−.31		
Cobb-Douglas							
Agr.	24.79	−25.01	−11.86	−109.90	51.45	−0.22	−19,239.23
Mfg.	2.16	−2.38	−5.01	4.75	−6.26		
Services	−.22	0.0	0.00	0.43	−0.13		

1. The utility functions assume negative own-price elasticities. With income constant, as the price rises, demand should fall. In the CGE model, the demand quantity falls in both scenarios.
2. The CDE demand system is nonhomothetic. AGR is a necessity good, SER is a luxury good, and MFG is a necessity that is more responsive to income changes

than AGR. The CD function so, holding prices constant, demand quantities of all three goods changes by the same proportion as income.

3. AGR/MFG: $(-25.01 + 2.38)/(2.16 - 24.79) = 1$
   AGR/SER: $(-25.01 - .00001)/(-0.22 - 24.79) = 1$
   Both indifference curves would be relatively curved.
4. The CDE demand system allows flexible budget shares. In the CDE scenario, the agricultural budget share rises because the price rises, and the quantity demanded does not fall by enough to compensate. The CD utility function imposes fixed budget shares, so the change in quantity exactly offsets percentage changes in price and income.
5. Both scenarios describe a substantial decline in imports and increased consumer demand for the domestic variety of AGR. This causes U.S. agricultural output to increase. Higher agricultural output will exert a pull on the productive resources used in MFG and SER, so their output will decline.
6. The Armington assumption implies that consumers differentiate goods by country of origin, and consumers' willingness to substitute among the varieties is governed by an import substitution elasticity. Both models include import substitution elasticities for AGR of 3.75. Consumer demand shifts to the lower-priced domestic variety, so imports fall and consumption of the domestic good rises in both scenarios.
7. For scenario one, the elasticity of import substitution is:

$$(-90.16 - 5.93)/(21.80 - 47.42) = 3.75$$

   For scenario two, the elasticity of import substitution is:

$$(-109.90 + 11.86)/(21.29 - 47.43) = 3.75$$

8. A change in EV welfare measures the income equivalent of the change in utility due to changes in prices. U.S. welfare declines in both experiments; the magnitude is sensitive to the choice of utility function.
9. The income results do not differ much between the two scenarios because food is a small share of the U.S. budget.

Model Exercise 5

1. See the technology tree in Figure 5.1. Your tree will look similar, with a value-added nest containing K, L, and Land, governed by a factor substitution elasticity of 0.2 and an intermediate input bundle that contains AGR, MFG, and SER inputs, governed by an intermediate input substitution elasticity of zero. The two bundles are combined to produce AGR governed by an aggregate input substitution elasticity of zero.
2. Price changes could lead to factor substitution in the CGE model, but no substitution among intermediates, or between the intermediate and value-added bundles.
3. AGR becomes more land intensive and less intensive in the use of labor and capital. This is consistent with land rents that are falling relative to wage and

Table ME 5.1. *Base and Updated Subsidy Rates (answer key)*

	Base Rate	Updated Rate
Production subsidy rto ("AGR", "USA") (negative value = tax)	−1.0	0
Land subsidy rtf ("LAND", "AGR", "USA") (negative value = subsidy)	−9.5	0
Intermediate input subsidy on domestic input rtfd ("AGR", "AGR", "USA") (negative value = subsidy)	−4.0	0
Intermediate subsidy on imported input rtfi ("AGR", "AGR", "USA") (negative value = subsidy)	−4.1	0

Table ME 5.2. *Effects of U.S. Agricultural Subsidy Elimination (% change from base) (answer key)*

		Base ESUBVA Factor Substitution Elasticity				
			Subtotals			
	Variable Name in GTAP	Total	Output Tax/ Subsidy Effect	Land Tax/ Subsidy Effect	Intermediate Input Tax/ Subsidy Effect	ESUBVA = 2 TOTAL
Agricultural output quantity	*qo* (AGR,USA)	−0.37	0.97	0	−1.34	−0.59
Agricultural producer price	*ps*(AGR,USA)	1.25	0.42	0.01	0.82	1.33
Land rent	*ps*(LAND,USA)	−11.31	5.07	−9.38	−7	−9.83
Labor wage	*ps*(LABOR,USA)	−0.02	0.09	0.01	−0.12	−0.04
Capital rent	*ps*(CAPITAL,USA)	−0.03	0.12	0.01	−0.16	−0.05
Household consumption	*qp* (AGR,USA)	−0.06	0.16	0	−0.22	−0.09
Export quantity	*qxw*(AGR,USA)	−1.61	4.19	0	−5.8	−2.57

capital rents. Intermediate input-output ratios are unchanged, consistent with the Leontief intermediate input technology in the U.S. 3x3 model.

4. The loss of the land subsidy effect has little impact except on land rents. The other two reforms have offsetting effects in many instances. Policy makers may want to select reforms with different impacts, or phase them all in together, knowing that they have off-setting impacts on AGR.
5. The total effects are only slightly larger when ESUBVA is higher. In this case, L and K more readily exit agriculture as farmers substitute toward the lower-cost land input.
6. Agriculture accounts for only 1 percent of U.S. household spending so U.S. consumers are not likely to be substantially affected by an agricultural reform program.

Table ME 5.3. *Change in Input-Output Coefficients due to U.S. Agricultural Policy Reform (% change from base)*

Output and Inputs	Output and Input Quantities	Change in Input-Output Coefficients (*qfe-qo*) or (*qf-qo*)
AGR output (*qo*)	−0.37	Not applicable
Land (*qfe*)	0.0	0.37
Labor (*qfe*)	−0.43	−0.6
Capital (*qfe*)	−0.43	−0.6
AGR intermediate (*qf*)	−0.37	0.0
MFG intermediate (*qf*)	−0.37	0.0
SER intermediate (*qf*)	−0.37	0.0

8. Land cannot be employed elsewhere, so a change in land use tax has no effect on quantity of land demanded, and therefore on AGR output levels. In the our simple 3x3 model, land is employed only in agriculture, whereas labor and capital are fully mobile across all three sectors; and all factors are fully employed.

Model Exercise 6

Table ME 6.1. *Effects of 10 percent Increase in the U.S. Supply of Unskilled Labor (answer key)*

Factor Price (*pfe*)			Demand for Labor (*qfe*) Unskilled	Skilled	Output (*qo*)
BORJAS – 10 percent increase in unskilled labor supply with high factor substitution					
Unskilled	−1.18	Agriculture	12.85	2.61	5.28
Skilled labor	−0.39	Manufactures	9.80	−0.16	4.42
Capital	−0.38	Services	9.99	−0.11	3.95
OTTA1 – 10 percent increase in unskilled labor supply with low factor substitution					
Skilled	−9.53	Agriculture	−2.19	−5.98	−4.91
Skilled labor	10.19	Manufactures	6.99	−3.06	1.49
Capital	9.28	Service	10.91	0.5	4.53
OTTA2 – 10 percent increase in unskilled labor, 6 percent increase in capital, low factor substitution					
Unskilled	−8.33	Agriculture	9.95	5.83	8.58
Skilled labor	10.93	Manufactures	10.34	0.30	6.42
Capital	−1.06	Services	9.92	−0.07	5.33

1. See Figures 6.2a and 6.2b in Chapter 6.
2. Change the factor substitution elasticities. A larger parameter value describes a more flexible production technology, with a relatively large substitution in factor input quantities given a percentage change in the inverse of their relative prices.
3. When firm technologies are assumed to allow easy substitution of among factors, a fall in the price of unskilled workers will lead to a fall in demand for and prices of the other two factors.

Table ME 6.2. *Real GDP Effects of a 10 percent Increase in U.S. Unskilled Labor Supply*

Scenario	% Change in Real GDP
BORJAS	4.04
OTTA1	3.90
OTTA2	5.56

4. See Figures 6.2c and 6.2d in Chapter 6.
5. Producers must hire more skilled labor and capital to complement their increased use of unskilled workers, which increases demand for and prices of skilled labor and capital.
6. An increase in the capital stock will shift the demand curves for both unskilled and skilled labor outward, if factors are assumed to be relatively complementary. Wages of both labor types will increase relative to the results of OTTO1.
7. The price of capital falls because the supply of capital increases.
8. AGR output declines in OTTA1 but expands in OTTA2. The difference between them is that the capital stock increases in OTTA2. AGR is the most capital-intensive U.S. sector. It expands because the factor cost share of capital is high in AGR, therefore an increase in capital that reduces rents lowers the production costs and price of AGR, compared to other sectors.
9. Real GDP grows because the endowment of productive resources grows. Real GDP growth is larger when the production technology is more flexible, allowing producers to better take advantage of an increase in an endowment and a fall in its price.

Model Exercise 7

Table ME 7.3. *Base Tax Rates in U.S. 3x3 Model (answer key)*

	Tax Rate					
	United States			Rest-of-World		
Tax type	Agr.	Mfg.	Services	Agr.	Mfg.	Services
Taxes on domestic intermediates used in agricultural production (rTFD)	−4.0	−1.0	−3.7	−1.4	2.2	−0.7
Taxes on imported intermediates used in agricultural production (rTFI)	−4.1	−2.0	−2.8	−1.5	0.4	−0.4
Export taxes (rTXS)	0	−0.3	0	−.4	−.8	0
Import tariffs (rTMS)	0.5	1.9	0	8.5	2.9	0

Source: GTAP v.7.0.

Table ME 7.4. *Welfare Effects of Trade Liberalization by Region and by Policy, $U.S. Millions (answer key)*

	Total	U.S. Agricultural Policy Reform	U.S. Nonagricultural Policy Reform	Rest-of-World Agricultural Policy Reform	Rest-of-World Nonagricultural Policy Reform
United States	14,565.39	−1,516.94	−10,632.93	7,860.50	18,854.70
ROW	−13,481.11	1,161.59	11,773.62	−6441.43	−19,974.88
World	1,084.29	−355.35	1,140.69	1,419.07	1,120.18

Note: Welfare is equivalent variation measure.
Source: GTAP model, GTAP v.7.0 U.S. 3x3 database.

Table ME 7.5. *Decomposition of the Total Welfare Effect, $U.S. Millions (answer key)*

	Total	Allocative Efficiency	Terms of Trade in Goods and Services	Terms of Trade in Savings-Investment
United States	14,565.39	1,030.0	11,909.5	1,625.9
ROW	−13,481.11	90.1	−11,941.0	−1,630.2
World	1,084.29	1,121.1	−31.5	−4.3

Note: Welfare is equivalent variation measure.
Source: GTAP model, GTAP v.7.0 U.S. 3x3 database.

Table ME 7.6. *Effect of Trade Liberalization on Exports (% change from base)*

	U.S.	Rest-of-World
Agriculture (*qxw*)	61.93	−0.77
Manufacturing (*qxw*)	8.07	0.71
Services (*qxw*)	−1.98	0.64

Source: GTAP model, GTAP v.7.0 U.S. 3x3 database.

1. The total world welfare effect is positive. The equivalent variation measure the income equivalent of the increase in utility due to the change in prices.
2. The main source is the benefit to the United States from ROW's non-agricultural policy reforms. A win-win strategy balances policies that benefit one country with policies that benefit its trade partner.
3. Export quantities increase most in sectors in which import tariffs are highest.
4. Both regions benefit from efficiency gains, but these are relatively small.
5. Terms-of-trade effects measure the price of a country's exports relative to its imports, or the import purchasing power of its exports. In this experiment, they are the most important component of each country's total welfare effect. The effects on USA and ROW offset each other, because in this two-region model, an increase in one country's import price is the same as an increase in the other's export price.

6. The import substitution elasticity has the most direct effect on terms of trade, because it influences the quantities of imports demanded when a country removes its tariffs, and therefore the supply quantity of its exports.
7. The toy 3x3 model's welfare effects are smaller because it is static, whereas theirs is a recursive dynamic model in which the economies have grown in size. Their model has more countries and commodities, and therefore more scope for efficiency gains.
8. Their tariff and subsidy rates are generally higher than in the 3x3 model, which may contribute to their higher welfare gains from reforms.

Model Exercise 8

10 a. Base tax revenue = 3,567,950
  b. Updated tax revenue = 3,690,278
  c. Change in government tax revenue = 122,328.

13 a. EV = −7,970.95
  b. Mean = −7,852.53
  c. Standard deviation = 935.67

Table ME 8.4. *Welfare Effects of a 1 percent Increase in U.S. Taxes, $U.S. Millions (answer key)*

Allocative Efficiency	Endowment	Technology	Population	Terms of Trade in Goods and Services	Terms of Trade in Invest-Savings	Preference	Total Welfare Cost	Change in Government Tax Revenue	Welfare Cost Per Dollar of Revenue
−3,509.1	0	0	0	−6,720.5	2,258.6		−7,970.9	122,328	−6.5

Source: GTAP model, U.S. 3x3 v.7.0 database.

Table ME 8.5. *Welfare Decomposition of the Allocative Efficiency Effect, $U.S. Million (answer key)*

Tax Type	Welfare Cost
Factor tax (pfattax)	−258.0
Output tax (prodtax)	−567.6
Input tax (inputtax)	−737.6
Consumption tax (contax)	−692.2
Government tax (govtax)	0.0
Export tax (etax)	−182.9
Import tax (mtax)	−1,070.7
Total	−3,509.1

Source: GTAP model, U.S. 3x3 v.7.0 database.
Experiment is a 1 percent increase in all U.S. taxes.

1. The direct burden is the increase in tax revenue of $122,328 million; its excess burden is an efficiency loss of $3,509.1 million.

2. Import tariffs have the most distorting effect and export taxes have the least effect.
3. The marginal welfare cost is the welfare change per additional dollar of tax revenue. This loss is 6.5 cents per dollar, so the government should be advised that its project must return at least 106.5 percent of its costs, or welfare will decline.
4. Terms of trade measures the price of exports relative to imports. It measures the import purchasing power of exports, so it is included in the EV welfare measure, which reflects the effect of price changes on utility.
5. The marginal welfare cost per dollar is lower than the Ballard, et al. finding. One reason is that the model has only three sectors. Taxes lead to allocative inefficiency by changing relative prices of goods such as groceries and autos. The more aggregated the model, the smaller is the scope for a tax to change relative prices. Another reason is that the GTAP model does not capture dynamic effects of income taxes on savings and capital accumulation or the supply of labor.
6. The U.S. 3x3 model's taxes are reported gross of the tax. Even so, sales tax and labor factor taxes are higher than in Ballard, et al. but the capital factor tax is lower. The effects of differences in tax rates on model results are therefore not clear.
7. EV mean value: –7,852.53
8. EV standard deviation: –935.67
9. 75% confidence range = –7,852.53 + / – 2 * – 935.67 = –9,723.87 to – 5,981.19
10. 95% confidence range = –3,670.09 to –12,035.95.

The negative sign of the EV result is robust with respect to the factor substitution elasticity.

Model Exercise 9

Table ME 9.2. *Cumulative Growth Rates (answer key)*

	Labor Force
USA	16
ROW	15
	Capital stock
USA	46
ROW	46
	TFP
USA	13
ROW	27

1. INCPAR is a parameter related to the income elasticity of demand, which describes the percentage change in quantity demanded given a percentage change in income. The model experiments introduce long-term income growth. Reducing

Table ME 9.3. *Role of Tobacco in Economywide Production (answer key)*

	USA	ROW
Share of tobacco in total activity output	0.55	.009

Source: GTAP v.7.0 3x3 tobacco database.

Table ME 9.4. *Base and Updated INCPAR Parameter Values (answer key)*

	Base Parameter Values		Updated Parameter Values
	USA	ROW	ROW only
Tobacco	0.7	0.7	0.4
Agr./Mfg.	0.8	0.8	*No change*
Services	1.0	1.1	*No change*

Table ME 9.5. *Private Household Budget Shares Under Alternative Scenarios (answer key)*

	Base		Income Growth		Income Growth with ROW nonsmoking Preferences	
	USA	ROW	USA	ROW	USA	ROW
Tobacco	.013	.029	.013	.027	.013	.025
Agr./Mfg.	.198	.387	.196	.373	.196	.374
Services	.789	.584	.791	.600	.791	.602
Total	1.000	1.00	1.00	1.00	1.00	1.00

Table ME 9.6. *Change in Rest-of-World Budget Shares for Tobacco (% change from base) (answer key)*

	Income Growth	Income Growth with Preference Change in ROW
Tobacco	−6.90	−13.79
Agr./Mfg.	−3.62	−3.36
Services	2.74	3.08

Table ME 9.7. *Industry Output with and Without Changes in ROW Smoking Preferences (% change from base) (answer key)*

	Income Growth		Income Growth with No-Smoking Preferences	
	USA	ROW	USA	ROW
Tobacco (*qo*)	39.38	56.38	38.98	48.46
Agr./Mfg. (*qo*)	44.03	57.91	44.02	57.93
Services (*qo*)	38.86	64.12	38.87	64.16

Table ME 9.8. *Systematic Sensitivity Analysis of Preference Change on Tobacco Quantities in ROW (answer key)*

	Point Estimate	Mean	Standard Deviation	95 Percent Confidence Interval	
				Upper	Lower
Production (*qo*)	48.46	48.53	4.03	66.55	30.51
Private consumption (*qp*)	43.93	44.00	5.57	68.91	19.09

Source: GTAP CGE model and v.7.0 3x3 tobacco database.

ROW's INCPAR means that the same growth in income will result in a smaller increase in its consumer demand for tobacco.

2. The INCPAR for tobacco and AG/MFG are less than one, and that for services is greater than one. All else equal, this means that demand for tobacco and AG/MFG will increase by proportionately less than the increase in income, whereas consumption of services will increase by proportionately more than the change in income. Therefore, the services budget share are expected to expand while the shares of tobacco and AG/MFG will decline in both scenarios.
3. Given consumer preferences for services as incomes grow, all else equal, services production will increase by proportionately more than other industries as their economies grow. However, other factors also influence output.
4. Economic growth causes the equilibrium demand and supply, and the tobacco price, to increase from the initial equilibrium. Antismoking preferences will cause the equilibrium quantities and price to fall.
5. The share of tobacco in both countries' total activity output is less than 1 percent, so economywide effects, such as effects on production in other industries, employment, and macrovariables like the wage and exchange rate, are likely to be minimal.

References

Anderson, Kym and Will Martin (2005). "Agricultural Trade Reform and the Doha Development Agenda," *The World Economy* 28(9): 1301–1327.

Armington, Paul S. (1969). "A Theory of Demand for Products Distinguished by Place of Production." *IMF Staff Papers* 16: 159–178.

Arndt, Channing (2002). "HIV/AIDS and Macroeconomic Prospects for Mozambique: An Initial Assessment," Department of Agricultural Economics, Purdue University, West Lafayette, Indiana. Downloaded on December 4, 2009 from: http://www.agecon.purdue.edu/staff/arndt/mozam_AIDS_dp.pdf.

Arndt, Channing, Thomas Hertel, Betina Demaranan, Karen Huff, and Robert McDougall (1997). "China in 2005: Implications for the Rest of the World," *Journal of Economic Integration* 12(4): 505–547.

Arndt, Channing and Kenneth R. Pearson (1998). How to Carry Out Systematic Sensitivity Analysis via Gaussian Quadrature and GEMPACK. GTAP Technical Paper No. 3. Center for Global Trade Analysis. West Lafayette, IN: Purdue University.

Auerbach, Alan J. and Laurence J. Kotlikoff (1987). *Dynamic Fiscal Policy*. Cambridge: Cambridge University Press.

Balistreri, Edward J., Christine A. McDaniel, and Eina V. Wong (2003). "An Estimation of U.S. Industry-Level Capital-Labor Substitution,"*The North American Journal of Economics and Finance* 14(3): 343–356.

Ballard, Charles L. and Don Fullerton (1992). "Distortionary Taxes and the Provision of Public Goods," *Journal of Economic Perspectives* 6(3): 117–131.

Ballard, Charles L., John B. Shoven, and John Whalley (1985). "General Equilibrium Computations of the Marginal Welfare Costs of Taxes in the United States," *The American Economic Review* 75(1): 128–138.

Bandara, Jayatilleke S. (1991). "Computable General Equilibrium Models for Development Policy Analysis in LDCs," *Journal of Economic Surveys* 5(1): 3–69.

Benjamin, Nancy, Shantayanan Devarajan, and Robert J. Weiner (1989). "The 'Dutch' Disease in a Developing Country: Oil Reserves in Cameroon," *Journal of Development Economics* 30(1) (January 1989): 71–92.

Bergman, Lars (1988). "Energy Policy Modeling: A Survey of General Equilibrium Approaches," *Journal of Policy Modeling* 10(3): 377–399.

Bergman, Lars (2005). "CGE Modeling of Environmental Policy and Resource Management," in Karl-Göran Mäler and Jeffrey R. Vincent, eds., *Handbook of Environmental Economics*. Volume 3. Amsterdam: Elsevier, North Holland.

Berrittella, Maria, Andrea Bigano, Roberto Roson, and Richard S.J. Tol (2004). *A General Equilibrium Analysis of Climate Change Impacts on Tourism.* Working Paper FNU-49, Research Unit on Sustainability and Global Change. Hamburg: Hamburg University.

Bhattacharyya, Subhes C. (1996). "Applied General Equilibrium Models for Energy Studies: A Survey," *Energy Economics* 18: 145–164.

Block, Paul J., Kenneth Strzepek, Mark Rosegrant, and Xinshen Diao (2006). *Impacts of Considering Climate Variability on Investment Decisions in Ethiopia.* EPT Discussion Paper No. 150. Washington, D.C.: International Food Policy Research Institute.

Borges, Antonio M. (1986). *Applied General Equilibrium Models: An Assessment of Their Usefulness for Policy Analysis.* OECD Economic Studies no. 7 Downloaded on June 12, 2010 from: http://www.oecd.org/dataoecd/52/32/35567467.pdf.

Borjas, George (2004). *Increasing the Supply of Labor Through Immigration: Measuring the Impact on Native-born Workers.* Washington, D.C.: Center for Immigration Studies.

Bouet, Antoine (2008). *The Expected Benefits of Trade Liberalization for World Income and Development: Opening the "Black Box" of Global Trade Modeling.* Food Policy Review No. 8. Washington, D.C.: International Food Policy Research Institute.

Bourguignon, Francois, Anne-Sophie Robilliard, and Sherman Robinson. (2003). *Representative Versus Real Households in the Macro-Economic Modeling of Inequality.* DELTA working paper 2003–05. Departement et Laboratoire d'Economies Theorique et Applique. Paris: Ecole Normale Superieure.

Breisinger, Clemens, Marcelle Thomas, and James Thurlow (2009). *Social Accounting Matrices and Multiplier Analysis: An Introduction with Exercises.* Food Security in Practice Technical Guide 5. Washington, D.C.: International Food Policy Research Institute.

Brown, Drusilla K. (1987). "Tariffs, the Terms of Trade, and National Product Differentiation," *Journal of Policy Modeling* 9(3): 503–526.

Browning, Edgar (1976). "The Marginal Cost of Public Funds," *The Journal of Political Economy* 84(2): 283–298.

Bureau of Labor Statistics (2009). *Preliminary Multifactor Productivity Trends, 2008.* Downloaded on May 13, 2010 from: http://www.bls.gov/news.release/prod3.nr0.htm.

Burfisher, Mary E., Sherman Robinson, and Karen Thierfelder (1994). "Wage Changes in a U.S.-Mexico Free Trade Area: Migration versus Stolper-Samuelson Effects," in Joseph F. Francois and Clint R. Shiells, eds., *Modelling Trade Policy: Applied General Equilibrium Assessments of North American Free Trade.* Cambridge: Cambridge University Press.

Burniaux, Jean-Marc and Truong Truong (2002). *GTAP-E: An Energy-Environmental Version of the GTAP Model.* GTAP Technical Papers 923, Center for Global Trade Analysis. West Lafayette, IN: Purdue University.

Cattaneo Andrea, Raúl A. Hinojosa-Ojeda, and Sherman Robinson (1999). "Costa Rica Trade Liberalization, Fiscal Imbalances, and Macroeconomic Policy: a Computable General Equilibrium Model," *The North American Journal of Economics and Finance* 10(1): 39–67.

Cline, William (2007). *Global Warming and Agriculture: Impact Estimates by Country.* Washington, D.C.: Center for Global Development.

Collier, Paul (2008). "The Politics of Hunger: How Illusion and Greed Fan the Food Crisis," *Foreign Affairs* 87(6): 67–79.

Condon, Timothy, Henrik Dahl, and Shantayanan Devarajan (1987). *Implementing a Computable General Equilibrium Model in GAMS: the Cameroon Model.* DRD Discussion paper No. DRD290, Washington, D.C.: World Bank.

Corden W. Max and J. Peter Neary (1982). "Booming Sector and De-industrialisation in a Small Open Economy," *The Economic Journal*, 92(368): 825–848.

Decaluwe, Bernard and Andre Martens (1988). "CGE Modeling and Developing Economies – A Concise Empirical Survey of 73 Applications to 26 Countries," *Journal of Policy Modeling* 10(4): 529–568.

deMelo, Jaime (1988). "Computable General Equilibrium Models for Trade Policy Analysis in Developing Countries: a Survey," *Journal of Policy Modeling* 10(3): 469–503.

deMelo, Jaime and David G. Tarr (1992). *A General Equilibrium Analysis of U.S. Foreign Trade Policy*. Cambridge, MA: MIT Press.

Dervis, Kemal, Jaime de Melo and Sherman Robinson (1982). *General Equilibrium Models for Development Policy*. Cambridge: Cambridge University Press.

Devarajan, Shantayanan and Delfin S. Go (1998). "The Simplest Dynamic General Equilibrium Model of an Open Economy," *Journal of Policy Modeling* 20(6): 677–714.

Devarajan, Shantayanan, Delfin S. Go, Jeffrey D. Lewis, Sherman Robinson, and Pekka Sinko (1997). "Simple General Equilibrium Modeling," in Joseph F. Francois and Kenneth A. Reinert, eds., *Applied Methods for Trade Policy Analysis: A Handbook*. Cambridge: Cambridge University Press.

Devarajan, Shantayanan, Jeffrey Lewis, and Sherman Robinson (1990). "Policy Lessons from Trade-Focused, Two-Sector Models," *Journal of Policy Modeling* 12(4): 625–657.

Devarajan, Shantayanan, Karen E. Thierfelder, and Sethaput Suthiwart-Narueput (2001). "The Marginal Cost of Public Funds in Developing Countries," in Amedeo Fossati and Wolfgang Wiegard, eds., *Policy Evaluations with Computable General Equilibrium Models*. New York: Routledge Press.

Dewatripont, Mathias and Gilles Michel (1987). "On Closure Rules, Homogeneity and Dynamics in Applied General Equilibrium Models," *Journal of Development Economics* 26(1): 65–76.

Diao, Xinshen (2009). *Economywide Impact of Avian Flu in Ghana: A Dynamic CGE Model Analysis*. IFPRI Discussion Paper 00866. Washington, D.C.: International Food Policy Research Institute.

Diao, Xinshen, Rachid Doukkali, and Bingxin Yu (2008). *Policy Options and Their Potential Effects on Moroccan Small Farmers and the Poor Facing Increased World Food Prices: A General Equilibrium Model Analysis*. Development Strategy and Government Division. IFPRI Discussion Paper 00813. Washington, D.C.: International Food Policy Research Institute.

Diao, Xinshen, Agapi Somaru, and Terry Roe (2001). "A Global Analysis of Agricultural Reform in WTO Member Countries," in Mary E. Burfisher, ed., *Agricultural Policy Reform: The Road Ahead*. Agricultural Economics Report No. 802. Economic Research Service. Washington, D.C.: U.S. Department of Agriculture.

Dixon, Peter B. and Maureen Rimmer (2002). *Dynamic, General Equilibrium Modelling for Forecasting and Policy: a Practical Guide and Documentation of MONASH*. Amsterdam: North Holland.

Dixon, Peter B., Maureen Rimmer and Marinos Tsigas (2007). "Regionalizing Results from a Detailed CGE Model: Macro, Industry and State Effects in the United States of Removing Major Tariffs and Quotas," *Papers in Regional Science* 86(1): 31–55.

Elliott, Joshua, Ian Foster, Kenneth Judd, Elisabeth Moyer, and Todd Munson (2010a). *CIM-EARTH: Community Integrated Model of Economic and Resource Trajectories for Humankind*, Version 0.1. Mathematics and Computer Science Division, Technical Memorandum ANL/MCS-TM-307, Argonne National Laboratories, Argonne, IL.

Elliott, Joshua, Ian Foster, Samuel Kortum, Todd Munson, Fernando Perez Cervantes, and David Weisbach (2010b). "Trade and Carbon Taxes," *American Economic Review* 100(2): 465–69.

Erkel-Rousse, Helene and Daniel Mirza (2002). "Import Price Elasticities: Reconsidering the Evidence," *Canadian Journal of Economics* 35(2): 282–306.

Francois, Joseph F. and Kenneth A. Reinert (1997). "Applied Methods for Trade Policy Analysis: An Overview," in Joseph F. Francois and Kenneth A. Reinert, eds., *Applied Methods for Trade Policy Analysis: A Handbook*. Cambridge: Cambridge University Press.

Gallaway, Michael P., Christine A. McDaniel and Sandra A. Rivera (2000). "Short-run and Long-run Industry-level Estimates of U.S. Armington Elasticities," *The North American Journal of Economics and Finance* 14(1): 49–68.

Gehlhar, Mark (1997). "Historical Analysis of Growth and Trade Patterns in the Pacific Rim: An Evaluation of the GTAP Framework," in Thomas W. Hertel, ed., *Global Trade Analysis: Modeling and Applications*. Cambridge: Cambridge University Press.

Goel, Rajeev K. and Michael A. Nelson (2004). "International Patterns of Cigarette Smoking and Global Antismoking Policies," *Journal of Economics and Finance* 28(3): 382–394.

Gottschalk, Jan, Vu Manh Le, Hans Lofgren, and Kofi Nouve (2009). *Analyzing Fiscal Space Using MAMs: An Application to Burkina Faso*. IMF Working Paper WP/09/277, Washington, D.C.: International Monetary Fund.

Goulder, Lawrence H. and Barry Eichengreen (1989). *Trade Liberalization in General Equilibrium: Intertemporal and Interiindustry Effects*. National Bureau of Economics Working Paper No. 2965. Cambridge, MA: National Bureau of Economics.

Hanoch, Giora (1975). "Production and Demand Models with Direct or Indirect Implicit Additivity," *Econometrica* 43(3): 395–419.

Harberger, Arnold C. (1964). "Taxation, Resource Allocation, and Welfare," in *The Role of Direct and Indirect Taxes in the Federal Reserve System*. Cambridge, MA: National Bureau of Economic Research. Downloaded on November 6, 2009 from: http://www.nber.org/books/unkn 64–4.

Hertel, Thomas W., David L. Hummels, Maros Ivanic, and Roman Keeney (2004a). *How Confident Can We Be in CGE-Based Assessments of Free Trade Agreements?* NBER Working Paper No. W10477. Cambridge, MA: National Bureau of Economic Research.

Hertel, Thomas W., Maros Ivanic, Paul V. Preckel, and John A. L. Cranfield (2004b). "The Earnings Effects of Multilateral Trade Liberalization: Implications for Poverty," *The World Bank Economic Review* 18(2): 205–236.

Hertel, Thomas W., Everett B. Peterson, Paul V. Preckel, Yves Surry, and Marinos E. Tsigas (1991). "Implicit Additivity as a Strategy for Restricting the Parameter Space in CGE Models," *Economic and Financial Computing* 1(1): 265–289.

Hertel, Thomas W. and Marinos E. Tsigas (1997). "Structure of GTAP," in Thomas W. Hertel, ed., *Global Trade Analysis: Modeling and Applications*. Cambridge: Cambridge University Press.

Hertel, Thomas W. and Terrie L. Walmsley (2008). "Chapter 1: Introduction," in Badri G. Narayanan and Terrie L. Walmsley, eds., *Global Trade, Assistance, and Production: The GTAP 7 Data Base*. Center for Global Trade Analysis. West Lafayette, IN: Purdue University.

Horridge, Mark (2001). *Run GTAP – Demo Version*. GTAP Resource No. 411. Center for Global Trade Analysis. West Lafayette, IN: Purdue University.

Horridge, Mark (2008a). "GTAPAgg: Data Aggregation Program," in Badri G. Narayanan and Terrie L. Walmsley, eds., *Global Trade, Assistance and Production: The GTAP 7 Database*." Center for Global Trade Analysis. West Lafayette, IN: Purdue University.

Horridge, Mark (2008b). "GTAPAgg Demo Version." GTAP Resource #807. Center for Global Trade Analysis. West Lafayette, IN: Purdue University.

Hosoe, Nobuhiro, Kenji Gasawa and Hideo Hashimoto (2010). *Textbook of Computable General Equilibrium Modelling:Programming and Simulations*. Houndsmills, UK: Palgrave MacMillan.

Huff, Karen M. and Thomas W. Hertel (2000). *Decomposing Welfare Changes in the GTAP Model*. GTAP Technical Paper No. 5. Center for Global Trade Analysis. West Lafayette, IN: Purdue University.

Hummels, David (1999). *Towards a Geography of Trade Costs*, GTAP Working Paper No. 17. Center for Global Trade Analysis, Purdue University, West Lafayette, Indiana.

Hummels, David (2007). "Transportation Costs and International Trade in the Second Era of Globalization," *The Journal of Economic Perspectives* 21(3): 131–154.

Jabara, Cathy, Mary E. Burfisher, and David Ingersoll (2008). *Wood Packaging SPS Regulations: Effects on U.S. Imports and Containerized Trade*. U.S. International Trade Commission, Office of Industries Working Paper No. 20. Washington, D.C: U.S. International Trade Commission.

Jokisch, Sabine and Laurence J. Kotlikoff (2005). *Simulating the Dynamic Macroeconomic and Microeconomic Effects of the FairTax*. NBER Working Paper No. 11858. Cambridge, MA: National Bureau of Economic Research.

Kehoe, Patrick J. and Timothy J. Kehoe (1994). "A Primer on Static Applied General Equilibrium Models," *Federal Reserve Bank of Minneapolis Quarterly Review*, 18(1). Downloaded on December 4, 2009 from http://minneapolisfed.org/research/qr/qr1821.pdf.

Keller, Wouter J. (1980). *Tax Incidence: A General Equilibrium Approach*. Amsterdam: North Holland.

Keogh, Marcus, Scott McDonald, Richard Smith, Melisa Martinez-Alvarez, and Jo Coast (2009). "Global CGE Modeling of Antibiotic Resistance: An Application of the GLOBE Model." GTAP Resource No. 3093. Center for Global Trade Analysis. West Lafayette, IN: Purdue University.

King, Benjamin B. (1985). "What is a SAM?" in Graham Pyatt and Jeffrey I. Round, eds., *Social Accounting Matrices: A Basis for Planning*. The World Bank, Washington, D.C.

Koopman, Robert, Hugh Arce, Edward J. Balistreri, and Alan Fox (2002). *Large Scale CGE Modeling at the United States International Trade Commission*. GTAP Resource # 1051. Center for Global Trade Analysis. West Lafayette, IN: Purdue University.

Kuiper, Marijke and Frank van Tongeren (2006). "Using Gravity to Move Armington," GTAP Resource No. 2044. Center for Global Trade Analysis. West Lafayette, IN: Purdue University.

Landes, Maurice and Mary E. Burfisher (2009). *Food and Agricultural Marketing Efficiency Gains in India: A Source of Growth and Equity*. Economic Research

Report No. ERR-89. Economic Research Service. Washington, D.C.: U.S. Department of Agriculture.

Lipsey, Richard G. and Kelvin J. Lancaster (1956). "The General Theory of Second Best," *Review of Economic Studies* 24(12): 11–32.

Löfgren, Hans, Rebecca Lee Harris, and Sherman Robinson (2002). *A Standard Computable General Equilibrium (CGE) Model in GAMS*. Microcomputers in Policy Research, No. 5. Washington, D.C.: International Food Policy Research Institute.

McDaniel, Christine A. and Edward J. Balistreri (2003). *A Discussion on Armington Trade Substitution Elasticities*. USITC Office of Economics Working Paper No. 2002-01-A. Washington, D.C.: U.S. International Trade Commission.

McDaniel, Christine A., Kenneth Reinert, and Kent Hughes (2008). *Tools of the Trade: Models for Trade Policy Analysis*. Washington, D.C.: Woodrow Wilson International Center for Scholars.

McDonald, Scott, Karen Thierfelder and Sherman Robinson (2007). *GLOBE: A SAM Based Global CGE Model Using GTAP Data*. USNA Economics Department Working Paper No. 15. Annapolis, MD: United States Naval Academy.

McDougall, Robert (2003). *A New Regional Household Demand System for GTAP*. GTAP Technical Paper No. 20, Revision 1. Center for Global Trade Analysis. West Lafayette, IN: Purdue University.

McDougall, Robert (2009). GTAP Research Memorandum No. 16. *Elasticities of Substitution in Nested CES Systems*. Center for Global Trade Analysis. West Lafayette, IN: Purdue University.

Nielson, Chantal Pohl, Karen Thierfelder, and Sherman Robinson (2001). *Genetically Modified Foods, Trade and Developing Countries*. TMD Discussion Paper No. 77. Washington, D.C.: International Food Policy Research Institute.

Ottaviano, Gianmarco I. P., and Giovanni Peri (2006). "Rethinking the Effect of Immigration on Wages: New Data and Analysis from 1980–2004," *Immigration Policy IN FOCUS* 5(8).

Paltsev, Sergey, John M. Reilly, Henry D. Jacoby, Richard S. Eckaus, James McFarland, Marcus Sarofim, Malcolm Asadoorian, and Mustafa Babiker (2005). *The MIT Emissions Prediction and Policy Analysis (EPPA) Model: Version 4*. Joint Program Report Series. Cambridge, MA: Massachusetts Institute of Technology.

Partridge, Mark D., and Dan S. Rickman (1998). "Regional Computable General Equilibrium Modeling: A Survey and Critical Appraisal," *International Regional Science Review* 21(3): 205–248.

Pearson, Kenneth and Mark Horridge (2003). "Hands-on Computing with RunGTAP and WinGEM to Introduce GTAP and GEMPACK." Resource Paper No. 1638. Center for Global Trade Analysis. West Lafayette, IN: Purdue University.

Pereira, Alfredo M. and John B. Shoven (1988). "Survey of Dynamic Computable General Equilibrium Models for Tax Policy Evaluation," *Journal of Policy Modeling* 10(3): 401–436.

Piermartini, Roberta and Robert Teh (2005). *Demystifying Modelling Methods for Trade Policy*. Discussion Paper No. 10. Geneva: World Trade Organization.

Powell, Alan A. and F. H. G. Gruen (1968). "The Constant Elasticity of Transformation Production Frontier and Linear Supply System," *International Economic Review* 9(3): 315–328.

Pyatt, Graham and Jeffrey I. Round (1985). "Social Accounting Matrices for Development Planning," in Graham Pyatt and Jeffrey I. Round, eds., *Social Accounting Matrices: A Basis for Planning*. Washington, D.C.: World Bank.

Reinert, Kenneth A. and David W. Roland-Holst (1992). Armington Elasticities for United States Manufacturing Sectors, *Journal of Policy Modeling* 14(5): 631–639.

Reinert, Kenneth A. and David W. Roland-Holst (1997). "Social Accounting Matrices," in Joseph F. Francois and Kenneth A. Reinert, eds., *Applied Methods for Trade Policy Analysis: A Handbook*. Cambridge: Cambridge University Press.

Robinson, Sherman (1991). "Macroeconomics, Financial Variables, and Computable General Equilibrium Models," *World Development* 19(11): 1509–1525.

Robinson, Sherman (2006). "Macro Models and Multipliers: Leontief, Stone, Keynes, and CGE Models," in Alain de Janvry and Ravi Kanbur, eds., *Poverty, Inequality and Development: Essays in Honor of Erik Thorbecke*. New York: Springer Science: 205-232

Robinson, Sherman, Maureen Kilkenny and Kenneth Hanson (1990). *The USDA/ERS Computable General Equilibrium Model of the United States*. Agriculture and Rural Economy Division Report No. AGES 9049. Economic Research Service. Washington, D.C.: U.S. Department of Agriculture.

Robinson, Sherman and Karen Thierfelder (2002). "Trade Liberalization and Regional Integration: The Search for Large Numbers," *Australian Journal of Agricultural and Resource Economics* 46(6): 585–604.

Robinson, Sherman, Antonio Yunez-Naude, Raul Hinojosa-Ojeda, Jeffrey D. Lewis, and Shantayanan Devarajan (1999). "From Stylized to Applied Models: Building multi-sector CGE models for Policy Analysis," *North American Journal of Economics and Finance* 10(1999): 5–38.

Rutherford, Thomas F. and David G. Tarr (2003). "Regional Trading Arrangements for Chile: Do the Results Differ with a Dynamic Model?" *Économie internationale* 94–95: 261–281.

Rybczynski, Tadeusz M. (1955). "Factor Endowments and Relative Commodity Prices," *Economica*, New Series, 22(88): 336–341.

Sachs, Jeffrey D. (2008). "Surging Food Prices Mean Global Instability," *Scientific American,* June. Downloaded January 3, 2009 from: http://www.scientificamerican.com/article.cfm?id=surging-food-prices.

Samuelson, Robert (2005). "The Endless Food Fight," in *Washington Post*, December 4, 2005, page A29.

Scarf, Herbert E. and John B. Shoven (2008). *Applied General Equilibrium Analysis*. Cambridge: Cambridge University Press.

Shiells, Clinton R. and Kenneth A. Reinert (1993). "Armington Models and Terms-of-Trade Effects: Some Econometric Evidence for North America," *Canadian Journal of Economics* 26(2): 299–316.

Shiells, Clinton R., Robert M. Stern, and Alan V. Deardorff (1986). "Estimates of the Elasticities of Substitution between Imports and Home Goods for the United States," *Weltwirtschaftliches-Archiv* 122(3): 497–519.

Shoven, John B., and John Whalley (1984). "Applied General-Equilibrium Models of Taxation and International Trade: An Introduction Survey," *Journal of Economic Literature* 22(3): 1007–1051.

Shoven, John B. and John Whalley (1992). *Applying General Equilibrium*. Cambridge: Cambridge University Press.

Sullivan, Evan (2010). "A CGE-based Analysis of the Effects of Piracy in Somalia on Global Markets in Grains and Petroleum." Unpublished research memo, Department of Economics. Annapolis, MD: United States Naval Academy.

Surry, Yves (1993). "The 'Constant Difference of Elasticities' Function with Applications to the EC Animal Feed Sector," *Journal of Agricultural Economics* 44(1): 110–125.

Taylor, J. Edward, Antonio Yunez-Naude and Steve Hampton. "Agricultural Policy Reform and Village Economics: A CGE Analysis from Mexico," *Journal of Policy Modeling* 21(4): 453–480.

Thierfelder, Karen E. (2009). "Tools for Undergraduates (TUG) CGE Model." Downloaded on October 1, 2009 from: http://www.usna.edu/Users/econ/thier.

Trostle, Ronald (2008). *Global Agricultural Supply and Demand: Factors Contributing to the Recent Increase in Food Commodity Prices*. Economic Research Service WRS-0801 (revised July 2008). Washington, D.C.: United States Department of Agriculture.

U.S. Census Bureau, Department of Commerce (2009). American Factfinder Data Profile. Downloaded on June 4, 2010 from htttp://factfinder.census.gov.

van der Mensbrugghe, Dominique (2005). *LINKAGE Technical Reference Document, Version 6.0*. Development Prospects Group (DECPG). Washington, D.C.: World Bank.

Verma, Monika and Thomas W. Hertel (2009). "Commodity Price Volatility and Nutrition Vulnerability" Markets, Trade and Institutions Division Discussion Paper No. 00895. Washington, D.C.: International Food Policy Research Institute.

Walmsley, Terrie L. (2006). *A Baseline Scenario for the Dynamic GTAP Model (For the GTAP 6 Data Base)*. Downloaded on March 16, 2010 from: https://www.gtap.agecon.purdue.edu/resources/download/2854.pdf.

World Bank (2006). *Global Economic Prospects: Economic Implications of Remittances and Migration*. Washington, D.C.: World Bank.

Author Index

Subject Index